Dear Uncles

DEAR UNCLES

The Civil War Letters of

ARTHUR MCKINSTRY,

a Soldier in the Excelsior Brigade

Edited by

RICK BARRAM

EXCELSIOR EDITIONS

Published by
State University of New York Press, Albany

Printed in the United States of America

Excelsior Editions is an imprint of State University of New York Press

For information, contact State University of New York Press, Albany, NY
www.sunypress.edu

Library of Congress Cataloging-in-Publication Data

Names: McKinstry, Arthur, 1839–1862. | Barram, Rick, 1959– editor.
Title: Dear uncles : the Civil War letters of Arthur McKinstry, a soldier in the Excelsior Brigade / Rick Barram.
Description: Albany : State University of New York Press, [2022] | Series: Excelsior editions | Includes bibliographical references and index.
Identifiers: LCCN 2022005758 | ISBN 9781438489971 (hardcover) | ISBN 9781438489988 (ebook)
Subjects: LCSH: McKinstry, Arthur, 1839–1862—Correspondence. | United States. Army. New York Infantry Regiment, 72nd (1861–1864)—Biography. | Soldiers--New York (State)—Correspondence. | United States—History—Civil War, 1861–1865—Personal narratives. | New York (State)—History—Civil War, 1861–1865—Personal narratives.
Classification: LCC E523.5 72nd .M35 2022 | DDC 973.7/447092 [B]—dc23/eng/20220308
LC record available at https://lccn.loc.gov/2022005758

10 9 8 7 6 5 4 3 2 1

The fact is this, volunteering is educating several hundred thousand pioneers in the very best possible manner. It is also fostering a military spirit among our young men which will never be extinguished and hereafter our county will never feel the lack of trained, disciplined, and ready soldiers. More than this, it is bringing the people of our wide domain in contact with each other and acquainting them with each other's characteristics and peculiarities in a manner and to an extent greater than any other cause could possibly have produced.

—Arthur McKinstry

Contents

Illustrations

Acknowledgments

Though it might be expected that bringing Arthur McKinstry's letters into the light they deserve by way of this collection would be a very straightforward sort of affair, there are still many people who deserve a hearty cheer of thanks for their help and inspiration.

The late Doug Shepard introduced me to the full extent of Arthur's Fredonia Censor letters while helping me research my earlier book, The 72nd New York Infantry in the Civil War. When I received in the mail a fat envelope full of photocopies prepared by Doug, who was volunteering at the Darwin R. Barker Historical Library at the time, I knew this was something special. The retired college professor had written extensively on the history of Chautauqua County and I can only hope that by bringing these two wonderful McKinstry letter collections together in one place would have made Doug proud and pleased.

Transcribing photocopied newspaper articles and scans of handwritten letters of course presents its own challenges. Blemishes on the originals, missing text, or just plain-old bad handwriting made converting Arthur's words onto a usable electronic format at times a consuming and frustrating chore. Helping with the thankless task of transcribing these pieces were Kimberly Schaible and Ed Cameron, both former students of mine though many years apart. Their hard work helped me make progress through what at first appeared a daunting task. With the transcriptions complete, proofreading the text was of supreme importance. In an effort to correct any earlier transcription errors, my brother-in-law and good friend Doug Compton read the entire work and compared it to the originals. This was a supreme effort that resolved discrepancies arising from unclear handwriting or stray marks on the printed pages. Doug's working knowledge of French and Latin phrases and familiarity with classical literature proved to be important help in deciphering some of McKinstry's more arcane references.

Another valuable asset in bringing this work to the page is my good friend Mark Richardson. As an engineer, he brings a keen and discerning eye to the proofreading process. As one familiar with the 72nd New York Regiment, Mark contributed to the overall scope of the book by providing input as to which words or phrases of Arthur's may or may not need further explanation or when and where judicious use of notes would be needed to help give context to the action or letters. In the end, Mark probably read more versions of this book's manuscripts than anyone.

Mark Dunkleman, author of a regimental history of the 154th New York, read early versions of the manuscript and was of great help in pointing out those of Arthur's references that needed more research and illumination. His input served to broaden the scope of work and make these letters more accessible to the twenty-first-century reader. Thank you, Mark, and another big thanks to David Brown. David is both a reenactor and officer in the Chautauqua County Historical Society, whose enthusiasm for this project served as a great inspiration and motivation. And yet another resident of Western New York who deserves my thanks is my friend Phil Palen. Phil has sent me a continual stream of tidbits about the 72nd New York for many years and has served as a ready resource for checking or double-checking information. His enthusiasm for the history of the region is unmatched.

Many thanks also go out the descendants and greater family of Arthur McKinstry. Throughout the process they accepted me and embraced my project, offering guidance and resources that would not otherwise have been available. Andy Rhodes, Robert Hawes, and Mary Frances Smith all made this book much more than it would have been without their support. How less complete this work would have been without their help.

Another round of recognition to those institutions whose resources are available to researchers like myself as they contributed greatly to this work: Emory Center for Digital Scholarship for making the resource of the wonderful images from the London Illustrated News available online; Heritage Auctions and the Union Drummer Boy for allowing the use of their images for this work; Adam Minakowski, special collections librarian at the Nimitz Library, US Naval Academy, for his efforts regarding Arthur's time at Annapolis; Maxwell Walters, curator at the Darwin R. Barker Historical Museum for responding to my small, clarifying questions about the Censor collection; and United States Library of Congress and its wonderful trove of images and documents.

Thanks too to my brother Scott Barram for his enthusiastic reading of this work. While not an expert in the Civil War, Scott's excitement over the immediacy of McKinstry's story informed his suggestions on how to help this work reach a wider, more general audience.

And finally, to my wife Rebecca, who while not always understanding my passion for Civil War history has learned to accept it. During the last months of work on Dear Uncles, Rebecca tried to keep the "honey dos" to a minimum, allowing me the time and space needed; thank you, darling, and I love you!

Figure I.1. Arthur McKinstry. *Courtesy of Ulysses S. Grant Presidential Library.*

Introduction

On a brisk morning in early fall of 1861, Stephen M. Doyle, adjutant in one of Brigadier General Daniel E. Sickles's five New York regiments, approached a young private. Doyle asked the private to accompany him on an inspection tour of the regiment's outposts and to write down his impressions. The 3rd Excelsior Regiment was deployed around the southern reaches of Washington, DC, part of the capital's defense during those uncertain early months of the Civil War following the Union's defeat at Bull Run. The private, twenty-one-year-old Arthur McKinstry, was thrilled both at the opportunity and that Lieutenant Doyle recognized him as a capable "writing man." But as thrilled as Arthur was, the invitation was not entirely unexpected since McKinstry's prolific writings were well known throughout the company and regiment.[1]

Arthur enlisted that June in a volunteer infantry company forming in Fredonia, New York, eight miles from his home in Forestville. Forestville is one of a number of small villages and hamlets that dotted Chautauqua County on New York State's western edge, which stretched along the shore of Lake Erie. Settlers began moving into the county in the late 1700s and in 1808 the limits of "Chautauque" County were established with the county government formed in 1811, boasting a population of around five hundred souls.[2] By 1861, with the onset of civil war, the population had grown to more than fifty-eight thousand, with much of the local economy focused on farming and the various opportunities provided by Lake Erie.

The Fredonia Censor, Fredonia's local newspaper, owned by Arthur's two uncles, Willard and Winthrop McKinstry, was one of several papers in and around Chautauqua County. From the day of Arthur's enlistment, the young McKinstry and his uncles had a plan; Arthur would send letters home describing the goings on within the company and regiment, with Willard and "Wint" publishing them.

The McKinstry family had had a long and integral relationship with the Censor. Willard McKinstry was twenty-six years old when he purchased part ownership of the paper in 1840. McKinstry was well experienced in the newspaper and publishing business and took sole ownership of the paper in 1847. Though Willard was a Democrat, he maintained the Censor as a Whig paper through the hiring of various political reporters and editors. In 1851, Willard's younger brother, twenty-three-year-old Archibald Winthrop "Wint" McKinstry, who had worked as an apprentice at the paper for the past seven years, became co-owner.[3]

Following Arthur McKinstry's enlistment, Arthur's "Dear Uncles" pieces became a staple of the Censor's war coverage as officers granted McKinstry unprecedented access to the inner workings of the regiment. Arthur concluded that his letters, combined with other material, had made the Censor the "military journal" of the region. Other soldiers' letters would be published in the Chautauqua papers, but none would have the detail, frequency, immediacy, consistency, and popularity of Arthur McKinstry's "Dear Uncles."

Arthur McKinstry was born on November 2, 1839, in Chicopee, Massachusetts. His father, William McKinstry, died of consumption when Arthur was five. His mother Mary remarried Austin Chapin and the family, including his sister Laura Jane (called Jennie by Arthur), along with half-brothers Francis (Frank) and Luther, moved to Forestville, leaving his extended family behind in Massachusetts. In Forestville the McKinstry-Chapin family took root.[4] Arthur was articulate and well read, and at age fifteen he was accepted to the US Naval Academy starting in the fall of 1854. The young cadet was eager for his instruction to move from the classroom to shipboard. In fact, so enthusiastic was Arthur that a poem he wrote called "A Sailor's Farewell" was printed in the Censor. Early on Arthur found the studies not as "severe" as he had expected, but by November his roommate had moved out and he had collected seventeen demerits during October alone. By January he was struggling in mathematics and was butting heads with the professor. His mother tried to console her son, speculating the instructor had "mistaken your pranking for insolence." Young McKinstry hoped if he could "pass a good examination" all could be set right in mathematics, making up for a host of low marks. However, by May, Arthur had accumulated 140 demerits as he prepared for a series of make-or-break examinations. But a second year at the academy was not to be. Finishing at or near the bottom of his class in nearly every subject, Arthur was deemed "unfit" for naval service and sent home. McKinstry would later call this time at the academy a missed opportunity.[5]

After his time at the Naval Academy Arthur traveled to Mexico and New Orleans. While it is unclear exactly when, for how long, or why he went, these visits were clearly impactful since he makes reference to both in later letters with his mother. What is clear is that, whatever the circumstances, his health suffered during his absence and he was likely not fully recovered by the time the country began to prepare itself for a looming civil war.

Arthur left for the seat of war that summer of 1861 and maintained a vigorous correspondence with friends and relations. Aside from the pieces intended for publication in the Censor, Arthur wrote frequently to his mother, sister, and Uncle Wint. These letters reveal Arthur's personal side, his joys and frustrations of being in the army; his relative success and failures in procuring a watch, respectable boots, a pistol, and the other equipage a proper soldier would need in the field. Arthur took what opportunities were afforded him to write home, be it in his tent with feet up writing by candlelight or at a picket post with the sound of Rebel artillery booming in the distance.

Before the war, Chautauqua County had already established a robust militia regiment in the form of the 68th NYSM under the command of David S. Forbes. When the first call came for three-year volunteers, the county filled its quota by sending five companies from the 68th. Many men and officers active at company and staff levels eventually became fixtures in the newly forming 3rd Excelsior Regiment. Arthur joined a company led by Chautauqua district attorney William O. Stevens. Stevens was a prominent figure in the county by virtue of his public service and his captaincy of the 68th's Company D. This company now formed the nucleus of the unit McKinstry joined and would retain its "Company D" designation in the new regiment. Stevens's reputation as a military man was well established, having led his company to victory in various drill competitions throughout the state. Stevens's quality as a leader was clear as soon as his company arrived for mustering near New York City. His Chautauqua men shone and Stevens was soon offered the position of major, a post he did not accept until receiving the consent of the men he had recruited. Stevens would eventually be offered his own regiment but would elect to stay. Remaining with the regiment initially known as the 3rd Excelsior, Stevens would rise to the rank of colonel, commanding the regiment from late 1862 until his death at Chancellorsville in May of 1863.[6]

Third Excelsior was just one of five regiments belonging to a brigade founded by former United States congressman Daniel E. Sickles. Sickles was a product of New York City's Democratic Party machine. Dirty political tricks and shady dealings were part of the political landscape and Dan was good at all of it, leading him eventually to a seat in Congress. Sickles may have very well stayed in Congress and ridden out the upcoming war on Capitol Hill except for a debacle that threatened to undo him both politically and personally. Though Dan him-

Figure I.2. Brigadier General Daniel E. Sickles. Daniel E. Sickles raised the Excelsior Brigade and eventually rose to the rank of major general with command of the entire 3rd Corps. *Courtesy of Library of Congress.*

self never believed much in the sanctity of marriage while he maintained various liaisons around Washington, DC, he never could tolerate the same indifference from his young and attractive wife Teresa. In February of 1859, once he discovered her affair with US District Attorney Philip Barton Key, Sickles murdered the unwitting paramour on the street as he attempted to signal Teresa. The following trial was a national sensation. And though Dan was acquitted on the grounds of "temporary insanity," his political career was wrecked. Perhaps only something as momentous as a civil war could redeem him?[7]

Sickles received approval in the spring of 1861 to form a brigade of five regiments, which he naturally would command. Dubbed the Excelsior Brigade, after New York State's motto meaning "Ever Upward," Sickles promised this brigade would represent the entire state. Sickles was eventually able to cobble together his five regiments, collected from twelve New York counties and five states; these were designated 1st through 5th Excelsior. Eventually these regiments received their official numerical state designations as 70th through 74th New York State Volunteers. And though affectionately still referred to as 3rd Excelsior, McKinstry's regiment would officially be designated the 72nd New York. Companies formed from preexisting militia units or those with strong company officers and hometown backing like that of Stevens's Chautauqua boys were the pride of their respective regiments, while many companies had been, as regimental chaplain Father Joseph O'Hagan put it, collected from "the scum of New York society, reeking with vice and spreading a moral malaria around them."[8] It was into this environment the articulate and well-read Arthur was thrust. He wrote:

> Those who were not uniformed when they left home are not yet any better off in that respect than when they started. We are of course in excellent trim, which we owe to the liberality of our friends and the active exertion of the ladies.
>
> Our boys, the Jamestown boys, and the few other companies, occupy the northern part of the ground, and the rest is occupied by, the Lord only knows who. They are the very dregs of humanity, and are raked up from the Points and other places of similar repute. Some are coatless, more hatless, and not a few have blankets girt around them to cover the deficiency of pantaloons. All are outrageously filthy, but as no object in nature is without its use, so they furnish an inexhaustible fund of merriment . . .[9]

Chautauqua County sent more than five hundred men into the 72nd New York Infantry, with many going on to prominent positions within the regiment. But the 72nd was by no means the only unit in which Chautauqua men served. The bulk of the 112th New York Infantry was formed from the county

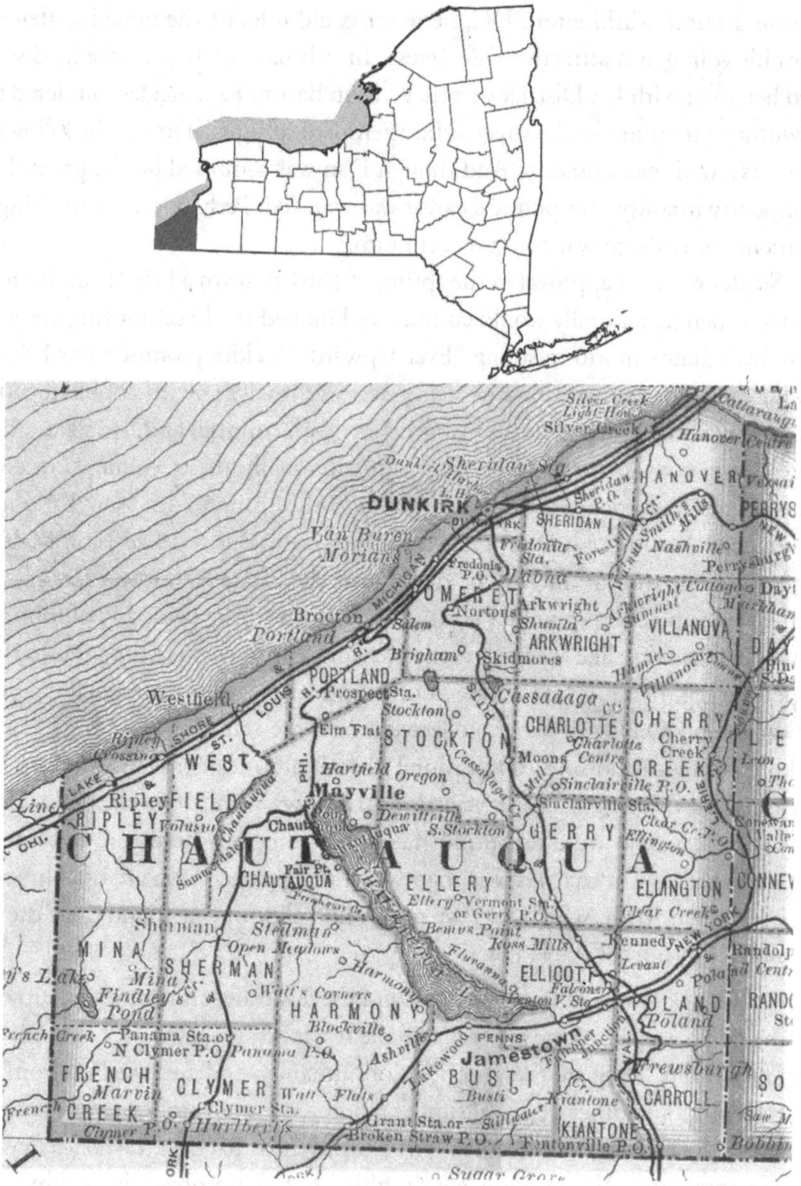

Figure I.3. Map of Chautauqua County. Chautauqua County is the western-most county in New York, tucked in between Pennsylvania and Lake Erie. This map from 1885 shows the various towns and villages within the county. *Courtesy of New York Public Library.*

as was the 9th New York Cavalry. Four companies of men were raised for duty in the 49th New York Infantry, while numerous other men joined regiments formed from outside the county, including two companies into the 154th New York. In all, almost 2,300 Chautauqua men served the Union in the Civil War, though some calculations put the number much higher.[10]

Because of Arthur's writings in the Censor, the Chautauqua companies and the entirety of the 72nd New York had become minor celebrities, at least in the western part of the state—and perhaps in their own minds. With Arthur's letters appearing almost weekly, officers looking to have themselves and their unit portrayed in the best possible light granted the twenty-one-year-old private firsthand access to some of the inner workings of the regiment. "I find that it is a very nice thing to be the correspondent of the Censor for I notice that the officers had rather have a good word there than a bad one. Take it all together I am about as well off as a private can be."[11]

This is Arthur McKinstry's story, told in his words and the words of those around him.

About This Work

Two collections are combined in this work. The first collection was published in the Fredonia Censor, most under the heading of "Dear Uncles," and is stored at the Darwin R. Barker Historical Museum in Fredonia, New York. The second collection, mostly letters to McKinstry's mother, is stored at Mississippi State University and included as part of the Ulysses S. Grant Presidential Library. This collection of letters made its way to Mississippi after the war when Arthur's niece, Lucy Chapin White, moved there to be near cousins who had migrated south prior to the war. All of McKinstry's letters are presented here in the sequence written, though it should be noted the "Dear Uncles" pieces did not appear in print until several days after Arthur penned them.

These letters are presented in their entirety in order to understand the full scope of Arthur's experiences. Unfortunately, because of the condition of portions of the letters, and some faulty storage of these papers, a few words and phrases are illegible. In these cases, the missing phrases will be marked with ellipses or a "best guess" effort will be made and set off by brackets. Arthur McKinstry sometimes wrote with a marvelous dramatic flair and often with a sentence structure to match. Unfortunately, Arthur's lack of punctuation makes understanding these passages difficult at first glance. In order to facilitate smooth reading, some punctuation has been added to tidy up a particular sentence's flow. Perhaps it was Arthur's "stream of consciousness" style of writing or his desire to save space, but there is very little use of paragraph conventions and subjects often change without notice. To help with this transition, a few paragraph breaks have been inserted. Other word use, such as "tomorrow" written as two words, "to" and "morrow," for example, will be left alone as they do not detract from the flow of the piece. Arthur also had a fondness for using foreign words and phrases, along with references to works of literature. While these phrases may have been common in the McKinstry household, many are somewhat obscure and arcane to the modern reader. Definitions or explanations of these words and phrases are included with each letter. Arthur also makes frequent references to friends, relatives, fellow soldiers, or characters from various pieces of literature. Every attempt has been made to identify these people or characters, but when Arthur provides too little information, the true identity of these references will unfortunately remain hidden.

While Arthur McKinstry clearly finds the institution of slavery immoral, he still remains a man of his times and occasionally uses racist terminology when referencing African Americans that would be deemed offensive today. These terms will appear unedited within the body of his letters, if for no other reason than to shed light on the dispassionate use of these dehumanizing terms even among more enlightened Northern men.

It is unfortunate this collection does not include the entirety of Arthur's writings. In letters home there are several references to letters sent to this or that friend or distant relative. It is reasonable to assume these letters, while personal in nature, will not shed much additional light on Arthur's personal trials, camp life, or politics within the company, regiment, and brigade.

This work also includes letters, reports, and newspaper pieces not written by Arthur McKinstry that are set off by the heading "Other Voices." These "other voices," along with a limited amount of notes, will serve to highlight, provide context, or to otherwise illuminate Arthur's writings and experiences. The final chapter will briefly describe the remaining experience of both Arthur's regiment, the 72nd New York, and the Excelsior Brigade after his death in May of 1862 and shed light on the fate of some of the men mentioned prominently by Arthur. An appendix includes additional primary source material, supplemental to Arthur's story. Material in the appendix includes items such as company rosters, officer reports, and newspaper pieces germane to Arthur's experience.

Please enjoy.

Sincerely,
Rick Barram

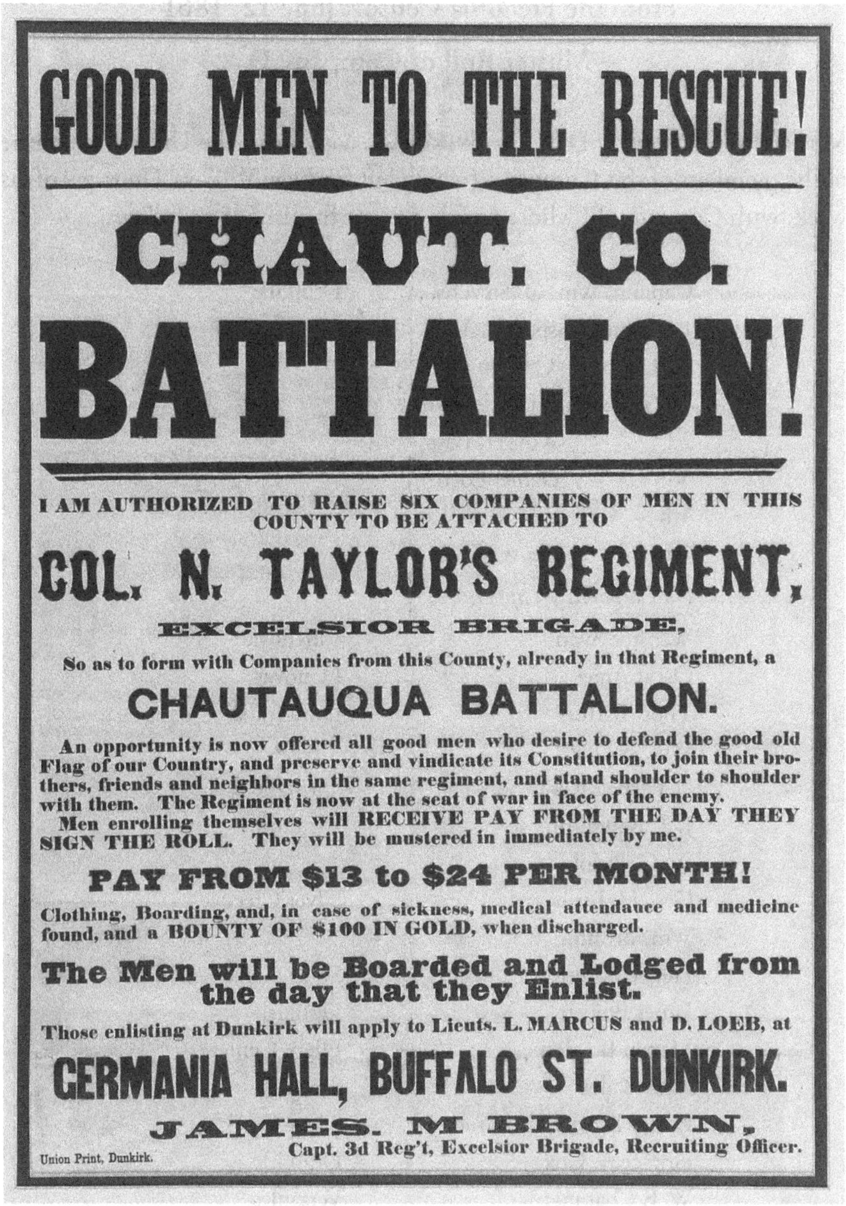

Figure I.4. Chautauqua County recruiting poster. Recruiting in Chautauqua County in spring of 1861. *Courtesy of Heritage Auctions, HA.com.*

From the Fredonia Censor: June 12, 1861

Muster Roll of Company D

Muster Roll Company D of Dunkirk—We copy from the Union, the names of the members of this Company, (which left for New York on Thursday of last week, with Company E, whose names are not furnished.) as follows:

Captain,		Wm. O. Stevens,	Dunkirk
1st Lieut.,		Caspar H. Abell,	"
2d Lieut.,		H. C. Hinman,	"
1st Sergeant,		J. H. Howard,	"
2d	"	Wm. H. Post	"
3d	"	Daniel Loeb	"
4th	"	Samuel Bailey	"
5th	"	George W. Fox	"

No Corporals yet appointed.

Webster Averill	Villenova
Oscar Ames	Hanover
Thos. Barton	Dunkirk
Wm. Babcock	"
L. H. Belknap	Springfield, Pa.
J. T. Boughton	Dunkirk
W. C. Brooks	"
Geo. H. Bush	Silver Creek
Wm. Bruning	"
Henry Beverly	Smith Mills
James Bowen	Dunkirk
Martin Boyden	Ellery Center
Milo Bailey	Stockton
Henry Brevier, drummer	Silver Creek
Horace A. Cox	Dunkirk
W. F. Chapman	Versailles
N. D. Clark	Laona
H. F. Ellis	"
C. A. Foss	Dunkirk
Frederick F. Francis	Centerville
Francis Ferry	Hanover

Marvin H. Farnsworth	Gowanda
W. H. Godfrey	Ellington
Hiram B. Gilbert	Cherry Creek
Onan Griswold	Sheridan
Mathew I. Gifford	"
B. Getz	Dunkirk
Frank Grey, fifer	Evans Station
Almond B. Hamilton	Fredonia
Frank Halsey	Laona
Francis M. Halsey	"
Alfred A Jewell	Dunkirk
J. Kennedy	"
J. Kramer	"
Harvey T. Lopez	"
Joseph Laughlin	"
Ira S. Lewis	Silver Creek
John Leroy	"
G. H. Lewis	Sheridan
Stephen H. Lines	Dunkirk
Otis B. Luce	"
Charles H. Ludlow	"
Chas. H. Miller	Silver Creek
Percival R. Moon	Villenova
Jas. D. Mount	Cherry Creek
Arthur McKinstry	Forestville
Daniel Nichols	Cherry Creek
John Neupling	Stockton
Lee O'Donaghey	Silver Creek
Allen Pickard	Ellery
F. A. Pickard	"
Augustus A. Page	Fredonia
W. H. Porter	Cherry Creek
Geo. F. Parker	Versailles
Jas. K. Palmer	Gowanda
David B. Parker	Ellery Center
Wm. H. Pugh	Dunkirk
R. Riley	Portland
Richard Ransom	Ellington

E. L. Row	Cherry Creek
Carmi T. Ryther	"
C. H. Sanborn	Dunkirk
Christopher Schutt	"
John Story	Cherry Creek
G. W. Shelly Fredonia	
W. Simpson	Dunkirk
Chas. H. Stillman	"
Wm. Schindler	"
R. Stafford	"
Jerome C. Sprague	"
Wm. H. Staats	Gowanda
Wm. Squire	Forestville
Chas. F. Sisson	Gowanda
August Schlutter	Buffalo
Henry Squire	Forestville
Daniel Tyrrell	Dunkirk
Chapin Tiffany	"
Frederick Tide	"
George Tate	Fredonia
S. Taylor	Portland
Jas. H. Vanbatten	Dunkirk
J. Vanhausen	Cherry Creek
C. Van Wormer	"
Claus H. Wriborg	Dunkirk
Jas. G. Warner	"
D. W. Worth	"
Ferdinand Weiler	Dunkirk
T. D. Walden	"
A. M. Wright	Elmira
J. Whitney	Portland
Melvin E. Wright	Villenova
Geo. Whitney	Fredonia
Chas. Youly	Dunkirk
Carl Zents	Dunkirk

CHAPTER I

Installed among Fine and Gentlemanly Fellows

End of May to Mid-July 1861— Joining Up and Departure for New York City

Off to New York to join the brigade • Impressions of men and officers • Rigors of soldiering • A nasty surprise at Bull Run and a call for capital protection

Dunkirk May 27th, 1861

Dear Mother,

I safely arrived here and am installed among as fine and gentlemanly a set of fellows as I ever have seen. Several from Forestville. Tom Brown, Frank Kennington and some others mean to join but they are too late for we are already over full and can take no more. I stand drill first rate and the erect position favors me. I have not yet been examined by a surgeon but I believe I can pass. I met Uncle Willard to day and I expect that he will give me a letter of introduction to the Captain to-morrow and take care of my citizens clothes. I could not get my portrait to-day owing to the crowd of similar applicants but will try to do so early in the morning and send it with this in time for the mail. We shall not go before Wednesday.

I am much pleased with my situation. We stop at the Eastern Hotel and there is no distinction made between us and the most wealthy guests.

Your aff. son
Arthur

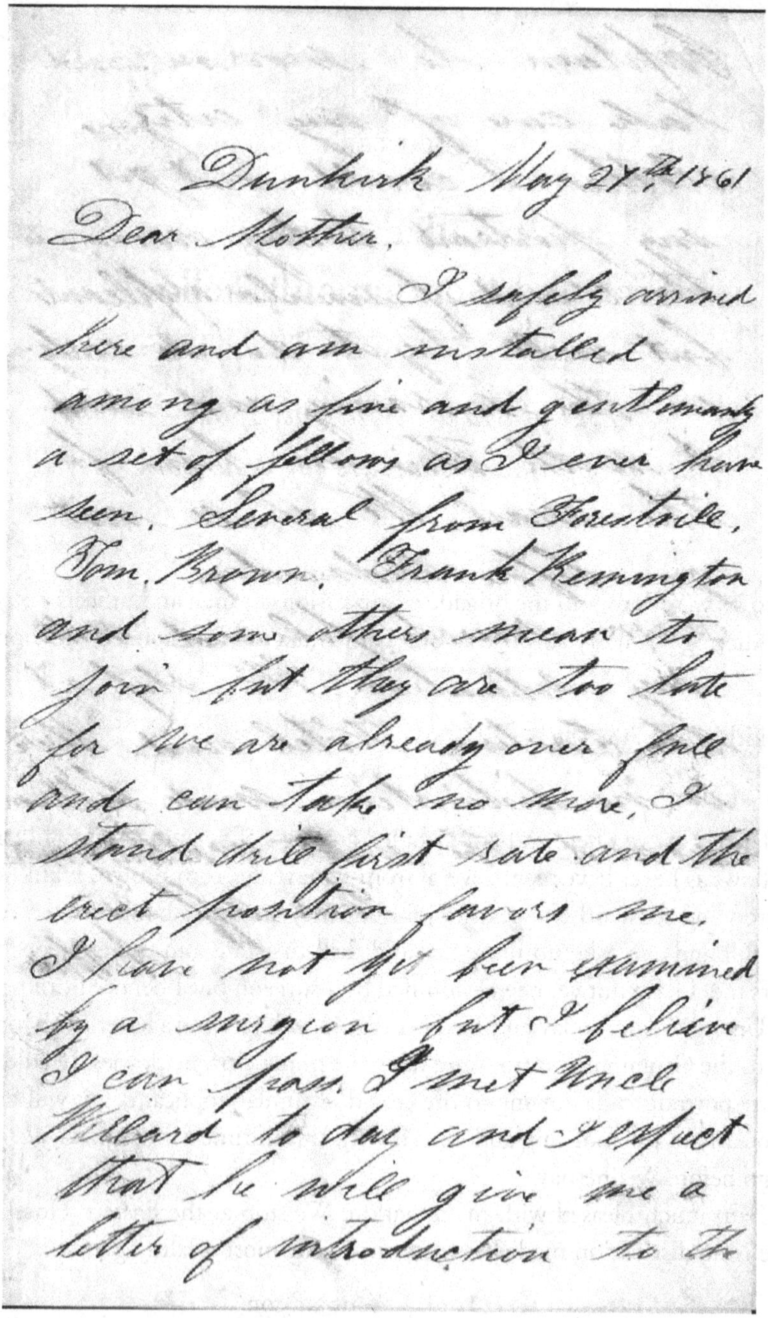
Dunkirk May 27th 1861
Dear Mother,
I safely arrived here and am installed among as fine and gentlemanly a set of fellows as I ever have seen. Several from Forestville, Tom. Brown, Frank Remington and some others mean to join but they are too late for we are already over full and can take no more. I stand tall first rate and the erect position favors me. I have not yet been examined by a surgeon but I believe I can pass. I met Uncle Willard to day and I expect that he will give me a letter of introduction to the

Figure 1.1. Letter to Mother. Arthur McKinstry's first letter to his mother after leaving home. *Courtesy of Ulysses S. Grant Presidential Library.*

Other Voices: From the *Fredonia Censor*
Published May 29, 1861

OFF FOR THE WARS

The first companies accepted from this County for service in the war are to leave for New York to-day. They consist of three volunteer companies, one commanded by Capt. Brown, of Jamestown, the other by Captains Stevens and Barrett, of Dunkirk, and go from that village. They are designed for Gen. Sickles' brigade, now organizing on Staten Island, which volunteers for the war. Under the arrangement each company is required to comprise at least 101 men, including officers and privates. We understand that Capt. Stevens' Co. has enlisted about 125 men, and that Capt. Barrett has also enlisted a surplus, sufficient to supply the places of those who may not pass inspection.

. . . The ladies of our village turned out patriotically, on Saturday last to make up the outfits for the soldiers, at Concert Hall. Through their exertions the recruits will be sent forward well clothed, and doubt not they will prove a body in which the County may take a laudable pride.

On Staten Island a camp of instruction is to be formed, of 60,000 men. Eighteen rifled cannon have been engaged for General Sickles' brigade . . .

Editorial Notes

By the end of May 1861, Daniel E. Sickles's Excelsior Brigade moves its base of operations to Staten Island and out of New York City, where the newly forming brigade was fast outgrowing their hastily organized accommodations. Fort Tompkins is a mobilization center located on Staten Island. While Sickles was originally charged with recruiting a regiment, his commission is soon changed to the formation of a brigade thanks to his successful recruiting. Sickles nominally holds rank of general since he commands the brigade, though officially still only a colonel.[1]

Nelson Taylor is designated colonel of Sickles's 3rd Regiment, receiving its numerical designation 72nd New York later on. Taylor is a veteran of the Mexican War and a prominent member of the early California political scene. Taylor eventually returns to New York, receiving a law degree in 1860 and failing in a bid for congress that same year.[2]

Other Voices: New York City Newspaper Coverage of Sickles's Recruiting Efforts

EXCELSIOR REGIMENT.

The headquarters of the Excelsior regiment is at the City Assembly Rooms, in Broadway, the whole of the building being devoted to the officers of the regiment, and it is needless to add that the spacious room is admirably adapted to the purpose of drilling the recruits. Our readers are already apprised of the organization of this regiment, which is to be under the command of Colonel Daniel E. Sickles. There are over five hundred members enrolled, and the good work is speedily going on. Captain Bradlee, the efficient recruiting officer, is exerting himself to complete the requisite number (1,200) as soon as possible. The men are undergoing thorough discipline under the instruction of competent military men, and if we may judge from their performances last evening, the name of the regiment will indicate its efficiency when it is called to active duty. A portion of the recruits are able to furnish themselves accommodations outside the building, but those who are not are kept in the Assembly Rooms, and furnished with comfortable sleeping apartments and substantial food.[3]

Fredonia Censor: Published June 5, 1861

From the Chautauqua Boys

We have received the following letter from a volunteer in Captain Stevens' Company.

Camp at Ft. Tompkins, near N.Y., Staten Island, June 2, 1861

Dear Uncles:

As I promised, I write to inform you at the first opportunity of our past adventures and present situation.—After leaving Dunkirk we passed the evening with song and music, and cheers from the crowds assembled along the line, in the jolliest manner imaginable. In the morning we arrived at the city, and were received by a battalion from Port Jarvis, and reviewed by our Colonel, and inspected by our Brigadier General, Sickles. This part of our adventures however, you have probably learned from the *Herald* of Saturday. As we entered the Park barracks I heard a citizen exclaim, as he glanced at our tall front files, "My God! There's men for you!" Our men were much admired by the crowd which lined the streets for their fine, erect bearing, and their straight lines. After dinner we marched to the Ferry, and were brought over to the Island and marched to Camp Scott, two and a half miles from the landing.

Here we were drilled a little—went through a dress parade, and finally marched through a dress parade, and finally marched to our present quarters, where we are very comfortable and in fine health and spirits.—Yesterday we marched down to where Capt. Brown, and those who previously arrived, were encamped. There we drilled until 11:35, when word came that we were selected as part of the escort of the famous 7th. Instanter we were in line and off at quick for the landing, which was two and a half miles off. We were there before the required time which was 12 P.M. We crossed over by the ferry, which is several miles wide. And after marching for some time through the principle streets, we were drawn up in line to receive the Seventh. After waiting for some time they appeared, and marched past in fine order by platoons, preceded by their howitzers which they took with them. We then marched after them with double files until we reached Broadway, when, as we reached it, we flanked by the left in platoons, and passed its entire length in lines which were unsurpassed by any on the ground, not even the Seventh its self, if I may credit the expressed opinion of spectators and my own critical observation. Twice we passed them in review, and each time they returned the compliment. Many inquired eagerly of our men to what regiment we belonged, and expressed much admiration at their fine marching order. After drilling pretty nearly until noon yesterday, we marched about twenty miles, and if the Seventh made half work for the enemy that they made for us, they deserved well for their country. On our entry Friday, we were greeted by roars of applause that drowned our music.

On our journey down the Captain telegraphed ahead for coffee, as occasion required, and thanks to the ladies, we did not lack for provisions, and first-rate at that. Indeed, even now, whenever we get hungry we nibble away at the contents of the baskets, and invoke a hearty blessing upon the ladies of Chautauqua. Thanks to them also for our Havelock's and housewives, which are stored with many usual things. The towels are in use, for we quarter upon the shore at the Narrows, and can bathe at pleasure. The Havelock's are a great protection against the sun, and yesterday they were very useful indeed. I will soon write again and enter more into minutia. It is not yet decided whether we receive the Minie or Enfield rifle.

Yours truly,

A. McK.

7th: the 7th Regiment of the New York Militia, aka the "Silk Stocking" regiment, was an infantry regiment also known as the "Blue-Bloods" due to the disproportionate number of its members who were part of New York City's social elite.

Instanter: immediately; without delay.

Havelock: cloth covering attached to a cap to protect the neck from the sun or bad weather.

Minie: probably shorthand for the Springfield rifle, or any rifle capable of accepting the Minie-styled conical bullet.

Enfield rifle: British import rifle considered equal to the Springfield.

Other Voices: *Fredonia Censor,* Departure and Arrival

Published June 5, 1861

DEPARTURE OF THE VOLUNTEERS.

The two Volunteer Companies of Captain Stevens and Barrett raised in Dunkirk, departed from that village on Thursday last, by Erie Railroad, for the encampment of Gen. Sickles' brigade on Staten Island. The acceptance of these companies is mainly due to the energy of Captain W. O. Stevens . . . Secretary Cameron [Secretary of War Simon Cameron] . . . was so favorably impressed with Capt. Stevens' energy and military spirit that he offered him a commission as Captain in the regular service, which the former with a true soldierly spirit of honor, declined to accept no less he could first secure the consent of his company. After his return from Washington a telegraphic dispatch was received offering to accept two companies from this section to be attached to Col. Taylor's Regiment in the Sickles Brigade. Within a week from the reception of the dispatch the men had been enlisted, uniformed, and equipped with havelocks, handkerchiefs, and other necessary articles, ready to march . . .

Published June 5, 1861

ARRIVAL OF TROOPS IN NEW YORK

The *Tribune* of Saturday notices the arrival of the troops in the city in the following complimentary manner:

Two companies of 108 men each, under command of Capts. W. O. Stevens and P. Barrett, arrived in this city from Dunkirk yesterday. They formerly belonged to the 68th Regiment N.Y.S.M., but the prospect of the 68th reaching the seat of war being very doubtful, they retired from the militia ranks and volunteered for the campaign. Their uniform consists of light-blue army overcoats and pantaloons, and brownish gray chasseur jackets and caps. They have brought neither arms nor equipments, as these will be supplied in the city, where they are to be embodied in the Sickles' Brigade.—

They were escorted from the Erie Railroad Depot to the Park Barracks by Capt. Bradley's and Capt. Mahan's companies of the Jackson Regiment with Dodworth's Band where they partook of a sumptuous breakfast of eggs, steak, roast beef, potatoes, bread, radishes, green onions, and coffee. At 12 o'clock, they were reviewed by Gen. Sickles and staff and Mayor Wood. During the afternoon they proceeded to Staten Island.—

The uniforms of the Dunkirk Volunteers are the gift of citizens of Dunkirk. Two handsome flags were presented to them by the ladies of Dunkirk on the eve of their departure. Their soldierly appearance is highly creditable both to the men and the officers.

Other Voices: *Fredonia Censor*,
Making an Impression in New York City . . .

Published June 12, 1861

From the Camp

June 6, 1861

Dear Sirs,

I embrace this first opportunity to write to you . . .

. . . Our Camp is situated on Staten Island, about twelve miles from New York. It is the most delightful spot on earth, so far at least as I have seen. The encampment comprises part of the Sickles Brigade, there being other camps of the same on Long Island and in New York City. Our Regiment is composed of 8 companies, so far—3 of which are from Chautauqua county,

Figure 1.2. WILLIAM O. STEVENS. William Oliver Stevens was the district attorney for Chautauqua County. He served as captain in Company D of the 68th New York State Militia. With the outbreak of war Stevens led what would become Company D of the 72nd New York State Volunteers, eventually rising to the rank of colonel and command of the entire regiment. *Courtesy of US Army Heritage and Education Center.*

1 from Delaware, 1 from Chenango, one from Orange county, N.Y., and 2 from New Jersey. The Colonel says he will have none but country boys in his regiment. Tell O. W. Johnson that there are a number of Otsego boys here in the Delaware and Chenango companies. I suppose you have seen the account of our reception in N.Y. in the papers. We astonished the New Yorkers, as well as ourselves, in that memorable (to us) march of 17 miles in the city, and the cheers and praise that were showered upon us by the crowds of ladies and gentlemen on Broadway and other streets had no other effect upon us than to draw tears to eyes that were unwant to wet. Not a head swayed to right or left, but straight forward, as inspired for the occasion, we marched. Capt. Stevens growing taller every moment. The next day, Saturday, while on parade, the fatigued men of our Company were ordered to N.Y. to escort the 7th regiment to their armory. When the Captain stepped in front and told them that any who did not feel that they could march could fall out, not a man left the ranks. After 4 miles to the landing in double quick time for we were late, we proceeded to the City where after landing, we marched to Courtland street, thence up Broadway to 14th street—to 4th avenue and back, amidst the largest crowd of people I ever saw. As we passed in column in the post of honor, we were cheered almost continually, and many expressions were made in our hearing such as "Them are none of your thirty day boys," "Good for old Chautauqua," "They beat the 7th," while many, supposing we were the advance of the 7th, showered upon us bouquets, bottles of wine, &c., all of which we bore meekly, as becometh good and faithful soldiers. On Sunday we volunteered for church, and attended at the village near the barracks, as the Colonel, for our good conduct, had given us parole of one day . . .

Yours &c.,

G. W. SHELLY

Camp Scott June 7th 1861

Dear Mother,

We are now pretty well settled in our quarters and so I again embrace an opportunity to acquaint you with my situation. We left Ft. Tompkins last Monday and now are dwelling in tents of about ten feet square and there are eight men to each. Our food is coarse but wholesome with the exception of the coffee which is so poor that I mean to stick to cold water henceforth. My health is now perfectly good and the drill though sometimes severe seems to toughen me and I am growing stronger very fast. The soreness is entirely gone and if I did not know that you were anxious about me I should not have entirely dismissed the subject from my mind for as I said before I am entirely well. I think that sea bathing has done me good, and we are yet within a mile of the shore. We may remain here for some time. There are I suppose 3,000 or more troops upon the island besides many more at another encampment up the river. The regiment of which I am a member is the third and contains the finest troops upon the ground. It is in fact the crack regiment. The Seventh returned from the south the day after I wrote you last and we were selected for a part of the military escort to receive them. They were a splendid set of men and looked I dare say more healthy and sunburnt than ever before. Twice they passed us in review and we returned the compliment. They marched in fine order but I heard many New Yorkers remark as they gazed upon our Dunkirk battalion—why they march as well as the Seventh!

I have not yet had time to visit the city except in the ranks but hope to do so before long. Our regiment as I said is a choice one but over on the right of our camp are the "roughs" from the city. They are a rascally set and we keep a constant guard which effectually prevent thefts. I was up nearly all last night on guard and though somewhat fatiguing we contrived to raise some sport.

I have written twice to Uncle Willard who without any solicitation on my part gave me on parting a portable ink stand and all sorts of stationery and writing materials—in order as he said that I might keep him posted as to our movements. Wint was no less liberal for he slipped a half eagle into my hand at parting, with some Windsor soap and a great supply of fishing tackle.

So as you see I am well provided for. We are very pleasantly situated on a grassy plain surrounded by beautiful country seats on three sides and on the east we see the ocean and the vessels passing to and fro. Our tents are perfectly rain proof and we each have an India rubber blanket to lay upon the ground and a pair of heavy woolen ones to wrap up in.

Well my sheet is coming to a close so hoping to hear from you soon and with love to all.

Good bye
Arthur

Editorial Note

Despite what the New York City papers may have written about the quality of the recruits filling the ranks of the Excelsior Brigade, Arthur concludes that not all men within the brigade are created equal.

Fredonia Censor: Published June 19, 1861

FROM THE CAMP.
Camp Scott, Staten Island, N.Y.
June 16th, 1861

Dear Uncles:

—I promised to write again as soon as possible; so here goes. Last Monday we left Fort Tompkins, and are now quartered as above mentioned, and we are now "dwellers in tents"—Our domicils are about ten feet square and lodge 8 men each. There is quite a little village here, with regular streets and a population of about 2,500, as near as I make out. We are supplied with rubber blankets, got up to be used as shawls in wet weather and we spread them on the ground under us, and then we ensconce ourselves in a pair of wool blankets, and this with our boots for a pillow constitutes a bed.

It is so rainy today that we do not drill, and the men have slept soundly this forenoon. Our friends must not take offence if we do not write oftener, for be sure that when our day's drill is over, we sleep as soundly as if on the softest beds cleanest linens. Besides we have no tables, nor as yet seats, and it is very awkward business.

Yesterday we had a very sociable growl about our commissariat, and an indignation meeting was held, and terrible resolutions passed. But the majority took Captain Stevens advice, and resolved to wait a few days, until we get utensils and do our own cooking. We have a pint of coffee (or more) morning and night, and ought to have soup at dinner, but do not build any great expectations, upon the fact that it is due to us. Meat we have enough of, but it is perverting one of the best gifts of Providence, to throw beef by the quarter into a cauldron kettle and boil it, when it is so much better roasted. Potatoes are few and far between; beans, good, naturally, but murdered in the cooking; and first rate bakers' bread, if we prefer it to "hard tack," either are very good. Our coffee reminds me of burnt bean soup, but having no other authority, I must take our room commissary's word for its composition. Our Captain does all he can for us and thus we are better off than most of the companies on the ground. Capt. S. is a great favorite with his men, and I regard our choice of officers throughout as an extremely fortunate one.

Those who were not uniformed when they left home are not yet any better off in that respect than when they started. We are of course in excellent trim, which we owe to the liberality of our friends and the active exertions of the ladies.

Our boys, the Jamestown boys, and a few other companies, occupy the northern part of the ground, and the rest occupied by, the Lord only (with one exception,) knows who. They are the very dregs of humanity, and are raked up from the Points and other places of similar repute. Some are coatless, more hatless, and not a few have blankets girt around them to cover the deficiency of pantaloons. All are outrageously filthy, but as no object in nature is without its use, so they furnish an inexhaustible fund of merriment, more especially when (as semi-occasionally happens) one of them is drummed out with shaven poll to the tune of the "Rogue's March," for some precious piece of rascality.

We have not yet received our Minies, but there are many revolvers and Bowies among us, and we keep a strict watch in camp, so that thieves stand no chance at all. The general health in camp is good, and though several are slightly unwell, there is no serious illness among us. We are now about a mile from the sea, and go nearly every day to bathe. All the Fredonia boys, I believe are well. There is a clam beach about two miles off—[There! I was sitting upon a folded blanket, writing, when I succumbed to Morpheus and slept soundly, when I was wakened by one of my chums, who wanted one of my blankets; and being a little rested, I resumed my letter.]

Notwithstanding our fatiguing drill, the boys are full of spirit, and occasionally during a pause of the double quick march, we rest ourselves by a sharp game of leap-frog. The sentries have a hard time of it, for somebody is always trying to run the line, and "Corporal of the Guard No.——" rings out continually. —Last night they kept me awake considerably by their alarms.

Our grounds are very beautiful—the weather tolerable—that is compared to the region of the lake winds. The men's watches, jewelry, &c., are changing color considerably from the corrosive qualities of the sea breeze. At the same time the same breeze is very refreshing, and as we have good society among the companies, we should enjoy ourselves very well if only we had good coffee and an occasional taste of butter, but the latter is *non est*, and we are no better off for the former on account of its quality. Butter is, I believe, a part of the ration, but we see no prospect of any. Yesterday, the hearts of our men were made glad by a barrel of tobacco from Dunkirk.—We are all impatient to take an excursion upon Virginia soil.

A. McK.

The Points: the Five Points area of Manhattan, a notorious, rough-and-tumble crime-infested neighborhood.

Non est: not available, not here.

Camp Scott June 19th, 1861

Dear Wint,

The [color-]bearer Mr. Francis M. Habey has been discharged by the Surgeon and not on account of any misconduct but on the contrary he is a general favorite both with officers and men. As he will return by the way of Fredonia, I send him to you that you may obtain from him details which would take too much time and space upon paper as well as a better general idea of our condition than any outsider could do.

As yet I have received only the first Censor and do not know whether you have received my letters (this makes I believe the fifth) or not. Just drop me a line now and then for letters are eagerly seized and read here. I sent you a day or two ago a corrected list of our officers and men (Corporals not yet selected). One of our men Nichols whose name is off our rolls, deserted a little while after our arrival but returned and gave up his uniform. The list I sent you was correct with the exception of the bearer (one or two others having run away or been discharged) and another, —honorably discharged to-day. We have still some sport with our sentries. It is a heinous offence in military eyes to surrender up a musket or yield it to any until relieved. Thus it is a standing joke to capture a musket from a guard. Once when on duty I thrust my bayonet into the ground and turned to speak with the sentry on my right. While thus engaged the sentry on my left seized my gun and was making off with it when I perceived what was going on and drawing my tooth pick I pursued him and compelled him to restore the spoil. The very next morning I caught a sentry sleeping and played off the same trick upon him. His dismay upon awaking may be imagined but I did not tease him long. I expected to have been in Chicopee by this, but we have not yet been sworn in which we expected to be last Monday, and so I am still waiting very patiently of course. I have had good opportunities to see Gen. Sickles—yesterday especially, being detailed as orderly for our Colonel and thereby seeing and speaking with him. He is a tall well formed man of quick energetic movements and courteous gentlemanly address. His hair is dark brown, beard lighter with long curling moustache. His general bearing impressed me very favorably. He is in the prime of manhood and displays corresponding talent and energy in the vast amount of labor required in the organization of this brigade. One of the great faults of the regular service is that the General officers and Naval Post Captains are raised mostly in their rank by their years of service rather than by acts of valor or commanding talent and thus when they arrive at a high command they are frequently superannuated. Fortunately this is not the case with Gen. Scott.

When you examine our archives you will find that many of our proudest victories were gained by men whose strength and force were not decayed by age but whose hearts were impulsive and whose brain unrelaxed—who were not restrained by that excess of caution so often found in aged men. I shall continue to write as often at least as once a week if unforeseen circumstances do not prevent. Give my regards to the family not forgetting Aunt Ellen and little Grace, or the young ladies whose kindly farewell at D. will be long remembered. My health is excellent and I endure hard marching better than many apparently tougher than myself. The company is in an excellent state of discipline and lines I think about the best of any upon the ground, besides wheeling and flanking with great precision.

Yours as ever

Tell Uncle Willard to write

Arthur

My tooth pick: common reference to a Bowie knife, or in this case Arthur could be referring to his bayonet.

I expected to have been in Chicopee by this . . . : perhaps a visit to the McKinstry ancestral home of Chicopee, Massachusetts, on furlough following enlistment.

Superannuated: retired or discharged because of age or infirmity.

Editorial Note

In mid-May New York governor Edwin Morgan orders Sickles to disband all but one regiment of his brigade. Undeterred, Sickles appeals directly to Lincoln, who eventually agrees to muster the entire brigade in as United States Volunteers.[4]

Other Voices: New York City Newspaper Coverage

Published June 24, 1861

GENERAL SICKLES' EXCELSIOR BRIGADE.

Camp Scott, on Staten Island, the quarters of the Excelsior Brigade, has been the scene of much activity during the past week, in consequence of the presence of the United States mustering officers—Captains Cogswell and Hayman. Twenty-five companies have been mustered since Thursday last, and in every instance the troops took the oath with great enthusiasm. The mustering will continue every day until the fifty companies composing the brigade are exhausted. Yesterday, at four o'clock, Rev. Drs. Berkeley and Twichell held Divine service at the camp, which was attended by the soldiers and a large number of their friends. The brigade formed a hollow square, with the general and his staff in the centre and the visitors outside, in which position the ceremonies were conducted. A full band of music was on the ground and assisted in the religio-military exercises. A dress parade followed and wound up the day's proceedings.[5]

Fredonia Censor: Published July 3, 1861

From Camp Scott

Camp Scott, June 24, 1861

Dear Uncles:

As one of our boys is going home on furlough, I take the opportunity to write again. As you have doubtless heard, we are now sworn in and committed for three years or the war. When the business was over, three rousing cheers were given for Co. D, one of the few which came out entire.—one or two did not take the oath, but they were not able-bodied men, and of course, were justifiable. Co. E—we kept our old Chautauqua letters as now organized—lost three men, and the Jamestown Co. five or six, but some of them enlisted in other companies.—This however, was of no great moment, as they were such as could be very well spared. The Michigan boys swore in to a man, and they are one of the best companies on the ground. It seems that we are still remembered in the city, for one of our lads who was over yesterday remarks that he heard many say that it was the finest body of men that had passed through as yet. I am digressing, however, from our subject. Our regiment—the 3rd, is sworn in, and indeed, I believe there are few who are not. The Pittsburg Zouaves are not, and wish to secede, but Sickles won't let them off without they pay the expenses incurred for board, &c. About twenty of our boys are now placed to bar their passage out. Whenever there is any disturbances our county boys are called upon for the purpose of putting it down, and they are always successful. There are now two Massachusetts companies on the ground, but as they were all militiamen and did not procure a proper discharge, they are liable to be recalled, Gov. Andrew having, it is reported, called for 10,000 more men. Many companies have left the place dissatisfied, and there are not so many men here by six or seven hundred, I think, as there was when the brigade was accepted. This is partly caused by insufficient or poor rations, and partly by one or two men of the Olean, and Delaware county boys being struck by Williamson, the Colonel late in command. This was certainly unjustifiable, but *we* have fared well and received good treatment so far. We have had a discussion just now by a committee of one from each tent, on the subject of Capt. Stevens' promotion to a Majority. It is certain that he has been offered that position, but declines the nomination unless the men vote their consent thereto. I think the men will consent, as they are unwilling to bar his advancement, though they regret to lose his services as captain.

We have had one recruit since I wrote last, named Cole, and a member of the disbanded Olean Company. He is now our *infant*, being only about six feet two. The *infant* of the Michigan boys is six feet five, but being well proportioned does not seem so large until you see the contrast of his height with that of others. Our infant is a short, square built chunk of a boy.

By late papers I see that business is getting pretty lively in Virginia. I should not wonder if we got marching orders before very long, and those high in authority are of the same opinion. We drill from five to six hours daily, and go through our evolutions on a quick, swinging step which carries us over the ground very rapidly. We drill but little in common time and we are so habituated to rapid motion that on brigade and regimental drills we gain so rapidly on the column ahead—we are on the left, that we have to mark time or halt very often. We do very well, indeed, upon the double-quick, and march in that

Figure 1.3. Jesse L. Walker. Jesse L. Walker was a member of Company E, which was raised in Chautauqua County. Walker is dressed in the New York State jacket typical of New York State troops. *Courtesy of US Army Heritage and Education Center.*

quite as often as in common time. In fact, on a double-quick wheel we can beat the Zouaves within our camp. We had a good rest yesterday, until about four P.M., when we were ordered to get ready for brigade drill.—The Colonel reviewed us passing arm in arm with Gen. Sickles, while Capt. Stevens commanded the regiment, and Lieut. Abell our company. First we went through dress parade, then we passed in review, (where company D bore off the honors on account of its beautiful company front and excellent wheels) and then—a rain coming on, we went to our quarters which were about a quarter mile off upon the double-quick, and every time we flanked or filed we did it with as much precision as if we were marching in common time. Company E does very well indeed, and marches admirably in double file, as do also the Jamestown men. Col. Nelson Taylor, our commanding officer, is a tall, dark complexioned man of fine military appearance, and pleasant and affable, though dignified, in address. He has served in Mexico and California and will therefore be just the man for a campaign in low latitude. Well I must close in order to look after my share of tent duty, in getting some boughs for bedding. I will try to write at least once a week, and shall be glad to hear from you. The *Censor* comes in Friday night.

A. McK.

Pittsburg Zouaves: a company in the 1st Excelsior (70th NY) that filed a court case against Sickles desiring to leave and join another regiment.

Olean: a town in Cattaraugus County, adjacent to Chautauqua County.

3d Regiment Excelsior Brigade
Care Capt. C. K. Abel
Camp Scott July 2nd 1861

Dear Mother,

Not being very busy just now I take the opportunity to write home again. I wrote some time since but have no answer as yet though Frank is fully capable of performing that office. I was sorry to hear that you had been sick but you will no doubt feel greatly relieved to know that I stand guard nights and do all the duties required of a soldier without any inconvenience whatever. We are pretty comfortable in spite of the attacks made upon the Brigade and its commanders by the Tribune, and its accounts of the state of things here are false and malicious in the extreme. The power of the press is however pretty fairly demonstrated for the Tribune must have caused the desertion of nearly 1,000 men. The Brigade is however mustered in and in good discipline, but I don't think it contains more than about 3,000 men. Capt. Stevens has been raised to the rank of Major of our regiment and is well fitted for the office. Oscar Ames I presume you have heard is in our company as well as two of the name of Squier from Forestville.

Company D is a fine one and some of favorites are from Fredonia. There are Lance, Ellis, Tate, Hamilton (John Jr.'s brother) Shelley &c. from there with whom I am more or less intimate. The other day I was astonished by seeing one of the Michigan boys bolt into my tent and exclaim—I came to see a namesake of mine. Why said I is your name McKinstry—Yes he replied, whereupon we took a stroll about camp and talked things over. He is a keen smart fellow with a face and head which bear a strong resemblance to the portraits of Tommy Moore. Like me he has wandered in the west but in a more northerly direction. His journeys extend as far as Santa Fe where he went as master of mail train. After all I associate with the Fredonia boys more than any other, having a description of them from Uncle Willard. The camp presented rather a scaly appearance as to society when I came here but many of the roughs have gone and the naked are clothed and at present the Brigade presents a fine appearance. Then we had few associates there being so many from the "Points" &c. but now the great body are respectable men from the country. One company is from Mass. and I call in now and then and spend an evening at the Revere House or some other Boston or Cambridge Co. tent. As we are likely to remain here some time I think you had better send on my trunk for I would like to have things convenient as the rest are now doing. I don't like to have everything mussed up together. If you will take it to Forestville you can send it on by express to me. Send on my white fine shirts and vest and black pants. The style among our boys is to dress neatly and respectably and thus as in other things appear a crack corps.

My best pants will appear very well as they can hardly be noticed beside the very dark army blue and I have the promise of a furlough to go to Chicopee before long. Soldiers on furlough travel free over most roads and I think over mine. As regards the trunk I shall need it in order to stow my camp kit at any rate for a satchel wont hold it and besides is very easy to get into by springing the jams. Put in my linen coat, straw hat and stand too, for cits clothes are often worn when off duty and our cloth uniform is pretty hot while the caps are no protection from the sun. I went over to N.Y. yesterday to see Byron Finch but he was home for vacation. Edward sent me his address and I left mine that he might call on his return. We are doing well and enjoying ourselves. I have just come off extra guard duty and am entitled to eight hours sleep and think I will improve them. I shall probably come on guard again the fourth which I devoutly hope for I fancy that the troops will get some very healthy exercise on that glorious day—give my love to the family and tell me how crops prosper for I am as anxious to hear from them as you from me. Send the trunk as soon as you can for I want it—as I don't like to have things lying about. It will not cost over half a dollar and I can better afford to pay that than to do without it.

Put the key inside and let the lid down for I can pick it.

Arthur

Tribune: *New-York Daily Tribune*. From the 1840s through the 1860s it was the dominant Whig Party and then Republican newspaper in the United States.

Michigan McKinstry: Robert McKinstry was not related to Arthur and served in a company from Paw Paw, Michigan, within the 70th NY.

Cits: abbreviation for citizens.

Fredonia Censor: Published July 24, 1861

For the Censor.

Camp Correspondence.

Camp Scott, July 6, 1861

Dear Uncles;—

I presume that by this time you would like to hear from the volunteers. In my last I think that I did not mention the fact that we now do our own cooking. This improves the quality of our food considerably, but the coffee is as much like burnt soup as ever, and even when we have milk it is not fit to use, and I believe it is the cause of half the cases of diarrhea in camp. I stick to cold water. The meat is very good, but we have to take it boiled. Of bread we have a loaf daily, which weighs about 18 ounces. As the ration is the same amount of flour, either the Commissary or the baker makes a very nice thing of it. We now have very good soup, and our full rations, I believe, in all other respects. At first we got things rather irregularly, and it cost me about $1.50 to get the food I required the first month, but now I can do very well upon my rations.

I see that the Tribune pitches into Sickles and the Brigade as savagely as a meat axe. Well, it commenced something as follows: The Tribune first published an article virtually warning the public that Sickles was unauthorized by Government, and that his contracts were not binding, for subsistence, &c. Sickles then produced the document, which you doubtless saw, which refuted the charge, and the Tribune could not very well refuse to print it. Gen. Sickles then forbade the sale of the Tribune upon the ground, and from that time he has been the object of its bitterest malice. That he was unwise in the prohibition is true, but that he has been deeply wronged is equally certain. The brigade was accepted just in the nick of time, for in a week after, the brigade was minus about 1,000 men, and I think that the point blank falsehoods of the Tribune contributed very much toward this. To be sure many left on the accounts I have before stated, and many because they had anticipated a pleasant holiday excursion, and found themselves slightly mistaken. If any intend to join with that expectation, they had better stay behind, but if they intend to do battle for their country, and they can endure some occasional privation and fatigue, why, let them come, and they shall have a cordial welcome. For we do not expect to bring back our banners untorn and unsoiled, but we expect that the next time you see them they will be discolored by smoke, and rent by bullets. Not a man of us is not eager to join in the strife, and the announcement by Gen. Sickles, day before yesterday, on parade, that in one week from the Fourth we shall be armed, equipped, and ready for the march, was greeted by the loud applause of the whole battalion. When we first came, we had few companies upon the ground which it would do to associate with, but no man need remain behind on that account, for he can mingle with his peers, be they of whatever class, though the greater part are fine young men from rural districts.

One of the Michigan men died a few days since, and was buried with all the honors of war. The whole brigade turned out as escort, while the flag was at half-mast.

One of the men has since died from a bayonet thrust received in attempting to escape from the guard house. There is a fine company of French Zouaves here, and I call upon them regularly, as also at the Revere House of the Cambridge, Mass., Co., and upon a namesake of ours in the Michigan company.

A fine battery is being constructed for the corps, and a few days since one of the guns, a rifled steel cannon, with Hotchkiss' ball, was tested. It put ball after ball into a space not larger than a man, at the distance of a mile and a quarter. It will throw a ball, or rather conical shot, from 2 ½ to 3 miles, though of only 2 ½ inch bore. The others are also rifled and of various caliber.

The Fourth passed off rather dull, and many thought it a poor celebration, but I came off first rate, for I was posted sentry at No. 11, and some good people seeing my situation, sent me a very good dinner, which Tate and I disposed of with great gusto, he being on post No. 12. The principal features of the day were parade at 4 P.M. and fire-works at 8. The last were very fine indeed. Being guard I did not go on drill, but observed Company D come wheeling around as squarely as a picket gate, and with every file closed to perfection.

Major Stevens is winning golden opinions in his new position, and his place with us is ably filled by Captain C. K. Abell, to whose care all letters to us should be addressed. Our company has the lion's share of regimental appointments, as you will see by the following list: Major, Wm. O. Stevens; Adjutant, Doyle; Surgeon, Irwin; Serg't Major, Bailey; Regt. Clerk, Wriborg; Drum major, Krevier; and this takes all the offices vacant when we came, except one clerkship, which is filled by Lord, of Jamestown.

We have as yet received no pay, and begin to feel pretty poor. Two or three days ago, private Kramer's revolver deserted, and as private Worth has not been seen since, we fear he was carried off by it. He could not have required much persuasion, however, as he had deserted twice before. We can do without him; but the pistol was sadly missed, it having been a present to Kramer.

Well, I believe you must be sufficiently bored by this time, so adieu.

A. McK.

Camp Scott July 6th, 1861

Dear Mother,

I received this morning a letter from Frank, Jennie, Wm. K. and you. I was surprised and greatly amused to hear how Ed. Graves performed. You can tell all inquiring friends that I can go a mile to two on the double quick without any inconveniences and hit straight out from the shoulder and fetch claret as soon as the next man, though I have never done so except in sport. We had rather a dull fourth and many remarked that it was very like Sunday. Gen. Sickles made an address stating that the brigade was to be completed, armed, and equipped in one week but it will take longer I think. You think things go on slow do you—well I don't think that so bad as to be too fast and though we are all burning with impatience yet we own that the slowly closing net of Gen. Scott will prove quite as effectual in the end and cost a far less amount of human life. I see that Gen. Patterson has routed 10,000 rebels with a loss of but two or three. I have had camp diarrhea a little but not so as to prevent my doing duty and I am now quite well.

Instead of being the consumptive looking fellow you saw last I am hardier to day than two thirds of our men though I am ten pounds lighter than when I left but as hard as india rubber. We have church and I attended last Sunday. We did not need chaplains for some of our officers stepped up and in full uniform of captains and Lieut's gave us preaching far superior to what we usually hear at Forestville or Fredonia. And then such grand singing—You can hardly realize the effect of the full choir of male voices varying from bass to alto (and we have some who can even reach treble,) there was a power which reminded me of the organ and I do not think instruments could have added to the music but would rather have marred. Well I am tired and as I wrote only a day or two since I will close.

Remember me to all. If you have not sent my trunk send it as soon as possible as my black pants will pass for uniform and if I have them I shall be entitled to their value instead of having it, all of it, expended upon very poor satinet. Hustle in my French as I wish to exchange reading with the French Zouaves whom I visit.

Much love to all
Arthur

Send the trunk first as soon as you can for I can take it.

Fetch claret: draw blood.

Gen. Patterson has routed 10,000 rebels: likely the Battle of Hoke's Run, also known as the Battle of Falling Waters, which took place on July 2, 1861, in Berkeley County, Virginia.

Fredonia Censor: Published July 24, 1861

FROM THE CAMP.

Camp Scott, July 11, 1861

Dear Uncles—

But little of note has transpired since my last. It is now so hot that we drill but three or four hours, daily, lying still from 9 A.M., until 4 P.M.—We drill in the morning as skirmishers, which requires a pretty active use of our legs, and in the afternoon we have brigade or regimental drill and dress parade, or if very hot, dress parade only. The first regiment has received their equipments and muskets, and ours are said to have been called for by requisition. I hope they will come to hand before long, for we are getting tired of the old routine of wheeling, flanking, and filing, and were it not for skirmishing we should be impatient indeed.

The men are generally quick to learn, and indeed very many are members of old military organizations, and as a week's drill will give a good practical knowledge of the manual—so that we shall be ready to meet the enemy as riflemen, while some at least are old cannoniers. The Sutler's department is now in running order and is rapidly absorbing the spare change and future pay of the soldiers. Any soldier can go there and get articles on credit and when pay day arrives the amount is stopped from the poor devils wages, and many who crave the little luxuries they were accustomed to at home will thus be robbed of one-half or two thirds of their wages. I say robbed because they do not get at best over half the value of their money, and generally not over one fourth.—Thus the sutler having the exclusive privilege of trading with the soldiers, makes in all probability, more than the commandant of the post, and does it by charges which reflect but little credit upon his patriotism. I am surprised that the general allows this thing to be carried on without looking to the tariff of goods a little closer. Our Colonel is absent and has been for some time, and it is pretty well understood that he is doing his best to get us into active service as soon as possible. During his absence Major Stevens virtually commands the regiment, though we occasionally see Lieut. Col. Moses stepping gingerly about and directing some file or other to dress up the sixteenth part of an inch. All orders to the battalion come, however, from Major. It is he who plans and directs the various movements, and conducts the view of parade. In one respect only we miss Col. Taylor and that is on account of his wonderful voice, which can be heard very distinctly at as greatly a distance as we are likely to get in any evolution. As a tactician Col. Taylor is evidently first rate, while his personal traits render him a favorite with all.

A few days since some of us, all I believe of Fredonia, went down to bathe, but having just come off guard we were entitled to the day until 4 P.M.; so, not being in a hurry we strolled of toward Ft. Tompkins, through some of the finest estates upon the Island. Nearly all orders of architecture were represented, and the surrounding grounds were ornamented by willows, cedars, Norway pines and various flowering trees, which loaded the air with their fragrance. Capt. Abell is back in camp and in better health. No one of our company is seriously ill, nor of Cos. B and E, so far as I know. Whenever we go out to take a look of the surrounding country our Chautauqua Co. gray jackets are a much better passport to a cordial reception than the dark blue which is worn by the city roughs, who when more numerous, got it into rather bad repute. Our three companies stick together like brothers, never quarrel with each other, but always observe the most cordial relations. Co. B is upon the right while D is upon the left, and E is next to us. I believe I forgot to mention in my list of regimental appointments that of H. T. Lopez who is Color Sergeant and carries the flag for the 3rd regiment.

I visited fort Tompkins during our stroll the other day, and went through the casemates and strolled along the parapets. It has circles for 108 columbiads, and is surrounded by a wide moat which is enfiladed by six heavy guns upon each angle. The shape is triangular, and like most of our fortresses it is weak upon the land side. There is however, a large fort in process of construction upon the hill which commands it upon the rear, which when completed will render approach by the landside impossible, while the columbiads of the masked batteries upon and along the hill-side by the Narrows could, from that elevation, sink the navies of all Europe, much more Jeff Davis' pirates, were they to endeavor to enter. The guns are not mounted, but there are ten ten-inch columbiads and some dozen of 32s, lying about which could soon be got ready, while opposite is the Diamond and in the rear, Ft. Hamilton.

I have been requested by the Fredonia boys, (and didn't require much urging,) to direct your attention to what I just spoke of, viz.: the extortion practiced toward those who require any little comforts besides the ordinary rations. Those who are unwell almost invariably require something more palatable, and if they do, cheese is 16 cents and very poor skim-milk at that, and butter is 30 cents which is just double the price at the city, while the cost of transportation cannot exceed one cent. Other things are still dearer, and it is from these causes that the boys request their friends to appoint someone to receive such luxuries as their relatives may give, and send them by express to some of our townsmen in camp—say Ellis or Luce, for distribution here. The proper address of boxes or letters is as follows: "A—— B——, 3d Reg't Excelsior Brigade, Staten Island, New York (Care of Capt. A. O. R. Abell)."

Yours, &c.,
A. McK.

Other Voices: *Fredonia Censor*

Published July 17, 1861

We have received a call from Mr. Geo. W. Shelley, of this village who is a member of Co. D, in the so-called Sickles Brigade, and is at present home on a furlough. Mr. S says that the number of men in Camp Scott who have now been mustered into the United States service is 41 companies of 101 men each. The men now well understand that there is no chance for the acceptance of the Brigade as such, and are content to go into service by regiments. Col. Sickles, it is reported, takes command of the 1st Regiment. The men have not as yet received any pay, though the Government is now responsible for it. The troops are very healthy, and eager to receive marching orders.

Published July 24, 1861

MORE CHAUTAUQUA RECRUITS FOR CAMP SCOTT

—We learn that Co. B of Westfield, was to leave yesterday for Camp Scott, Staten Island, where it is to be incorporated in Col. Taylor's Regiment. This will make the fourth Chautauqua Company which has gone into the Regiment. The Jamestown *Journal* states that eight members of the Jamestown Cornet Band left that place on Wednesday last for Camp Scott, where they are to form a nucleus for a band for the same regiment. The Dunkirk Regimental Band has had an opportunity offered for enlisting in this band, but we have not learned their decision with respect to it.

Fredonia Censor: Published July 31, 1861

Camp Scott, July 21, 1861

Dear Uncles:—

It seems to be pretty definitely settled that by Saturday next, at the very latest, we shall be en route for "Dixie." We are having manual drills and very fatiguing battalion drills daily. Our muskets we have had for some days, and they prove to be the altered guns of 1833. This will prove a sad disappointment if they are used for any other purpose than for drill. We have, however, some hope that we shall exchange them for rifles. Last Thursday, Shelley and some others came in from Chautauqua, bringing some creature comforts, which were thankfully received.

I am very glad to hear that our County is to furnish two more companies. This, though not sufficient to reach the maximum, will yet exceed the minimum number required for a Regiment. They will find themselves mainly under staff officers from our own county, for we have had all the offices there were, excepting Col., Lt. Col., and the Quartermaster's Dept. Our Chaplain, Rev. Mr. Norton, of Jamestown, preached a very fine sermon this morning, and was listened to with great attention. The Jamestown members of our regimental band are here and furnish the music for divine service.

The old order of things is now entirely broken up, and each regiment has its own sentries, while the brigade guard, which was a perfect nuisance is withdrawn. The 3d is now at liberty to come and go at will, taking care to be present at drills or roll call, and I am happy to say that the liberty is not abused and that no irregularities are caused thereby. The other regiments are surrounded by guards, and none are allowed to pass without a permit signed by the officer of the day. There is no reason in such strictness, for if a man really wishes to get out, he does it by night, and after a high pressure bender, come back at about 4 o'clock pretty well used up, and in just the frame of mind to shirk duty on the ensuing day. During the daytime, to be sure, the guard is pretty effective, but then the horse has been stolen and it is of no use to fasten the door, while the men who really have occasion to leave the lines for water or upon other errands, must go to the circumlocution office, for a pass. Our guards simply do policeman's duty and do not, until 9:15 P.M., hinder the passage of any one. From that time until morning the countersign is required.

Our men take very naturally to the musket drill, which is probably owing to the fact that so many have drilled before, that patterns are plenty for the uninitiated. I think that we can give a pretty fair account of ourselves and we are all burning with impatience to try it on.

Well we shall soon "look away for Dixie," and this may be the last you may hear from Camp Scott, though. I shall probably have the opportunity to acquaint you with the time of our departure. Until within three days we have slept upon the ground, but Thursday we tramped to Ft. Tompkins and took mattresses, since which our officers have had unprecedented difficulty in gathering their lambs together at reveille roll-call. Our Duties for the day are as follows, 5 A.M., reveille,—one hour's drill as soon as the roll can be called, and on our return, street sweeping and general setting of things to rights—at 7 o'clock breakfast—at 8, sick call, when those who are ill report to the surgeon. At 8 ½ o'clock guard mounting, when the new guard is formed and the old dismissed—also at 8, drill for one hour—at 1 P.M., dinner—at 3, company drill—at 5 battalion drill, which lasts generally until sunset, more or less, and we close our tasks by dress parade, supper immediately follows, and at 9 come tattoo, when the roll is called for the third time, and in fifteen minutes after, "taps," when all are expected to be in bed and the lights out. N.B. 24 hours extra guard duty to the poor wight who does not comply with the last requirement, or who absents himself from drill or roll call.

22d.—I see by the morning papers that a great battle has been fought and an important victory won. I am very sorry that we could not be there, but hope for better luck next time. The 1st are getting ready to depart, and will do so very soon. Our orders are, if I may credit one of our men, who heard Col. Taylor read them to be off by Saturday at the latest, and as much sooner as we can.

Why has not Co. A of Fredonia, come into this brigade. Shelley reports them as being in a very good state of drill, and if they would fill up and come on they would just about fill up the 3d to the maximum number. That they would be accepted I do not doubt. Yesterday evening we had a very fine brigade drill. A large number of spectators were here and it was a splendid affair. Almost every imaginable evolution was performed except retreating. I believe that we march to the right about once or twice, but that is something we do not expect to practice before the enemy. The first and second are full; we shall exceed the minimum when our Chautauqua re-enforcements come; and the fifth will soon receive six companies from Maine, which will complete that regt., and when the rest are off it will be easy to fill up the fourth. There are but few men upon the ground who have had no uniforms. All nearly, are armed, and so the brigade makes a splendid sight when upon review, with the long lines and marching columns, and their polished weapons gleaming like silver in the sun.

The discipline is now excellent, and all have become familiar with their duties. I am sorry to say that we have had two deserters. They were not regretted for their personal qualities however, and perhaps the watch which *Boughton*, (J. F.) and the revolver which disappeared when *Worth*, absconded could better be lost than we could keep the offenders within our camp. Boughton had tried for several days to borrow a watch, and when at last he succeeded, he disappeared as promptly as Roderick Dhu's Clansmen.

He had been a corporal, and might have been a sergeant: but for his utter disregard for rules, and for his lawless conduct, he was degraded to the ranks.

We understand that letters go free from here, and certainly many do, but a young gentleman writing hence to a young lady received in return some stamps, with a hint that it was cheaper to pay postage in advance. Does this proceed from the ignorance of P.M.s or are not the letters legally franked? Many write from here without stamping letters, who would be greatly mortified to hear that the recipients have to pay their postage. Please let us know about this and look into the matter.

There have been many cases of diarrhea in camp, but I think they were caused by the coffee and by the bread; the latter is light and sweet, but I do not regard it as being as good as fermented bread, and I think that it will be better for us when we get biscuit only. None are seriously ill, and if we were in the enemy's country, every man could and would turn out instanter for a fight. Trifling cases are common, but nothing serious.

Yours as ever,

A. McK.

Altered guns of 1833: a model 1816, .69 cal., smoothbore flintlock musket converted to percussion.

Wight: a living creature, especially a human being, especially one regarded as unfortunate or unlucky.

Roderick Dhu's Clansmen: from the epic poem *The Lady of the Lake*, where the character Roderick Dhu's band of Scottish warriors, his clansmen, disappear with a wave of a hand.

Editorial Note

On July 21, 1861, the Battle of Bull Run is fought, the first great land battle of the war. Instead of it being an "important battle won" like Arthur had heard, it is a shocking defeat for Union forces. Soon every available unit, fully ready or not, moves to defend Washington.

Other Voices: Regimental Command

General Order, No. 8
Headquarters Third Reg't.
Excelsior Brigade
Camp Scott, Staten Island, July 23rd, 1861

The Regiment being under marching orders for the seat of war will make the necessary preliminary arrangements for the march. The personal baggage of officers and men will be reduced to the minimum. Every article will be marked with the name, company and number of the owner. Tents, poles, axes, hatchets, cooking utensils, &c., &c., &c., will be distinctly marked with letter of the company and No. of the Regt., and the tents folded with the mark on the outside. The commandants of companies will make requisition for hams and hard bread for two days. If rations are supplied on the transports then rations will be reserved until the arrival of the Regiment at the point of destination to avoid the suffering and delay which would otherwise in all probability occur. The baggage and tents will be prepared for transportation immediately after Reveille.

Commandants of companies will see that their men are furnished with overcoats or woolen blankets, rubber blankets, tin cups, plate, knife, fork and spoon. The Regiment will hold itself in readiness to march at 2 p.m. precisely.

By order,

Nelson Taylor,
Comm'dg.[6]

Editorial Note

On the evening of July 24, 1861, the regiment boards boats, taking them off Staten Island on to New Jersey and eventually through to Washington.

In the July 24 edition, the *Fredonia Censor* reported: "We understand that the 3d Regiment at Camp Scott, since the Manassas battle, has received orders to march, and was to leave for Washington last night. Success to our gallant boys!"

Figure 1.4. Nelson Taylor. Nelson Taylor was colonel of the 72nd New York. Taylor often commanded the Excelsior Brigade during the frequent absences of Daniel Sickles. *Courtesy of US Army Heritage and Education Center.*

Chapter 2

As Far as the Eye Can Reach

Late July to End of August 1861—
Moving to Protect Washington, DC

Arrival in Washington after passage through Baltimore • Realities of slavery • A soldier's routine and unpleasant truths • Confidence in Scott and McClellan • The enemy near collapse

Editorial Notes

Initially only the 1st, 2nd, and 3rd Excelsior regiments move to Washington, leaving on July 22 and 23. Remaining behind to continue to fill out their ranks and finalize their command structures are the 4th and 5th Regiments. Many of the debts run up by Sickles during the formation of the brigade are yet to be settled. Captain William Wiley, who was with Sickles from the earliest days, is left behind to settle the "pile of judgements" totaling in the many thousands of dollars and taking more than a year to resolve. But for now, Sickles has his brigade and they are off to the "seat of war."[1]

Fredonia Censor: Published August 7, 1861

Correspondence of the Censor

DEPARTURE FROM CAMP SCOTT

Washington, D.C., July 28, 1861.

Dear Uncles.—

Now that our tents are pitched and matters again settled, I must again acquaint you with our location and narrate our adventures. Last Tuesday, the 1st got under motion and the 2d and 3d escorted them down to the landing. At the same time we were directed to be ready to vamoose at 30 minutes notice.

After our return that evening we had the hardest battalion drill we had yet passed through.

The next morning we set our things in order, struck our tents and got ready for our journey. A little about 10 the 2d departed, the 3d escorting them down to the ferry. At noon, while they were gone, the Westfield and Tidioute companies came in. The Westfield men were mustered in but these from Tidioute could not be accepted, as a company, the number not being sufficient. As they would not consolidate with any other companies, they returned, or at least left camp.

After dallying, as usual for a long time, we finally, at sunset, left Camp Scott southward bound. As we passed down toward the landing we received the kindest adieus from the ladies and gentlemen of Staten Island. After a hot and dusty march we finally got the last man upon the boat and steamed rapidly down the lower bay. We took supper and after getting hold of our plunder again, settled down for a short nap. At about midnight we arrive at Perth Amboy, and were soon speeding along toward Philadelphia.

In the morning we arrived just about in season for breakfast in the city of "Brotherly Love," which we found to be no misnomer, for, almost the first thing which met our eyes was a mammoth sign reading "Coffee and refreshments free for Union Volunteers." Along in front was a roof or awning under which was a long range of wash basins, where we were overjoyed to perform our abolutions [*sic*]. Then we adjourned to the spacious saloon and partook of a bounteous repast which had the merit of a neatness which we who had dwelt so long in camp, knew full well how to appreciate.

We were served by ladies whose courteous bearing and evident refinement declared them to be of the first class of society. I learned that they had fed no less than 85 regiments since the association was formed, which is still free to all volunteers and is maintained by the city.

One regiment of the returning three months militia came in while we were there, and they looked brown and healthy, as did the 7th when they arrived at N.Y. some time since. Several others we passed upon the way. Our journey from daylight until dark was one triumphal procession, in which every house within view waved its greeting from the windows and the cheers of spectators rose above the roar of the engine as we sped along from station to station.

At Wilmington, Del., the enthusiasm began to cool considerably, but still we received friendly greetings all along, though some didn't seem to owe us any particular good will.

Above Baltimore the bridges were guarded by soldiers who cheered us as we passed. At dark we arrived in Baltimore. Here there seemed to be a great diversity of opinion for some cheered us lustily, while others hurrahed for Jeff

Davis—these last being children. The parents were evidently smothering their hate, for but few adults cheered, but maintained a sullen silence while we passed. No doubt they would have liked to attacked us, but dared not for a simple flank movement on our part would have pinned every man to the wall for a distance equal to our battalion front, say 25 or 30 rods.

At Baltimore we were delayed for some time but got off at about midnight. We were offered water, lemonade &c., *but judged it prudent to decline until we arrived at the station.* Late the next morning we arrived in the city. We rested near the station for some time, but finally removed to Camp Marsh, where we now remain.

We are now encamped about a mile I should think, nearly north of the Capitol. Camp Marsh is situated upon the side of a hill, and the summit overlooks the city, the Capitol, and most of the Public buildings. South west of us lies the Potomac; a little farther north the national monument's unfinished shaft, and beyond them Arlington heights, while far off in the distance we can see the spire of Fairfax C.H. All around as far as the eye can reach are scattered our encampments, and we often hear the roll of drums, or the heavy jar of cannon from across the river.

To day all has been pretty quiet. We saw some old friends who belonged to the Olean and other seceded companies from Camp Scott who had been in the battle of Bull's Run. They said that Gen. McDowell's division was hurried for a long march without water and upon the double quick for some miles, and that they did a hard day's work before engaging the rebels. Here they met, and routed a foe far more numerous than themselves, and were only beaten by reinforcements which outnumbered them four to one, and who were fresh and strong. The Fire Zouaves have immortalized themselves by their gallant charges upon this occasion. The Virginia Black Horse charged and fired, when every Zouave fell apparently dead, but upon the other turning they sprang up, fired and charged; and of the famous Black Horse cavalry, the pride of Virginia, but six were left to tell the tale. The masked batteries were piled with the rebels our soldiers had bayoneted in their firery charges, and in fact everywhere that our men charged they scattered the foe like leaves before a whirlwind. Their loss is far heavier than ours our volunteers say. Bull's Run and Manassas might now be ours had not McDowell advanced contrary to his instructions, and thus he was just one day too soon, and could not be supported, his division alone being engaged. Gen. Scott, it is said does not mean to trust out the job next time, but to go himself. Lieut. C. B. Halsey of the first Maine regiment called here yesterday and his account, as do all others, agrees with that of my informant. His sword was stained with secession blood. He is a brother of Frank Halsey of Co. D of ours.

We do not know at what time we may cross the Potomac. Troops are arriving as fast as they can come and the railroads are tasked to their utmost capacity. Some times eight or ten thousand come in in a day. We were filled up by a company from Flushing, L.I. Address letters to the camp as follows: A—— B—— Care of Capt. C. K. Abell, Col. Taylor's 3d Regiment, Camp March, Washington, D.C.

Your's Truly,

McK.

Judged it prudent to decline . . . : as mobs had previously attacked Massachusetts troops traveling through Baltimore, Arthur and his mates were no doubt suspicious of any offers of drink or refreshments from unknown sources.

Fairfax C.H.: Fairfax Court House is thirteen miles from Washington and the site of a small skirmish between Confederate and Union troops on June 1, 1861.

Other Voices: Chaplain Joseph Twichell, 2nd Excelsior Regiment

July 27, 1861: Letter home

. . . From the time our friends waved us adieu from the shores of Staten Island, all along the route by the Camden & Amboy R.R., we met enthusiastic receptions—the stridulous notes of small boys mingling with the deeper shouts of men who knew wherefore they hailed us. The women especially favored us with clouds of fluttering handkerchiefs at every station. Everybody on board was in high spirits, save now and then a lengthened face betrayed that the dark side of our errand was not wholly lost sight of, nor the lonesome folks left at home forgotten. We arrived in Philadelphia at about dark, or rather Camden . . . We met hosts of vociferous friends, and if a guard had not been posted at the door of every neighbouring rum-hole, the regiment would have been made a drunken one by mistaken liberality. As it was bottles were circulated somewhat . . .

Chaplain Joseph H. Twichell,

2nd Excelsior Reg't.[2]

Stridulous: A shrill, grating sound or noise.

Other Voices: Report of Colonel Nelson Taylor

Brentwood, Camp Marsh, July, 28th, 1861

Major:

In accordance with Par. I, Genl. Orders W. D., I have the honor to report that my regiment is principally from the State of New York, about one-half from the Western part, and the other from the city.

They were transported from the place of muster, Staten Island, New York, by the Perth Amboy route through Philadelphia and Baltimore, and arrive on Friday at 5 a.m., July 26th, and are now encamped about one mile north of the City of Washington, the encampment having been called Camp Marsh.

Seven companies are armed with the smooth bore percussion musket, 1842. (Altered.)

Seven companies have a fair knowledge of company and battalion drill, but are deficient in the manual of arms. Three companies having joined within a week are almost raw recruits.

The drill has been "Hardee" with such modifications as required by the musket.

No Skirmish drill has yet been practiced.

No target practice has yet been commenced.

No bayonet exercise has been practiced.

The regiment is nearly complete on what is absolutely necessary for the field. The Commissary, Quartermaster and Medical Departments will be sufficiently complete in three days for campaigning, except in wagons and ambulances, of which there are none.

By order,

Col. Nelson Taylor

Commd'g.[3]

Direct thus to me.

Write and tell me all the news—your last came safely here and I was glad enough to get it.

Col. Taylors 3d Regt. Co. D
Camp Marsh
Washington D.C.

Washington July 30th 1861

Dear Mother,

Having got a very little leisure I improve it by writing again to you. I got here last Friday but have been very busy or else very tired ever since. To be sure I felt in duty bound to send one letter to Uncle Willard for the paper and that you can get from Uncle Sabine, that is if he ever got it. We expect to be paid at least one month's wages pretty soon—our pay roll is made out at least. I suffered very much from diarrhea during the last part of my stay at Camp Scott. Now however I am in splendid health and spirits and can stand as hard a day's drill as the next man. We are quartered upon a hill about a mile north of the Capitol and upon the southern slope of a hill which commands a view of that and of most of the city. I learn from the men who returned from Bull Run that the southerners could not begin to stand a northern bayonet charge, that a portion of our van was out of ammunition and that Gen. McDowell disobeyed his orders which were not to engage until the following day. If he had obeyed orders he would have had support enough on the ensuing day to have crushed down all oppositions. As regards the result the southerners won the victory it is true but their loss was far heavier than ours—the men who were there say that their southern dead were piled upon the batteries by the hundred. Ellsworths Zouaves annihilated the famed Black Horse of Virginia. This corps was the "crème de la crème" of the F.F.V's. and they fired upon the Zouaves and charged. The Zouaves dropped to all appearance dead. The cavalry then turned upon the 27th N.Y. when the Zouaves jumped nimbly up and fired—charged—and but six of the cavalry remained to tell the tale. These also I believe were taken prisoners. Even the enemy were forced to admit that their loss was double ours at the least. Our men fell back when tired by the severest labor and out numbered four to one by perfectly fresh troops besides the army they had routed. It was all McDowell's fault. We have now within 5 to six miles of here at least 150,000 men who can take the field at an hours call. McClellan or perhaps Scott himself will head the next advance. It may take place in a month, or within an hour. We have the old muskets yet but all who have gone over the border lately have taken minies with them and left their muskets.

Before we go into action our officers must be examined by a board to see if they know their duty. Ours will stand it but I should not wonder if our company should furnish some for others who have not good drill masters. Well I must fall in for roll call pretty soon. I am stout as need be. I think I may get over into the city in a day or so—to morrow perhaps.

The climate is very fine though rather hot and agrees with me better than Chaut. Co. I wrote to Aunt Eliza and got a letter from her, all well.

Love to all and I will soon write further. Make Frank write and fill out the sheet, my regards to Bill K. and Nerofoa.

Generally either at work or resting.

Arthur

Tell Frank Hopper that as a general rule I have as little time and less conveniences than he—I have neither seat nor table. But if he will write I will answer as often as I can—Mother and the "Censor" have first claim upon me.

F.F.V.'s: First Families of Virginia.

Washington Aug. 1st, 1861

Dear Mother, (We get pay in a day or two)

It rains very hard to day and so I have a first rate chance to write to you once more. We are all well and in fine sprits. I think the water here agrees well with me for I have not been so well before since I left school. The climate is delightful. We are kept very strictly and it is difficult to get a pass outside our regimental lines. Being dead broke I have no object to go except to wash, and that is allowed.

I see by the Balt. Sun—as rank a secesh paper as can be found, if they only dared to show it—that there was a row the other day in Western VA. and the rebels were routed with a loss of 1,500 while our loss was only 600. A great force is now collected here and the next blow must sweep the "Old Dominion" clean of rebels. I went out to wash the other day and went over to see the 2nd Rhode Island reg't. Gov. Sprague goes with them and fares not so well as our colonel. That's the man for me. The banner stood by the tent and was torn by cannon and rifle balls and splashed with blood. They had a splendid gray eagle chained to his perch in the midst of the camp. Overhead was a delightful grove and all seemed to enjoy themselves amazingly. They were a very fine corps of men and idolize their gallant governor, who led them at Bulls run. Fenton as you see kindly franks our letters and even furnishes considerable stationery. It rains like the mischief to day and so we don't drill or do anything else. I suppose that by this you are nearly or quite through haying. Is grass good with you. I am glad to hear how you get the wheat cut. It is very well arranged. I suppose that you will sell nelly now. I should think that the great demand for horses in the army would improve the market. At any rate she ought to sell now better than you could by keeping her over. Hate I presume is as cute and saucy as ever. She will make a good farm horse. Our reg't. is alone as yet but if it had not been so wet we should have removed and encamped with the other two reg'ts. which came on before us. I shall be right glad to see Bob McKinstry for he is a splendid fellow. Your caution about intimacy is decidedly wasted. Home or home affairs are about the last thing a soldier thinks of conversing about. It is the present—the future that engages our attention and only the vicissitudes and adventures of the past are alluded to—not the quiet scenes of home, or home affairs. As for reading I get little except papers. If I was liable to any injury from such a source it would have been long ago. As for society I may feel the need of good when I return to the hill, but not here where the scions of the first families of our county shoulder their muskets at my side. The average of society in our company is better than with you, and I find no difficulty in choosing my friends—some of them especially pointed out by Uncle Willard. When I go to visit outside our company you cannot suppose that I should go to seek more questionable friends. So just dismiss all concern about my associations.

We are often stinted in our food and just kick up a row and get more. We don't get all we are entitled to and if things don't mend I will get transferred to the Naval Brigade. I think however that these things will be righted soon and offenders punished. I do not like our new captain—Caspar K. Abell very well. I have not a thing against him personally but his treatment of many is so arrogant and harsh that he is rendering himself very unpopular. I am determined not to shirk duty and don't do it—thus when I ask anything—I can get it if any one can but when he reproves any slight offence he does it in very harsh terms and so the company are down upon him. He is not at all severe in punishments but his harsh manner does injustice to his actual disposition.

As I said before I have been punctual, have sustained no reproof, and have nothing against him but rather the contrary—but he is very unpopular with the most of the men. The orders were strict about baggage and as I was liable to march at once into Va. I judged it most prudent to send back my trunk but keep almost everything in it. I sent it to Uncle Willard's care and when you go there you are pretty sure to find it. The lock has got worn and though locked it will open by working the lid up and down and sideways a little. The pants, vest, shirts, and hat I was very glad to get. The pants alone will save the charges for they are good and fit well while the others are mere satinet and shrink and fade abominably. The coarse blue pants we wore off are very good every day wear and very tough, and we have also very good linen pants so that I am abundantly supplied with good clothes. We have a fine cool breeze during the heat of the day and it is just right and I don't take cold as by the lakewinds. By ascending the hill back of our tents I can see most of the city—the Capitol and other public buildings, the Potomac—and Arlington heights and even to Fairfax C.H. spire which is seen far off in the south west. Love to all at home. Remember me to Pete's folks and other friends and write as soon and as often as you can. My address is Co. D Col. Taylor's 3d Reg't. Washington, D.C.

A row the other day in Western VA . . . : probably the fight at Rich Mountain and Laurel Hill. While a Union victory, McKinstry has greatly exaggerated the numbers.

Gov. Sprague: Governor William Sprague of Rhode Island accompanied the 2nd Rhode Island to battle and had his horse shot from underneath him at Bull Run.

Fenton: Reuben E. Fenton was the local congressman for that part of western New York and would send the boys' letters on for free using his congressional franking privileges.

Caspar K. Abell: Abell was born in Fredonia, New York, on November 27th, 1827. He mustered in as first lieutenant of Company D on June 20th. Five days later the commander of Company D, William O. Stevens, was promoted to major, resulting in Abell's advance to captain. Abell served as captain of Co. D until May 3rd, 1863, when he was promoted to major as a result of casualties suffered at Chancellorsville. Abell served as major for the remainder of the war and was mustered out with the regiment.

Figure 2.1. Caspar K. Abell. Caspar K. Abell commanded Company D after William Stevens was promoted. Abell was considered an excellent disciplinarian who nonetheless won and held the affections of his men. Abell would eventually rise to the rank of major. Source: Henry LeFevre Brown, *History of the Third Regiment, Excelsior Brigade, 72nd New York Volunteer Infantry, 1861–1865* (Jamestown, NY: Journal Print, 1902).

Other Voices: Letter from Emerson Merrell, Co. I, 3rd Excelsior

Aug. 6th 1861

Washington

Districk of Columbia

Dear Sister . . .

We occupy as splendid a position as there is in the United States. We can see the whole city of Washington, Fairfax, Washington Heights and Georgetown Heights. We have a splendid view of the Capitol and the White House, also the patent office. I have seen plenty of niggers but never have I seen a cecession flag not with standing. We are encamped on a cecessionista farm stocked with thirty nigroes. He has got about 20 acres of corn that stands 12 feet high average and may be we can have an ear of roasted corn now and then and once in a while a few new potatoes and cucumbers and apples.[4]

Other Voices: Charles Gould, Company I, 72nd New York

Washington DC.
August 7, 1861—Wednesday

Dear Sister . . .

We left Staten Island two weeks ago in good spirits. I however was never so disgusted before at the effects of rum. All the officers were drunk. Half of the companies were lying around like a bunch of brutes.

Many a mother bade her son adieu. Sorry to expose him to the temptations that he must meet in the Army. While they are praying for them their sons are playing a game of cards or lying around drunk on the ground. I sincerely thank god for giving me parents who taught me, by Godlike example, to shun all vice. Their prayer I believe will not go unanswered . . . [5]

Other Voices: Orders from Sickles

Headquarter Excelsior Brigade

August 8th, 1861

Colonel:

The President having expressed a desire to see the several regiments of this Brigade now in Washington, you will dispense with the Evening Parade, and report with the Third Regiment at the Executive Mansion at seven o'clock p.m. this day.

D. E. Sickles,
Col. First Regt. & Act. Brig. Genl.[6]

Fredonia Censor: Published August 21, 1861

[Correspondence of the Censor.]

FROM THE THIRD REGIMENT.

Camp Caldwell, Aug. 11, 1861.

We have again pulled up stakes and planted them in another place. On Friday last, we struck our tent and started under a burning sun for a march of six miles, but we took a wrong road and made ten of it. We passed quite near the Capitol, and crossed the Anacosti[a] river, close by the Navy Yard. After getting well over, we took a good rest, and gave the stragglers who had given out a chance to close up. The men were in poor condition to travel, for they had been to the White House the night before to be inspected by **President Lincoln**, and the heat was so great that about forty gave out; completely exhausted. This time a far greater number were overcome upon the second stage of our journey, and men whom I supposed endowed with strength far greater than my own, either fell back or lay panting upon the ground by way. The camping ground it appears was not decided upon, and we halted near our present location.

It was now getting late in the afternoon, and to add to our pickle, a soaking rain set in and completed our confusion. A house and barn nearby were quickly filled; and I deposited myself upon a hay-mow where the outer man was all right, though the inner was both hungry and thirsty. The rain continued to pour, and at last I decided upon a new plan of operations. The 1st Regiment of our Brigade lay near us, and I went up to their line of sentries as bold as a sheep, and to the challenge of the sentry (it was pitch dark) I answered "Friend from the 3d Regiment." The corporal was called and I was brought before the Officer of the Day. Here I gave an account of myself, and in a short time I was ensconced with my old friend Rob't McKinstry, of Schoolcraft, Michigan, and enjoying his blankets and a comfortable snooze.

The next morning I was out early and came back to our regiment. All was in confusion, for each mess had got hold of a tent and pitched it where it came most convenient. This was soon remedied and the streets laid out geometrically, and a better ordered city than ours a short time after, could not be found, even where Napoleonic architecture is in vogue, and the streets are so straight that they can be enfiladed by cannons six abreast. The stragglers soon came in, and now the world wags with us pretty much as before. We lost one man from our regiment a few days ago, but he was not from Chautauqua County. The general health is good. The 1st in its last journey had two or three hundred drop out exhausted. The thermometer was at 105 in the shade the two days before we started, and I think full as hot when we marched. It must not be inferred, however, that all who fell back were used up, or ill. Many were getting tired and took the license of the occasion to have a little more freedom, but in reality did not suffer much, and could have marched much farther if necessary.—To-day we have had straw hats served round, and they are a most excellent article.

In the country about us I think a good many secessionists may be found. Our sentries now load their guns, and any man, who attempts to escape, or enter after dark without permission, will be fired on. Ten rounds of ball cartridge are served out to each man. We fired at targets for a few days at Camp Marsh, and got a little acquainted with our weapons. Each day the bull's eye was hit at ten rods, and the guns did better than we expected. Most of them shoot in line, but very shockingly in elevation. The best rifle shots of our company shoot no better than novices, and chance seems to rule more than skill. Hon. D. E. Sickles' position now seems pretty well defined. He is Colonel of the first, which is the highest command our soldiers could confer upon him. During his stay at camp Scott he acted as Brigadier General, and probably drew pay accordingly, but we are now broken up as a brigade and he now commands the 1st only. I hope that we may be re-united, for we have many friends in the 1st and 5th regiments, though we do not care much about the 2d and 4th. There are in the 1st the Michigan men and those from Pittsburg, and a finer body of men than these is rarely to be seen.

In the 5th are the French Zouaves—many of whom were in Algeria, and some in Crimea, and a company of splendid fellows from Cambridge Mass. These last begged to be placed in our regiment, but they were not uniformed, and the Flushing, Long Island Company got the preference. These last are a fine company, but had our wishes been consulted the Cambridge Company would have entered our regiment. I do not think it impossible that we may yet be re-united under Col. Sickles' command.

The country here is hilly, and not fertile. Corn generally is poor. The water is very good, but not very convenient. Most of what we use is brought by teams, in barrels. Some of the letters we have received have wandered like Telemachus in search of his father. This is caused by the fact that there are three colonels about here named Taylor, and one N. Taylor at that. There is also another Camp Marsh. Out present camp is named after S. D. Caldwell of Dunkirk, and Dr. Irwin is its godfather. Last night the Censor—for some weeks a stranger, came in, and we were glad to hear again from home. Our friends must write us often.—Letters thus addressed will stand a fair chance of reaching their destination. "______, Col. Taylor's 3d Reg't., Excelsior Brigade, Camp Caldwell, Washington D.C."

We expect pay soon, and have been doing so for some time. I must finish up to go out on dress parade. We are to have new uniforms very much like the old one of Co. D of the 68th Regiment.

A. McK.

Telemachus: son of Odysseus who searched for him.

Address—Col. Taylors 3d Reg't. Excelsior Brig.

Camp Caldwell, Washington, D.C.

Camp Caldwell Aug. 12th, 1861

Dear Mother,

I received Frank's letter day before yesterday.

I am glad to hear from you again. I was then acting as orderly, which post I have often been selected for, in place of standing guard, a most agreeable substitute for I do not have to carry a musket, and get the whole nights sleep. We struck our tents last Friday and came to our present location which is about six miles further on. I am well and sound but have felt rather sleepy for a day or two. We had a hard night of it Friday for before we could pitch our tents or even select our location a drenching rain set in. As I told you I was Colonels orderly and thus exempt from roll calls, only looking out to be on hand when Col. Taylor wanted me to carry orders. He had dismissed me for the day and so I put out for the 1st Reg't. which was encamped near by and staid with Robert McKinstry who gave me a hearty welcome, and with Capt. Hugo's aid, a dry bed. Next morning I was on hand in good order only very tired. I will complain no more of weakness for I kept up with the head of the column—and whiskey circulated pretty freely among them at that—while several hundreds—and many of our stoutest among them—fell back overpowered by heat and fatigue. The only thing which troubled me was the sweat which ran into my eyes until they were sore. I always prided myself on my endurance of heat but I stand it even better than I expected. The thermometer was at 105 in the shade the two days before we moved, and quite as hot the day we marched. I do not feel it myself more than I used to do at 80 to 90. I do not shave, for, though I look rather rusty it saves my skin, which peeled off several times at Camp Scott from exposure to the sun. We have not yet been paid but expect it daily. I must get between 30 & 40 dollars for we get an allowance of nearly twelve dollars for provisions for our trip to Camp Scott, the allowance being 2 ½ cts. per mile, when rations are not furnished by "Sam."

The planters about here are really secession but dare not show it. The negroes here and all around are very favorable to us but are still as mice when their masters are about. The planters pretend to be union men but the slaves say that when any southern success is reported they are hugely delighted. Milk, vegetable, and fruits, can be got of the darkeys who are invariably our friends. Slavery here assumes its very mildest form. The negroes are well fed and clothed and as comfortable as the poorer classes at the North. For all this they all long for freedom and hail our advances with delight. One little rascal ten or twelve years old ran away from his master at Washington and came here with us. I don't think his master will see him right off for he is now dressed a la zouave and waits upon one of the officers messes. He is called Sam. The boys get passed out now and then to wash clothes and some how they get lots of apples, peaches, pear &c. which are not laid down in the U.S. rations. Green corn and new potatoes also stray away from home considerably.

Our wages are now $15 which is just about a fair price. Of this $2 are kept back until our discharge when we draw it with all arrears of pay or clothing and a bonus of $100 beside. It is now sprinkling and I hope it will continue on in that state until night, so that we will not have to drill. We have just got some very fine straw hats. They are braided panama style and have broad brims. The straw is fine and tough and you can not get such for less than six or more likely eight, shillings. Military rule is beginning to work a little and what we get in the way of clothing or equipments is of the very best.

There are no hostile troops near that we know of but each man has ten ball cartridges and a large guard is posted. The zouaves say that the southern cavalry is splendid but that it can not do anything with the northern bayonet charge which no horse will face. Cavalry is only useful when pursuing the flying. The Zouave and the rifled cannon are the order of the day. Our men pass for light Infantry but can come the Zouave drill in splendid style. For a while we did not drill much in ordinary time but lately we have done so more as we have no good parade ground.

I got a letter night before last from Thomas Chandler. He expressed a desire to enter the army as an assistant surgeon but felt the impracticability of the thing on account of his lameness. One of his college friends, Dr. Foster Swift, was taken by the rebels while ministering to the wounded. He might have escaped but nobly refused to desert his suffering charge.

I think precisely as you do about Ally Cushings letter. There is little good feeling between the regulars and the volunteers. The regulars consider the volunteers as raw and undisciplined, while we look upon them as mere mercenary hirelings. In point of fact there is no regular corps which has so good material as a volunteer force. What is called lack of discipline is more frequently the license which is always given to volunteers beyond what the regulars may expect. No volunteer officer dare arrogate such supreme power as regular for his office is elective and those who gave it can oust him. Well it is about time for my Siesta. Our Adjutant S. M. Doyle is a very fine specimen of the better class of Irish society as described in Jack Hinton and Tom Burke of ours. He is humorous, well, yes very highly bred and has a very slight brogue which has nothing coarse about it but is both prepossessing and comical. He is the first thoroughly cultivated Irishman I ever got acquainted with. I haven't got a stamp so I must even let you pay the postage on this. Write soon dear mother and tell me how you all prosper. I suppose by the time this reaches you all your crops will be housed. Bill Rockwell I suppose and hope is prospering well. If he liked to join us he could do it yet and his bad eye could be smuggled in easily enough. I have not time to write him just now but he can read this which contains all I could tell him and enclose a slip in your reply.

Much love to all,
Arthur

Staid: archaic use for stayed.

Zouave: military units dressed and drilled in the style of French colonial troops stationed in north Africa.

Come: to take on the aspect of.

Jack Hinton: title character in midcentury Charles O'Malley stories.

Camp Caldwell Aug. 16th 1861

Dear Mother,

I have just got and read through Frank's letter of the 14th. I find that the report among you is that Oscar Ames is dead. If so his ghost is a voracious one and eats regularly once and a half its live weight of roasting ears and other delicacies of the season. He is fat as a hog and about as useful as that animal would be in harness. We have at last got our knapsacks and haversacks and are fully equipped for war. I had quite a compliment yesterday. While engaged in some conversations with my comrades the Adjutant, Doyle, beckoned me to one side and proposed that we should go together and visit the outposts of our regiment—which extend to Alexandria—and that I should make good use of my pen and record whatever we should see worthy of note, being as he was pleased to term me a "writing man," that our friends at home might have the pleasure of reading from a county paper some incidents of our first actual service—we are the outer post in this direction—and get some idea of our actual duties and situation. This will require a pass from headquarters but it is very possible that Doyle may get it. I am I believe at present the only regular reporter from our county.

I am on the sick list today from the weakening effects of diarrhea. Very few suffer from any other disease. I feel better and intend to go on drill again to-morrow. The right and left companies of our regiment have minie rifles and no doubt we shall all get them in time.

Our drill is a very severe one and tasks the strength of the men to an unnecessary extent. It would do at Dunkirk very well but a commander ought to know better than to work his men so hard in a hot climate where they drink new water. If the drill was reasonable I should not have gone on the sick list yesterday nor to-day but I won't drill so when weak from diarrhea. I hear that we are to go out before daylight to relieve Capt. Austin's company who have been out scouting for the last five days. I like the idea first rate. We must of

Figure 2.2. LITHOGRAPH OF THE CAPITAL AND THE SEAT OF WAR. Arthur enclosed this map with his August 31, 1861, letter to mother. This lithograph shows the Capitol dome construction as complete, something that did not happen until late 1863. *Courtesy of Ulysses S. Grant Presidential Library.*

course get more freedom and we can rely upon the negroes who would never suffer the enemy to approach without warning us. They would do us anything in their power. One of our boys asked a negro who had been telling of the secession sentiments of his master how old he might be. "Old enough to be free" replied the gray headed old man.

Tell me that the negroes are a happy contented race and I will believe it as well as if you said that powder would not ignite when brought in contact with flame. The very mildest existing form of slavery is found here but there is not a negro to be found, of whatever age, who does not feel like this one, who had grown gray in servitude, "old enough to be free." To be a northern soldier is to be the object of the friendliest feelings in a negro breast and when alone they speak in the most unreserved manner of their masters and betray in every look and word their hatred of bondage and their rising hope of freedom.

I must slip in a word to Newton so with love to all and hoping to soon hear from you.

Good bye
Arthur

Capt. Austin: Captain John S. Austin was born in June of 1812 in New York. The forty-four-year-old Austin enrolled into the 72nd New York State Volunteers on May 15, 1861; a month later he was mustered in as captain of Company K, which formed out on New York City. From December 18, 1861, to June of '62, Austin also served as acting brigade quartermaster, on Sickles's staff. On October 25, 1862, Austin was promoted to lieutenant colonel of the 72nd New York with the resignation of then–lieutenant colonel Israel Moses.

On May 4, 1863, Austin ascended to colonelcy of the 72nd New York with the death of Colonel William O. Stevens at the Battle of Chancellorsville. During the fighting at Gettysburg on July 2, 1863, Austin received a wound in his right hand, wrist, and forearm from an exploding shell while fighting along the Emmitsburg Road. It is not clear his exact role within the regiment after his wounding as effective command fell to Lt. Col. John Leonard.[7]

Other Voices: Open Letter Appearing in the *Westfield Republican*

ATTENTION LADIES.—

We, the undersigned officers, non-commissioned officers, musicians, or privates, valiant, gay, and gallant Chautauqua County bark-peelers, having faithfully served our country since the formation of the grand Army of the Potomac, do hereby advertise, through the columns of the local press, as the last resort by which to obtain the much coveted correspondence of some of those noble daughters of Chautauqua, who have so kindly assisted us thus far in our efforts to crush this cruel and unnatural rebellion, that—If any of the above said Ladies, of that noble and patriotic County, "which we have the honor in part to represent," should choose to write, they will receive a hearty response from the subscribers.

FRANK RURAL,
FRED LYNN,
LONELY.
Co. "Y" 72d Regt. N. Y. Vols.
Washington, D.C.[8]

Editorial Notes

By the second half of August, four of Sickles's regiments are in position on the southeast side of Washington, stretched out along the eastern branch of the Potomac River. The 5th Regiment has arrived from New York while the 1st, 2nd, and 3rd Regiments were repositioned. The 4th Regiment remains in New York, plagued by recruiting problems and an ongoing feud between its colonel, James Fairman, and Sickles.[9]

Chaplain Twichell explains their duties are to "cut off communication between the Secession part of Maryland and Virginia." Twichell adds, "We are in secession country. Everybody but the vegetable peddlers refuses us any greeting. All look glum. The man on whose land we are pitched has a son—an officer in the Confederate Army—and he protested against our stopping here."[10]

Fredonia Censor: Published September 4, 1861

Correspondence of the Censor.

FROM THE THIRD REGIMENT.

Camp Caldwell, Aug. 26.

As it is Sunday, and we have a short period of rest, I will improve the opportunity to post you up in what little news is current in camp. Last Tuesday we received orders to fall in with our muskets to take them to the city and exchange them. This we did with alacrity, for we were not partial to the old flint lock, and desired most heartily to get rid of them. We were soon under way, and after a rapid tramp we at last arrived at the arsenal, which is situated upon Potomac, some distance below the Washington monument. This is an extensive affair, and is enclosed by high brick wall, except along the river shore. The buildings are large, well, and tastefully constructed. In the open space in the center, many hundred cannon are lying upon skids. There are a few old style 24s, 18s, and even lighter ship guns, not over a dozen or two at most, but the balance were 32 pounders, which is the lightest gun now cast for vessels, and 42 pounders and columbiads. Besides these ship-guns there were some batteries of rifled cannon, which are served with the Hotchkiss ball, for the field.—Boat howitzers were also found there.— These are used mostly for Shrapnel shells and rarely exceed 12 lb. caliber. The Shrapnel shell, which is named after its inventor, is filled with both powder and balls, and is thus the most destructive weapon in modern warfare. There were some howitzers manufactured by Ames & Co., of Chicopee, of 32 lb. caliber, for field use.

After waiting a short time, we were taken up into the Arsenal by companies, and there we exchanged our guns for Harper's Ferry muskets. Though these are a decided improvement on the old guns, we were bitterly disappointed that we did not receive rifles. There were muskets enough there to supply an army, but I did not see rifles enough to arm a single company.

After our company were armed, I took a stroll about the yard to examine the ordnance. The rifled field guns were mostly of steel, and of 10 and 12 pound caliber, (conical shot.) I also visited the cartridge manufactory, and admired the expeditious manner in which power and ball were got ready for our hands. It was a significant fact, that to the bullet which is commonly put up was added three buck shot—and four of us loaded on one of our wagons 30,000 of these cartridges, with 5,000 of ball only, for target use. We have fired at target a little and find that our guns are a hard hitting arm, *at which ever end the mark may be.* They are very inaccurate, but shoot with great force, and the fire of buck and ball by a battalion must prove terribly destructive. Four regiments of our brigade are now in camp in this vicinity—the 4th only remaining at Camp Scott. We are not together, and it is better so, for it would be very difficult to supply so large a camp with good water. The weather is delightful, and the health and spirits of the men rise in proportion. We have cool, clear mornings, sunny, but not oppressively hot, days, and glorious moonlight nights. Colonel Taylor improves this state of things by having battalion drills, that we may not forget the timely lessons of Camp Scott. I never before fully appreciated the rare chance which we then had of maneuvering in brigade drills. The grounds there were superb for that exercise, and many a corps has won high honors in the war which cannot compare with the regiments of this brigade in the military evolutions required of men assembled in large force. I am not so egotistic as to ascribe this to any superior qualities of our men, but simply to their good fortune in having such an opportunity.—The dark blue blouse of the infantry and rifle corps has been served out to us, and they are just exactly the thing we needed. They are well and neatly made, of fine wool, (no satinet or half-cotton humbug,) and I know by trial on a former occasion, that they are a splendid thing to wear. There are a lot of satinet coats at the Quarter Master's, but don't think we shall take them. The Government pays for and required fine blue broadcloth, or at least that quality for our fall dress, and nothing but connivance by inspectors could ever get the coarse, satinet article accepted. *Somebody's* axe is pretty well ground, it is quite evident. We now get the increased ration of bread, and I do not find much evidence of potatoes in it for a few days. The meat which we get is as good as you will find on an average at any good market, and the only trouble lies in the cooking apparatus.—The vegetables are of all sorts pressed together, and make a first rate soup.

As we were on our way to the Arsenal we met our band from Fredonia, Dunkirk, and adjoining places, and a cheer ran down the line at sight of their familiar faces. On our return we shook hands, and there were joyous greetings all round. Among them I was glad to find my old school-mate, "Hearty Dick," as we used to call him at the Academy, in those good old days when "King David" reigned with undisputed sway, and Daniel was only Premier. Not that I consider it a misfortune that the mantle of royalty has fallen upon the latter, for before the rebellion it was my cherishen design to come once more under his sway; but I only recall old times and old friends, of whom so few remain—the rest scattered far and wide, by land and sea.—Now, instead of extracting obstinate-roots, or conjugating "Amo," I am performing far less congenial duties, but those which no true patriot should shrink from. I see by letters from home, that there are still a few secessionists among you. Whether cowardice, or, as an Arkansas man would term it, "a sort of general cussedness," is the matter, I do not feel much disposed to pity them, even if they do make the acquaintance of Judge Lynch.

I am glad to hear of the organization of new companies, and only regret that the movement was not simultaneous, so that we might be embodied as one regiment. It makes no great difference to us, however for the staff, as you know, is furnished mostly from our county, and Maj. Stevens represents us ably as a field officer.

We have not yet received our pay, and I hear that the rolls are again not made out in proper order and must be filled out again. It takes a great deal of writing to pay a regiment of volunteers. I really wonder if it cost Floyed as much trouble to steal his millions as it takes to collect the well earned pay of a few volunteers from our circumlocution office.

The Jamestown boys are back again, and Company E relieves them. Our boys are much exercised at this arrangement, for they wish to get out before all the *melons* are gone. Those who have been out far have been liberally treated by the planters to fruit &c. Peaches are getting ripe, as also are pears. Milk can be got for ten cents a quart—if we only had the ten cents. Some of the boys, who have the needful, indulge in hoe-cake, biscuit, milk and fruits which are not very dear. Roasting ears of corn, and potatoes are also seen over the fire now and then, for some of the boys have not forgotten how they used to go "cooning" in the *melon*choly days of August. It seems hard that a soldier whose rations cost enough to procure his board at one of your hotels should be compelled to steal vegetables, and then not get as many as the law allows him, or as are necessary to sustain his health, which at least risks much when confined to animal and stimulating diet.

Under McClellan's rule, great advances have been made toward order and discipline. His rigid rule not to give a pass toward the rebel lines without the oath of allegiance, is doing good service, but it is a bitter pill to those of rebellious proclivities. Information seems at last cut off from the rebels concerning our movements. It is reported that smallpox and measles are ravaging their forces fearfully, while we, strongly posted and well armed and equipped, are daily improving in military science and discipline. Every day places us upon a better footing and them upon a worse.

Shelley is detailed as regimental saddler, which greatly improves his situation and pay. N.B. We get about all the spoils.

A. McK.

Harper's Ferry muskets: by this time some of the companies had already been issued the Model 1842 while indications are the rest may have been using old flintlocks that had been converted to percussion. McKinstry is probably referring to the M-1842 in this passage.

Cherishen: old form of word "cherished."

Floyed: probably John B. Floyd, who was asked to resign from his post as secretary of war in the Buchanan administration in 1860 after being implicated in cases of misappropriation of funds. Floyd, before his resignation, had transferred over one hundred thousand older muskets from armories in northern states to those in southern states. A native of Virginia, the former secretary became a brigadier general in the Confederate Army.

Figure 2.3. Excelsior Brigade. Formation of an Excelsior Brigade regiment early in the war. *Courtesy of Library of Congress.*

Camp Caldwell Aug. 26, 1861

Dear Mother,

Your letter came safely in yesterday. I think that the danger for us is pretty much over. The rebels no longer press upon our pickets on the Virginia side and the rumor of their having crossed below seems to be unfounded. Things are going finely with us at present. We did not go out scouting but our other Dunkirk Co. did. This was too bad for we would have liked to get out before all the cantelopes, watermelons, peaches, &c. on which our scouts have waged a war of extermination are entirely gone. I felt very dull for a while since our arrival at this camp but the weather is now delightful and our health and spirits rise in proportion. We drill from six to eight hours exclusive of the time it takes to clean our arms. I was over to the 1st to day and was sorry to find McKinstry in poor health. He has had a run of fever and they have no separate arrangement for the sick men's food. We have a chance to diet and this is much to our advantage. The 1st expect to be paid off to-morrow. We expect one months wages in a day or two and very shortly after two months pay more. We have just got some jumpers like those I brought home from here only much better cut and made. The flannel is first rate.

Sure enough Bob is of the Ypsilanti family. Look over our records and give me his genealogy. His father is named Samuel and has two brothers David and William. Just look it over for me won't you. I sent to Lewis Osmer, formerly foreman of the Censor and now editor of the Dunkirk Union, a plan of our camp and the Union has been in great demand ever since. Our rations have improved considerably of late. We are to have dark blue uniforms that we may not again be confounded with the rebels as at Bulls Run. This will leave us a first rate uniform which we can't carry and I think I can afford very well to pay a few shillings freight and send it home as it will make a very good business and everyday suit. My black pants will now come handy for they can't come their shapeless satinet humbugs upon me and they must pay me the contract price for clothes I dont draw. The coat pants and cap are called worth $19.50, so I shall get all the pants ever cost. My watch is at the city to be cleaned and regulated. It was nearly regulated a few days since and the jeweler pronounced it a very good timekeeper. Our mails come much more regularly here than at Camp Scott and as our regimental postmaster lives in the next tent I get mine punctually. He is named David B. Parker and his father kept the water cars at Forestville. When we get paid off I mean to get myself a good Colt's Navy revolver and some few other more trifling articles and then I shall be apt to have some to send home. I make little use of thin shirts now but those flannel shirts are the very thing for a soldier. I have bought no shirts, socks, or drawers and shall not want anything of the kind except socks this winter. These I can get at any time and I have three pairs allowed—or their value if not drawn. So Bill has had a nice little family row has he. Well tell him never to mind it for a young man can get at any time just as good a family ready made by taking a wife. And Dan has another little responsibility has he. "What will the line stretch till the crack of doom," cried Macbeth and so say I. I am getting on very well with officers and men and as I never shirk duty or miss roll call I can get any favor which any one can. Discipline is very strict but I get out now and then in spite of guards and I always take the proper measures to escape any possibility of detention. I never fail to get back in time for the next duty and so I never have been missed.

We have a fine mess here in no. 7 with one exception. This is an old Crimean soldier who has but little decency or common sense. He is from Ireland and as pig headed as the race usually are. On these glorious moonlight evenings we just raise Ned. A few days since we were all quiet and all in bed. Now there are eight of us in this palace 10 ft. square and we are named a fellows Corporal Pugh of Dunkirk, Laughlin (Paddy), Miller, Silver Creek, Moon, Villenova, Myself, Neapling and O'Donoghay of Silver Creek and our Drum Major Bevier, also of S.C. Well all was quiet and temptation growing stronger and stronger. I shoved my head out from under the canvas and opened the concert with a lusty crow. Directly crows began to caw—cows to bellow, calves, sheep and lambs to bleat while I continued on alternately as a sucking lamb and a stout old chanticleer while Moon followed as the old sheep varying the entertainment by playing upon the jackass. In three minutes the whole camp was in a perfect uproar of domestic beasts and fowls and we lay shaking our sides in No. 7 but keeping as whist as mice that the officers might not find out whence it all originated. Every beast you see or hear on a farm from a horse or ox down to a chipmuck were heard as natural as life. If our mess are not a jolly and pleasant one there never was such on earth. We wear our hats in every style. Mine is turned up continental and I think that the best for if the brim is not turned up it is in the way of the musket. Others simply loop up one side, or cock them military style with but two points. I think the continental the neatest way of having it fixed for drill. Sometimes we get on a regular gale here and carry on pretty extensively so that it is as good sport as cooning.

A drunkard is very rarely seen for McClellan has made a wonderful reform in all matters of discipline. He is, I fully believe, the right man in the right place. He gets at the very "root of the matter" and if any one is known to sell or give a soldier liquor he puts him through by law to the extent of a smart fine, and destroys all liquor found on the premises, a proceeding for which the law gives no redress. All is quiet here and will be I think for some time. It seems that the impression is general that this brigade will continue here to guard the city—an easy but inglorious task. I stand roughing it about as well as any. I can think of no especial news. I heard from Aunt Eliza not long since. Set Frank and his pen at work again as soon as you can.

Lots of love to all,
Your aff. son Arthur.
I glory in the spunk you show in your last.

Shillings: no specific amount, used here as colloquial for a small amount of money.

David B. Parker: Parker rose through the ranks to second lieutenant and eventually was supervising the mail delivery for the entire Army of the Potomac with the title of acting assistant quartermaster.[11]

Raise Ned: Raising the Devil, an old folk expression.

Whist: hushed, quiet.

Camp Caldwell Aug. 31st 1861

Dear Mother

Having got a little leisure I improve it by writing again to you. The regime have subscribed and bought a fleet horse so our mails go twice a day. Day before yesterday we got one months pay which was a great joy to us. It sufficed for all that I want with the exception of a revolver and as next week we get two months pay more beside our mileage and I believe a few dollars for the use of our Dunkirk uniforms. I need not wait long for that. I have a small neat portfolio and a reasonable amount of writing materials and a pocket filter and number of other small compact articles very useful upon a campaign. The weather is very delightful and I have the health and spirits to enjoy it. Your Censor came to hand and I did not admire Ally's letter any more than you. I think Porter Bliss' letter must have been far more palatable to the public. A few nights since we got orders from McClellan to be ready for a short march and a fight at a moments warning. 40 round of buck and ball cartridge were served out and all were ready in short metre. We lay on our arms that night—and I never slept better in my life. We have had no orders since and all is quiet. This can not last much longer. The rebels are near our lines across the river but there are none on this side. They are melting away by small pox, measles, and desertions. We on the contrary are constantly improving in discipline and our food is getting to be very good as things get more regulated. What clothing and equipment come in now are very good. I have seen some of the new cloth pants and they are just the thing. We have not got any yet but when we—that is the others get them I shall send my ole uniform home. There is lots of wear in it yet. I got a letter from Aunt Eliza two or three days since with lots of good advice and such wishes for my future welfare as affected me not a little—hardly less than your own letters which was just such a letter as the mother of a union volunteer should send. I am proud of your firmness and patriotism and will never shame them by a cowardly or unworthy act. I think the rebels must soon make their last stand—as hopeless as a tiger in the anaconda folds but not less fierce. McClellan is all action and his vigilance is unfailing. Beyond this he has the prestige of a brilliant and successful campaign in Western Virginia. The confidence of his soldiers and the terror of his arms to the enemy. His administration has effected wonderful reforms and I have not seen a drunken soldier for weeks. Aunt Eliza—good old soul, offered me money if I needed it—or in short any thing she could do for my comfort. Fortunately I need absolutely nothing and have money enough for some time.

I have everything I can carry for a campaign except the revolver and I could buy three of them next week if I wanted.

The Censor has just come in and lies at my elbow. It has another good thing of the Mass. boys, "When the 12th Mass. Regt were coming through Harrisburgh the rumor was current that the rebels were attacking the Capital. The engineer was urged to make speed but replied that the engine was out of order and five mile an hour was the best he could do. A committee of five machinists were called by Col. Webster and they replied that it was in good order. Then the engineer was arrested and the engine steamed up to 30 miles an hour by the Yankee mudsills." Lency is expected home but I doubt if she can get there as things are now.

As I am tired and my time short too I will close but will write again soon as I have now the conveniences. Tate—who is a good scholar and I mean to study Geometry a little, he is a good steady fellow but too well bred or rather too exclusively used to first rate society not to be the object of the dislike of the "canaille" as the French would say. I have seen more of the rougher ways of the world and can bend to circumstances, however distasteful better than he. I don't know that I have an enemy here, while he has many but it is only the antagonism of two different degrees of society, and inferiority and jealousy that cause it. Give my love to all round and write soon. The crisis will probably come within the coming month—may come within the hour, but that is not likely,—and it must be short but decisive. The rebels are concentrated so near us that once routed they are lost forever. McClellan by his genius of combination can bring us forward at the right time and place in overwhelming force. I have full confidence in our commander in the reg't. Write soon.

Your aff. son
Arthur McKinstry

Mudsills: persons of the lowest social order.

"Canaille": common people, the masses.

Editorial Note

Washington is fast becoming one of the most fortified cities in the world as the men of the brigade are detailed to building a number of forts in that part of the country. But soon McKinstry and his comrades will take a more active role in throttling rebel activities: extended patrols into the heart of southern Maryland.

Figure 3.1. James Hall. James Hall of Company B, also from Chautauqua County. Hall would be killed at Malvern Hill on July 1, 1862. Source: Owen Street, *The Young Patriot: A Memorial of James Hall* (Boston: Sabbath School Society, 1862).

Chapter 3

Into the Doubtful Part of Maryland

September to Mid-October 1861—Camp Near Washington and Patrols into Maryland

The capital is safe as patrols into Lower Maryland begin • The Army takes shape: a division under Joseph Hooker is created • Preventing rebel activity in Lower Maryland and illicit traffic across the Potomac

Editorial Note

Since early summer, a small squadron of Navy ships known as the Potomac Flotilla had been patrolling the Potomac River below Washington. The flotilla's commission is twofold: keep Confederate gun emplacements on the Virginia side of the Potomac in check as to ensure uninterrupted ship traffic in and out of Washington, and to quash communication between the secesh-leaning Maryland and the fully seceded Virginia. Up till now there is some assistance from the Army to intercept those wishing to cross the river in the form of the occasional cavalry patrol into Lower Maryland, but results are meager. The Navy is clamoring for help if their mandate is to be fulfilled.[1] Help will soon be on its way in the form of multiday infantry patrols conducted by the Excelsiors deep into what McKinstry calls "the doubtful part of Maryland."

Fredonia Censor: Published September 11, 1861

Correspondence of the Censor.

FROM THE THIRD REGIMENT.

Camp Caldwell, Sept. 1.

As I have been very busy for a few days I have not been able to write since I informed you of marching orders. On the night of Tuesday last, we were ordered to be ready to march, but not receiving further dispositions we lay on our arms that night, and have been in a state of readiness ever since. On Wednesday, the 1st Regiment were paid off and on Thursday we also signed the pay roll and get pay up to the 30th of June. The peddlers found it out in short matter, and baskets, packs and go-carts of every description were congregated like turkey buzzards to a feast. The first apple pie vendor reaped a rich harvest, and were beset by crowds of eager purchasers, who seized their [purses] and were loudly vociferating for "change." The perplexity of the sellers and the [desiring] of the purchasers were irresistibly [mixed] and such a supreme indifference to the value of gold and silver was never exhibited except upon similar occasions. The appetite for home delicacies appeased, the next thing was to pay up some debts and subscriptions, and then all parties paused a moment and drew a long breath of immense satisfaction. Many of the boys very prudently sent by Capt. Abell to the city what money they could conveniently spare, to be sent home by Adams Express. On Saturday we were again mustered for the next two months' pay, and fell out with knapsacks and all equipments as for a long march. A rigid inspection of dress, arms and accoutrements followed. This over, we were dismissed until dress parade. Gen. Sickles was present, and went through the ceremony of a review. He wore the full uniform of a Brigadier General. The ground was such that we could not pass in review except at great disadvantage, so we only went through the manual of arms and inspection.

Yesterday, (Sunday) I was on guard, but it being my hour off post, I was electrified by the order to fall in, as the President and Secretary Cameron were expected, and the guard were of course expected to receive them at a present. The carriage soon came but not passing near us, (the guard,) we broke ranks and watched the progress of events. The cortege drove up to Col. Taylor's tent, where they alighted and entered. The assembly was at once beaten, and in the time that I require to describe it, the Regiment were formed upon the color line. The President and suite, accompanied by Col. Taylor and staff, passed down the [main] avenue and in front of the center of the battalion. The order was given to prepare for review, and ranks opened to the rear. On the party facing us, we at once recognized our old acquaintance, Hon. Wm. H. Seward and he inquired with considerable interest after the Chautauqua companies. The President then reviewed the regiment to the stirring music of our band, which played to perfect time and unison. I really like their music better than that of any band which I've heard at Camp Scott or at Washington. They had just got acquainted with the instruments a little, and also with each other, and played with great sweetness and poise. I was in the rear of the center, and had an excellent view of the whole proceeding. Col. Taylor is of a tall, commanding form, but the President towered half a head above—yet was he ill-proportioned—but he had a decided stoop of the shoulders, the result, evidently of severe bodily labor. I should think that the bust owned by Judge C——, of Fredonia, was a fair likeness, but his whiskers too much improved his personal appearance. His gait seemed somewhat unsteady, like that of an overtasked accountant, who is constantly at his desk. As when reviewed by Gen. Sickles, we only drilled in the morning and I was greatly pleased to observe the machine-like precision with which the [paces] were handled by the battalion. Capt. Brown was chosen senior Captain, which was perhaps due to his former service and of years, but so far as a thorough military education is concerned, I think our officers second to none here, from Captain down. At battalion maneuvers, whenever Col. Taylor is absent, Major Stevens takes the lead, but however good an executive officer Lieut. Col. Israel Moses may be, his voice is so deficient in power that he is utterly unable to take any effective command. Thus while this Lieut. Colonel only performs the proper duty of a Major, (that is in the field,) he gets a higher pay than these duties should entitle him to, while with the Major the case is vice versa. In all camp duties, however, Lieut. Col. Moses is well posed and prompt in their execution.

It is wonderful what a check Gen. McClellan has placed upon drunkenness and its attendant vices, by his order respecting furloughs and passes, and his prompt punishment of all who are convicted of selling liquor to soldiers.

Our new State jackets have come, and they are really a first rate article. They are a dark blue, and are far more tasty than gay. Pants of the same have come, but only a few have been served round, and I do not think there are enough as yet to uniform the regiment. While at Camp Scott we did not suppose ourselves recognized as State Militia, but the uniforms and other things seem to indicate that we are. Can you inform us on that point?

Yesterday a large number of boxes came in containing uniforms for the regiment. This morning they are served out to the companies. The jackets are dark, and the pants like those we brought from Dunkirk, excepting that they have no stripe down the seam. They fit extremely well. We have no new caps as yet, but many have bought these saucy little fez caps which the French Zouaves wear. They are of a deep crimson color with heavy dark blue tassel. I think the company will obtain them, if not the regiment. They contrast strongly with the dark blue jacket; and a body of men so uniformed look both soldierly and picturesque. As I am on guard to-day I have little time to write. Letters and papers come to us more punctually than at Camp Scott.

Yours as ever,
McK.

Hon. Wm. H. Seward: Secretary of State William H. Seward came to Chautauqua County (living in Westfield) in 1836 to serve as agent for the Land Company. He left in 1838 to run for governor of New York, which he won.

Other Voices: From the *Censor*

Published September 11, 1861

Correspondence of the Censor.

FROM THE THIRD REGIMENT.

Camp Caldwell, Sept. 2.

Dear Censor;—

As I was once a reader of your columns, and would be so now, but that I am now in the army of the Potomac, where the Censor rarely penetrates, unless sent to the Chautauqua volunteers. I take the liberty of sending you a few lines. When the Censor does come, it is warmly welcomed, and it is read and re-read until it has been passed through a hundred hands. If one receives a Chautauqua County paper he is soon surrounded by a hundred eager listeners, each anxious to hear from home.

I joined the Fredonia Company last spring, when it was expected that the 68th Regiment would be called upon to fight their country's battles. When it was decided that the 68th was to stay at home, I went to Jamestown and joined the company of volunteers that Capt. Brown was getting up. We went to New York along with two Dunkirk companies, and joined the 3d Regiment Excelsior Brigade.

We are now encamped across the east branch of the Potomac, or the Anacostia, and about two miles from the city. Our camp is very pleasantly situated, and is the farthest from Washington in that direction. We keep one company on picket duty all the time; the companies relieve each other every five days, that are stationed down the river about four miles, opposite Alexandria; their duty is to block up the road to Washington, and allow no one to pass, without a written pass from Gen. McClellan. The other day a party of 300 cavalry went down to Port Tobacco and arrested some prominent secessionists, who were known to be aiding and sending information to the rebels.

Last Tuesday, the 27th of Aug., Gen. Sickles came into camp, his horses covered with foam; he gave orders to have the Regiment in readiness to start at a moment's warning. The companies immediately formed in line, and 40 rounds of ammunition given to each man, and such other things as were necessary for a march. We waited patiently, expecting every moment to hear the *long roll* beat; but the morning came, and the 3d Regiment was still there. The cause of the alarm was 2,000 of the enemy who crossed the river below here, but went back again. Gen. McClellan thought it was a blind of the enemy to cover some movement toward Washington, and immediately gave orders to have all of the troops in readiness to start at a moment's warning.

The next day there was a skirmish at Bailey's Cross Roads. We could hear the firing quite plain, our troops are in possession of the place. Quite an amusing incident occurred during the skirmish; some of the Michigan boys got a stove pipe and mounted it upon some cart wheels, and partly concealed it in some bushes, this soon attracted the enemy's attention, they took it for a deserted gun, after firing a few guns to drive away any men who might be near, they charged upon it with 200 cavalry, but they soon discovered their mistake and went away without their prize.

While we were encamped at camp Marsh, one mile north of the city, we went down to the city to be reviewed by the President. We arrived there about sun-down, and drew up before the White House. Abraham soon came out, dressed in a linen coat and plug hat, both the worse for wear. After review, he told Gen. Sickles that it was the best Regiment but one (a Maine Regiment,) he had seen.

The department of the Potomac under the hands of Gen. McClellan is fast assuming a formidable aspect. The troops as soon as they arrive are put under strict drill and military discipline. This drilling men until they are mere *machines*, subject to the will of their superiors, I judge from my own experience and observation, to be injurious. Take a man from his work-shop or farm, he is running over with patriotism, and is ready to shed the last drop of blood in defense of his country's honor; let him enlist, and put him under strict military discipline, and in less than three months he will be a mere machine, which must work perfect in all its parts, he does his work mechanically, his patriotism drilled and starved out of him. We gain nothing by drilling; while we are drilling and perfecting our army, the enemy are not idle, they can drill as long as we can. The best fighting that has been done was done by undisciplined troops, who had no chance to drill. There are now four companies of Chautauqua County boys in the Regiment, and it is needless to say that they are the best. It is very healthy here at present, there has been but one death in the Regiment since we left Camp Scott. Our rations are now as good as can be expected. We are now under marching orders, and may leave any moment.

H. B. Taylor [Henry B. Taylor, Private, Co. B, Jamestown].

Letter to Jennie . . . [undated, appears a page is missing, early September of 1861]

We have lots of meat but it is not cooked fit to eat. It is wholesome but I never liked boiled meat and almost all ours is cooked that way. So Charley is ensign is he, well good for him. That rank is not recognized in the U.S. service but there is a non commissioned officer called Color sergeant instead and there is but one to a regiment. As a N.Y. militia officer however I think Charley can draw his pay and come out all right. Well he is the only tolerable one in the crew and I wish him good luck. Pete I presume howls piteously for his dear Journal of Commerce.

There are 150,000 men in this little cluster and as many more in other parts fighting to repair the mischief such traitors have made. I think it would do good to make an example of one or two leading softs and tar and [feather] them least. Are there any meaner class on earth than "Northern men with Southern principles." I am very brown and hairy so I have shaved but once since I left Dunkirk because I need the beard to keep the sun from skinning me alive.

I have been unwell for a few days but I think I can do duty again to-morrow. I stand the heat like a salamander and I think I can fight upon as hot a day as any secesher. While we were scouting we had for three days but one meal a day and that for a trip of not less than 15 miles. We didn't starve though—oh no we sort of found what was needed and went on our way with well filled bellies and rejoicing hearts. As a general rule our officers and men presented a marked contrast to the Irish Company from the 2nd, and the Zouaves by their order, decency, and discipline. I think you are lucky in getting rid of Frank Remington for the war but Jerome seems to stick to you yet. Don't you wish it was necessary to draft that you might get rid of him too.

So Millie wants you to tell me that she loves Artie. Well Artie has heard it and is glad of such news. I shall be glad to see the little thing again when the war is over. Millie is a kind good girl and a pretty one too if she is not so almighty gristly as John junior.

McClellan makes his plans so secretly that we cannot ourselves tell anything where we are going when under marching orders. When we stop we know what the order must have been. If the enemies know what we are about they are better posted than our colonel. Finally McClellan in the East and Fremont in the West are sure to conquer.

The enemy talk of retreating but if they do it they are ruined at once for nearly [unreadable] men would be after them very [seriously] with abundance of flying artillery and cavalry. I don't try to send you [unreadable] except so far as concerns myself for any new [unreadable] goes by telegraph to Forestville in less time than a horse can travel five or six miles from the city and bring it here. The reporters of the [unreadable] that paper as soon as it goes to Washington offices. I see that Justus McKinstry has been promoted to brig. gen. U.S.A. in Fremonts division. Well Jennie I have done you a long letter. Its good bye.

Arthur

Justus McKinstry: McKinstry was appointed a brigadier general of volunteers on September 2, 1861, but the appointment expired without confirmation by the United States Senate on July 17, 1862. McKinstry was kicked out of the army in January of '63 for cheating the government out of many thousands of dollars (apparently no relation to Arthur).

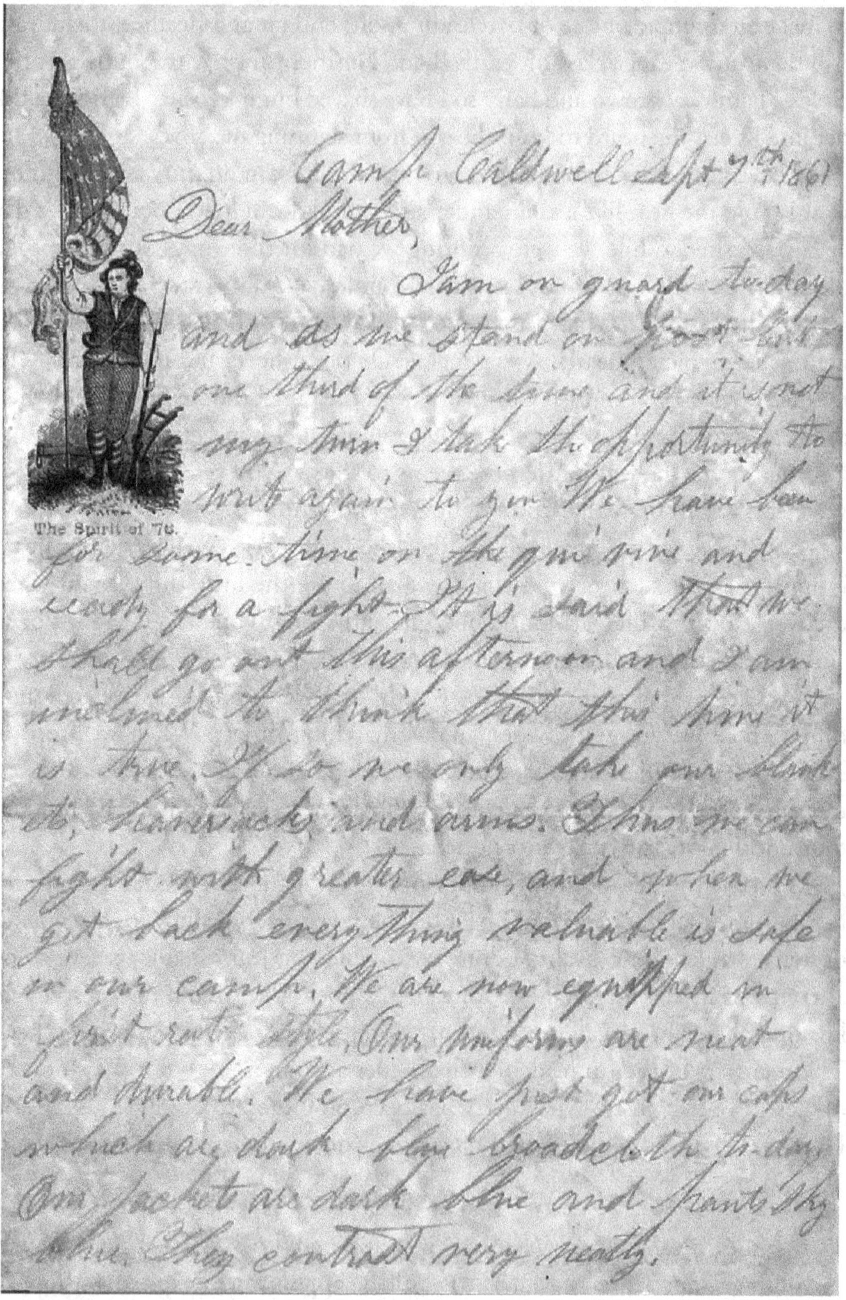
The Spirit of '76.

Camp Caldwell Sept 7th 1861

Dear Mother,

I am on guard to-day and as we stand on guard but one third of the time and it is not my time I take the opportunity to write again to you We have been for some time on the qui vive and ready for a fight. It is said that we shall go out this afternoon and I am inclined to think that this time it is true. If so we only take our blankets, haversacks and arms. Thus we can fight with greater ease, and when we get back everything valuable is safe in our camp. We are now equipped in first rate style. Our uniforms are neat and durable. We have just got our caps which are dark blue broadcloth to-day. Our jackets are dark blue and pants sky blue. They contrast very neatly.

Figure 3.2. Letter to Mother on Patriot letterhead. *Courtesy of Ulysses S. Grant Presidential Library.*

Camp Caldwell Sept. 7th 1861

Dear Mother,

I am on guard today and as we stand on post but one third of the time and it is not my turn I take the opportunity to write again to you. We have been for some time on the qui vive and ready for a fight. It is said that we shall go out this afternoon and I am inclined to think that this time it is true. If so we only take our blankets, haversacks, and arms. Thus we can fight with greater ease, and when we get back everything valuable is safe in our camp. We are now equipped in first rate style. Our uniforms are neat and durable. We have just got our caps which are dark blue broadcloth to-day. Our jackets are dark blue and pants sky blue. They contrast very neatly. My Dunkirk pants are at the washerwomans and when they get back you may look out for a budget by express. The pants want a little fixing but the jacket and cap are of very fine and soft grey cloth and will stand a years ordinary wear. Instead of sowing my clothes about I mean to establish a rallying place for them so that I can use them when I return. I am now feeling as strong (There goes a cannon) as ever I have done since my return from Mexico. I live mainly on bread and butter, with rice vegetable soup, hominy and, coffee. Meat is plenty but I use very little. We have butter by paying for it so each of the mess buys it for one day in his turn. We use a pound a day among eight of us which is not very extravagant. The other night I went out on the countersign, after standing one tour, and went over to the first regt. to see Bob who was unwell the last time (Another cannon shot) that I saw him. I did not see him for he was worse and in the hospital. The next day I got a pass from Col. Taylor and went over to see him. He lay in great distress and the steward called the case bronchitis. I thought that he was in the same fix that I was last winter, he breathed very short, his pulse was high, and he raised just such phlegm as I did. Coughing exhausted him much and he cared for no victuals (Cannon again). I got him a fat tender chicken about the size of a partridge and cheered him up so that he looked much more encouraged when I left. The steward told the cook to prepare the fowl to Bobs own liking. If the sutler gets some currant jelly to day I will try to carry him some of that for he is a good fellow and gave me useful and costly medicine when I was sick and exhausted with diarrhea. I shall get the pass word on post and I could go all over McClellans division on the strength of it when I get off. All I want to look out for is to be ready to go on post again in four hours after being relieved. Four of us went out a while ago and finding our way into a melon patch we each carried off four large ones and shortly after there was nothing but some very thick rinds (we were dainty and only ate the ripe red heart) to tell the tale. I am now quite satisfied and mean to engage in no risky adventures hereafter. We are drilled very hard and it is easier to do guard duty which keeps one busy nine or ten hours than any other.

They are preparing splendid winter quarters for our brigade. We seem to be recognized as state volunteers at last if I may judge by our uniforms which are furnished by N.Y.S. I am on the whole as well contented as I could be on any farm and am getting pay clothing to amount to $16 ½, per month. I do my duty and I do it well. Why don't you write.

Love to all,

Arthur

Budget: leather pouch, package.

Other Voices: Orders to Move into Lower Maryland

HEADQUARTERS HOOKER'S BRIGADE,
Camp Union, September 8, 1861.

Colonel COWDIN,
Commanding First Regiment Massachusetts Volunteers:

The major-general commanding the Army of the Potomac is informed that two companies of rebel troops and other small portions were seen this morning in the direction of Upper Marlborough and extending down the Patuxent towards Lower Marlborough. For this and other reasons the brigadier-general commanding the brigade directs that you proceed with your regiment to Upper Marlborough by the most direct route, and from that point send out scouting parties in direction of Alexandria and Lower Marlborough. For this service two companies of cavalry will be ordered to report to you, and the whole of your command will march, provided with five days' rations and forty rounds of ammunition and with a dozen axes and spades. Your men will take their overcoats and blankets, and you may require five or six wagons. Let their loads be light, so as not to embarrass your progress. You will watch the enemy and report at once anything of importance that may occur. It is possible that the parties seen were local troops, which should be captured; also, all supplies intended for their use or that of the rebel forces. You will use your cavalry freely, and collect all the information possible about the enemy's movements, and will also hold your force in hand and not permit them to commit depredations upon the citizens.

As General Sickles will send the same amount of force to Patuxent as your own, it is desirable that your parties should connect between that and Upper Marlborough. You will exercise great care to prevent your scouts firing on those of Sickles' brigade. You will report to me regularly twice a day, and will make special reports of anything of consequence that occurs.

Very respectfully, your obedient servant,

JOS. DICKINSON,
Assistant Adjutant-General[2]

Fredonia Censor: Published September 25, 1861

Correspondence of the Censor.

FROM THE THIRD REGIMENT.

Camp Caldwell, Sept. 14.

As we have just returned from a long and fatiguing scout in the doubtful part of Maryland, perhaps some of the readers of the Censor may feel some interest in the adventures of Company D. Last Sunday, Sept. 8th, we received orders to prepare to leave with one day's rations in our haversacks. Every man was all astir with excitement, the sick, who could walk, suddenly got well, and the biggest company was turned out that had ever been seen since pay day. At about 2 P.M. we marched off the ground and headed for the cross roads at Good Hope Tavern. Here we found two companies awaiting us; one from the 2d, and the French Zouave company from the 5th. We took our position between these and marched in a south-easterly direction, the Zouaves in the rear. At some considerable distance, two or three miles, perhaps, we found a company from the 1st, stationed as pickets. Immediately after passing these, we halted and loaded our pieces. We then immediately got under way and tramped rapidly on. After a long heat we halted, and a cavalry company, which had followed in our rear, passed to the front and rode forward to reconnoiter. Zou-zou now began to cut up all sorts of antics, and to dance and sing right merrily. First came "Viva Garibaldi." As this was Italian, I cannot pass any comment upon it, save that it was sung with great spirit by the old Italian campaigners, and that it seemed very musical. Then came the "*Zouave, Mourir pour la patria,*" and other stirring national airs. I send you the Zouave and meant to have copied *Mourir pour la patria,* but had not had time. The last I like the best. As very many readers of the Censor are proficient in languages, even a French song will not come amiss to them.

Some pigs were seen in the wood, and forth with a Zouave had one in the circle, and great amusement was derived from it by mercurial Frenchmen. *Le gallop, La pastoralle,* and other dances were performed to the sound of bugle and drum. Soon the order came to fall in again, and away we dashed. It was nearly night when we halted again at a cross road. Here Capt. Abell started out with Billy Post, Lopez, Mount, Van Houton and Simpson, to seize upon some arms said to be concealed in the house of a secessionist named ______. We awaited their return for some time, but as we heard nothing of them, we at last resumed our march, and after a long and severe tramp, arrived at a place we called Cross Roads. This village consisted of two ginger-bread and whiskey stores, and one dwelling house and barn. Here we posted guards, and stacking our arms, lay round our guns to sleep. The next morning we awoke in good season, and were very glad to see Capt. Abell report himself and party to Lieut. Col. Potter, of the 2d, who was in command. They brought in a fine London twist, double-barreled shot-gun, and an antiquated musket with flint lock, which looked as if it might have figured in the battle between the Cavaliers and Puritans of Cromwell's time. ______ was at not home, but they secured the arms, and soon after they arrested a fellow whom our pickets had been looking after. He was handed over to Col. Potter. ______'s house was about two miles from the corners where Capt. Abell left us.

The Zouave's had a roaring fire, and were proceeding to roast therein some corn which they had *confiscated.* The Negroes whom we had met thus far on our journey hailed us with delight, and told us the unvarying story that every planter was secesh but dared not own it. While Capt. Abell was at ______'s, two horsemen approached, but seeing our party they rode quickly away. The 4th Regiment company left us at the same time that our scouting party did.

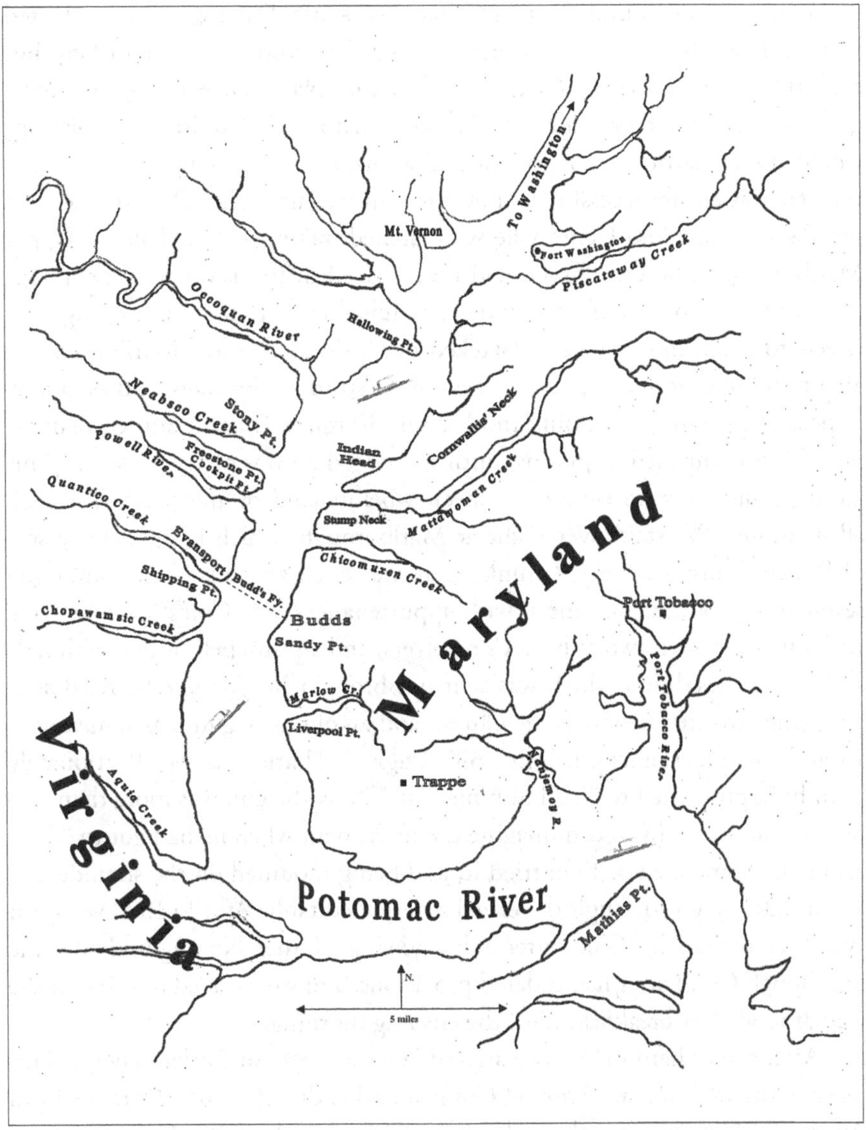

Figure 3.3. Map of region. Area of operation for Hooker's Division and the Potomac Flotilla from Washington, DC, to beyond Mathias Point and all of Lower Maryland. *Courtesy of the author.*

Soon we were again under way and marched some distance, when we halted to rest. There being a fine grove at Centerville, however, we staid here but a short time, when we pushed forward to that place. Here we laid off for a good rest, and took a good meal. Thinking that a little "spiritual consolation" would do no harm, Col. Potter treated all hands.—The only act of hostility thus far was an unsuccessful shot at our Calvary last night. The offender was not discovered. From Centerville we marched, taking a short halt, to Upper Marlborough. The Frenchmen had been placed in front, on account, I suppose, of their showy uniforms, and we marched in first rate order through the streets to a common where we stacked our guns and rested. Marlborough is about 15 miles from camp, but as we traveled through by-ways, and as quietly as possible, we made, I should think 25 or 30 miles. Every mounted man we found was compelled to join us, until we judged he was pretty well out of his latitude, and thus we were not expected beforehand of any place, but took all unawares. We staid over night at Marlborough, which is the county seat of Prince George's county, I think. Here we seized an arms chest containing seven very good dragon sabers, with appurtenances, one Colt's revolving rifle with saber bayonet, two Whitney's revolvers, and a pistol belt or two with holsters.—An expedition which was sent out brought in a double barreled shot gun, (the favorite weapon of the Chivs,) and an old duck gun which measured six and a half feet in length. This, Billy Pugh, or "Barley," as we affectionately term him, proceeded to "load in nine time." Now the gun was more than two feet the tallest, and you can imagine the merriment when he had got to "draw rammer." Someone else then tried it, and being mounted on the shoulders of a comrade, he got through the exercise very creditably. At 3 ½ P.M. we again "vamosed the ranch," Col. Potter only knowing whither. No wagons had come up, though Col. Potter had ordered provisions, and we received nothing in the way of food after breakfast, until the ensuing morning.

After a very hard march, we arrived late that night at Butler's tavern. This place is situated in Ann Arundel County, and is distant about 11 miles from Annapolis. Here we slept through what remained of the night. Col. Potter was astir, however, and foraged right well for his command. An army of niggers lost their sleep that night to bake our hoecakes, and one or two beeves were cooked. Some raw meat was also brought in, which we broiled, as we had done at Marlborough. This is the best way to enjoy meat, for boiled meat is poor food for a company upon the march. A number of persons were brought in here. One had in his house a Southern captain's uniform, and Col. Potter desired the pleasure of his company back to headquarters. This invitation was unhesitatingly complied with. I have heard that some letters southward bound were here intercepted, but, as I have no reliable authority, I think this statement very doubtful.

As it is very uncertain where the next meal was to be obtained, a great number now went out to forage. On our part this was done in a law-abiding manner, but *Jean Crapau* had no such idea in his head—going into every hen-rooster orchard for a circuit of miles and taking what he thought he could conveniently carry. As regards fruit, we were not so very punctilious ourselves. This section abounds with peaches, and they were very nice. After staying long enough to recruit a little, we again dug out, and a long, hard tramp we had. We visited Queen Anne upon on our way. Just before our arrival we forded stream, well swollen by rain, and the first intimation I had of ducking in store, was the wild yelling of the Zouaves, who plunged gallantly in, and came out with a large amount of the "drink" in the slack of their inexpressibles. Their passage fixed me in the opinion that however good Turkish trowsers are, on the march, they are not exactly the thing to ford rivers in.

We crossed the main branch of the Pautuxent just before entering Queen Anne. On entering this village we passed a neat house, in the doorway of which, a lady stood, waving a small Union flag.—This was the only hearty Union sign that we saw in the place, and was greeted by our boys with rounds of applause. As this lady kept somewhat within her dwelling, I concluded she desired to escape the observation of the neighbors. After halting for a rest, we put out again and journeyed until very late toward Good Hope, our headquarters. During this day, I was frequently requested to take notes as we crossed the "Maryland bridges," as the boys termed the mud puddles in our way. I cannot particularize, for their name is legion, so let one note for all. Late at night we arrived at Brooks' plantation, about 14 miles from camp. Here the men slept in some large tobacco sheds, and were securely sheltered from a drenching rain which fell that night. This was the first night they had slept under cover, and they were in the nick of time.

The next morning things looked rather squally, for we could not get half a breakfast. As it is pretty well known that large quantities of bacon are kept by planters to feed their Negroes with, our boys began to think forbearance no virtue. The Zouaves started to scour the country, as was their wont. I was convulsed with laughter to see the desperation of one of the hungry soldiers. "By G–d," cried he, "if they won't give nor sell us anything, I will have the satisfaction of killing something." An unlucky Muscovy duck waddled up as he spoke, and was instantly knocked over by the butt of his gun. Then seizing the bewildered fowl he wrung off its head and cast it upon the body. He then strode fiercely off and soon after I saw him in hot pursuit of a flock of screaming chickens, with a very long stick in his hand. I committed no act of depredation here—upon honor I didn't—but if the partaker is as bad as the thief, I must settle up a date which I hope is still very remote, for the breast of a chicken which I broiled and ate for dinner. Opportunity makes the thief sometimes—this time it was stern necessity; but I don't blame the man who killed that chicken, for it was very nice and tender, and as Little Mice would say, it made a "mizzible good brile."

From Brooks' we soon got under way, with but very little thanks in our hearts for hospitality so faint and so grudgingly bestowed. That they had ample resources to supply us, no man can doubt. It was not necessary that they should cook for us; that we could do ourselves; and Col. Potter's order would have been honored by the proper disbursing officers. It is true that they did at last unbend a little, but it was the screaming of poultry and not the necessity of the soldiers which reached their hearts.

After a march of three Maryland miles (7 in your dialect,) we halted once more. As for two days I had felt dizzy and unwell, I started on after a short pause, knowing that I was not well enough to keep my place in the ranks. I plodded slowly on until past Oldfield, which lay about three miles ahead. At some distance beyond, I caught a ride, and was pleased to find the driver a Yankee. He was a native of Salisbury, Conn., and he had been for 25 years a teacher. He owned a large tract of land, and had a good, substantial, but unfinished house. "I do not finish it," said he, "because it is very possible that the rebels, or their sympathizers, might burn it." He had been attempting to supply our soldiers with milk, but gave it up because the planters would rather feed it to their hogs than to sell it for 40 cents per gallon to Union volunteers. "The people here," said he, "are all secessionists, and it is only the presence of an overpowering Union force which causes them to feign loyalty. They are all ready to take the oath of allegiance; that doesn't hurt them a bit; but just so soon as they think they can help Jeff Davis, so soon their dispatches will be sent on." He further stated that he was aware of a good deal of aid and comfort being given to the rebels. At this period of our conversation we reached his gate. Here we were received by his wife and two children, who were quite refreshing to behold, from their neatness and evident intelligence, as contrasted with the ignorance and almost beastial degradation of some of their neighbors.

Here I staid long enough to fill my canteen and again plodded on until I reached the camp of the 2d Regiment, where Col. Potter's command overtook me. Here we were received with presented arms by the Jackson Guards, as their regiment is called. We marched past and filed into their encampment, where we received some more "spiritual consolation," and were treated to an excellent supper by the generous Irishmen. Being sick I obtained leave to remain, and soon after Company D started on the home stretch, amid thundering cheers from the Jackson Guards. I staid that night with the boys who were out with us, and was filled to the lips with coffee and whatever else they imagined was good to eat or drink. They almost killed me with pure hospitality. The next morning I jogged into Camp Caldwell.

While at Marlboro we saw the 1st Massachusetts Regiment, which we left in occupation of that place. A more intelligent looking body of men I have never seen. They fought at Bull's Run, and their Colonel and Lieut. Colonel fought like brave men, with their muskets in their hands.

The 1st of our Brigade has gone down to Port Tobacco. With regard to the distance we traveled, I can make no estimate, but I think the last day's journey, in which we accomplished 14 miles, altogether the easiest. This, too, under a broiling sun, which made our clothing wringing wet with perspiration. We took circuitous routes to avoid observation, and as we seized every horseman we saw, we were always unexpected. The Negroes wished to go with us, but this they were sternly forbidden to do. Today we have received our pay up to the 1st of September. Capt. Abell has received a considerable amount to be sent to our friends by express. We are well clothed, and though I have not drawn my full allowance I shall send some home to get them out of the way. When I turn my bayonet into a drag tooth, they will be found very useful no doubt. While upon our march, Capt. Abell was found to be good and jovial company, and the unbending rules which he enforces in camp were relaxed. Indeed a common sense of duty and of danger kept every man in his place, ready to attack the foe or defend our expedition. The men all bore up bravely, while toward the last the Zouaves dropped behind us by the dozen. The baggage wagon was loaded, but by other men, and I believe that but one of our men was in it, and he was violently sick with cholera morbus. He was in the ranks again in less than 24 hours, and marched stoutly into camp. No man here likes to have his plantation cut up by roads, and we never marched two hours together without heading for each point of the compass—rarely without crossing a "Maryland bridge."

The roads were abominable. The soil is mostly poor, but a good climate has produced all the corn that this state can possibly consume. In some fields the corn stood twelve or even fifteen feet high. We passed large fields of tobacco, and some of the boys decorated the points of their bayonets with "bands" of the weed, which closely resembled the knot of Pocahontas, as represented in my juvenile school books. There were no fields of better tobacco than I have raised in Forestville; while the valley of the Connecticut throws them quite into the shade; but their corn is first rate.

A. McK.

Garibaldi: prominent Italian nationalist who supported the Northern cause, especially the end of slavery.

Mourir pour la patria: dying for the fatherland.

Little Mice: the black coachman in *Harper's New Monthly Magazine's Virginia Illustrated, Adventures of Porte Crayon and His Cousins*, February 1855 edition. "Presently he [Little Mice] returned, his face illuminated with a triumphant grin, carrying the bird by the legs. 'Bullet tuck him right through the neck; mizzible good brile he'll make; fat as butter.'"

Maryland mile: McKinstry joking about the poor conditions of the roads, so that "three Maryland miles" would be equal to seven miles anywhere else.

Chivs: probably Arthur's shorthand for his term "chivalrous planters," referring to the locals.

Drag tooth: a drag tooth harrow is a type of soil cultivating device.

Other Voices: From the *Censor*

Published October 9, 1861

Correspondence of the Censor.

FROM THE THIRD REGIMENT.

Camp Caldwell, Sept. 27th, 1861.

Dear Censor:—

The Regiment is still here, and will probably be here for some time to come judging from present appearances. We have now a regimental bakery, and consequently, our rations in that line are very much improved. We are now building a log magazine after the style of an old fashioned block house, for the accommodation of the prisoners during the cold weather. It is not decided whether we shall stay here this winter or not, though arrangements are being made to that effect. The barracks at the Arsenal and Navy Yard are unoccupied and Col. Taylor has the privilege of quartering his regiment there if he thinks proper. Whether we shall spend the winter in the city, yet remains to be seen. The Buffalo regiment, Col. Bidwell, arrived in the city the 21st, and Monday they left for Meridian Hill, where they are now encamped.

Everything is quiet across the Potomac, more so than usual, but as a storm succeeds a calm, this deceitful quiet may be broken at any moment, and break out into a terrible battle between nearly 400,000 men, which will shake the continent to the center, and will probably decide the fate of the Union. We have had a prisoner in camp, a secession Captain, who was taken by Co. D, while they were out upon a scouting expedition. The prisoner was treated more like a friend than as a prisoner, and was allowed greater liberties than any of our other captains.

The Excelsior Brigade is at present employed upon some fortifications on the top of a hill across the East Branch, and opposite the Navy Yard. It commands the river, Arlington Heights, and the whole of Washington. There are about 300 men employed upon it every day: Major Stevens has the superintendence of the work at present. Contrary to the orders of Gen. McClellan commanding the observance of the Sabbath in the army, our Colonel puts us through a course of drilling every Sunday, which precludes all possibility of forgetting when that day of rest comes around. I will take last Sunday as a fair sample. We were busy all the morning until 9 o'clock, cleaning our guns and putting our tents in order for inspection at 9 o'clock which lasted until 10 o'clock. From 11 to 12, we had preaching. At 2 P.M. we had to fall in for knapsack drill. We have to march about 1½ mile to our drilling grounds with our knapsacks on. It was after sun down when we came back to camp. Then came dress parade, and it was dark before we were dismissed. Our Colonel probably intends that we shall not forget the Sabbath.

I shall have to close, as news of any kind is a scarce article.

[Unsigned]

Camp Caldwell Oct. 7th '61

Dear Mother,

I was very glad to hear from you yesterday for I had been getting very impatient as well as anxious. I am in hospital on account of the same old fever but it is broken now and I am doing well. The hospital of our regiment is very neat and well arranged. The food is suitable and well cooked and great care is given to the sick.

I could not do our scouting justice for I had a smart fever on me the day I wrote it and I should not have stirred in the matter if it were not for the sake of Uncles Willard & Wint and the anxiety of the Company that I should write an account for publication. Capt. Abell wanted the worst kind that I should send it to the Dunkirk Union but this was no go you may be sure. The more I see of Capt. Abell the better I like him. A prompt man who never fails to do his duty may look for anything in reason, while the shirks get fits I can tell you. My watch got horribly dirty and a good deal out of order at Camp Scott and I sent it down to the city for repairs. It was sent back looking very neat but it had a trick of resting four or five hours at night. I sent it back and the jeweler agreed to set it right without further cost. (He had got $1.75.) Well he gave up his business to another who assumed his liabilities. My watch was righted and marked $1.25. Our Postmaster who did the business for me very coolly told him to look to his predecessor for the dollar and a quarter and brought me the watch, and I don't know that there is a much better time keeper here than my poor abused old turnip. The whole secret is, the jeweler who repaired it this time understood its machinery which none heretofore have done.

Tell Lute the crescent should be worn in front. You will now see the wisdom of my holding on to my money when I tell you that for some time previous to my admission here I could not eat the coarse food allowed the company but went out and got food more suitable for a sick man and of course I had to pay roundly for it all. I only ate as much as a good sized family eat and did not desire any dinner so it did not count very fast but still I find it a great thing not to be short of funds. A man who is well needs but a third at most of his pay but one who is unwell had not better send a great deal home till he gets well. Here in the hospital a man is well provided for and money is not needed. Well I am tired and will quit. I wrote to Orra and received a cordial answer in which she told me that Cousin Cyrus and Uncle Henry visited Ft. Porter to see if I was there, having heard that I had enlisted.

Uncle Henry it seems has a daughter 3 months old and Orra says that he and Aunt Mabell do not visit at all but that they enjoy themselves hugely at home. Love to all and write soon.

Arthur

Other Voices: *Fredonia Censor*, Forming a New Company

Published October 10, 1861

Adjutant S. M. Doyle, of Dunkirk, has returned to that village for the purpose of raising a new company of Chautauqua men for the 3d Regiment Excelsior Brigade. It is designed to create a Chautauqua battalion and raise the strength of the Regiment to 1,600 men. The Dunkirk Journal states that Adjutant Doyle's company "H" is already nearly filled and the uniforms have been received. Capt. Brown, of Jamestown is engaged in the like effort in the southern part of the county.

Editorial Note

On October 11th, Joseph Hooker is promoted from brigade commander to divisional command, a command which includes the Excelsiors. Though a brigade of regiments from New Jersey will eventually be added, the new Hooker's Division is composed of:

Cavalry.—Eight companies Third Indiana Cavalry.

Artillery.—Elder's battery (E), First U.S. Artillery.

Infantry. Hooker's former brigade: First and Eleventh Massachusetts, Second New Hampshire, Twenty-sixth Pennsylvania, and First Michigan Volunteers.

Sickles' brigade: First, Second, Third, Fourth, and Fifth Regiments Excelsior Brigade (Seventieth, Seventy-first, Seventy-second, Seventy-third, and Seventy-fourth), New York Volunteers.[3]

EXCELSIOR
BRIGADE!
3D REGIMENT
COL. TAYLOR!
50 ABLE BODIED MEN
WANTED!
For the above Regiment, to go immediately into active service for the term of 3 years, or during the war.
PAY FROM 13 TO 24 DOLLARS PER MONTH!
FROM THE DAY OF ENLISTMENT, AND ALSO
A Bounty of $100 & 160 Acres of Land
AT THE EXPIRATION OF SERVICE.
This Regiment is composed principally of men from Chautauqua Co., and is encamped near Washington, D. C. Good men capable and willing to serve their country, can be enrolled, by applying immediately to the undersigned at Sinclearville.
Lieut. SAMUEL T. ALLEN,
Recruiting Officer.
Oct. 10, 1861.

Figure 3.4. RECRUITING POSTER. Poster used during the formation of Company H of the 72nd New York. *Courtesy of Union Drummer Boy.*

Fredonia Censor: Published October 23, 1861

FROM THE THIRD REGIMENT.

Camp Caldwell, Oct. 12.

Dear Uncles:—

I have long been silent on account of a long and tedious spell of intermittent fever, which is now the most prevalent disease in the camp, and, indeed, I was suffering severely from its effects when my last letter was written.—The disease is seldom fatal, and we have no patients who are in danger from it or any other complaint. I was in the hospital a few days, and was well pleased with the neatness of the same, and the care of those who are in charge. Dr. Irwin has been very fortunate in his selection of assistants in his department.—There is a Hospital fund derived from savings of the past, I believe the saving of flour at the Bakery is one of the sources. This fund has never at any time been exhausted, but on the contrary, it is increasing all the time, and at present it amounts to upward of seventy dollars, although the sick are furnished with every delicacy reasonable in every case.

The men are having a severe course of drill, mainly on account of the incapacity of some company officers of the regiment, whose ignorance of military science would shame the privates of any of our Chautauqua companies. They are sadly in want of all the drilling they receive, but it seems hard to make those who are efficient in their drill, do double duty on their account. On the day of our National fast, humiliation and prayer, we had plenty of the second, but as for the first, no man could do it and expect to live. The prayers were all "over the left"; for the benefit of the Colonel, the men did if, possible, a harder day's work than ever, which is the case almost every Sunday, notwithstanding Gen. McClellan's order to the contrary.

We have just finished our earth work fortification. It is called Fort Stanton. It has many angles, where cannon can be mounted and enfilade the ditch, which is 16 feet wide, and 10 feet deep, as nearly as I can judge. By mounting heavy guns on circles, it could be made very formidable. It commands the best view of Washington and Arlington Heights, and even as far as the enemy's camps beyond, of any spot that I have yet visited. I used to scout the development theory of La Place, but since I have come south, I have changed my opinion materially.—I see but one thing which confirms his tenets, but that is confirmation strong indeed.—I notice though everything else is at a stand still, the negro race is undergoing a *bleaching* process, which brings each successive generation still nearer to the Caucassian standard. Poor, abused La Place, how much easier his bones would rest in his coffin if he only knew how triumphantly his theory was vindicated in the far-off country towards the setting sun. I not only see that they are gradually whitening, but also that they in many instances bear strong resemblance to the more aristocratic families of Maryland.

The 1st is back from Port Tobacco, where, according to their report, they had a jolly time and succeeded in capturing considerable contraband property on its way south, together with several secession prisoners. Frank Stevens arrived here a few days ago, and has commenced whipping the sheep-skin severely. Our band is progressing finely, and our dress parade is a very different affair, as enlivened by the sweet strains of "Annie Laure," or some equally pleasant tune, from what it was in the old times when we had only the fife and drum. The Fredonia boys are all well. I understand that Adjt. Doyle is to take command of the new company from Dunkirk. I congratule them in the selection of a commander so capable, for he is every inch a soldier, at the same time the regiment will be deprived of the services of an officer whose place can hardly be filled.

Yours, as ever,
McK.

La Place: Arthur probably confused Pierre-Simon Laplace, a French scientist/mathematician, for Jean-Baptiste Lamarck, a French naturalist who put forth a theory of evolution based on acquiring and discarding various traits based on environment. Lamarck's theories were eventually overshadowed by Charles Darwin.

Congratule: French for congratulate.

Other Voices: From the *Censor*

Published October 23, 1861

[The following is an extract from a private letter received from a young man of this village, now connected with the 3d Regiment Band.]

Camp Caldwell, Oct. 17

I arrive at Washington about 1 P.M. The first, and about the finest sight I saw, after getting off the cars, was the 6th Connecticut Regiment going into camp. They had a good Band with them. I went to the capital, and then went around the city, but the soldiers were so thick that I could hardly see anything else. On my return to Camp Caldwell, there was Regiment after Regiment of Cavalry and Flying Artillery passed me, and they did look fine. I reached camp about 3 or 4 o'clock, and the boys were glad to see me. I was surprised to find so many of my old acquaintances here. Willie Cushing came to our camp the second day after I arrived here and spent three days with us. Our camp is situated about 2½ or 3 miles from Washington, but our drill grounds are about 2 miles from here, in the State of Maryland. The Regiment goes over there every day, right after dinner, and the Band go anywhere from 3 o'clock to 5, and escort the Regiment into camp. We take it easy going over, and gathering chestnuts which are in great quantities and very large. I like it first rate, and would not come home if I could. We have large wall tents with a flyleaf over the top, (an extra piece of heavy duck clothe, the same as our tents) which covers the whole top, making it a double top and perfectly water tight.

This week, Tuesday, the whole Brigade was reviewed by Gen. Sickles and staff, on our drill grounds. It was the greatest military display that I ever saw. Our regiment had the position of honor in the Brigade, (the right of the Brigade,) as it is the best drilled. We are the only regiment that has got a Band and that sets us up a peg or so. Talking about your Zouaves, you ought to see a company of French Zouaves that belong to this Brigade, if you want to see drilling. Well, they ought to do it up right, for they are at it all the while.

Yesterday our Band went over to the 2d Regiment, N.Y. Fire Zouaves, (now the 4th Regiment in this Brigade,) to a flag and banner presentation. We had a gay time. The colors were presented by Chief Engineer Decker, of the New York City Fire Department. He made a fine speech, and was replied to by the Colonel of the Regiment, after which, General Sickles made a good and somewhat lengthy speech. Then the Band escorted the color officers, Gen. Sickles and staff, to the Colonel's headquarters, where we partook of a very nice supper. There was every kind of liquor on the table, and the corks popped from the Champaign bottles sounded like the discharge of a volley of musketry.

In the General's speech to the Fire Zouaves, he said he hoped and knew they would not dishonor their colors. At any rate, it would not be a great while before they would get a chance to fight; and he was right, for we leave here to morrow, with the rest of the Brigade for some place unknown to me. We take six days ration, and the boys are all packing their knapsacks. It is now raining hard, and we will have a muddy march, but that don't make any difference, for we are going, "sure as shooting."

Yours truly,

Frank G. S.

Editorial Note

By mid-October occasional patrols through Lower Maryland are successful in rounding up some disloyal citizens and little else. As far as the Navy is concerned, this is far from adequate if the Potomac is to remain open. For months, naval commanders and even the president are requesting action be taken by the Army to help reduce threatening batteries along the Virginia shore, all to no avail. For the Navy, a critical juncture is fast approaching and the Excelsiors, and indeed the entirety of Hooker's Division, will be part of the hoped-for solution.

Figure 3.5. AVOIDING UNION BOATS IN THE 1861 POTOMAC. Confederate blockade runners attempting to evade Union ships. Both the Potomac Flotilla and troops stationed in Lower Maryland were tasked with stopping communications between Virginia and secessionists in Maryland trying to cross the Potomac. Source: *Illustrated London News.*

Other Voices: Letter from the Navy Department to General McClellan and Reply

Navy Department, October 18, 1861
The Department is advised that the navigation of the Potomac River is becoming daily and almost hourly more dangerous. Commander Dahlgren telegraphs this morning that "some measure is needed to lessen the risk of the passage. Lights are shown on the Maryland shore to give notice of our vessels coming and should be seized. Small parties of troops should be distributed near the locality to observe and check communication by boats between the shores."

Similar views are expressed by Captain Craven, in command of the flotilla. The Navy has exerted itself to keep open this important avenue to the city, and thus far with success, but the erection of extensive batteries and stationing troops to the amount of many thousands in their vicinity, imperatively requires the action of the Army, unless communication by the river is to be abandoned, which on many accounts would be unfortunate and almost disastrous. I deem it important to communicate to you these reports and suggestions from the officers named and would add my concurrence.

I am, respectfully,
Gideon Welles.

Headquarters Army of the Potomac,
October 18, 1861.

Sir:

I have this minute received your letter of this date with reference to the navigation of the Potomac, and in reply have the honor to inform you that a command composed of infantry and cavalry started this morning for different points below here on the Potomac River, accompanied by a staff officer, with orders to examine the country thoroughly, to ascertain whether or not it is necessary to erect heavy batteries for the protection of navigation and to accomplish the object asked for in your letter.

I am, sir, very respectfully, your
obedient servant,
Geo. B. McClellan,
Major-General[4]

Figure 3.6. General George McClellan. George McClellan was slow to respond to the threat of Confederate batteries along the Potomac. Not until President Lincoln issued direct orders to McClellan were troops then stationed in Lower Maryland. *Courtesy of Library of Congress.*

Chapter 4

Down the River and Opposite the Rebels

Late October through November 1861—Arrival in Lower Maryland

Moving into Maryland to squash Rebel activities • Rebel batteries threaten Union ships and health of Excelsior men • Building proper huts to survive the coming winter • Heartening letters from home • Notoriety for the Chautauqua boys thanks to Arthur's writings

Editorial Note

On the night of October 18th, Dan Sickles's brigade begin their movement from the outskirts of Washington twenty-eight miles or so into the heart of Lower Maryland. Joseph Hooker intends to use the move as a large-scale infantry exercise. While the 1st Brigade seems to manage fine, Sickles's 2nd Brigade encounters one difficulty after another, most notably, the near collapse of the 1st Regiment after too little food is packed for the trip and the ranks devolve into an unruly mob of foragers. The performance of the Excelsiors serves only to reinforce Hooker's low opinion of political generals and of Sickles in particular.[1]

As for Arthur McKinstry, the regiment moves without him as he stays behind while on the sick list, traveling by boat to rejoin his comrades two weeks later.

Fredonia Censor: Published October 30, 1861

FROM THE THIRD REGIMENT.

Camp Caldwell, Oct. 23.

Dear Uncle:

I have pretty much forswarn, writing, but the events, of the last few days have been too interesting not to be served up to the patrons of the Censor. On the 18th, six days rations were drawn, two of which the men carried in their haversacks, and four were loaded upon the wagons—of which a large train had arrived during the night. At noon the regiment got under way, and started for port Tobacco, which lies about twenty-five miles down the Potomac, and opposite to the rebel batteries at Matthias Pt. It is situated at the head of an estuary, and is therefore at some distance from the river. The 1st Regt. men, who have been there, describe it as a stirring, active, business place. The Surgeon made out a list, not only of the sick, (upon which your correspondent figured,) but also of those who were weak from previous sickness, or in any way unfit for a hard march, and for any or all kinds of exposure. Eight tents were taken for each Co. A show of guards was kept up for the first day and night, and then Lieut. Holmes, who now commands the post, withdrew all except that over the prisoners in the guard house.—The next morning after the departure of our boys, the Commissary Sergeant came round and informed us that there were potatoes enough to suffice for two meals daily. Now we did not wish the potatoes to spoil, and have acted accordingly—. There being but few of us, our food has been well cooked and we have lived much better than heretofore.

After all, it went very hard to see our comrades off, and not be able to share their fortunes, whether good or evil.—I cannot as before take notes for your paper, for if I had gone, I should have given out at the first hill, if not sooner, but nevertheless notes will be taken, and your readers will have full benefit of them when the regiment returns.

Yesterday our hearts were made glad by the sight of the new Dunkirk Company, headed by Adj. Doyle and our old friend Charlie Loeb, who looks as jolly and rotund as ever. The new company are a pretty promising set, and seem to be of a far different material from those recruits which are picked up in our crowded cities. They are now on drill; and considering their limited experience, they do very well indeed. To execute a good wheel is the hardest thing, perhaps, which a recruit has to learn, and frequently one poor sap-head will spoil it in spite of the pains the rest may take, but I have just seen the thing done very neatly.

I am glad to see the Chautauqua interest growing stronger, for we are the majority of the regiment. If Doyle exchanges his Adjutantship for a Captaincy, I do not think the former will be lost to our county. At present, Lieut. Willard of Jamestown, fills that station, and, as he does it well, there is no reason to expect a further change. We had a Brigade review the other day, and to the chagrin of the 1st and 2nd, our regiment had the post of honor, upon the right.—At Camp Scott, we had the second post, which is the left. Our boys have a good name as regards foraging; very little of that business being laid to us. I have heard all sorts of absurd reports about one or another of our boys being taken prisoner or some other evil befalling him; indeed I was greatly edified by the news that I myself had deserted. As we have never been in action, no lives are lost or captives taken. The only death which has occurred in the Chautauqua battalion, was that of one of the Westfield men, who died in one of the city hospitals, while we were at Camp Marsh; several of our men are seriously ill, but none, I believe, dangerously ill. The only deserters from Co. D since it was mustered into the service, are J. T. Boughton, D. W. Worth, and Frederick Francis, and I don't think we have a man now who wishes to desert. The other companies have lost but very few, whose names I do not know, and whom it is their business to publish, not mine.

We take all the papers and get our news of campaign from the *Tribune*, *Times*, and other papers. From the *Herald*, we get news of McClellan's plans and movements long before they are conceived by that famous General. We also read the most virulent attacks upon Fremont, whom Bennett is on the point of Court Martialing, and whom he will doubtless cashier. If I were in Fremont's place, I would give the venerable mosstrooper of the literary world, his customary black mail, to any amount not exceeding $50,000, for the sake of being exempt from his infamous slanders. For a far less sum, I fancy that its praises would become as fulsome as its falsehoods are notorious.

Perhaps you have wondered why I do not give you more war news. The reason is plain. The news flashes along the wires to you more quickly than a messenger on horseback can reach our camp; and as for details, you get them fully in the New York Dailies as soon as we.—We can hear the roar of cannon, and that is all the advantage we have over you.—Many are impatient for the dance to open. Let them wait till the leaves which are already of the bright hue of Autumn, have fallen. *Then* we can see the cannon, now veiled by the leafy underbrush.

The habits of a Southerner unfit him for the close discipline of camp. So far as my own observation goes, the constant use of whiskey predisposes a man to fevers, and other complaints incident to camp life. Now, in my wanderings, I have traversed several thousand miles of road and river in the South, but if ever I saw a "Chiv" refuse his whiskey, it was because he preferred "hardware," vulgarly called *brandy*. I advise a soldier never to use whiskey, except in cases of extraordinary fatigue or exposure.

I have done a little growling before in this communication and I have not done yet. We have a Brigade Sutler here, (an officer and monopoly, wholly contrary to the Regulations, which prescribes that the sutler of each regiment, when apart from others, and, like ours, a post by itself, shall appoint its own sutler,) named Seymour, and a citizen of Dunkirk. Now, I know nothing of his antecedents, and as little, but the fact is plain, that he practices a system of extortion upon the soldiers of the Brigade which is shameful to him, and to those who authorizes it. A sutler is a storekeeper for the convenience of a military post, that all necessaries can be got without the soldiers leaving the lines therefore. Now with a monopoly so exclusive, he could well afford to sell cheaply, but the fact is quite the reverse. For butter which we can get shipped to us from home, and, after paying Express charges and all, not exceed 13@15 cents outlay, we pay, here 30 cts., Envelopes, 25 cts. a pack, and paper, a penny a sheet, if you buy a ream and everything in like proportion. A branch store is with each regiment, and the sutler's income is probably greater than that of any of our public officers.—Many of my comrades have desired me to state the facts.

Hartwell Dickenson is with the regiment, and was denied the privilege of following his gallant fathers remains to their final home.

Yours as ever,

ARTHUR.

Bennett: James Gordon Bennett was the Scottish-born founder-publisher of the *New York Herald*. He waged war on numerous prominent figures and was considered to be pro-Southern early in the war but eventually supported the war and endorsed Lincoln in the 1864 election.

Mosstrooper: a marauder who operated in the mosses, or bogs, of the border between England and Scotland in the seventeenth century.

Other Voices: From the *Censor*

Published November 6, 1861

FROM THE THIRD REGIMENT
Camp Taylor, Oct. 23d, 1861.

Dear Censor:—

Last week Friday, the 17th, our regiment received marching orders, and accordingly prepared for a march down the Potomac. The next day at 10 o'clock P.M., we took up our line of march. Our regiment numbered 700; and two Cavalry Co.s belonging to the brigade that accompanied us. Twenty pioneers, with axes and shovels, went ahead to repair the roads and make bridges; besides these we had a wagon train of over 50 wagons. We marched ten miles this afternoon, and encamped on the banks of Broad Creek. Within twenty minutes after we halted, our tents were up and a new camp appeared as if by magic. The next morning by 8 o'clock, we were again on our march. We had to halt frequently for the pioneers to build bridges. It rained nearly all day, and the mud was ankle deep all the way. We passed through the village of Piscataway, and I must say that I never saw its equal in any of the Northern States. Its appearance would indicate that it was built some time during the Revolution. The roofs of the houses are covered with moss, and the whole village presents a decayed appearance. Two thirds of the houses, a Northern farmer would not allow to disgrace his farm.

Our road lay through plantations, and no fence on either side of it. To look ahead, the road appeared like a yellow streak through the fields. To-night we camped by the side of a Catholic Church, of which there are a great many in this section. The next day our road lay through pine barrens, and not a house to be seen for miles. Not a *decent* house was seen to-day. Everything wore an ancient air. The inhabitants of this country are at least fifty years behind their brethren of the North. It is enough to make a man sick of soldiering to know what a miserable good for-nothing country he has got to fight for.

To-night we camped by the side of the Piscarasic [Piscataway] Creek, about five miles from its mouth. This is quite a large creek, and is navigable some ways above where we were encamped. The next morning a captain of a gun boat stationed on the Potomac came into camp, having heard our drums the night before. We marched ten miles this forenoon, and encamped about half a mile from the river. Right opposite to us are three rebel batteries, one of which mounts an Armstrong gun. The river here is three miles across. They fire at most every boat that goes by, but seldom do any execution, and the balls come over this side. Several have struck in a field and passed through a house close by the camp. There are rebel batteries all along the river, from here down as far as we can hear the report of the guns. We are the only regiment on this side within thirty miles. We have got a captain of engineers with us. He is down to the river nearly all the time, with men disguised as citizens, looking out a place for a battery. We have got some artillery on the road. Some of the boys picked up some of the Armstrong balls and brought them into camp; they are conical, 18 inches in length, and seven in diameter; there is a small cavity, inside which is filled with an exploding substance; a cap is placed upon the small end, so that when it strikes anything solid it explodes; those that we picked up did not explode.

Yesterday afternoon, one of the men belonging to Co. E, from Dunkirk, was at work at one of them; after taking out all the powder, as he supposed, *he dropped a live coal into it.* It immediately exploded, scattering death and destruction through camp. The man who touched it off was entirely *blown* to atoms. Five others were so badly wounded that it is thought they cannot live. Seven others are wounded, some badly, and some slightly. We have just received orders to pack up ready to start at a moment's notice, for a *rebel* steamer has anchored *opposite our camp*, and we expect every moment she will commence throwing shells. Our rations are poor, and not enough of them. We have pilot bread and paving stones, as the boys call them, hickory, beef, tea and coffee. The probability is that we shall have a brush of some kind before many days.

H. B. Taylor

Camp Caldwell Oct. 25th 1861

Dear Mother

I got your letter day before yesterday and should have replied sooner but we are having stirring times. Our regiment are down the river and opposite the rebels. Eleven regiments and 17 cannon are on their way to join them. I have been out of hospital these two or three weeks and mean to join the regiment soon. Send your box as soon as may be and I wish you would send me some white woolen drawers and my comforter, my throat needs protection and I need it now, put no strings on the drawers but buttons, just as for a wristband. Stockings I would like but they are of no consequence compared with drawers, for our pants are not lined and we are pretty cold. Our men will suffer a great deal this winter. Any such little matter as a good home made Thanksgiving cake would be joyfully received and as the boys are mostly away I should not have so many eager eyes to ask a share. I am weak but shall go to the regiment as soon as your box comes and I can get a pair of winter boots made. I dare not attempt duty without these. If your box comes by the way of Dunkirk (send by John or Abel) it will come most of the way free.

I never yet knew a man to die of intermittent fever but it always wears out at last.

It is very cold and my fingers are getting stiff so I must close. I am doing well and am able and have been all the time to walk all around. I now walk quite a distance if I desire.

Lots of love to all. I helped Leute Jones to pack his kit and got him a cup. There were none given out to the company. Doyle and his men went yesterday, as did the other four regiments of the brigade.

Leute was plucky as a gamecock and will make a good soldier I will bet. Write soon and hurry up the box that I may get it as soon as I am fit for duty.

Your aff. son.
Arthur

Fredonia Censor: Published October 30, 1861

Camp Caldwell, Oct. 26, 1861.

Dear Uncles:—

My prediction that our boys would smell powder has been verified. They are in full view of the enemy, and the other day they were obliged to remove

Figure 4.1. Lucius Jones. Lucius Jones Jr., a friend of McKinstry's from back in Chautauqua County, was not admitted into Company D when it formed because he was considered too young and small. Jones was later able to join Company H as it was added to the 72nd New York. Source: Lucius Jones Jr., *In the War of the Rebellion from 1861 to 1865* (Fredonia, NY: [No. pub.], 1913).

their camp on account of the rain of shot and shell. No one was hurt on that occasion, but a most lamentable affair has resulted from the carelessness of one of Co. E's men named Rouse. It seems that he took a shell which had failed to explode, and unscrewing the fuse poured out as he supposed, all the powder. Now the shell was a shrapnel, and there is no doubt that some powder still remained among the enclosed projectile. He then screwed in the fuse, and putting his foot upon the shell lighted it with a burning coal. The shell exploded, and Rouse was so badly injured that he soon expired. O. Donahue and Sergeant Daily of Co. E were severely and perhaps mortally wounded. In all, there were about a dozen men injured by this careless and rash act. The sufferers are so far as I can learn, confined to Co. E with exception of A. Page, and Martin Boyden of Co. D. The left hand of former was hurt, but the last, our postmaster (from whom I gather the greater part of my information,) saw of him, he was carrying his musket as defiantly as ever.

Boyden's hurt was a flesh wound in the hip or side. I have heard it stated both ways. His wound is not considered dangerous.

A rebel steamer and two sloops made a demonstration on our boys, but there was something so very uninviting in the stead line of battle which was instantly formed that they withdrew without effecting a landing upon the Maryland side.

Strong reinforcements are now on their way, and ere long you may learn of the demonstrations being made upon the other side. Doyle's company received their arms this morning, and are speeding on their way. Soon after, the whole brigade got under way, and were followed by the 1st Mass. and two other regiments respectively from Penn. and Vermont. In addition to these, three or four batteries of rifled steel cannon are also on their way. I cannot give the exact location of our men, but David Parker, who had just came up with the mail, says that it is near Bidder's [Budd's] Ferry.

In about three days I shall probably be able to get further information, and if important I will transmit it to your at once.

Yours as ever,

Arthur

Other Voices: Chaplain Twichell of the 1st Regiment Regarding March

In Camp, Saturday night. Oct. 26th 1861.

Dear Folks at Home,

I should make rather unintelligible work of it, were I to undertake to tell you just where I am now, for I have only a faint idea myself . . . Suffice it to say that my humble tent is pitched on a broad level plain . . . in Charles Co. Md., about 1 ½ mile from the Potomac River. We struck tents at Camp Selkirk early Thursday morning and after two and a half days march are here, a part of a comparatively large army comprising the Excelsior Brigade, the 1st Massachusetts, 26th Pennsylvania, 4th [2nd] New Hampshire, 11th Mass., 1st Mich., which regiments (10 in all) compose the Division of General Hooker . . .

Our march here was not accomplished with as much credit to the Regt. as I could desire. By some great neglect a good part of the boys started without rations even for one day. The result may easily be imagined. They had to get something to eat as best they could. At one time not more than two hundred men were in line, the rest being scattered over at least five miles of the road cooking pigs, turkeys and geese etc. which they had shot. I never felt so bad for any state of affairs, in my life. The Col. [Hall] has been placed under arrest, for the condition we were in . . .[2]

Figure 4.2 (facing page). GENERAL JOSEPH HOOKER. Joseph Hooker commanded the 2nd Division of the 3rd Corps, which included the Excelsior Brigade, and by extension, Arthur McKinstry. Hooker considered political generals, and especially Dan Sickles, as being unworthy of command. Hooker was able to get Sickles fired, but after Sickles was reinstated by an act of the Senate, Hooker and he found common ground; both men favored strong offensive action against the enemy and a taste for strong liquor accompanied by beguiling women while in camp. *Courtesy of Library of Congress.*

Editorial Note

Following the poor performance of the 2nd Brigade (the Excelsiors), Hooker issues a stern rebuke to Sickles. Feeling such a reprimand is unjust, Sickles replies by going over Hooker's head and complaining directly to General McClellan, prompting the following clarification by Hooker.

Other Voices: Hooker Regarding the Conduct of Sickles's Brigade

HEADQUARTERS HOOKER'S DIVISION,
Camp Baker, Lower Potomac, Maryland, November 1, 1861.
Brig. Gen. S. WILLIAMS,
Adjutant-General, Army of the Potomac:

GENERAL:

I very much regret to find myself involved in a correspondence on the subject of ambulances . . .

My order requiring all ambulances except one to a regiment to be placed in depot has been before you. The reasons for its issuance I have stated in the presence of both of those officers, and I will now state them again.

During the march from Good Hope I found them overloaded with lazy soldiers, officers, and women's trunks and knapsacks to such an extent as to lead me to fear that if they reached camp at all, it would be with crippled horses and broken-down ambulances, and in consequence I repeatedly ordered the men out of them, some of whom would heed me and others would not. With such an undisciplined crowd, with no assistance from a single officer of the command, I abandoned my purpose and passed on to camp. When the troops reached their destination I directed the ambulances to be put in depot, with instructions to Surgeon Bell to receive them and to report to me their condition, which is herewith respectfully enclosed. The First Brigade had but one ambulance to a regiment to accompany them, and those they retain.

When you reflect that the Second Brigade had but 28 miles to march, you will be able to form a just appreciation of the perils to which the ambulance train was exposed. Had the march been double that distance, I question if I should have had one serviceable ambulance among them remaining.

Among new troops, as you doubtless know, there is a feeling of destructiveness towards everything belonging to the Government, and I must say that I never saw it more fully expressed than during my late march. This is one of the outrages committed by some portions of my command, as you will be informed in due time. In some regiments there appears to be a total absence of anything like authority. The officers are on the same footing with the men, and I have yet to receive the first report from any officer of the outrages and depredations committed by their men . . .

In my official intercourse with veteran politicians suddenly raised to high military rank, I have found it necessary to observe their correspondence with especial circumspection.

If with these facts before the major-general commanding it is his wish that the ambulances should be put in the hands of the Second Brigade, I request that you will inform me.

Very respectfully,

JOSEPH HOOKER, *Brigadier-General, Commanding Division.*[3]

Fredonia Censor: Published November 20, 1861

FROM THE THIRD REGIMENT.

Third Reg't. Sickles' Brig., Nov. 10, 1861.

Dear Uncles:—

Last Monday, we the lame and the lazy, who had been lying at Camp Caldwell so long, were on the *qui vive*, getting ready to start. "Great bodies move slowly," and so did our wagon train; but by Tuesday night, most of our stuff was at the landing, or on a river schooner, to be brought down by water. I slept that night at the marine guard house, between a small dog named *Beauty*, (whose beauty I will surely spoil if I ever get a fair chance at it with my revolver,) and a drunken corporal of Co. C, (not Bliss, that is G now,) who was altogether a worse nuisance than the dog. The next day we got off at about 11 ½ AM, and soon beat up the channel and out into the Potomac. As we passed the Navy Yard we saw several small gun boats mounting a 32 pounder at the bow, and another at the stern. They were pivot guns, and could be aimed from either side. It has always been my fortune, whether on fresh water or salt, to travel in a furious gale, and a petrel is not a surer forerunner of a storm. The wind freshened, and we eased off under mainsail and jib, and our fleet craft ran pretty nearly with a steam tug at that. Soon we passed a U.S. war steamer which was being brought up by a large tug.—As the latter was between us and the vessel, I could not ascertain her force. At 1 o'clock we shot past Alexandria, where the sloop of war *Pensacola* lay at anchor. There were but 14 guns aboard, but she is pierced for 22, and is fully capable of carrying that armament. Just below lay the brig *Perry*, and here we were required to heave to and show a pass. I should imagine that a man of common sense would have let a skipper known to be in Government employ, and with camp equipage and uniformed soldiers on board, pass, but no; heave to we must, and off came a boat with two blue jackets and a pair of coat tails, with a "midshipmite" inside of them. The pass was examined, and we fell off before the wind, nearly capsizing the boat, and wetting the aforesaid coat-tails nicely.—We ran down past Fort Washington, and as the schooner low heeled over to the gale till her gunwales were often six inches under, we finally lowered our sails and anchored off Mount Vernon. Here we lay all night, and I assure you it was a fine thing, for we shivered all night long in a tremendous gale. There were two women on board, and it was Serg't Chapman's *ex officio* duty, he commanding our squad, to play the part of ladies' man. He did his duty like a major, but as they were both sea sick we didn't envy him his task. Chapman and I felt greatly tempted to visit Mt. Vernon, but as we were not certain in whose hands it was, the skipper would not let his boat go.—Long before sunrise our sails were spread to catch the light cat's paws into which the previous storm had died away. Another boat followed us from the wharf soon after our departure, but her sails were torn to ribbons in the gale, and her crew and cargo were taken off by a large schooner which opportunely came to her aid. They passed us, as we lay at anchor, under reefed mainsail and jib. Even under this short sail, she fairly flew over the waves. After a short time, the light morning breeze freshened to a gale, but we still kept all sail set, and soon reached Indian Head, where our fleet lay at anchor. There were nine gun boats, (tugs) mounting 32 pounders, beside a schooner and a steam ferry boat. Our Captain and his business were known, so we passed with a brief challenge and went our way. In a short time we passed Freestone Head, where there was a rebel battery, which has been playing a sort of pop-gun game at our vessels, but they did not open fire upon us. They would have been very silly if they had done so, for only the heaviest fortification guns, and the best of gunners, can do execution at such long range. A few more minutes and we were round into Maitawoman [Mattawoman] Creek, where we spared ourselves the trouble of dropping anchor, by running into the mud to the depth of about three feet. We then got ashore in the boat, and made the best of our way to Camp Baker, where the 3d now are encamped. Here I was glad to meet once more my old companions in arms, and I am now so far recovered that I hope to ask no further remission of military duty. We are daily expecting to move down nearer the main rebel batteries. I find that our regiment has the post of honor, not only of the Brigade but of the whole Division, and that Gen. Hooker, who commands the Division, stays with us. Gen. Sickles' Headquarters are at a private house, and of course a body guard is necessary.—The French Zouaves were dreaded; the fame of their depredations having preceded them, so that it was requested that they might not be employed for that purpose, as heretofore. A guard was then tried from the 1st, and they were also found wanting. The request was then preferred by the landlord that a guard might be taken from our regiment, and Company D furnished the detail. As they have been on duty some time, I presume that they give satisfaction. It makes all the difference in the world, I can assure you, whether a man belongs to this regiment or not, for the rest have pillaged so extensively that they are looked upon with hatred and suspicion, while ours has the reputation of abstaining from such lawless practices, and our men are treated with civility everywhere. We now sleep twelve or thirteen in a tent, and not less than six or seven in a tier. Our tents are now old and rotten, and leak like a sieve, and much sickness no doubt results from this cause. One of the men of Company A died last Friday, and was buried with the honors of war.

Figure 4.3. View of Indian Head. Union ships at Indian Head north of Mattawoman Creek just across the Potomac from Confederate positions at Freestone Point. *Courtesy of Library of Congress.*

To-day, being Sunday, we went out to the beautiful grove of pine and cedar and listened to an excellent sermon from Chaplain Norton, which well repaid those who came. There is a grandeur in a full chorus of male voices which instrumental music not only fails to add to, but sadly mars. The most impressive service I have ever seen was at Camp Scott, where an immense choir united in the vocal music, and then I wondered no longer that none but the unaided voices of males were heard in the Sistine Chapel's magnificent choir.

The last I heard of Daley and O'Donahue, they were in a very critical situation. Boyden and Page, of Co. D, are doing well. It may be a source of gratification to their friends that they were in their own tent at the time of the explosion, and were not tampering with the shell.

Capt. Brown having left the regiment, Capt. Barrett succeeds him as senior Captain, and company C takes the right. Capt. Abell of course ranks a little higher by the change, and so far as military science, and what is highly important, a good, clear, distinct style of giving orders, are concerned, he should stand at the head of our line officers. A private in our company was offered a Captaincy, and several of our non-commissioned officers have been offered commissions outside our regiment.

I might find much more to write of, but I have not time.

Arthur

Qui vive: lookout.

Cat's paw: a light air that ruffles the surface of the water in irregular patches during a calm.

There were nine gun boats . . . : reference to the Navy's "Potomac Flotilla," which had responsibility to intercept insurgent traffic upon the river and to suppress Confederate batteries on the Virginia shore.

One of the men of Company A died . . . : Max Lowe died of disease; he was thirty-five years old. Company A was a German-speaking company raised out of New York City.

Editorial Note

While the presence of Hooker's Division (soon to be expanded by the addition of a third brigade of infantry) in Lower Maryland no doubt helps to throttle disloyal activities, the few field guns that were brought along do little to reduce the threat of Confederate batteries on the Virginia shore. As the Navy commanders on the Potomac see the situation, the lack of decisive action by

Fredonia Censor.

ESTABLISHED IN 1821.

VOL. XLII. NUMBER 5. FREDONIA, WEDNESDAY MORNING, MARCH 19, 1862. WHOLE NUMBER 2187.

Figure 4.4. *Censor* BANNER. Front-page banner of the *Fredonia Censor. Courtesy of Darwin R. Barker Historical Library.*

the Army's highest commanders and scanty naval resources impeded efforts to prevent the expansion of Rebel batteries, let alone destroy them. So exasperated in fact is Potomac Flotilla commander Thomas T. Craven that at the end of October he declares the Potomac River closed to large ships heading in and out of Washington. The fight against enemy shore installations, however, will continue.[4] For Arthur McKinstry and his mates, a massive, cross-river assault seems like the inevitable next step in the war, a step greatly anticipated, despite the intentions, or lack thereof, of George McClellan.

Camp Wool Nov. 16th 1861

Dear Aunt,

I have received two letters from you which I have not been able to answer until to night.

Since I received your first we have moved twice—the last time I managed to carry my knapsack & gun and all my things for a march of seven or eight miles.

We have been busy for several days in fixing our tents for winter. We have two bunks in our tent which have each room for four men and in which two sleep on a lower shelf and two on the upper. We have a floor of pines which we split in halves and laid down with the flat side up. We have a good fire place which warms us well and while there is a stick of wood in Secessia we mean to keep warm.

The boots I presume are at Washington unless already taken from the office. There has been no express stuff brought down here as yet but I fixed it with the sutler to bring the box and I expect it within two or three days. As regards the price I don't care what a thing costs if it is worth the money. Such a pair as I sent for are worth seven or eight dollars here and as Mass. boots are better than N.Y. the latter price would not buy them of me. So far as my experience goes it is all humbug about having boots very large to march in. I want plenty of room for the toes but a perfect fit is what a man needs. The best thing a soldier can have is a fine made boot of stout but soft calf skin, broad soles will wear longest but are not nearly so convenient for military exercises. Broad heels are very bad to face upon as a man does it by turning upon the heel as upon a pivot and does not turn by stepping. The things in the box are just what I stood in need of. Gloves are in great demand just now and as we don't get enough to eat sometimes, all that goes to appease hunger is very acceptable. Reading of all sorts is in great demand and when your papers come to hand there is no danger but that they will be handled by a great many. I won't try to describe our life here in this letter as I shall do it for the Censor where you of course can read it. I don't know that I can pay the postage upon this for the want of stamps. I have twenty dollars in my pocket but can't get a stamp. I shall write to Mother and send for a lot as well as remit a little something for her private purse.

As soon as I can get a chance I will send that money by express. As large amounts will be sent North we shall send a trusty agent to the city and probably in a day or two. As there is a good deal of stealing at the Post Office I dare not trust it by mail.

Arthur

Fredonia Censor: Published November 27, 1861

FROM THE THIRD REGIMENT.

Camp Wool, Nov. 17.

Dear Uncles:—

Amid the changes which are going on at this stirring period you will not be surprised that I again date from a new location. Last Tuesday we once more got under way and traveled seven or eight miles to our new camp.—We are now two miles below Budd's Ferry, and can hear not only the cannon but the rushing of the shell, when the belligerent batteries pass the compliments of the day. As soon as we get our tents pitched, we turnpiked our street in beautiful style, and then set ourselves to work to build stoves and fire-places. First, Sanborn, Brooks, and the other machine-shop boys, made a very neat stove of clay, and worked over the front the U.S. arms, and upon the sides of the door two very neat tall chimneys, the smoke of which curling upward, formed a fanciful wreath encircling the arms above. Upon trial the stove smoked and cracked beyond all endurance, but by plastering on a little more clay and building the chimneys a little higher these defects were remedied and the tent is now very comfortable. Fire-places of all imaginable patterns, with stick and stone chimneys, are all in full blast, and Co. D is now pretty comfortable, and the rest of the regiment is rapidly taking pattern. If [it] had not been for the patterns which companies B and D set, I believe the whole parcel of Gothamites would have frozen to death.

It would be tedious to tell of all the shifts which we soldiers make, but I will simply describe the tent in which I reside—No. 7. over which Corporal Pugh presides. First, we have a tent ten feet square, in which eight of us are expected to have lots of room. Just as you enter you will see a cheerful blaze upon your right, which is found to be in a hole 18 inches deep; the draft goes under an inverted three pail iron kettle, which makes a splendid drum, and thence under ground outside the tent and up a stick chimney into outer air. On each side of the tent stands a double-decked bunk, upon each shelf of which two men sleep. The heads are toward the farther end, so that our feet may be toasted over our stove drum—that incomparable old iron kettle, which excites the envy and admiration of the whole regiment. The kettle has a hole in the very center, which is surmounted by a can labelled "Fresh Chesapeake Oysters," which serves to heat dish-water; and an ingenious man would probably discover how exceedingly well it is adapted to the manufacture of hot whiskey punch. The space between the beds is floored with split pines with the flat side up, and this extensive territory of 6x3 feet serves for a dressing room, and as there are usually only eight of us we get along swimmingly. Our company officers wisely excused us from a good deal of drill that we might complete these arrangements, and when we had got pretty well settled, stole our best models and set a squad of men at work to build their fire-places in like style.

I believe that it is positively settled that we are to have a French rifle, which though heavy, is the most practical thing I have seen yet. It will pick off a man beautiful at five hundred yards—indeed Maj. Stevens put several shots successively through a cap at that distance. It is the best gun for off-hand sight I have ever seen used for military purposes.—Our Harper's Ferry muskets do not shoot as accurately, nor as far, as the abused old Springfield altered flint locks.

I took a walk down to the ferry yesterday afternoon, and took a view of the rebel batteries and our own. The guards would not allow us to approach our little battery of two twelve pounders, but I cared very little for that, as I got a description of it that answered my purpose just as well. It is a little earthwork with embrasures for the muzzles of the guns, and the gunners have succeeded in exploding several shells in the enemy's batteries. The river bends around the point where our guns are situated, in the form of a pretty regular crescent, and in the center and opposite them is a large rebel battery. On the left of this battery is a creek where the Steamer Page and two rebel schooners lie.

The masts of the schooners and the smoke pipe of the Page are plainly visible. They dare not come out for our rifled cannon face them, and the 1st Massachusetts Regiment have a fine battery, and, for the field guns, a heavy one, which can be got down in time to have something to say if occasion demands. A new earthwork was commenced on Saturday night, a short distance to the left of the first one. The pickets told me that some mortars were on the way down. These are better suited to the business of shelling an established battery than long guns, for when once the line and range are found, it is impossible to tell which way the fragments may fly, while there is some chance of dodging a ball or shell from a cannon. The shell from a cannon flies in nearly a horizontal direction and with such force that when it bursts no fragments return upon its path, but they separate upon its onward way like the diverging hairs of a painter's brush. On the contrary, the mortar is pointed at a great elevation; for very great distances at forty-five degrees; and when the shell at last descends it is almost vertically downwards, and then the walls which protect against a horizontal shot are useless, and it is impossible to calculate which way the fragments may fly.

Every time that an oyster boat passes, it is made a target for the rebel batteries, but as they do not hit them, it affords great amusement to the crews, who dance, yell and gesticulate in contempt of the gunners. Our guns sometimes reply, and beyond doubt with effect. There is certainly one pretty heavy gun opposite us, for one of the Mass. 11th informed me that some of his comrades weighed a shell which struck on this side, and found its weight to be ninety-nine pounds.

It is a standing amusement on a still day for the pickets to blackguard each other across the river, which cannot be much over a mile wide in some places.—While we were down, we noticed the numerous columns of smoke which ascended from their camp-fires, and heard the measured beat of their drums. But few tents were seen, and it seems pretty evident that the most of them have none, I think by the smoke of the camps, that their numbers are exaggerated, and their force immediately upon the river does not exceed our own.

What force may be behind the hills it is of course impossible to conjecture.—Our boys, who have been acting as a bodyguard to Gen. Sickles, have astonished the natives considerably by their explanations of the way the telegraph operates. Gilbert was on duty not long since and saw a negro jump very suddenly on hearing the oeolian music on the wind acting upon the wires at Headquarters.—With fear and trembling he came up to Gilbert, and inquired about the cause of the mysterious sounds; "Oh," replied Hiram, "that's a secessionist officer they are sending to Washington." "Lor bless de telegraf," exclaimed the delighted darkey, "if dat's de way dey sends de seceshets to Washington."

Slavery does not wear near as mild an aspect here as in the vicinity of Camp Caldwell. Here there is little to distinguish the negro from the brute, and the masters are generally, though naturally more intelligent, but little better educated than the slave. They use the same *patois*, and are shamefully ignorant.—There are of course marked exceptions, but I am speaking of the middle and more numerous class. Part of the regiment was paid off Friday and Saturday last.—The weather here is milder than at Camp Caldwell, but it is pretty cold, and the Chautauqua people would do well to find out whether their friends are supplied with flannel underclothes, for we need something better than the government shirts and drawers, which are not fit to be worn, and which are not at all comfortable. They are made of cotton and wool (I mean dog's hair) and are very harsh. The government socks are a very poor thing, and the shoes, however good for summer, are not at all suited for the deep mud we must pass through whenever we move. Every man ought to have a pair of stout calf boots, reaching about to the knee. We have each a pair of thin blankets, (one good wide blanket with a good nap, is worth a dozen of them) and that is all we can very well carry. The postman is here and I must close. We live mostly on hard bread and coffee, but as the bakery is now set up, we expect soon to have our own workmen's bread.—Sometimes we get enough to eat and sometimes we don't.

Yours, as ever.

Arthur

French rifle: probably a Belgian copy of the French Model 1859, which was a .61 cal., accepted the Minie ball, and considered equal to the '61 Springfield rifle. This rifle was widely imported for use by Federal troops.

Steamer Page: CSS *George Page* was a 410-ton sidewheel steamship operated by the US Quartermaster's Department until captured by the Confederates in May of '61 and renamed *Page*. She operated in the Potomac River in the vicinity of Quantico Creek and was destroyed by her crew on March 9, 1862.

Oeolian: archaic for Aeolian, as in relating to or arising from the action of the wind

Camp Wool Nov. 17th

Dear Mother,

I have watched and waited for a very long time for a letter from you. I don't often write where a letter is due me but as Leute Jones got one which says that you sent me a box, I presume that you sent it in that. The box was sent too late to find me at Camp Caldwell and is I suppose at Washington. I have sent for it but I sincerely hope that you did not pay the freight for in case it rots in the office I don't want to be the only loser. If you bought any flannel for drawers let me know what it cost, I will send you the money to pay for it as soon as I can do so by express and I will also add something for your private benefit. I am doing well and doing full military duty. I brought my full kit upon my back on the last march of seven or eight miles and it must weigh thirty or forty pounds. Leute is looking well. As a man can not cut up very much here I should not wonder if enlisting was a good thing for him. As our bakery is set up I suppose that we shall stay here some time and we have built bunks and made a fire place and even made a floor of split pines with the flat side up. We are pretty comfortable but we don't owe it to Uncle Sam for we paid for our boards out of our own pockets and indeed for pretty much all we have that is calculated to make us comfortable. We use mustard, butter, pepper and other little niceties for which we pay. Butter I mean to have cost what it may for our crackers are very dry and don't slip down very easily. We are to have the genuine Minie rifled musket in a day or two. I find that it is a very nice thing to be the correspondent of the Censor for I notice that the officers had rather have a good word there than a bad one. Take it all together I am about as well off as a private can be. As regard liberty I can get passed outside the lines about at pleasure which is better than most can do. I was down to the river this afternoon and took a view at the Secesh batteries across. They fire at all the vessels that pass and don't hit any. We have two 12 prs. there which throw rifled shell across and several have burst in the rebel batteries.

The Sutler agreed to bring my box and I hope to see it soon—in a day or two but I am afraid that something will be spoiled. Still it is very cold at Washington it may all be well. There will soon be an express run down here. Ephraim Smith, Mrs. Bumppus' son is dead. He died of fever. Visitors are not much allowed in the hospital and I only saw him once and then was not allowed to stay long.

I hear often from Aunt Eliza and answer accordingly. My friends there have sent me a box she tells me with eatables, papers, books etc., that is very nice for the list she gave was just and all I wanted besides what I think you sent.

It is getting late so I must close. Give my love to the boys and Father and to Jinnie and John, she ought to write to me and I insist that you and she get your likenesses taken and sent for me.

Your aff. son
Arthur

Direct to Washington

Other Voices: Chaplain Twichell of the 1st Regiment Regarding Proximity of the Enemy

In Camp—Sandy Point—Md.
Sunday night, Nov. 17th 1861

My dear Father,

Our position opposite the enemy and in sight is the occasion of some interesting incidents. Our boys do a great deal of impudent shouting across the river, which is responded to frequently with more force than elegance. Letters tied to boards, or the boards themselves inscribed, are occasionally sent across both ways according to the wind. Some that we have received were rare productions and showed that neither the schoolmaster nor the Preacher had been much abroad where the authors were reared. The rebels keep popping away at oyster schooners etc. passing down and up, never inflicting any injury however. This is a source of much amusement. A gun is fired. The ball strikes wide of its mark. A score or 20 of our boys looking on, raise a howl of derision, responded to immediately by a howl of defiance from the other side, and so we go for the present, exchanging nothing worse than ill wishes and windy words. Some day there may be less speech and more work . . .[5]

Fredonia Censor: Published December 4, 1861

FROM THE THIRD REGIMENT

Camp Wool, Nov. 23d, 1861.

My Dear Uncles:—

My last was hurried up for want of time, or I should not be violating rules about extinguishing lights at eight and a quarter. The weather is not very cold, but still I feel very much the want of certain boots, gloves and flannels, which have been for some weeks on their way by express, and the only reason I do not press our Northern friends to send us something to wear, and something fit to eat, is that we never get them until the clothes are outgrown and the eatable ruined. Jesting aside, our express matter is singularly long in coming, and I shall pay for no more things to rot in some intermediate station. Packages have been received which have been six or eight weeks on their way, and others have been on their travels still longer, which very likely never will come.

Very little of moment has occurred since my last, but I was compelled to omit then some data of interest to some, at least, of your readers. Since we last moved, we have heard of the death of young Willard of the band, who was left at camp Caldwell sick. He was a fine young man, and many will miss him among his old companions. His brother, Lieutenant Willard, now succeeds to the captaincy of the Jamestown Company vice, Capt. Brown, promoted. Mason is now 1st Lieut., and Sergt. Major Bailey is promoted to a 2d Lieutenancy in that company. Private Ephraim Smith, of Arkwright, died here in our regimental hospital, about eight days since; like Willard he died of intermittent fever. He marched here while very weak, and on his arrival, lay quite exhausted upon the damp ground. This exposure aggravated his disorder and the result proved speedily fatal. Our Chaplain, Rev. Levi Norton, has been to visit our sick at Washington, and reports that Daley was not expected to live, but Donohue was in a fair way to recover. Boyden, who was hurt by the shell, is able to walk about, and will soon be all right. Page's hand is nearly well. At the time when the regiment were in line of battle and expecting a fight, he was told to fall back. "No," said he "I can load by holding the gun in the hollow of my left arm, and I can sight across it" (the arm.) He accordingly stood it out, as did J. Whitney, who was pretty sick at the time, but thought if there was any fighting to be done he ought to have a chance to pop at them too. That is the kind of timber which is found in the "mudsills" of Co. D, and I doubt if the Palmetto state can produce its equal.

Doyle is now fairly installed as Captain of Co. H, and Lieut. Wm. J. O'Neil acts as Adjutant in his place. The latter officer has not such a powerful voice as Capt. Doyle, but no one who has seen him commanding Co. E, on drill or review, will doubt his qualities as a soldier and a gentleman. Lieut. Twomey is now 1st Lieut., and 1st Serg't Wallace, who had just been made Sergeant Major in Sam. Bailey's place, is again promoted to the rank of 2d Lieut. in Co. E. Capt. Doyle is putting Co. H through a pretty lively course of [sports], and they drill very well. If you were to see our regiment on drill, you would not discover Co. H by its mistakes, for it does about as well as many who began at the commencement of three years enlistments. The company seems to be mostly of foreigners, but of the more intelligent class.

We have heard heavy firing yesterday and the day before. We have since been informed that it was the rebels practicing gunnery upon our vessels. The result was that nobody was either scared or hurt, and that the rebels wasted a good deal of powder and such a valuable quantity of conical shell in the Potomac, which the vessels passed securely by. Co. E, U.S. 1st Artillery, passed a few days since toward Port Tobacco, with a fine battery of brass field guns. I was not near enough to be certain, but I should think they were 32 pr. howitzers. Some of our officers have been sent to Piscataway to examine the claims of many people who have been injured by the robberies committed by our soldiers when they passed through. My informant stated, (and I believe him reliable,) that about $1,400 had been demanded, *not one of which had been charged to the 3d Regt.*, and he thought that a good share of the amount was really due. Our own regiment had won the good opinion of all on account of its sobriety, good order, and neatness, and was distinctively known as Col. Taylor's. Our bakery is now in full operation, and we get as good bread as at home.

We were taken by surprise the other evening, when we heard an order read upon parade forbidding all soldiers from going beyond the regimental lines without a pass from their captain, signed also by the commandant of the post. Yesterday I went out, armed with the proper pass, and as soon as I reached the store I had started for, the mystery was solved. A lot of soldiers had got pretty "glorious," and had cleaned out the store very thoroughly. As it was a whiskey doggery, I did not pity the storekeeper, but at the same time Col. Taylor's order was most appropriate, and as Gen. Sickles was absent, and Taylor in command, the order was general, and is in force throughout the brigade. I wished to purchase cooking utensils and a hatchet, and on my inquiring for hardware, the man looked at me in a doubting, puzzled manner, and then inquired if I meant something to drink. Hardware, you remember, is brandy at the South. I replied in the negative, and explained myself. Neither frying pan, skillet, nor hatchet could be got. I also went to a store about two miles distant, with no better success, and returned to camp greatly disgusted. While we were on guard, the other night, an old darkey came up with a roast duck and some chickens to sell. It was night, and he could not be admitted to the camp, but to save him from pecuniary loss, our boys bought him out, and ate the fowls off-hand. While with us, he told us that the corn planters along the river had agreed to have corn shuckings along the bank, whence it could be at once taken over to the rebels in boats. This nice little arrangement was spoiled by our pickets being extended along the river, one of these "happy and contented" Africans having disclosed the plot.

They also attempted to send some of the slaves across to work upon rebel fortifications, but like the Irishman's flea—when they went to put their fingers upon them they were not there, and ever since the negroes are very fearful about approaching the shore. We asked him if he knew of any Union men about here. Upon reflecting he replied that he did know of one man, but he was a poor man and of no account anyhow. His master did not know that he was away, and would be very apt to whip him if he did.

Yesterday we turned out in light marching order, and formed in line in an adjacent field. Soon the rest of the brigade fell in on our left and we were ready for a review. Our guns shone like silver, and all had white gloves and were clean and tidy.

We waited until sunset, but Gen. Hooker did not arrive, and finally Col. Taylor assumed command and marched us off the field. Such beautiful marching I have never seen before, and better I cannot well see in time to come, for all the companies were so well aligned that a chalk line could have been snapped upon every head from right to left. It is very likely that we shall have the review completed before long—perhaps to day.

We have not received the last Censor, and indeed, papers are pretty uncertain at best. Our friends must write, for our letters generally reach us. A log hospital is in process of erection, and will soon be completed. This will be a great advantage to our sick, for a log is warmer than a frame house, and as regards attendance, there is no doubt that our sick are better off than they would be at the city hospitals. As regards sending clothing for the sick, it is a humane and a wise thing, but in my opinion an ounce of prevention is worth a pound of cure, and it would be well worth while to try what good flannels would do toward keeping the men out the hospital. Government shoes are not fit for a campaign like this, where we must march by roads where the mire is often up to the axletree of a wagon. All our stores come by boat, for the simple reason that the roads are impassable for heavy loads. Still, as I said at the beginning of this letter, it is only an aggravation to feel that things are lying in express offices which we may not see for months.

Yours, &c.
Arthur

Camp Caldwell Nov. 26th, 1861

Dear Aunt,

I meant to have written to you before but I have been very busy of late. Your box had not arrived at the city three or four days ago. If it is there now I shall learn of it by our mail carrier. If it don't come by the last of this week I shall have to buy a pair of the sutler and sell those you sent which I can do for a pretty fair profit.

I am now in very good health and feel fully able to stand the fatigues of a campaign. I am pretty well acclimated and if we should be sent to Carolina I feel myself well prepared. We expect some new blankets very soon and I can assure you we need them for the old ones are not fit to blanket a horse if we may credit what Gen. Hooker said when he inspected our regiment yesterday. There is some expectation that our regiment will go south to Carolina but at last we have a general in chief who can keep his own counsel and none know for whom a blow is intended until it falls. When we move we do not know where we go and a planter told me that a soldier asked him in all simplicity where he was going. He thought the planter might conjecture by the direction travelled which way he was going which was more than he could do. I sent the V [$5] for those boots in a very heavy letter for the Censor where I thought the color of the note could not be seen by holding it up to the light and asked Uncle Willard to forward it to you. I sent it also in a Government envelope so that it looked more like a Congressional speech than anything else—more especially as it was franked. I presume however that you have it by this time, if not tell me at once. At any rate write soon for there is no telling how long or short our stay will be but when we move at all we shall be very apt to make such an advance that mails will be uncertain and irregular. The late Union successes will do much I think toward shortening the war.

We have our bakery now in running order and get very fine bread. 27th I was busy and did not get a chance to finish but it is just as well for I could not have sent it. Our Quartermaster has been to the city and the box has come. I cannot get it however until he is here to deliver it in person which will probably

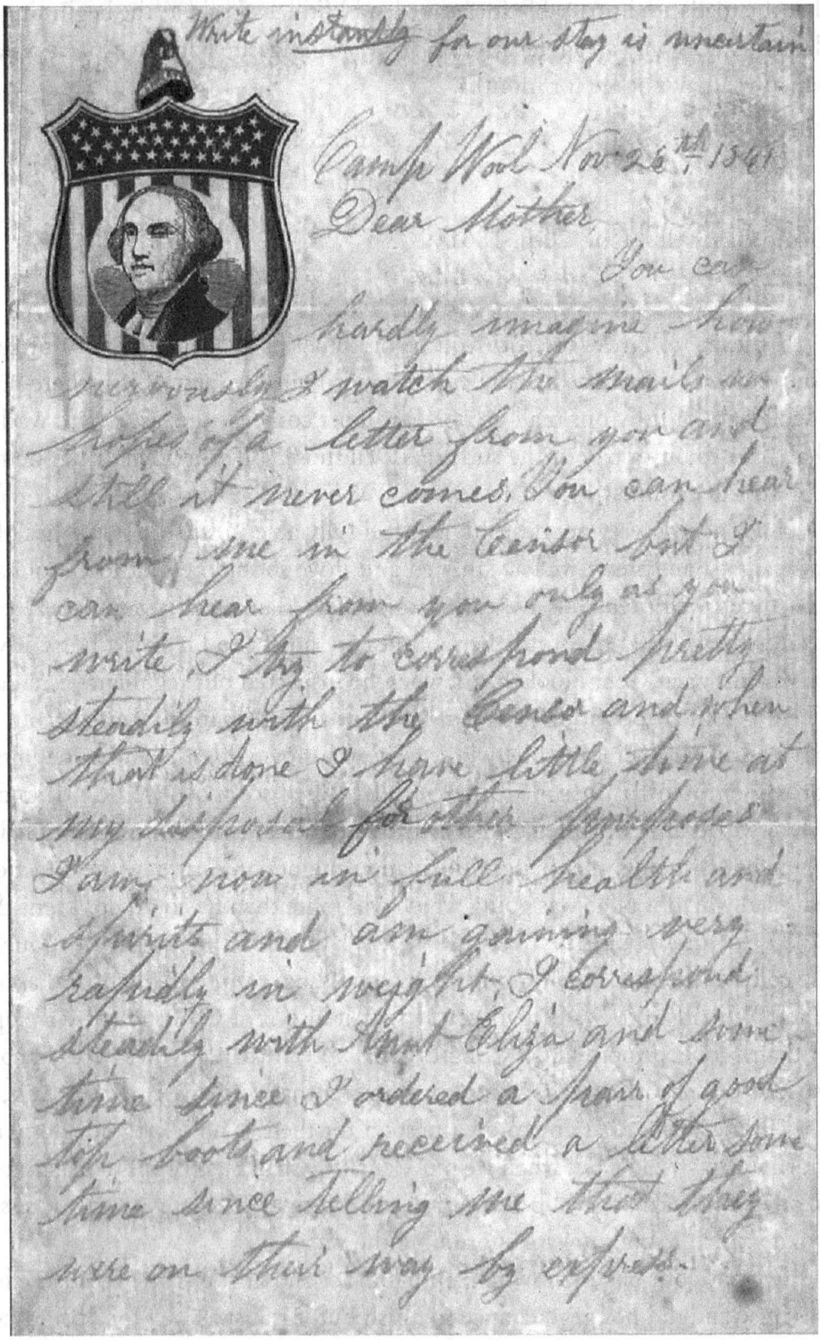

Write instantly for our stay is uncertain

Camp Wool Nov 26th 1861

Dear Mother

You can hardly imagine how anxiously I watch the mails in hopes of a letter from you and still it never comes. You can hear from me in the Censor but I can hear from you only as you write I try to correspond pretty steadily with the Censor and when that is done I have little time at my disposal for other purposes I am now in full health and spirits and am gaining very rapidly in weight. I correspond steadily with Aunt Eliza and some time since I ordered a pair of good top boots and received a letter some time since telling me that they were on their way by express.

Figure 4.5. Letter to Mother on George Washington letterhead. *Courtesy of Ulysses S. Grant Presidential Library.*

be to night. Mothers box too has come and you see how handy it is since the Thanksgiving for N.Y. State comes to-morrow. I have fixed it with some boys who own a clay stove (the one I described in the Censor) to take Thanksgiving with them and as it makes a splendid oven by drawing the coals out we shall have baked beans, roast chicken with oyster stuffing, hot biscuits and butter, and various other luxuries of the season.

When Mother got up her box I told her to send me a good Thanksgiving cake and I presume that she has done so. We have been paying the sutler 35 cts. for butter but I fancy Mothers box will spoil trade in that quarter.

I will reserve the rest of the sheet until I can report upon the condition of the contents.

29th Those boots fit and are first rate. [They] are pretty but I shall keep them though I could sell them at once for eight or nine dollars. We celebrated Thanksgiving yesterday in great style and those preserves of Aunt Theodosia helped amazingly. Moses gloves are first rate and the papers you sent are just what we want. As I have no accommodation in this crowed tent and it . . . I will close. Thank Aunt Jane for those cakes . . . very good and still more for her papers.

Your aff. nephew
Arthur

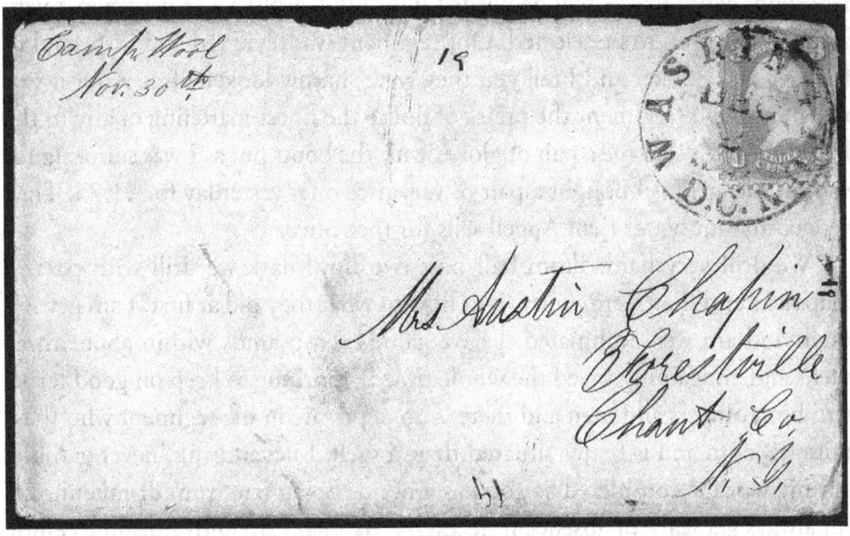

Figure 4.6. Envelope of November 30th. *Courtesy of Ulysses S. Grant Presidential Library.*

Write instantly for our stay is uncertain

Camp Wool Nov. 26th, 1861

Dear Mother

You can hardly imagine how nervously I watch the mails in hopes of a letter from you and still it never comes. You can hear from me in the Censor but I can hear from you only as you write. I try to correspond pretty steadily with the Censor and when that is done I have little time at my disposal for other purposes.

I am now in full health and spirits and am gaining very rapidly in weight. I correspond steadily with Aunt Eliza and some time since I ordered a pair of good top boots and received a letter some time since telling me that they were on their way by express. I have sent her the money, 5.00, but have not yet received the boots. If I don't get them this week I shall buy a pair of the sutler. I sent five dollars for a pair of calf boots which were to be stout and durable and to come up to the knee. Here I must pay seven dollars but as the boots are really worth it I don't care. If my other boots come I can sell them for a good profit by waiting until next payment for the money and if they do not the express Co. is responsible. The Sutlers boots are of very superior Russia calf and I am willing to pay a good price for an article which is worth it. They come to the knee, and a little higher in front. Mother I think that we shall be away from here soon. More troops will be needed in South Carolina and we are in a very favorable position to be selected. Our regiment was reviewed and inspected to day by Gen. Hooker and I tell you they were sharply looked after. After it was over he gave our regiment the praise of doing the finest marching of any in the division. Moses sent me a pair of gloves with the boots but as I was suffering for want of the articles I bought a pair of very nice ones yesterday for $1.75. They were costly but better than Angell sells for that price.

We drill very hard. From half past two until dark we drill with packed knapsacks and they seem pretty light now to what they did at first. I am getting tough and am well acclimated. I have gained ten pounds within about three weeks and am gaining speed the whole time. I continue to keep on good terms with both officers and men and there is not a private in the regiment who [has] more freedom and is better situated than myself. I never drink, never gamble, and my word is considered as good as a bond. Being free from drunkenness I can always get leave of absence if necessary. As I gain strength I begin to enjoy myself and do not wish to return to Mutton Hill except that I long very much to see you all. Cash is pretty plenty just now and I send you three dollars for private pin money. If you like though you may send me three or four shillings worth of postage stamps. At all events write as soon as may be for a soldier never knows where he will sleep till he gets up in the morning nor where he is going till he stops. Direct as before. Your box has not yet arrived at the city. If you put six cents worth in it makes the Express men hunt it up out of spite.

Lots of love to all

Arthur

Pin money: women's money for small incidentals.

Other Voices: James Rusling, 2nd New Jersey Brigade

Near Washington, D.C.
Nov. 30, 1861. Saturday

Dear Father:

I have only time to write you a single line. We are under orders to move this afternoon or tomorrow morning. We go down the Potomac on steamboat to Budd's Ferry. Land there on the Maryland side, and join the division of General Hooker. The Fifth, Sixth, Seventh, and Eighth New Jersey Regiments all go: under the command of Colonel Starr, as acting brigadier general. I suppose it is intended for Hooker's division to cross the Potomac and storm the Rebel batteries . . . All is confusion and clamor. Good-bye, and God Bless you all.[6]

Editorial Note

As fall begins to move into winter, any chance of active campaigning goes with it. For McKinstry and the other volunteers of Hooker's Division, settling in and preparing for harsher weather along the Potomac is their only option.

Chapter 5

Where the Bon Vivants Assemble

December 1861—Duty along the Potomac

Arthur and mates make a cozy camp despite harsh weather • A resourceful Christmas dinner • Pain of a growing sick list • Hooker's Division grows with addition of a New Jersey Brigade • Concerns about an enemy attack as Rebels continue to fire at passing Union ships

Editorial Note

With winter close at hand, company sick lists begin to grow longer as the days grow shorter. The weather is surprisingly warm and pleasant for the beginning of December but as the month wears on, the pace of war slows as the cold, wet, mud, and ice force the men's attentions toward defense against the elements rather than an offensive against the Confederates. Despite the hard conditions along the Potomac, Arthur and his mates exert themselves toward making the most of Thanksgiving and Christmas.

Fredonia Censor: Published December 11, 1861

FROM THE THIRD REGIMENT.

Camp Wool, Dec. 3, 1861.

Dear Uncles—

Although we do not drill as much as formerly, we have but little opportunity to write. In the first place we must bring and cut wood, and in the next, we are having such a course of Inspection and Reviews that we must work most of the time to keep our arms and accoutrements in order. On the 1st we were out for inspection, when Gen. Sickles' Aid came in with a message to the Colonel, and soon after, Gen. Sickles himself appeared, and our inspection was changed to a review. The principal feature of the occasion was the formation of the solid square, which was repeated several times upon the run. Not over half a minute was consumed in converting our long line of soldiers into a dense mass, all bristling with bayonets, and as impenetrable to cavalry as a solid rock.

A week ago yesterday, we were inspected by Gen. Hooker, and overhauled pretty sharply. The impression seems prevalent that we shall go South to Carolina, but we only *know* where we are going when we *arrive*. It is certainly one of the chief requisites of a commanding officer to keep his own counsel, and McClellan seems to do this, for if the rebels get any certain knowledge of any intended movement, they are wiser than we by far. To day we expect a review of the whole division.

And now I suppose you would like to know how we spent Thanksgiving. Well, I knew where the "facilities" were, and speedily arranged it with the machine shop boys, whose superb clay stove had already proved its capability of baking beans, and hence came the conclusion that it would bake turkey, too. The turkey was secured and stuffed with oysters, and "Ote Luce" baked it to a beautiful brown. A mighty pot of pork and beans was also sent upon the board, and Chautauqua butter formed also part of our bill of fare. Fricasseed chicken was there, and toast as well, and a very nice desert was provided; but the latter proved a fizzle, for the attraction of the turkey exhausted our powers in the epicurian line.

I was on guard, but contrived to get another to take my place at the all important hour of 2, and I repaired at once to the tent where the *bon vivants* were assembled. "Bones" took his place at one end of the table, and your most obedient at the other, while "Ote," with his patriarchal beard took the center, and did the honors of the feast. The thing was a decided success. "Bones" twisted his and expatiated eloquently upon the merits of *pork and beans*, while the *turkey* upon the plate evaporated or disappeared in some manner or other with great rapidity. Brooks' emotions were too deep for utterance, so he wisely forced them down together with a leg, a wing, and a little of the oyster stuffing. "Swinburne" proved himself a right valiant trencherman, and struck off at a tangent, which eventually centered in a dish of the fricassee, "Tommy" bearing him company. "Barley," too, was there, and when the feast was over, his equatorial circumference was one inch greater than the meridional. No snow white linen graced our table, and the neat china which you ate from was here replaced by the regulation tin plates and iron spoons. The knives and forks were mostly adapted to the pocket. Thanksgiving dinner, like all other good things, was soon over, and we separated, I to my post, where I ended the night in a soaking rain, and the others to their various duties or amusements, never, in all human probability, to reunite upon a similar occasion.

Since I wrote you last, we have lost three more men, one a member of Co. B. I think I told you in my last, that Daley, of Co. C, was dead. Though our comrades did not fall in battle, they died not less honorably but more painfully than if by shot or shell, Daley alone excepted, and he suffered most of all. The last I heard of Donahue, he was doing well.—We have now tight and warm log houses for the sick, and they are as well cared for as circumstances will admit of. Dr. Irwin gave them oysters, at his own expense, for their Thanksgiving feast.

We do not drill over two or three hours now, in the day. The maneuvers in which we have drilled mostly of late, have been the formation of the hollow square, and doubling files in four ranks for the solid square. The regiment is certainly now a fine corps, and it is a splendid sight to see them advance in line, which they can now do with a straighter front than many a company can present. The odds, as you see, are ten to one in the company's favor, since it is ten times easier to keep 100 men in line than 1,000.

Col. Taylor is a very prudent man, so far as the health and comfort of his men are concerned, and few men could enforce such strict discipline, and exact so severe a drill as he has done until lately, and yet retain so thoroughly the love and confidence of the men. He is very severe upon gaming, and in this he is ably seconded by Capt. Abell, who gave out the word that if any of his men were caught playing for money they would get lodging at the guard house forthwith, and that if the offender was a non-commissioned officer, he should be degraded to the ranks. As regards punishment of ordinary offences, our officers have pursued a very wise course. Instead of sending a culprit to the guard-house, he is required to pack his knapsack and walk to and fro with one of the sentries down in the woods. This punishment, while more severe than imprisonment, is more private, and in proportion less prejudicial to self-respect. Drunkenness also is an offence which Col. Taylor has little leniency for. At present it is almost impossible to procure liquor, and the man who returns home an inebriate must indeed be lost to all sense of honor and self. As a whole, I think that the effects of military life upon the minds of young men will be generally good, and certainly, habits of idleness are not apt to be acquired under Col. Nelson Taylor.

Yours as ever,
Arthur.

Ote Luce: Otis B. Luce.

Daley, of Co. C, was dead: actually, it was Sergeant Michael Daily of Co. E who died in hospital on November 24. Daily was among those soldiers hurt when a live coal was placed inside an errant enemy artillery shell back on October 22.

Camp Wool Dec. 5th, 1861

Dear Mother,

I received a letter from you a day or two since which must have been written before my last. I have been very remiss in writing to you personally but my letters to the Censor must of course give a pretty good idea of my situation. You inquire about rations—well the allowance is just about enough for a man to eat if he has no hard labor to perform and is well lodged and gets all of it. Owing to the bad state of the roads and the fact that all we get must be hauled for a least seven miles we don't always get our stores punctually. Firewood and straw are all this god forsaken country affords and everything else even to a board is sent from Washington in a boat to the mouth of the Mattawoman Creek whence it is hauled to us over roads which are here hard and good and next mud axle deep. A man whether mounted or on foot can get along without any trouble but a team which must keep the road has hard times. Thus you see sometimes meat turns up missing and sometimes bread even. What we do not get is credited to the company but whether it will ever do us any good I don't know. We have a new sutler here and he is more reasonable than the old.

I feel it a matter of nescessity [*sic*] to get provision of him occasionally when short. You can hardly think how good your butter tastes. The cake was very good but I disregarded your advice as to eating by portions. We had a regular Thanksgiving feast which I have duly described and which you can read of in the Censor in a week or two and as the feast was really sumptuous and I was an invited guest and could not make them assess my share, I put on the cake which was about the only edible wanting to make it complete. As regards our situation you will see upon the map of Maryland Ft. Washington which commands the Potomac at some distance below the Capital. We are not over two miles from the river and Ft. Washington is about half way between us and the city. By the road we are about 45 miles distant from Washington. One of the 3rd Indiana Cavalry has just been here and says that there are one hundred wagons a few miles off and that the teamsters say they are coming to move the Sickles Brigade to Annapolis whence it is to embark for Carolina.

This may be an idle rumor or it may be true. For my part I had rather go for I had rather winter there by all odds and as regards supplies we can get them there as well as here if not better. Leute Jones has been troubled with asthma and the Brigade Surgeon recommended Dr. Irwin to send him home. He is not unwell enough to be confined to his tent but as his breath fails him upon any severe exertion he can not be of any service in a campaign in winter in which a man must be exposed continually. I have gained seventeen pounds since I was sick and am in high health and spirits and still gaining. Yesterday I was detailed for guard but while we were having our guns inspected I saw Capt. Doyle stepping about very gingerly and whispering to Adjutant O'Niel [O'Neill]. The latter soon after came up to me and selected me as orderly, or messenger for Col. Taylor in place of standing post. By this arrangement I awaited the Colonels orders in his tent and had a beautiful opportunity to see what was going on. The Bourbon Count of Paris and Maj. Davis who have been reviewing our brigade and inspecting arms, equipments, tents, hospitals &c. and even all the accounts, were staying at Col. Taylors. The Count is a captain upon McClellans staff and is of course the hon of the day. Maj. Davis is an old campaigner and is [a] very critical inspector. He is a regular and hence we value the high compliment he paid us after inspection. I think very much of Captain Doyle and frequently spend an evening at his tent. He is one of the Jack Hinton style of Irishmen and is high souled and a thorough gentlemen. There is something in his eyes and his smile which reminds me of Moses. Those drawers you sent me are first rate. I am now well provided with winter clothes and that is the reason I have only sent a V to you. I sent another to Aunt Eliza for those boots. Exposed as we are whenever we move and until we get settled in a new location, I need plenty of good clothes and I've got them. When warm weather comes I shall have a lot of good clothing which I shall not wish to carry and if near an express office I can send spare things enough for six months wear at home. I am not very hard upon clothes and my pants and shoes are about all that shows wear at all. I have now a pair of very nice boots which are just the thing to keep a mudsill out of the wet. They are fine firm leather and come up to the knee.

I cautioned Aunt Eliza that it would not do to have thick leather because that grease was not always available and when a man's boots get stiff and he must march with his knapsack on, it almost kills him. The boots came and they were a staring good pair but just stiff enough to hurt my right foot. There was no appeal and I had to sacrifice my five dollar boots for only seven-dollars. They bought those I now wear and by the trading I have got my boots cheaply.

With regard to butter &c. we don't get an ounce from Gov. Our bill of fare is usually when settled and quiet a loaf of bread to last for the day and coffee at morning soup at noon and coffee and tea at night. The rice, beans etc. we do not often get and we do not of course get soup when we have no fresh beef to make it of. The regulations allow 1 ¼ lbs. fresh meat but I don't recollect ever getting that amount or anything like it. When we have it we have enough for one meal and rarely more. Generally we get one meal of meat daily and bread is the substance of the remainder of our fare. Thus you see it resolves itself into bread and coffee or tea for breakfast, bread and meat for dinner and bread and coffee or tea for supper. We should have potatoes three times a week but would like to be sure of them once. Spare eaters can live upon rations but I can not. When we get all that we are entitled to I only need butter and pepper and mustard in addition and then I wont eat all I get. We have an iron over or rather two which we cover with clay to retain the heat and which can bake 1,800 loaves daily. We have bakers in the regiment and they make the bread so we are all supplied with the best hop yeast bread. Each company cooks its own food otherwise than bread and two men to cook and one to bring the rations from the commissary are sufficient for a company of a hundred men. It needs however about three more to bring wood and water.

I do not know whether Dr. Irwin will discharge Lucius or not. At any [rate] he has good officers for Doyle and his lieutenant all take an interest in every man. Doyle speaks well of Leute who he seems to think considerably of. If you are likely to get cramped much in paying your taxes let me know it. If you have not to pay before Jan. about the 20th give yourself no uneasiness at all. If sooner let me know when and don't sacrifice over a dollar to meet it for I can get money if needed. Give my love to the boys, Father and Jennie. Write again and direct as before to Washington. If we move the answer will be forwarded.

Your aff. Son
Arthur

Bourbon Count of Paris: Prince Philippe, Count of Paris, served on the staff of Major General George McClellan after his family fled France.

Other Voices: From the *Fredonia Censor*

Published December 18, 1861

[Extract from a private letter from the 3rd Regiment]

Camp Wool, Dec. 7, 1861

Friend Hurlbut:—

I have undertaken to keep you partially booked up in regard to the movements in this quarter. I propose to overstep the rules of corresponding so far as to write when there is anything new, which would be likely to interest you, regardless of the fact that you owe me a letter, which you can not have had time to answer, however.

We have been strongly reinforced lately. The 5th, 6th, 7th and 8th New Jersey Regiments have been assigned to Hooker's Division, and they have come down within 5 miles of our Brigade, occupying the left of the line. I saw some of them today. They informed me that they were to be followed by McLeod Murphy's Reg. of Engineers, with pontoon bridges, &c., preparatory to *what*? Well, we must be patient. There are now 15,000 men on this side of the river, swearing, scolding, praying, and in every way showing much impatience to cross over, and wipe out the rebels. This feeling assumes a very malignant form, when the boom of the rebel's guns is followed by the hissing sound of the shell intended for the destruction of some unarmed trader, who is intent upon making the trip to Washington to supply the needy inhabitants of that city with wood or coal, which has from the earliest period found its way to the city by this route only. At such times, you will hear very many expressions of rage, which find vent in words not found in the catechism. But today it came out that a deserter from the rebel camp was at Head Quarters, and we were all very anxious to know the report he gave of things on that side. Soon we learned that he was a Marylander, who, becoming sick of rebellion, and following the example of Jeff & Co. determined to secede, this time, from Secessia. Accordingly, he left his post last night, and by some means which I did not learn, (I had this from Sickles' attendant who overheard the examination,) reached this shore, and was in the hands of our pickets. The report which he gave, I am not able to give in full, but some parts of it I can state, with the assurance of truth. There are, within reach, ready to receive us, 25,000 men, with artillery fully equal to our own, protected by works of great strength, and facilities for reinforcement far superior to ours. This satisfied the soldiers that our commanders knew their business, and have acted prudently in not risking an attack, which, from the nature of the case, must have resulted fatally. When we go over there, I think we will go to stay. The news he brought from the rebel army confirms previous reports, that the soldiers are becoming very much dissatisfied. He said there were ten in his company that was to attempt to leave last night, but he took his chances alone. There are two Maryland Regiments that want to return to their own State and lay down their arms, and submit to the action of their own people. But to attempt this, will be sure death, so says [the] deserter, and his statements are credited here. He has been sent to Washington. You will see some account of him, probably, before this reaches you.

Yours Truly,
G. W. Shelley.

Editorial Note

The composition of Hooker's Division:

1st Brigade (Cowdin)
1st Massachusetts
11th Massachusetts
26th Pennsylvania
2nd New Hampshire
3rd Indiana Cavalry

2nd Brigade (Sickles)
1st Excelsior (70th New York)
2nd Excelsior (71st New York)
3rd Excelsior (72nd New York)
4th Excelsior (73rd New York)
5th Excelsior (74th New York)

3rd Brigade (Starr)
5th New Jersey
6th New Jersey
7th New Jersey
8th New Jersey

Figure 5.1. Reconnaissance with General Sickles on the Potomac. General Sickles and his staff survey enemy positions across the Potomac from the shore of Lower Maryland. Source: *Illustrated London News*.

Fredonia Censor: Published December 18, 1861

FROM THE THIRD REGIMENT

Camp Wool, Dec. 9, 1861.

Dear Uncles:—

We are still at Camp Wool, and as busily engaged in drilling as ever. That, however, is a mere rest, after the course of reviews and inspections we have had to undergo during the past two weeks. First we were reviewed and inspected by Gen. Hooker, and a very sharp inspector he proved. Upon this occasion Sergeant Best and private Nuepling, of Co. D, were complimented for having the cleanest guns in the regiment. Afterward we were reviewed by Gen. Sickles, and exercised in forming the solid square in double quick. [*Mem*—that was a pretty heavy gun just fired down at the river—and that last one, too; ah! There goes yet another. Fifteen minutes later—I have just been out of the tent to witness the rebel firing. It is now nearly half past eight, and the flashes of the guns are very easily seen, amid the darkness of the night. The interval between the flash and the report is from seventeen to eighteen seconds, and as sound travels probably about 1,100 feet per second, the firing must be more than three and a half miles distant] *Mais reveuonsa nos montous.* Capt. Abell and some other officers have gone down to witness the firing, and, until he returns, I will stick to the news current. After being inspected, (dissected would apply about as well to the case,) by Gen. Hooker, we found that we had only just begun. Last Monday, if my memory serves me right, we turned out with arms looking the very best, brasses brightly polished, and blacking applied *ad libitum*, to our understandings, for still another review by Major Davis, of McClellan's staff, and also by the Count of Paris, who is also of the General's staff, and who holds the rank of Captain. The Count is of the Orleans family, and were the Bourbons the dominant power in France, would stand pretty near the throne; but under the present dynasty, his title is all that remains. As regards his *personnel*, he is of unusual height, and finely proportioned. There is nothing of reserve or *hauteur* in his manner, but, on the contrary, he is very quiet and unassuming, though evidently a man who has traveled, and who has acquired much general information.

While in this vicinity, the Major and the Count were Col. Taylor's guests.—While here, they inspected arms, quarters, hospital, and regimental and company books. That the investigation was a searching one, I can bear witness, for I was orderly that day, and was sent to summon the Captains to meet. An orderly, or messenger is selected from each guard that is formed, and, as the duties are light, it is the usual custom to select the one who comes out with the cleanest and brightest gun. My gun-lock gave out at the time we met in our street, so I borrowed Charley Foss' for the occasion, and on inspection I was picked out upon the superlative merits of Charley's gun—and that is how I was smuggled in among the lions, and inspected the Inspectors.

The review will be long remembered by the Excelsior Brigade, for we turned out at 8 a.m. in complete heavy marching order, upon a field which had about an inch of snow upon it, and a soft stratum of mud below. To prevent the men from freezing their feet, Col. Taylor marched and countermarched them by flank until the ground was of about the right consistency for plastering stick chimneys, and then selected a new spot to pursue the exercise. Military etiquette, of course, required white gloves, and as the thin cotton was no protection at all, we suffered not a little in remaining at a shoulder for any length of time, with the cold iron in our hands. Finally we got ready and marched in review. We were already heartily sick of the affair, and the regiment moved in a lounging, free and easy way that looked really laughable. When, however,

Figure 5.2. SIGNALING FROM THE RIGHT BACK OF THE POTOMAC. Federal troops signaling Washington from the Lower Maryland shore. Source: *Illustrated London News.*

we approached the reviewing officers, the irregular lines straightened as if by magic, and every man marched exactly and squarely to the front. After getting a good distance from the inspectors, the old free and easy style was resumed. After marching in review we were inspected by regiments. At dinner time we stacked arms and went to camp. After dinner we were drilled upon the soft, muddy ground until our turn came. When we were fairly through, we were glad to march into camp and get our suppers. The condition of our arms was highly approved, but the quality as strongly condemned. The result is, that the French rifles have come this evening, and now that we have a really serviceable arm, we shall feel disposed to take better care of it than we have done heretofore. These Harper Ferry guns are a miserable thing, and I would not have one about me unless for shooting pigeons. For ducking even, I prefer a rifle.

We have balloon reconnoissances, and it seems to tantalize the rebels not a little to see the aeronauts so coolly and securely overlooking their operations. They have fired at the balloon again and again, but though they have thrown shells over and beyond it, they are too distant to stand any chance of hitting it.

Since I wrote you last, we have lost three more men by fever. The last who died was young Williams, of Dunkirk who came as drummer in Co. H. At present the sick number, probably, a little less than ten per cent. of the whole. All those now in hospital are in a fair way to recover, though some are very weak. Corporal Ellis, and Sprague, of Co. D are convalescent, and I believe there are no others in the regimental hospital from this company. At the hospital at Good Hope, near Washington, are two patients from our company, Redmond Riley and Franklin Pickard. Pickard is about ready for duty, and may come here at any time, but Riley did guard duty before he had fairly recovered, and suffered a relapse. This will enfeeble him for some time, but I do not apprehend his case to be dangerous. There are others of Co. D ill, but not so as to need removal to hospital. As a whole, we have lost fewer men in proportion than any other regiment in the brigade, and fewer than most in the service.

Our Indian summer has just begun, and the extra blankets we so anxiously looked for a short time since, are now scarcely needed. They have arrived, however, and they are a first rate thing, being seven feet long and five-wide, and very substantial. Indeed, the new single weighs more than the old double blanket. Other clothing has also arrived, and we are comfortable and in good spirits. The constant succession of knapsack drills has rendered us quite indifferent to the weight of that article, and when we are really called upon to journey, we can do it as easily as at first with muskets and canteens only. Capt. Abell has got back, and reports that the heavy and prolonged firing was by the rebels at some oyster sloops, which ran by unharmed. There was considerable ground plowed up on this side by the balls, and the officers made a foot ball of a hollow shot which lay in the road. Quite recently, some of our gun-boats had been down, and it seem[s] that as they ran the gauntlet they gave the rebels a good deal better than they sent, and closed the business by shelling the town of Dumfries, which lies a little below us. The result was that the town was knocked about like a basket of chips, and set on fire. Capt. Abell could plainly see the glare of the burning ruins, when down at the river this evening.

I really think, from the present appearance of things, that this war will eventually prove the death blow of Slavery.—When I entered upon this campaign, I was a non-intervention man as regarded the existing institutions of States, and still am as regards the rights of loyal citizens, though then, as now, utterly opposed to the further extension of slavery; but I do not see why the old world system of confiscating the property of those who are found in arms against their lawful rulers should not be followed by our Government, as well as that of all the principal civilized nations on the earth. I do not see why we should give to rebels and to traitors a security which is denied to loyal citizens

Figure 5.3. LOWE BALLOON. Thaddeus Lowe and his fledgling balloon corps conducted aerial observations of Confederate positions starting in the summer of 1861. Though many Union officers were skeptical of the new technology, Dan Sickles was among the first to embrace it. *Courtesy of Library of Congress.*

of seceded States; and yet more, I wonder that they who are giving freely their treasure and their blood for the restoration of the Union, should seek to perpetuate the cause of the disruption.

But the old order of things is fast passing away, and the Southern planter with his smiling family of domestics around him, over whom he exercises so mild and benevolent a sway, and who would go through fire and water for their beloved master—this picture, so charming in the perspective, upon nearer approach, fades away into a dirty-looking farmer, in a coarse suit of clothes of antediluvian cut, and a ragged parcel of chattels, who look eagerly to us for one ray of hope for their delivery from their present thralldom. It was indeed painful, on our scouting expedition to Marlboro, to turn back the eager slaves, who hailed us as their expected deliverers, and entreated that they might follow us back to camp. All volunteered whatever information they were possessed of, and undoubtedly many of their backs smarted in consequence—Here, I know it to be the fact, that the planters forbid their slaves from visiting us from fear that their disloyal sentiments and acts may be disclosed.

We have now several hundred thousand young men who have just come upon the stage of active life, who see things now in their true light, and who will hereafter, in all political conflicts between Slavery and Freedom, refer to their own fresh memories, rather than political tracts, or ingeniously got up speeches, for the knowledge of the true relation between master and slave, and between the results of slave and free labor. And yet they have seen only the fairest page of the book. The difference between the slaves in Washington and those here is not nearly as widely marked as between those here and in the extreme South.—Time, however, presses, and I must close.

Yours as ever,
Arthur

Mais reveuonsa nos montous: this may be misspelled but probably intends, "But let's return to our subject."

Editorial Note

McKinstry's mention of the balloon reconnaissance does more than tantalize the Rebels, it influenced their thinking. "I believe you are nearly correct with regard to your conjecture as to the future movements of the enemy," wrote Confederate General P. G. T. Beauregard. "Those balloon ascensions indicate either offensive or defensive movements, most probably the former."[1] So while at the same time Confederate planners anticipated a cross-river assault, Arthur becomes increasing frustrated at the lack of offensive preparation. It would seem an attack is expected by everyone except the man who can set events into motion—George McClellan.

Camp Wool Dec. 10th 1861

Dear Aunt,

As all is quiet just now I will improve the opportunity to write you a note though it may have to be cut off short by afternoon drill. I am well and hearty and we have I believe no very sick men just now. We took great pleasure in reading those papers and when through I gave them to the chaplain to take to those in hospital. The boots I had finally to sell for they were too stiff for a man who must daily carry upon his back for several hours the weight of a heavy knapsack. I sold them for seven dollars and that was sufficient to pay for a lighter and easier pair. The fact is a soldier needs an easier boot than any other man and must have it cost what it may. As however I sold them at a price great enough to purchase a suitable article I am no loser and not the less indebted to you. Has Uncle Willard sent that five dollar bill yet. I have not heard from him since and that makes me think he may have shown as little punctuality toward you. The cakes and preserves were duly discussed and received unqualified praisc.

The gloves were of great service for a short time and I think will wear well but just now it has settled down into as quiet an Indian summer as ever you saw.

13th Yours of the 10th has just come to hand. We are very busy—that is our tent building a log home. We have the rafter up and shall get through in a day or two. Our stay is uncertain but is as well to work at that as anything else. Our tent is inside and undisturbed but when we get all the rest done we shall take it down roll it up, take it out doors and stretch it on the rafters in place of shingling. As it is late I will quit but when the house is done I will write again. Give my love to uncle Lyman and Aunt Jane. I wrote a few days ago to Edward but unluckily directed to Amherst.

Your aff. Nephew,
Arthur

P.S. I am well off for clothing in every particular and have a mattress.

I have not heard from home for a very long time but I learn by a letter which another young volunteer from our neighborhood received, that Mother had sent a box of under clothes and some butter. No doubt there is a letter in it but it came too late to reach me without considerable delay. I expect to get it at the same time that I do yours. I am very grateful to you all for the things you have sent me. I got a letter from Edward the other day.

As it is ten and a quarter—just two hours later than lights are allowed if known of I must quit. I will write again when the box comes.

Your aff. nephew
Arthur

(Direct to me Co. D 3rd Regt. Ex. Brig. Washington D.C.)

Figure 5.4. ALONG THE POTOMAC, BOAT EVADING FIRE NEAR EVANSPORT. Despite the Confederate batteries firing hundreds, if not thousands, of shells at passing Union shipping, only a few rounds ever found their mark. Source: *Illustrated London News*.

Other Voices: From the *Fredonia Censor*

Published December 25, 1861

FROM THE THIRD REGIMENT
(From a private Letter)
Camp Wool, Dec. 12

Friend Hurlbut:—

When you become bored beyond endurance by my indefatigable efforts to furnish you with news from the seat of war, you will please inform me, and I will try some more invincible temperament, for write I must. I have got the writing mania, and I must give it vent. A person with a vivid imagination could with ease find much in camp life that would interest to write, but if I succeed in furnishing you with a few items of interest I shall consider myself amply repaid.

Since my last letter was written, there has been heavy cannonading almost continually. Until last Monday, the rebel batteries were allowed to monopolize the business almost exclusively, but on that day it became evident to us, by the rapid firing, and the report of the constantly exploding shells, that Uncle Sam had taken a hand in the game. From our camp to the river, in a direct line, is perhaps one and a half miles. The rebels used the 64 pound Parrott guns taken from us at Bull Run, and each discharge shook the ground like the shock of an earthquake. The voices of the guns which seemed to reply, if less loud, seemed more sharp, and were far more frequent. The excitement in camp ran high; curiosity was raised. Now you know that I am not the least curious of mortals, and you will not be surprised to learn that I was resolved not to let this opportunity of witnessing a battle, slide without making an effort to see it. Having obtained permission, I started for the river. On my way down, several soldiers were met, from whom I learned that three of Uncle Sam's gun boats were engaging the enemy's batteries. There was a large volume of smoke arising from a point about 2 miles up the river, which it at first occurred to me might be from the burning of one of the boats, but my fear was father to the thought, for upon emerging from the woods, the sight which met my eyes was one that filled me with extreme pleasure. There, on the bosom of one of the finest rivers in the world, in all the majesty and pomp of battle-array, lay two of our heavy gun-boats, while the third had just landed and set on fire a dozen buildings, used by the rebels for store houses. From these issued the smoke which I had observed before. A new battery had already been demolished by the boats, and now lay a mass of ruins. On the bank of the river, in front of where I stood, the 1st Massachusetts regiment had planted two ten-pound rifled cannon, and during the fight had kept up an occasional fire upon the battery on Shipping Point, which is about four miles below the one which the boats destroyed. This last one was, I think, on what is called Freestone Head, opposite Mattawoman Creek, the point from which our division is supplied. As the river is clear from this point to Washington, it was the purpose of the rebels in building this battery, to cut off our supplies. As the point commands the mouth of the creek, it would have annoyed us exceedingly, but after working for months to build it, they had the mortification of seeing it knocked about their heads, in about two hours.—We could not learn how many of the enemy were killed, I think not many for they vamoosed the ranch early in the action.

After the boats had done their work, they headed in shore on this side, and sent a boat ashore. After conferring with Gen. Hooker, I think the boat went back, and after looking down stream toward Shipping Point, they turned head[ed] up stream, and were soon out of sight. Not one man injured on our side.

Of course the rebels on Shipping Point were very angry at the result of this, and whenever a group of soldiers gathered on the bank, they would send a 65 lb. shell at them, but they failed to hurt any body, although they made some good shots for the distance, considering the guns are smooth-bore, and throw round shot or shell, of course.

I stated, in a former letter, that the river was one and a quarter miles wide; now, as you may wonder why we cannot get a nearer range than three miles, I will try to explain it. The river bends on this side opposite Shipping Point, in such a way as to make it impossible to get a position for a battery directly opposite. So you see by drawing a line straight across the river from where our two little guns are, you strike the Virginia side one and a half miles above the battery. Our artillery, which is attached to this division, is lower down the river, and have never, I believe, paid their respects to this battery. After the boats had gone away, I turned my attention to this part of the fray. I walked up to where I saw a crowd of men, which proved to be a detachment of the Massachusetts boys. They had their little guns loaded and were just in the act of firing. I got a good position, and watched the battery. Simultaneously with the report of the gun, I saw the shell explode, short of the enemy and on the water. The day was still, and when the enemy saw the failure, they set up a terrible cheering, and hallooed back, "How do you like Bull Run," &c. But they did not halloo as much, when the other shot reached its mark. I was looking at the battery, and when this shell exploded, it was in their very midst. It was our turn to cheer now, and we did it right lustily. The rebel ire had been kindled now, and "take care boys," was the next word from the officer in charge. I had not thought of this before. What he meant by taking care, I did not know. I did not see any place to dodge, but as they had seen the thing before, I determined to do as they did, which was to throw themselves on the ground, and crawl under an old hovel which stood near. I was not long in following suit, and scarcely had I got my position before the death dealing missile came roaring, whizzing through the air. It passed directly over us, and exploded some 60 rods from our position. We came out of our hiding place, and I took a look to the rear to see if there were any more a coming, and suddenly recollecting that I had business in camp, I took double quick for home, or any other place of safety. There is something about these shells that I cannot fancy. I don't think I would mind being shot with a nice smooth musket ball; I abhor the idea of being hit by a fragment of these things. If there were no one hurt on our side, there was one man terribly scared. Two more shells came after me but fell short, for I made good time. Some of the boys dug them up, for they went into the ground after exploding, five or six feet. I got a piece of the one that frightened me. So, if I ever come home, I will show it to you. One was dug up whole, and boys of the 4th carried it into their camp. Our boys don't [need to go far] to have 64 lb. shells to play with.

We have got our new rifles, they are a nice article. We are to have a prize on Christmas day for the best shot. So says Major Stevens.

Yours truly,
G. W. Shelley

Other Voices: James Rusling—Death of a New Jersey Man

Camp on Lower Potomac, MD.
Dec. 16, 1861

Dear Friends:

How rapidly time flies! Another week gone, and I scarcely know it. It is over three months, almost four, since I left home; and yet it seems but yesterday. Have been sad and pensive all day, and have thought more of home than for a long time. I supposed it has been caused by the death yesterday of one of our men. He was a German, with no friend in America. Was taken with typhoid fever; lay some time, and yesterday afternoon dropped off before anybody knew it. *Hard drink* was the principal cause. Of all other places, drunkards should shun the army, and yet we have "lots" of them. Nine tenths of the sickness and suffering in camp comes from habitual drunkenness, either directly or indirectly. Poor fellow! We made him a rough board coffin; and hard by a little country chapel, a mile away, we buried him beneath the trees, to await the resurrection morning. Our men hardly seemed to notice it. Such is the hardening and dehumanizing effect of camp life . . . [2]

Fredonia Censor: Published January 1, 1862

FROM THE THIRD REGIMENT.

Camp Wool, Dec. 17.

Dear Uncles:—

As little of importance is going on I propose to give a list in detail of men we have lost and the sick list of to day. The lists are of our county only:

Co. G, —Geo. Rhynehart.—Nov. 28
" H, —John Williams.—Dec. 9
" E, —Ephriam Smith.—Nov. 15
" " —John Rouse.— Nov. 24 (By shell explosion)
" " —Michael Daily.—Nov. 24 (By shell explosion)
" " —J. P. Henderson.—Nov. 13 (Gen. Hosp't. at Wash.)
" G, —J. McWilliams.—Aug. 6 (Gen. Hosp't. at Wash.)
" " —C. W. Bennett.—Nov. 10 (Gen. Hosp't. at Wash.)

Sick list of Dec. 17, 1861. Condition.

Co. B, in Hosp't.	E. L. Homer—Doing well
" " " "	Otto Nelson—Helpless
" " " "	Ed. Porter—Convales.
" " " Quarters	Wm. Dowd
" " " "	C. Pickard
" " " "	John Thomas
" " " "	B. B. Slater

"	"	"	"	E. B. Bishop	
"	"	"	"	James Young	
"	"	"	"	Wm. Marvin	
"	"	"	"	G. Sanford	
"	"	"	"	——Hobart	
"	"	"	"	——Richardson	
"	D,	"	Hosp't.	J. C. Sprague—Convales.	
"	"	"	"	A. A. Page—Feverish	
"	"	"	"	Sergt. C. A. Foss—Intermittent fever	
"	"	"	Quarters	J. Kennedy—Sprained ankle	
"	"	"	"	H. F. Ellis—Convales.	
"	"	"	"	W. Averill—	"
"	"	"	"	L. O. Donaghey—	"
"	"	"	"	Noah Clark—	"
"	"	"	"	J. Van Housen—Catarrh	
"	"	"	"	Dan. Terrell—	"
"	"	"	"	A. B. Hamilton—	"
"	E,	"	Hosp't.	None	
"	"	"	Quarters	G. Smith—Convalescent	
"	"	"	"	W. H. Smith—	"
"	"	"	"	——Fleming—	"
"	"	"	"	R. Dindsley—	"
"	"	"	"	Wilbur—Fever	"
"	"	"	"	Mathews	"
"	"	"	"	Wilcox	"
"	"	"	"	Webster	"
"	"	"	"	Lynards	Catarrh
"	"	"	"	Connoly	"
"	G,	"	Hosp't.	D. Berry—Typhoid fever	
"	"	"	"	C. Thornton	
"	"	"	"	Strain	"
"	"	"	"	Bowdish	"
"	"	"	"	Bond	
"	"	"	Quarters	Steward	Convalescent
"	"	"	"	Van Dusen	"
"	"	"	"	Hall	"
"	"	"	"	Jones	"
"	"	"	"	Bliss	"

"	"	"	"	Barrows	"
"	"	"	"	Sutton	"
"	"	"	"	Hunt	"
"	"	"	"	Neff	"
"	"	"	"	Huff	"
"	"	"	"	Cross	"
"	"	"	"	Warren	"
"	"	"	"	Wheeler	"
"	"	"	"	Wilson	"
"	"	"	"	Schaffer	"
"	H,	"	Hosp't.	Rogers	Gen. Debility
"	"	"	"	Butcher	Fever
"	"	"	"	Laport	"
"	"	"	Quar.	Bowers	
"	"	"	"	Snoble	
"	"	"	"	Baker	
"	"	"	"	Crane	
"	"	"	"	L. Jones	
"	"	"	"	McGwinn	
"	"	"	"	Williams	
"	"	"	"	Coleman	

Band in Hospital—D. C. Smith, recovering from fever.
" Died at Good Hope—Henry Kirk Willard, Nov. 12

Those marked in quarters, include all who are weak from recent illness, or who, from cases often trifling are unable to do full military duty. As soon as a patient needs nursing he is removed to the hospital. Thus a man who cuts his finger so that he cannot use a musket is marked *quarters*, though very likely in a day or two he will be all right.

IN GEN. HOSPITAL AT WASHINGTON.

Co. B, Chapin Tiffany—Able to go out.
" D, Redmond Riley—Relapse of fever but recovering.
" E, O'Donahue—Recovering from shell wound.
" G, Frank Lilley—Inflammatory Rheumatism.

These in general hospital are all doing well, and remain there only because they can not yet do full duty, and are better off where they are. I shall not again send a list of those in quarters, as the cases are mostly too trivial for mention, but I propose to send you a weekly list of those in hospital, and to send you also a record of all deaths.

We are preparing for winter, though the weather is now remarkably mild. I live now in a substantial log house, and the company propose to build also for all hands. I really enjoy myself very well: though I should receive with joy any orders which would transfer us from our comfortable quarters to a field where we should be of more efficient service than simply holding the rebels in check. Lieut. Hinman, who sent to Piscataway to determine claims against the United States on account of soldiers' depredations, tells me that the people of that locality were making a very fine speculation out of it for the preferred claims, to the amount of about $5,000. "I notice though," said Hinman, "that I cut them down a little, for they could not fool me on the cost of rail fence much." The rebels still fire at our vessels and do not harm, but once in a while when *our* shells burst they do some tall capering. One of our largest gun boats came down yesterday and stirred them, up to the great delight of Capt. Doyle and some other spectators. The firing unmasked a battery, but what damage our shells did, we cannot tell, as they exploded amid the thicket which concealed the rebels. One thing is certain, and that is that they introduced some new figures in dancing which we don't feel disposed to imitate. I do not see any prospect of our removal from here.

The list I give you of the sick is from the official records, and may be relied upon. All whose names are not down are fit for duty. When the regiment left Camp Caldwell, it left without much camp equipage, and, as was supposed, for a tramp of six days only; thus no hospital tents were taken, and as the days lengthened into weeks their need was felt. That they were not procured earlier was due to the fact that transportation could not be obtained. As soon as possible, things were set to rights.

Yours as ever,
Arthur

Camp Wool Dec. 19th 1861

Dear Mother,

Your last came in after a journey of two or three days only but I have not had before [now] a fair chance to reply. The night I read your letter I sat in front of our house which we had just raised, I now live in a log house with canvass roof and am probably more comfortable than you so far as cold is concerned. I am lounging upon a bunk as I write this and enjoying the cheerfull blaze of our fireplace. My health is fair and I am really enjoying myself very well—as much as at home. As the correspondent of the Censor I have access to what is going on to a greater extent than many officers. Day before yesterday I sent in place of my ordinary letter a list of all the Chautauqua men who had died in the regiment with the dates of their decease. I also sent a list of all the men now sick from our county and mentioned the disease or condition.

As many very desponding letters have been written home I thought it my duty to relieve the anxiety of friends and I can assure you that Dr. Irwin was very glad to place his books at my disposal, for he wished facts to be known rather than the opinions of private individuals. Thus you will have in the next Censor a list of all who are not ready to do full duty, who came here with us. We drill very little now but we use up most of the forenoon in target firing. Our rifles do tall shooting I can tell you. At twenty rods the other day I fired three shot which averaged four and three quarters inches from the centre and the best of which was within only half an inch of it. This however is better than I usually do. The Brigade Surgeon has just been here and was much struck with our comfortable domicil. He is inspecting the regimental quarters.

We have bright sunny days and such glorious moonlight nights as I used to see in Mexico. At about this time when I was at Annapolis we had a foot of snow upon the ground and the harbor was frozen over but it seems as if this weather was for the special benefit of the soldiers.

Oscar Ames is fat as a pig. I was very glad to see that Republican you sent me. Papers are very uncertain now and I only get about half of my Censors. I am pretty well off for clothes now and I am able to carry them. I got a letter from Aunt Eliza since yours. All well. Cyrus and I correspond a little.

Well there has just been a corporal after me to get water so I must close. Give my love to Father and the boys. How is George Hopper. Lucius Jones is unwell but not in hospital. His officers look after him pretty well and he does not suffer for lack of attention. I think he will come out all right but if he don't he will be discharged. Capt. Doyle holds on that he may get stout here if possible. Write soon. I think we may stay some time and we are building winter quarters.

Your aff. Son.

Arthur

Other Voices: Charles County Maryland Delegate and Slave Owner Augustus Sollers Regarding His Arrest and Detention

. . . My arrest was a simple outrage only to be excused upon the ground of over zeal in the officer who ordered it . . . he had been informed that I and others had formed a plan to take the polls on the day of the election and prevent the Union men from voting . . . but it was a pure a fabrication as ever was invented by wit and malice combined, and I have certificates and affidavits from nearly all the leading Union men in the district and count to that effect. The truth is I took no part in the election; never attended a public meeting and never publicly or even privately expressed any opinion about it or the question upon which the canvas was.

Colonel Welch says he was also informed that I had forced my son to go to Virginia and join the Confederate Army. This is equally false, and I produced to General Dix abundant proof of this. My son and my only son did join the Confederate Army, but against my earnest entreaties and the tears of his mother and sisters. I commanded him not to go. I held out every inducement for him to remain that I was able to hold out. In truth when he did go I denounced him for doing so and ordered him to hold no further intercourse with me or any of the family. But he was twenty-four years old and beyond my authority.

. . . when the First Massachusetts Regiment and Colonel Cowdin visited this county some two months ago they sought to arrest men. I was driven from my home, family and business and lived in the woods for weeks. They visited my house the night of their arrival and searched for me; they placed a guard of 150 men around it; they killed my hogs, sheep, poultry and wantonly shot the best horse on the farm, for all of which I was never offered a cent nor have I since received a cent. Now, all this has been endured by as loyal a citizen as any in this State; so help me Heaven I have never perpetrated or dreamt of perpetrating an act that malice could construe into treason . . . but notwithstanding all my persecutions I have sternly refused (although importuned very often to do so) to aid those in arms against the Government. Many person have passed through this county on their way to Virginia, and contraband of many kinds have also been sent by the same route and I have been called upon to assist in the work. I have always refused to have anything to do with such matters . . .

For all this I have incurred the displeasure of some of my best friends and looked upon with suspicion and distrust by many others. But for my loyalty I have received nothing but persecution . . .[3]

Fredonia Censor: Published January 1, 1862

FROM THE THIRD REGIMENT.

Camp Wool, Dec. 22.

Dear Uncles:—

Since I wrote you last there has been little going on except target shooting with our new rifles. A week or ten days since, a notice was posted upon the bulletin board, signed by the Col., Lieut. Col., and Major, that at 2 P.M., on Christmas, the man who made the three best shots, string measure, would receive a $50 gold medal. The target is to be at 300 yards, six feet high and 22 inches wide. Of course all the regiment cannot complete, but all are having a chance to try their skill now, and a record of their practice being kept. The best marksman of each company will strive for the prize. Our rifles are a first rate arm, and are easier to clean than the muskets. Of our practice thus far, the best has been done by Hiram Gilbert, (I speak of Co. D only) he having upon one occasion fired three bullets in succession through a bull's eye of about four inches in diameter, at 100 yards. The best shot of the three bent the nail, and had it not been for the conical shape of the ball, would have driven it. As it was it bent the nail, and glanced a little to one side. Van Houten, Post and Lewis, have also done some very fair shooting, but I think Gilbert will be the champion. When we fired at 100 yards the target was cut so that it hardly held together while it was brought in. The last distance we fired was at 250 yards, and of course, it took the best marksmen to do much execution.

We are now very busy in preparing our winter quarters. We build log walls about twelve feet long and ten wide and put two tents over them for a roof.—In the habitation thus formed, twelve men are lodged. The walls are chinked and are filled with clay, and are as warm as we need or desire. The canvass

Figure 5.5. Civil War winter quarters. Though the details may have varied slightly, the general design of winter quarters built by soldiers on both sides was about the same. *Courtesy of Library of Congress.*

overhead lets in light, and the ample fireplace with its blazing fire is an excellent ventilator. We suffer but little from cold even when the weather is inclement, having become by our constant out-door life hardened like Gipseys or Indians.—Indeed, such is the indurating effect of this unconstrained life, that it is to me no hardship to stretch myself upon the ground wrapped in my blanket, and so pass the night. The last night I was upon guard. I did so rather than to be in the crowded and uncomfortable guard house. Another of our men kept me company, and declared that he had spent a very comfortable night. Thus you see that "dormer au planair coma un brave" is an accomplishment not confined to the Zouaves or the Chasseurs d' Afrique.

There are probably very few men in the regiment who have not read the speech of Senator Lane, and it is most enthusiastically endorsed. We are now earning our money very easily and are very comfortable; but ease and comfort are not what we enlisted for. We enlisted for the prosecution of the war, and we do not desire any rest and idleness which defers the forwarding of that end. Gen. Lane is right; we *do not* desire winter quarters. The season has been thus far wonderfully favorable for a campaign. Indeed, I may call it providential that we have had so little rain, and such bright, sunny days. Why, then, is prompt, vigorous action delayed? Gen. Lane spoke truly when he said that idleness was the bane of the volunteer. We left our homes cheerfully at our country's call, and we will remain until it no longer needs us, but not a day—not an hour longer. I do not believe that there is in the service, a brigade of volunteers drilled as our own; I do not believe that there is in the service better fighting material than ours. Why, then, are we placed here in a position where the prospect of *real* service seems hardly less remote than doomsday itself. It is true that we are not absolutely useless, for we hold the rebels in check, but a couple of brigades of comparatively raw recruits could do that, aided as we are by such efficient artillery.

As regards vigilance, there is no such faithful sentry as a raw recruit, and no such exacting and watchful officer as one who is new to his position, and is endeavoring to prove himself capable and worthy of it. I hope, for the good name of our commanders, that it will prove that this apparent apathy is assumed, and that we shall soon hear of some decisive blow having fallen.

As regards the health of our men, I send you the hospital list of Co.'s B, D, G, H; Co. E, having no men in the hospital. The result of its perusal will show you that not over three per cent of our men require hospital attendance—surely not a bad account for a regiment;

Of Co. B, in Hospital—E. L. Homer, Convalescent; E. Porter, Fever, serious; Hosier, Convalescent.

Of Co. D—Sergt. C. A. Foss, Fever—doing well; J. B. Sprague, Convalescent; A. A. Page, Convalescent.

Of Co. G—Berry, Typhoid fever—doing well; Strain, Remittent fever; Bowdish, Convalescent; Bond, Fever; Wheeler, Diarrhea.

Of Co. H—Rogers, doing well; LaPort, doing well; Butchers, doing well.

The health of the Metropolitan companies is still better than ours, for the fellows who used to sleep on coal boxes, and who never owned a decent suit in their lives, are better fed and clothed, and in some instances, better lodged than when at home.

Last night we were gladdened by the news that our friends S. D. Caldwell and Dr. Benedict had arrived in camp. This morning they attended the regimental inspection, and can tell you upon their return what they think of us and our arms and equipments, and our quarters. This afternoon we had a battalion drill, and I suppose for their especial benefit. While out we went through a great variety of maneuvers, and formed square several times. To give you a fair idea of our capacity to guard against cavalry, we ought to have formed the square upon the run, but this Col. Taylor unfortunately omitted. Perhaps, however, he reserved that for another day. Capt. Doyle, who had been unwell, was out, and is apparently all right. Lieut. Howard, I regret to say, is still very ill. The rebels still fire at passing vessels, but I have not heard of their hurting any one as yet. The pickets still continue to blackguard across the river, and whenever a new company goes down they tease the rebels until they fire a few shots—"just for the sake of seeing the fun." "What are you here for, you Yankee sons of b—s?" sings out a Confederate picket across the river; "do you want the knapsacks you dropped at Bull Run?" "No," cries the Federal, "we found them at Port Royal." And so it is kept up whenever the state of the wind will allow. Col. Graham and his regiment are held by the rebels in especial detestation on account of their daring excursion upon the "sacred soil" a short time since, and particularly because they slipped through their fingers so cleverly when they retreated back to the Maryland side.

The rain is now pattering overhead, and the beautiful weather we have enjoyed of late is, I fear, at an end. The roads are now hard and good, but if the rain continues long they will soon be as bad as ever. We are using up a vast amount of firewood and timber, and I suppose that our planter landlords will bring in a bill of damages against the Government to a much greater amount than their estates would have sold for even in the palmiest days of corn and tobacco planting. At the same time I suppose a terrific howl will be raised about ruined homes and wasted forests, though the impudent rascals know that for every dollar's worth of property wasted they will get two eventually. The Southern people speak of us as a nation of pedlars. Well, perhaps we are, but if I had a relative who would charge such prices for such farm products as we soldiers buy, and need, as those "chivalrous planters" and their high bred ladies and children do, I would, if possible, conceal that any tie of relationship existed. "We waste farms!" Why, that recalls to my mind what Ira Lewis, our ambulance driver said: "I am ready," quoth Ira, "to die for my country, but I don't want to die here, for I don't believe that any one buried in such a miserable soil as this would ever come up, not even at the call of the last trump." I don't really believe that anything covered with such poor soil would ever come up. It is a plain and undeniable fact that this war is a source of immense wealth to Maryland, even to its traitors.

Arthur.

P.S.—We shall now get a daily mail from the Capital.

"Dormer au planair comme un brave": "Sleep in the open like a courageous (person)."

"Call of the last trump": the final trumpet call that will awaken and raise the dead on the Day of Judgment.

Camp Wool Dec. 23rd, 1861

Dear Mother,

As it is a rainy day I take the opportunity of writing once more to you. My watch having again got out of order I sent it this morning by Risley French of Dunkirk to Uncle Willard of whom you can get it. I have got a hunter case lever with a compass upon its face which is better suited for a soldier (or a schoolmaster) than an open faced watch. I paid $15.00 for it but took care to have it examined by a jeweler and a particular friend of mine who is a judge of such things, first. Both appraised it at the price I paid and it keeps exact time. I have just written a letter to Leucy which will go to Fortress Monroe and will there be examined and forwarded. Many letters are sent in this manner under flags of truce and the manner prescribed is as follows—

The letter must be sent open for examination and must be confined to one page only. The postage is ten cents. S. D. Caldwell of Dunkirk and Dr. Benedict of that place—both prominent citizens are here and have been taking a good look at our quarters and have seen us drill. Major Stevens called me up and I received a special introduction as the nephew of the McKinstrys' and the Censor correspondent. I used to be very much embarrassed about writing but Dr. Irwin tendered me to the use of his desk so that now I can write a long letter very conveniently. All this writing improves my position and I don't see how on earth a private soldier can enjoy himself better than I do.—nor a non-commissioned officer either. You see that I save a little for I have made a watch and revolver at least and clothes enough to last a good while beside. My shirts are just about as good as when I left home and I wear no others. Give me the good home made yet.

Lucius Jones continues just about so—able to be about but not fit for duty. Capt. Doyle agreeably to Mr. Jones request, applied for a furlough but Dr. Irwin replied that it was of little use for it takes so long to do these things that the patient generally dies or gets well before any action is taken. First you see Dr. Irwin recommends the furlough in writing—then the Brigade surgeon takes it up and sends the recommendation (with his written approval) to the division Surgeon and this last sends it in the same ceremonious manner to Washington.

There it is deliberated upon and the answer returned in the same manner. Now you know what red tape is dont you? Lucius however is well cared for and gets his food from the captains mess tent—an unusual favor. Furthermore Doyle says if he don't get better he will get his discharge at any rate. I got that Republican with your letter and I tell you I devoured it. We get the N.Y. journals but the Republican is ahead of them all in everything that makes a family paper acceptable. I would not however advise you sending them for very many papers miscarry. A little sleet has fallen to day but melting as it fell. When you get that watch of mine just take it to the village and get it fixed. It will cost five shillings and then you will have a watch to carry with you whenever away from home. I will see that you get more spending money next pay day and that is not far off. And now tell me how Frank and Lute get on, how is Father. Have you money to meet your taxes. If you have not let me know how much you are short, and at once too. How does Newton progress with his school. How do Petes folks sagaciate. How do Abert Knapp and wife get on. Lot of love Jennie and John. I wish I could see little Milly. She was getting to like me a good deal when I came away.

We get a daily mail now and letters get here within two or three hours of the Camp Caldwell time. They come by steamer and perhaps one will come to-night.

Your aff. son Arthur.

Sagaciate: thrive.

Fredonia Censor: Published January 15, 1862

FROM THE THIRD REGIMENT.

Camp Wool, 35 miles below Washington, Dec. 30, '61.

Dear Uncles:—

Still we jog on pretty much in the old way, putting up log houses; we are now at work on the last one in our company, and cutting firewood to keep us warm, and "cleaning house" and washing clothes or cooking for the rest of the time.

Last Christmas dawned upon us cold and gloomy, and for a while I thought that it would turn out a terribly dull day. After a time, however, I saw sundry turkeys, geese and chickens being carried over to the bakery, where they were baked nicely. In all these, however, I had no share, and, being on duty, my holiday amounted to little enough. The day, however, wore slowly around, and at last I was back in our house, and then the prospects brightened very materially. First, Bevier popped in with a package of raisins, and Moon immediately dragged forth from its hiding place a large pan of flour. Earnestly and faithfully did Moon labor upon the growing lump of dough in the center, and at last the whole mass was of the proper consistency. Meanwhile the pot was heating over our fire, and soon the water boiled and bubbled right merrily around a giant plum pudding. With what fond expectations and growing appetites did we watch that pot, and how liberally did we feed that fire; and picture, if you can, the excitement when the pot upset and rolled out upon the floor; imagine, if you can, our joy when we found that the pudding had already risen so as to fit the sides of the kettle as snugly as a minie bullet in its grooves. The pudding could not come out, and was safe. Well, we added more water, and after a while our pudding was done. By this time Lewis had prepared some capital sauce, and all hands fell to and ate it. The pudding was loudly extolled by all, and Pugh and Moon thought that if they had only just such another between them, they could go to sleep contented. After unanimously voting in favor of having another, New Years, we put away our dishes, heaped on more wood, and seated ourselves around our blazing fire, where we chatted and told stories of the remainder of the evening.

Late as it is we still enjoy fine, open weather. A few years ago I skated upon some of the estuaries of the Chesapeake Bay, where the ice was five or six inches thick. It is now as late in the season as then, but I have not seen ice sufficiently strong to bear a man's weight. All this, however, seems to make no impression upon the Rip Van Winkles at Washington, and we are still running up bills, which we must pay in after years, to an extent large enough to buy our public buildings at Washington over and over again. As the 200,000 men who compose the army of the Potomac, simply a special police guard, detailed as watchmen for the Capital, or are they a body of thinking, reasoning, active men, who volunteered to quell insurrection, and not to stand idly upon their arms while such a mighty struggle is going on around them. We have seen brave Generals and gallant men defeated by overwhelming odds, and we have felt that it was not their fault, nor the enemy's merit which lost us the day, but the incapacity of those who sent them into danger without an adequate support. We have heard much of the probability of England's interference, but like the stroke of steel upon a flint, it only elicits fire. The sentiment, and the unvarying sentiment here is, that if England wants Slidell and Mason she can take them—when our vast army of volunteers is annihilated, and not before.

Which will be the gainer, she or we? Perhaps before they had advanced far in our matters, they would find business enough at home. How long would a war between England and the United States continue, before the green banner would float over Ireland, and yet another realm be lost to the British Lion. Too many exiled heroes have made our soil their home for Ireland to deliberate long which side she will espouse in the struggle.—Such men as Col. Corcoran and Thomas Francis Meagher could at a word rouse a storm that England could never quell, if backed by the United States. In our New York companies the Irish element is largely predominant, and a hate of England and a love of Ireland seem to have been imbibed with their natal air.

As regards clothing, we are tolerably well off. For a time, after we left Camp Caldwell, we were very short of under clothing, but four or five hundred suits were distributed among us a while since, making a suit per man, and that improved our condition considerably. Last summer we got under clothing of a very poor quality of flannel, but still by courtesy supposed to be wool, while now we get very nice *summer* shirts and drawers of white cotton. They are very good, but I must say they are very unseasonable, and by no means the thing for a winter campaign. If we remain here during the winter we shall not suffer, but if we should be required to make any long or forced marches, we should wish that our cotton was turned to good home made flannel. A soldier can carry but little clothing, but that should be the very best for durability and comfort. I sent north for flannels in preference to taking the stuff which was, for a while last fall, palmed off upon the soldiers. As regards our food, I do not believe the average of our men get enough to satisfy hunger, though the imperative demands of nature may be supplied. Our bill of fare for the day is substantially as follows. For breakfast, a pint of coffee and a loaf of bread weighing from twenty to twenty-two ounces, which must last all day. For dinner, meat, and if fresh, soup. For supper, coffee. Now and then we get baked beans, but not *too* often. Vegetables (dried and pressed,) we get in our soup, but not to the extent the law allows. Potatoes we get at irregular intervals. On the whole, we do not fare quite as well as State prison convicts, but I do not feel disposed to complain much, so long as my allowances and pay together suffice for my support. I think a man can lay up about one half of his pay, if he is economical and prudent, but he must possess both qualities in a higher degree than I do, if he saves more than that.

Yesterday I borrowed Major Stevens' glass and went down to the river. Very few rebels were to be seen, and there was no firing. On approaching Budd's Ferry we (Bevier and I,) were stopped by a picket, who told us that we could not be permitted to approach the battery. A judicious application of soft soap, and a good long look through the spy-glass, however, mollified him so far that he ventured to hint that a rather circuitous route, which he pointed out, would take us to the desired point without his seeing us. We followed his advice and were soon down by the river side, a little to the right of our battery. Across the river in a north westerly direction, (it here runs nearly north and south,) we saw a battery the rebels were erecting, and were pretty confident that we made out two heavy iron guns. Further up I thought I saw a field battery, but the distance was too great to be positive. We then sauntered along down to our own little two-gun battery at the ferry. This was situated in a pit upon the brow of a hill, and dug down in front of the muzzles of the guns, for embrasures. Opposite was the rebel battery on Shipping Point.

Here the glass enabled me to detect the glitter of their brass field pieces. There were no other cannon in sight, though the works were apparently in an unfinished state, and others might have been near. Farther down and at some distance from the river rises a lofty hill, whose summit is crowned by a rebel Fort. Upon a level flat, near the river, I saw a number of soldiers in dark uniforms whom I supposed to be pickets. At the battery was a sentry in a light blue overcoat like our own, and an F.F.V. cit. in the inevitable dirty white "nigger cloth" coat. I also saw a ferry boat plying to and from between Shipping Pt. and Quantico Creek, where the Page still lies. The passengers were evidently in uniform. The sound of the oars in the rowlock could be heard, though the boat was barely distinguishable by the naked eye. The pickets are no longer allowed to converse with the rebels on the ground that they provoke them to throwing shells a little too thick for their safety. Directly in front of our battery was a hole which would hold at a moderate estimate ten bushels. Around were a lot of other holes of various dimensions; all caused by shell explosions, hence I admitted the cogency of the reasons why pickets should not swear at each other. The rebels appear to have only two batteries which are fortified viz.: The one opposite Budd's Ferry and one perhaps two and a half or three miles up the river and opposite the mouth of Chickamoxen creek. This last was unmasked by one of our gun boats when Capt. Doyle and Lieut. Mason were down a couple of weeks since. Bevier and I now began to get tired of straining our eyes at such distant objects and started for home. On our way we ascended a high hill and paused a while to gaze at the beautiful panorama at our feet.

Beneath us like a map lay the beautiful valley of the Potomac and for miles every bay and inlet of the river could be seen sparkling and glittering in the light of the slowly setting sun. Very rarely indeed have I gazed upon a fairer landscape

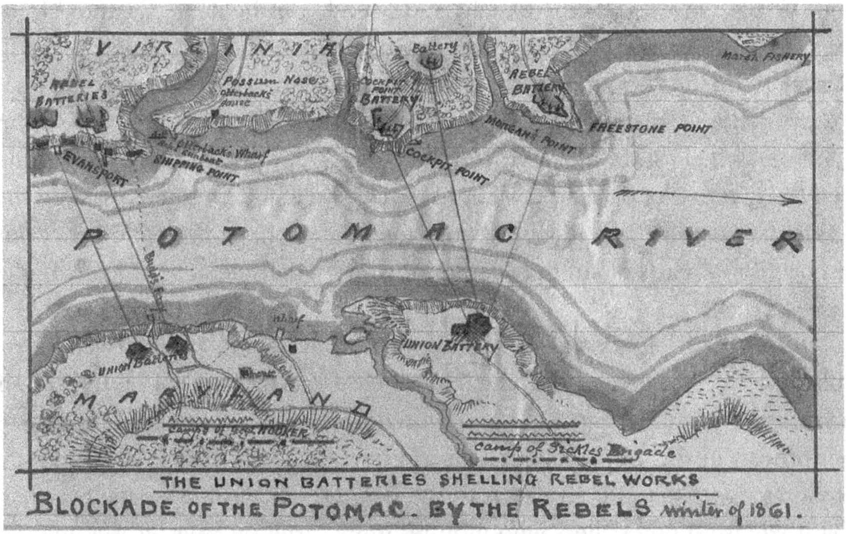

Figure 5.6. Blockade map drawing. In this sketch by Robert Knox Sneden, the position of the Confederate batteries relative to the Union camps is clear. Sneden fails to identify Chicamuxen Creek, which separates Hooker from Sickles, nor does he include Mattawoman Creek, which forms the northern edge of Sickles's camp. The 3rd Regiment moved to Camp Wool, which by Arthur's estimation is about seven or eight miles farther south and two miles or so below Budd's Ferry. *Courtesy of Library of Congress.*

and no one unacquainted with the facts would suppose that two hostile armies lay encamped so near. After I had taken a rough map of the river we started once more for home. On our way we passed two batteries of rifle guns—six guns being a battery. We passed very near the 11th Mass. Reg. and saw them out on dress parade. They were drilling in the manual, and I never saw pieces better handled in my life. They were building houses—regular hotels—which shelter whole companies and give plenty of room to all. I was in one a few days since, and admired it very much. Upon one side of the building were the bunks three tiers high and looking—though abundantly large—like the pigeon holes in a post office as you looked at them in connexion with that immense building. Upon the opposite side were their minie rifles standing in their racks, while at each end of the building was a huge fireplace. The walls were of logs, and the roof was of boards, and the only item of expense in the whole arrangement.

We have lost several men lately, and I send you the names of those from Chautauqua County: Of Co. B, Porter died upon the 25th. Of Co. G, J. Wheeler and D. Warren, on the night of the 29th. There is no doubt that much of the sickness in our regiment has been really contracted at Camp Caldwell. Much, I am inclined to think, came from drinking of and bathing in a creek near that place, the waters of which were not considered safe by the residents, even to bathe in. It does not follow that the fever would break out at once, for a man's blood may be poisoned for a considerable time before he suspects the fact.

In our new log houses, those who are not severely ill are pretty comfortable. A fair degree of attention is paid to their wants by their comrades, and, if necessary, by their officers. Of course I am not posted in all that goes on among our officers in this respect, but so far as I have seen, the officers of Co. H are ahead as regards careful attention to the sick. Dr. Irwin informs me however, that there is no officer here who inquires more earnestly after his sick men in the hospital than Capt. Abell, and here it may not be out of place to add that his men feel the utmost respect for him as a commander, and confidence in his abilities. His stern manner at first made him many enemies, but now that he is better known no man could fill his place. There are very few men with whom Co. D would feel satisfied, but if we were to ballot for officers there would be no change whatever. Perhaps you will think this rather a grumbling letter, and that I am a little blue. In good sober truth, I should enjoy myself capitally were it not for the fact that I feel, as all must feel, the necessity of something beside this "masterly inactivity." By the by what a capital joke upon the "Home Guards" it would be, should a war with Great Britain ensue. It is true that we stand upon rather unstable ground with regard to the Mason and Slidell affair, but I think that England of all nations should be the last to complain, and of all the opinions I have heard expressed upon this camp ground, not one has differed. All seem ready to stand by the Stars and Stripes to the last.

Yours as ever,

Arthur.

Slidell and Mason: the US Navy captured two Confederate envoys (John Slidell and James Mason) from a British Royal Mail steamer, *Trent*; the British government protested vigorously. The "*Trent* Affair" threatened war between the US and the United Kingdom. The United States ended the incident by releasing the envoys.

Col. Corcoran and Thomas Francis Meagher: Michael Corcoran and Thomas Francis Meagher, both officers in the 69th New York, both strong Irish nationalists/activists.

Editorial Note

While the Navy may have declared the Potomac River closed to large vessels, many smaller craft still navigate the river and draw the occasional shot from Rebel batteries on the Virginia side. Arthur and his mates now settle in for winter.

Chapter 6

All Frivolous Subjects Are Avoided

January 1862—Occupation of Lower Maryland

Maintaining morale is the focus of Arthur and his mates • Artillery duels between Reb batteries, Hooker's cannons, and Navy ships continue • General Dan Sickles is frequently gone from camp

Editorial Note

With the pace of the war slowing in the face of winter, both men and officers look for ways to maintain morale. The regiment-wide shooting contest, sponsored by the top commanders, finally is held, with its outcome delighting the men of Company D.

Fredonia Censor: Published January 22, 1862

FROM THE THIRD REGIMENT

Camp Wool, 35 miles below Washington, Jan. 2, 1862.

Dear Uncles:—

The shooting match which was given out for Christmas was finally postponed till New Year's. So yesterday, at 10 A.M. the ten best marksmen of each company marched out to compete for the golden prize. There was a good deal of excitement, and bets ran high. Co. I of Delaware County, counts some capital shots among its members, and they had even been so confident as to declare that the yellow metal would hereafter grace one of their company. Alas for human calculations. The First Sergeant of Co. D managed to put in three telling shots (purely accidental of course) and that evening Wm. H. Post of Dunkirk was called out, when the parade was formed and received from Col. Taylor the beautiful trophy. Billy has been the object of all sorts of abuse since, from the disappointed competitors, who have all along been of the opinion that "the Chautauqua element was the ruination of the 3d Reg." and are now more convinced of it than ever.

They accuse Post of taking private practice (which was not permitted) and in fact of every species of unfairness. All this of course amuses us vastly, and, as for "Chautauqua monopoly," our county not only has the ascendency but it is likely to keep it for an indefinite length of time. And why should we not? At the time when the Tribune attacked Sickles so savagely, it cost the brigade a thousand men, and had the Chautauqua boys given way, the stampede would have become general and the 3d Regiment would not to day have existed.

But I am digressing. The day was clear but rather cold, though overcoats were not exactly indispensable, and the wind pretty strong. The target was at full 300 yards and, though the sun shone fair upon it, the wind crossed our line of shot in such a manner as to make it very difficult to take aim. Markers were established near the target, and also men to pass the numbers of the shots between the umpires and the markers. The umpires were Captains Doyle, Willard, and Chadwick.

The marksmen were drawn up in line, and numbers written upon bits of paper were handed round in a cap. Each man drew one, and, when the number upon his ticket was called, stepped forth to shoot.

Post's number was 49, and the manner of procedure was as follows: Capt. Willard called "No 49." (Post) stepped forth, aimed, and fired. No. 49 was passed down the line to the marker, who found the bullet hole and marked that number by it. He then stepped aside and called out "49 marked." Had Post missed he would have called "49 blank." No. 50 was then called and Post retired. All cheating and deception were rendered impossible by this arrangement, and the markers did not know for what persons the numbers stood. In shooting we were allowed to fire in any position except from a dead rest. Post shot off-hand, taking a very quick aim. The trial took over three hours, and three rounds were fired.

Our New Year passed off pleasantly enough, and very quietly. The new cook house is completed, the clay oven in first rate running order, and, for the first time since its entry into active service, Co. D had a good, hearty, substantial dinner of roast beef. Extra rations of bread were served out. Pork and beans were baked in quantities proportionate to the occasion, and all was done that could be done to give the opening year a fair commencement. Ote Luce deserves credit for his oven and we expect that roast will hereafter supersede boiled beef, whenever suitable pieces are allotted to us. Luce is a sort of steward, and draws the rations, and has the general superintendance of cooking arrangements. Wright and Neupling do the cooking, and "old Joe" who is a graduate of the British army, brings them the water. Joe thinks these volunteers a hard set, and declares that they are no soldiers at all.

Jan. 3d—The upper battery of the rebels was silenced yesterday by our gunboats. The battery on Shipping Point opened to day at a schooner which was going down, and gave her a shot that made her stagger, but she stood on and run the blockade. Our battery was not silent. When they (apparently) hit the vessel they (the rebels) ran up the Confederate flag. Our battery replied to the taunt with a shell which burst in the rebel battery, and when the smoke of the explosion cleared away *the flag was gone*. The rebels cheered lustily when they fired, but when our shell burst they did not, apparently, see "where the laughter came in," and they have been very quiet since.

Post wears his honors with all proper humility, and is not so far set up but that he still deigns to converse now and then with us "high privates in the rear rank." The medal is a very fine one and would pass current for $50 anywhere. It bears upon one side this inscription. "Presented by the Field Officers of the 3d Reg. Excelsior Brigade, U.S. Volunteers, to ________ the best marksman. Dec. 25th, 1861." Upon the reverse is the likeness of Washington. The whole is very finely executed.

Jan. 5th—I sit down this evening with a firm determination to bring this letter to a close. Our last log house is now up, and Sergeant Brooks and his machine shop boys are still ahead and have by all odds the best and neatest house in the regiment. Among its other extras it has an oven for private pork and beans, and fowls. Of a verity, Brooks and his comrades will never die of cold or hunger. And this is precisely as it should be; an invading army should contain within itself the elements necessary to sustain itself, unaided if need be, in a hostile country.

It is one of the disadvantages under which a correspondent labors when at such a distance, that it is so long ere a mistake can be corrected. In the sick list of our regiment I see the following one which I myself am to blame for. Instead of Chapin Tiffany at General hospital, it was Chapin Lyon, of Co. B. We have not heard from those in that hospital for several weeks, or I would include them in this list of to-day.

In regimental hospital:

Of Co. B—E. L. Homer, convalescent; Richardson, convalescent; Bliss, sore throat.

Of Co. D—Sergeant C. A. Foss, J. B. Sprague,[weak only] and will rejoin their company soon.

Co. E—None in hospital.

Co. H—Bauer, Wild, Fever.

Co. G—Bond, Strain, convalescent, Mason, Tail, Jones, Fever.

Died of Co. G Miles Jones this morning. I report the death of Otto Nelson Co. B who died on the night the first sick list was made out, is not recorded.

We drill but little lately and occupy ourselves mostly with "internal improvements." Among the latest is a plan for the company to engage a good professional cook, and pay him by assessing the company. The plan meets general favor, and ought to have been adopted months ago. A box has arrived, I hear, from Dunkirk, with clothing for our men. I have not yet seen its contents. Co. H had one some time since.

Yours as ever,
Arthur

"Old Joe": likely Joseph H. Mewhiney, age thirty, from Dunkirk. He was the only "Joe" in Company D at the time.

Tail: likely John H. Teale, died January 8, 1862, of disease in Camp Wool, Maryland.

Editorial Note

With winter setting in and the chance of any offensive action nil, Arthur and his mates focused on the routine of camp life and various pursuits to ease the boredom. Sadly, the sick list continues to lengthen as do reports of men who had succumbed to the many ailments of the season.

Camp Wool, Jan. 6th 1862

Dear Mother,

I have been very busy of late in helping to fix tents or rather houses for the company, but I think it is time to turn over a new leaf and tell the best friend I have how I prosper. On New Years eve I got a very long letter from Wint. In which he told me that my articles were looked for by many with interest and that they were becoming an attractive feature of the paper. I have endeavored all along to make the Censor the military gazette of the county and I believe that I am succeeding. There is no other paper which has a regular table of the sicknesses and deaths and I have a private opinion of my own that there is no

Figure 6.1 (facing page). McKinstry letter on 72nd letterhead. *Courtesy of Ulysses S. Grant Presidential Library.*

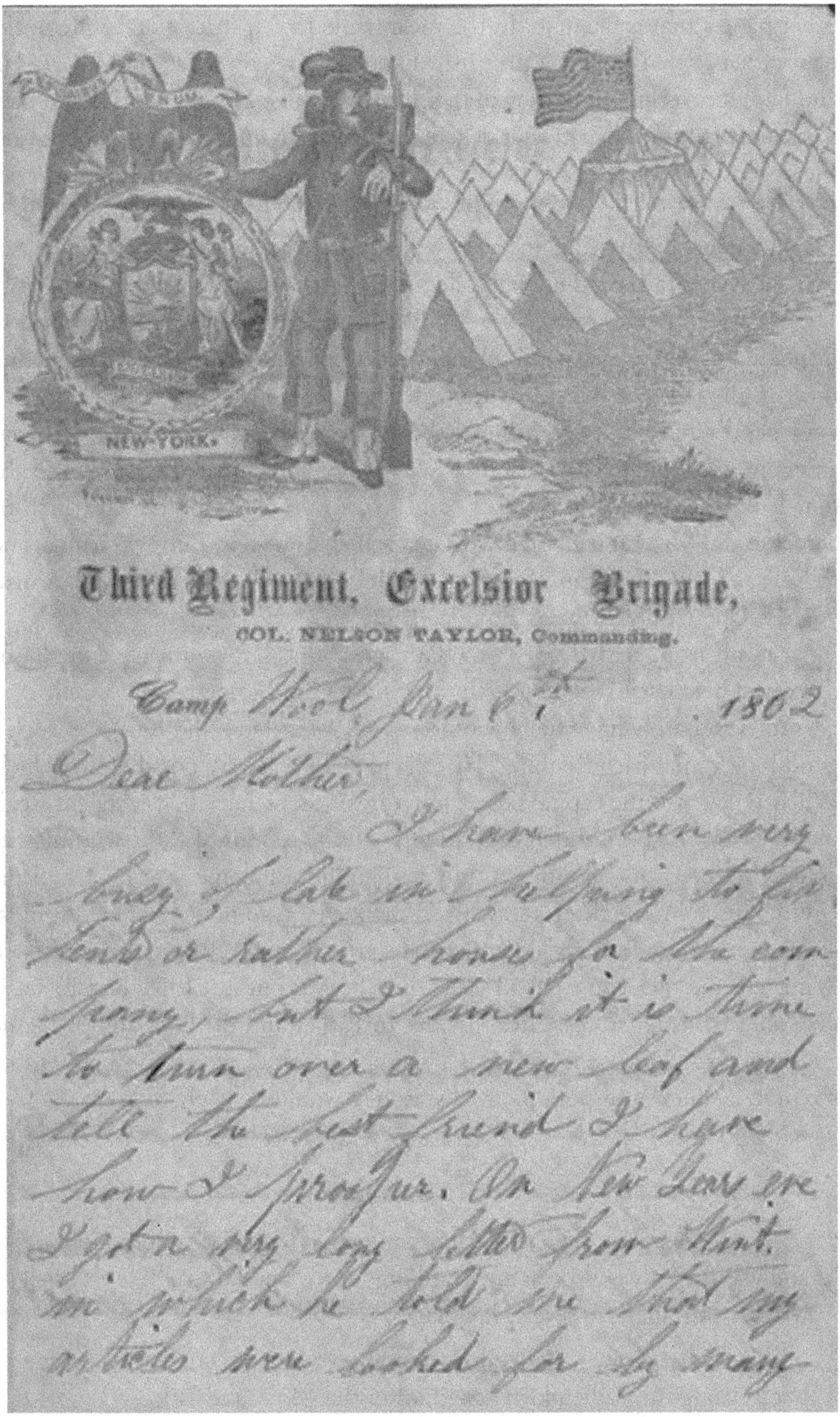

Third Regiment, Excelsior Brigade,

COL. NELSON TAYLOR, Commanding.

Camp Wool, Jan 6th . 1862

Dear Mother,

I have been very busy of late in helping to fix tents or rather houses for the company, but I think it is time to turn over a new leaf and tell the best friend I have how I prosper. On New Years eve I got a very long letter from Matt. in which he told me that my articles were looked for by many other papers that is likely to. In the meanwhile I keep strictly up to the duties of a soldier so that when I want a little liberty I can get it. My health is very fair and I am recovering something of the elasticity which I lost in Mexico and have never enjoyed since in a greater degree than now. There is just snow enough on the ground to whiten it a little but I am so hardened to this life that I do not suffer as much as I used to at home under the most favorable circumstances.

Just now I am writing upon my bed and the backlog is getting well ablaze, while we have oak wood enough piled up to last 24 hours.

My watch proves to be a very good one and I could sell it at a profit if so disposed but when I get a good thing it is my general disposition to keep it and not run the risk of having a poorer article palmed off upon me. If I only had your pantry and library to run to I should feel very contented. As it is I have access to a few French books and as we have a pretty smart Dutchman in the tent I mean to get an "Ollendorf" and make him teach me Dutch which he agrees to do. My tent is floored with heavy plank hewn by our own hands, and so long as I have an ax, an auger, and a jack knife I will agree to live as warm as you do. Upon a pinch the ax alone will answer.

I heard from Aunt Eliza a few days ago and as letters must eventually be destroyed here I send it along with this, and Cyrus' business card as well.

You can hardly imagine how much good Wints letter did me it was such a good long genial friendly thing. He tells me that it is very possible that Uncle Willard may visit the capital before long. If so I hope he will visit the 3d Regiment. There has been much exultation here on account of Posts winning the gold prize medal for shooting. Old Chautauqua still comes out no-1 and the city roughs are more disgusted with us than ever. And now Mother you must either write yourself or make Frank do it so that I can hear from home oftener. Wint tells me that you were all well when he was out but I like best to see it over your own signatures. Give my love to Father and the boys and to Jennie and John. Lute Jones sent home for a box, if it has not been sent just remember me in it. A chicken or pork pie well seasoned would be likely to keep.

Your aff. son

Arthur.

Smart Dutchman: Claus Wriborg migrated to America from Holland and was the only child of a high-ranking Dutch naval officer. He was well written and fluent in several languages.

"Ollendorf": Henri Ollendorff produced a series of language-learning books using the "Ollendorff" method in the 1830s and '40s.

Camp Wool Jan. 10th 1862

Dear Uncle Wint,

I believe that I will consume an inch or so of candle in private confab with you this evening. Roll call is over and the boys are tumbling off to bed so that I shall be very little disturbed in the operation. All without is wet and nasty and the road are getting to be abominable but our fireplace is filled with good honest oak—the roof of canvass is impervious to the rain—and we are enjoying as complete comfort as yourself. In fact however glad we might be to see the old familiar faces of our friends, I am pretty well satisfied that at least nine tenth of this regiment enjoy themselves quite as well as at home while the remaining tenth for the most part enjoy themselves better. Our duties have become so familiar that we do not mind them and we are all getting to be pretty fair cooks as well as carpenters and joiners. I can put up a good log house with fireplace and oven attached and all the tools required are an ax and auger. An ax alone will do tolerably. The fact is this volunteering is educating several hundred thousand pioneers in the very best possible manner. It is also fostering a military spirit among our young men which will never be extinguished and hereafter our county will never feel the lack of trained, disciplined, and ready soldiers. More than this it is bringing the people of our wide domain in contact with each other and acquainting them with each others characteristics and peculiarities in a manner and to an extent greater than any other cause could possibly have produced. In a word it is a school of military tactics and political economy and general information which we have long needed and whose benefits are worth their price, dear even as it is. The greatest objection I have to soldiering is that I cannot study to any great extent here. No matter! When I get back I can go to the academy and brush up old and attack new studies with all the keener relish from my long and unexpected vacation. To be sure I am getting to be rather old to take such a course but better late than never. We have little enough of reading matter here and if you would pack up a lot of old magazines and such matter our tent would be very glad indeed to pay the express. It does not pay to send good bound books for we might have to abandon them, but if you could find an old German "Ollendorff"—no matter how dilapidated I think I could put it to good use as we have a pretty well educated German in this tent and I mean soon or later to learn that tongue. Easy acquisition of languages you know is one of our family traits and I don't like to let even a campaign pass wholly unimproved. Mathematics is hardly practicable for I am liable to interruption at any time and Algebra and Geometry require an uninterrupted train of thought. I am getting to be pretty stout and tough so that I can bring our heavy loads of wood which we get at some distance—having already used up five or six acres—as well as the best of us. I must however admit that my lungs are rather irritable for I have not seen a day even during the past twelve months that I was entirely free from hoarseness. That is disagreeable but it has not interfered much with the performance of my duties, and for the past two months not at all. As regards food we have to buy a good deal or else go hungry. This is owing in part to the half gipsey life we lead and in part to the fact that the Comissary falls a little short now and then. A life so much of which is spent in the open air will cause a man to eat at a low estimate at least one third more than if lodged in a city and leading a comparatively idle life. We are pretty well off for clothing and our comfortable quarters have been the principal means of reducing our sick in hospital to seven only, about 1/150 of our regiment. G Company (Westfield) has lost two more men. I don't really see how so many miserable soldiers were ever collected in one town. There is no life—no vitality—no ambition in the company, and they have at least twice as many sick as any other. There seems to be no stamina there, and when a man gets sick he gives up at once and lies upon his back a helplessly as a turtle. I have little patience with such for I know that a stout heart and a determined will is worth more than medicine sometimes. Some men will live on despite the predictions of medical men and against all probabilities through the force of their own unyielding will. They will not die, and their unfailing courage sustains the sinking forces of nature. You smile perhaps at my earnestness but I formed my opinion at New Orleans, during the yellow fever season, when men died around me like rotten sheep, and I have seen some of the same characteristics in this acclimating fever.

Our mail has not come for three days. I supposed that the failure for the last two days was occasioned by the dense fog which must have rendered it difficult to pilot a vessel safely down. As I shall write you my customary letter for the Censor I think I will quit to night. That hospital list is something all cannot get access to with any such accuracy as I can and you are likely to remain its sole publishers. "Kerleighs" nose was broken in respect to all hospital news weeks ago but the present Ward Master is a friend of mine and Dr. Irwin is also very obliging.

Please send some magazines &c. &c. if you can and don't pay freight for the others in the tent will gladly do that. Write soon.

Your aff. Nephew,

Arthur

P.S. Love to Aunt and all.

Fredonia Censor: Published January 22, 1862

FROM THE THIRD REGIMENT.

Camp Wool, 35 mile below Washington, Jan. 14, '62.

Dear Uncles:—

We now jog along very quietly and contentedly in our log houses, drilling little, but still pretty busy in bringing wood and water, and occupying ourselves in those numberless little additions and improvements which are within our reach over here. We have made a good reservoir, which is fed by a fine spring, and which we keep a sentry over. The whole regiment is thus amply supplied with tolerable water. The good effect of our improved style of living is very manifest in the decrease of the sick list. There are now eleven men in our regimental hospital, and so far as I can learn, only two in general hospital. The list for our county is as follows:

In General Hospital, at Georgetown, O'Donahue, of Co. E. The last I heard from O'Donahue, he was doing well.

In General Hospital at Alexandria, Redmond Riley, of Co. D. Riley had two relapses, but is now able to walk upon the street, and will probably soon rejoin us.

In Regimental Hospital, of

Co. B—Hosier and Hubbard, fever.

Co. D—Stafford, cold.

Co. G—Bond, and Mason, convalescent.

Co. H—Wild, convalescent; McKernan, measles.

It may be a matter of interest to the readers of the Censor to know who nurse their sick, and something of the organization of our hospital. Our hospital steward in Fincke, of Co. B. Fincke has charge of the medicines, and by the by, is no mean doctor himself. C. L. Ryther of Co. D is Ward Master, and superintends the nursing of the sick, and sees that they do not lack bedding or clean clothing. The latter requisite has been abundantly supplied by our Chautauqua ladies, and our sick do not feel the need of clean shirts, drawers, and towels. John Finch of Co. B is head cook, and if I am any judge, he is a good one. When sick with fever, I could not eat my company rations, but while in hospital, unreasonable as a sick man will be, I never had reason or disposition to complain. Finch is assisted by Hanchett, of Co. C, who is also a very good cook. Ryther is assisted in nursing the sick by Dudley Fuller of Co. B.

Night before last I was informed that the sloop of war Pensacola,[1] was expected down that night, and was very much tempted to forego a night's sleep

Figure 6.2. USS *Pensacola* POSTWAR IMAGE. The USS *Pensacola* caused a stir when on January 11, 1862, she sailed from Alexandria, managing to evade Confederate batteries in the dead of night to join the fleet forming in the Gulf of Mexico. *Courtesy of Library of Congress.*

to witness the brilliant fireworks which were sure to attend her passage. After deliberating awhile, I gave up the project, for I had been hard at work carrying wood for Sunday and felt pretty tired. At about 5, however, on Sunday morning, I was awakened by heavy firing and whizzing shells. The course of the Pensacola was as easily traced by the ear as by the eye, and the distant flashing of the rebel guns was plainly seen through the canvass roofs of our houses. Each battery, as she passed, hurled its quota of cold iron, but the Pensacola had sent down her topmasts and lighter spars, and protected herself by a barge filled with bales of wet hay, which were as effectually a protection as Gen. Jackson's cotton bales. In respect to this caution, however, it was apparently needless, for I do not hear that a single shot was accurately aimed. Maj. Stevens was on the shore, and witnessed the whole affair. The Pensacola shot silently past the batteries in our immediate vicinity, but some time after, we heard a couple of rattling, crashing, broadsides down the river, which led us to suspect that she had at last assumed the offensive.

Yours truly,
Arthur

USS *Pensacola*: screw steamer launched in 1859. She was 3,000 tons and 230 feet long. She carried 17 guns. Pensacola was decommissioned in 1911.

Gen. Jackson's cotton bales: at the Battle of New Orleans in 1815 (War of 1812), Andrew Jackson incorporated cotton bales into his defensive breastworks against British attack.

Other Voices: Report from USS *Pensacola* Regarding Potomac Passage

U.S. [STEAM] SLOOP PENSACOLA,
At Anchor off Liverpool Point, January 12, 1862—5:45 a.m.

Dear Sir:

We got abreast of Cockpit Point about 4:30 a.m. That battery fired three shells; the first passed directly over our smokestack, and only a little above it. None of their shot or shells struck us.

In passing the batteries of Shipping Point they fired about fifteen shot and shells at us, chiefly shells; most of them passed over the ship in a line from the starboard quarter to the after part of the fore rigging, a little above the tops. None of our rigging was injured or cut away. We did not return their fire at all, as we did not wish to indicate our position.

I have written a short telegraph to the Secretary of the Navy and given it to Lieutenant Commanding Magaw, who will send it to General Hooker to transmit.

Please send this letter to him immediately.

Very respectfully,
Henry W. Morris
Captain[1]

Other Voices: Confederate Dissatisfaction with Transit of USS *Pensacola*

HEADQUARTERS, *Evansport, January* 14, 1862.
General S. Cooper,
Adjutant and Inspector General, Richmond, Va.:

GENERAL:

On the morning of the 12th instant, between the hours of 4 and 5 o'clock, a vessel was discovered floating down under cover of the darkness of the night. She was then a little above the battery known as No. 1. The sentinel reported it to the corporal of the guard in the battery. He waited to see her, and then went to summon the guard for the guns always in the battery, but before they manned the guns she was so far past the battery that all the guns could not be brought to bear on her. From two guns, the new guns, and battery No. 2, a fire was opened, and it is certain she was struck several times. After she was discovered here a shot was fired from Cockpit. Had that battery seen her pass it and fired sooner, our men could have been at their guns in time; or had the corporal at once summoned the crews many more shots could have been fired.

The men were slow in getting to the guns until the first gun opened. As soon as fired at she put on all steam and, with the assistance of a tug, passed rapidly down . . .

Again I directed the officer of the guard of the infantry force which guards the river at night and which acts as a supporting force against surprise to instruct the pickets, in case of anything being seen on the river, to first warn the batteries and then their main guard. This duty they performed. Between 11 and 12 o'clock at night Captain Collins and I went with our glasses and made a long and careful survey of the river up and down, but could discern nothing. But notwithstanding my taking all these precautions, the vessel was not discovered until nearly abreast of Battery No. 1. She passed Cockpit undisturbed, and I presume unobserved, and whether the darkness did completely conceal her until the moment she was reported I cannot tell. One thing is certain, the corporal should not have waited to see her before he summoned the men. I mention all this, because I am very much dissatisfied that, with the unusual precautions for the night, the men were not more prompt, and that she escaped many shots that should have been fired at her. It was the third time the men had to man the guns during the night, but that is not uncommon.

As regards the blockade of the river, not a sail has passed for weeks. The river would be lifeless and desolate except for the eight or ten steamers always in sight above and below.

The plan of the Pensacola seems to have been, with the assistance of a tug, to float silently in the darkness by the batteries. She did not return a shot. I presume she left Alexandria and came directly down.

Very respectfully, your obedient servant,
S. G. FRENCH,
Brigadier-General, Commanding.[2]

Fredonia Censor: Published January 29, 1862

FROM THE THIRD REGIMENT.

Camp Wool, 35 miles below Washington, Jan. 14, '62.

[Continued from last week.]

After Inspection I got leave to go down to the shore. I struck directly across lots, and reached the river a mile or more below Budd's Ferry. Here were the inevitable pickets, whose orders were to allow no one to approach within hailing distance of the river, but they do not always live strictly up to orders, and I was allowed to enter an old fish house upon the shore, which furnished a capital post of observation. Here the Major's glass came into play once more, and all hands took a good look at the new battery in process of construction just below Shipping Pt. At present it consists of shapeless piles of dirt like a railway embankment, but the situation is a capital one, and if not looked after it will soon become very formidable. A large party were at work, but knocked off for dinner while I was gazing. While looking from this point I saw a white puff of smoke from the battery above Shipping Pt. followed soon after by the report of a gun. Pretty soon the sergeant of the pickets began to fear a visit from the

Lieutenant, so I started up toward the ferry. While at the fish house, however, I made a careful map of the vicinity, and would have made a sketch had my limited time allowed. Fortunately my watch contained a compass, so that I was able to place the cardinal points upon my map. I now hurried up above the ferry to ascertain the cause of the firing. It turned out to be some small vessel which had run into Chickamoxen Creek. I now began to edge carefully round toward the ferry, and to approach our own battery there. This required caution, for the pickets allow none to pass, but I avoided them and get pretty near. While taking a peep at Shipping Pt. I heard a roar from our guns and a shell went whizzing over the rebel battery and exploded in the woods beyond. The "Chivs" took up the gauntlet and three or four rebel guns enveloped their battery with dense volumes of smoke. In five or six seconds—perhaps more—the report came crashing over the water, followed by the peculiar rushing sound of coming shells. This sound resembles the blowing off of a good head of steam as much perhaps as anything. Soon after, the sound traveling evidently with about twice the speed of the shells, the missiles began to divide their attentions between our battery and a group of fifteen or twenty in which I was standing. I was greatly amused by the spectacle which followed. Some immediately assumed the position of a swimmer who is practicing his first lessons upon dry land. Others dodged behind trees or banks, some took to their heels, and others stood and took it as cool as cucumbers. As for myself, I was looking through the glass at the rebels, but the smoke was so dense that I got very little satisfaction. As I stood enjoying the treat, the fun grew fast and furious, and shells came whistling over and around us and buried themselves in the earth—followed immediately by a tall jet of sand forced upward by the exploding shell. Each shell which burst in the ground excavated a very respectable potato hole, but they did not remain long undisturbed, for there were many amateur soldiers beside myself who eagerly dug out the fragments to send home as souvenirs of their campaign in the land of secesh.

Our battery fired but the shells, one of which went beyond the rebels into the woods, and the other, which was extremely well aimed, burst about two seconds too soon. Our Artillery men cheered lustily at each successive failure of the rebels to do any harm and at last the latter got tired, and knocked off for a rest. As my watch admonished me that I must do some tall walking in order to get into camp in time for battalion drill, and the Captain had given me a pretty strong hint that I had better be present at that interesting ceremony, I now started for home, and thereby lost a view of another heavy cannonade.

My bunk has just jarred from the roar of a gun from the battery opposite Chickamoxen Creek. While looking across from the fish house, I got a good

Figure 6.3. A Federal ten-pound battery. A Federal ten-pound battery in action at Budd's Ferry firing at Confederate works on the far side of the Potomac. Arthur McKinstry estimated the width of the river here to be no more than a mile. Source: *Illustrated London News*.

flank view of Shipping Pt. battery and could see that it was well constructed, having a good wall and angles. Nevertheless I think a well planned expedition might take it without serious loss, and I am *sure* that a U.S. steam frigate could very soon silence it. There are embrasures for five or six guns. The battery is an earthwork only, but it is a very good one.

We have just got some new clothing—all having had a chance to draw whatever they were in need of—drawers excepted, there being none. There is a good deal of difference in these government clothes—some being very cheap at the prices for which they are allowed, and others proportionately dear. For instance, you may take up one jacket and you will find it of fine, thick, substantial cloth—in a word a first rate article—while the next may prove thin and coarse, and not worth so much by several dollars as the other. As a general rule our clothes are pretty fair, but I think the most of us will be obliged to use more than the amount allowed by the regulations. The old allowance was calculated for the idle life of a regular, who lived almost as systematically as a citizen, and not for the active life and increased wear and tear of a volunteer. The case is precisely the same with regard to rations. When a man who leads as idle a life as a regular does in time of peace, gets his full allowance, he gets all he needs and more too. But the volunteer is out upon a campaign, and such a thing has happened before now as a train of provisions being delayed a day or two, perhaps longer. A regiment in the field does not generally carry a great supply of provisions, or any other baggage, and the soldier esteems himself fortunate, indeed, if he gets his "salt horse" and his hard bread and coffee, without interruption. Suppose that the wagons are delayed a couple of days when there are but one day's rations on hand. This does not occur very often, but it is a contingency which may occur, and which did occur on our Marlboro trip. Now we enjoy comparative ease and plenty, and wherever our regiment is, there is *home*. But even here, many complain that they have not enough food. Others, again, waste food. In looking at this matter you should remember that a man in our situation will eat upon an average at least one third more than at home, and you will find—if you try it—that this estimate will generally fall short of rather than exceed the fact. Taking these things into consideration, you will not wonder that many soldiers would like exceedingly to step into "mother's pantry," especially when a ration of meat or bread turns up missing. As regards our joys and our regrets, I do not know but that they balance about as nearly as at home. Home looks charming enough in the perspective but were the 3d Excelsior disbanded and sent home, I think that but little time would elapse before the greater part would again shoulder their rifles in the army of the Potomac. We are familiar with our duties, and long practice has made them sit lightly upon us. We are hardened to cold and fatigue, and we do not mind them, in fact regard them less than the ordinary amount which we must endure at home. We have learned to prepare our food with regard both to economy and health, and this is one of the most important things which a soldier has to learn. We have confidence in the ability of our *immediate* commanders, and we are ready to follow wherever Col. Taylor leads. I do not know of a brigade, or regiment even, which has drilled so constantly as we, and I do not think that the drilling has been thrown away. We used to think two or three hours drill with knapsacks a pretty tough exercise. *Now* we consider it a mere bagatelle, not worth mentioning. If any of your readers have any curiosity to try that drill, let them fasten a bushel of wheat upon their shoulders, a half gallon jug of water and a days provision at their side, and shoulder a crowbar of medium weight, for a walk of about three hours duration. The amount of labor required for a drill in heavy marching order is not under the sample I have given, or but little if at all.

I must say that we are very much in the dark as to what is going on in the political arena, or any where else outside Gen. Hooker's division. Here we eat at stated hours, bring wood and water, sleep or stand guard. Apropos as to the guard, perhaps you would like to know something of the system by which it is regulated. *Imprimis*. At Reveille roll call, the 1st serg't. of each company announces the names of those who are to stand guard for the next 24 hours. The five or six named persons immediately prepare their arms and accoutrements for a rigid inspection. At 8 ½ A.M. the call is beaten for guard mounting, when all guards detailed step out into the company street, and are inspected by their 1st sergeants, or orderlies as they are often called. The guard turns out with his overcoat on and in full dress, white gloves, boots polished, and cartridge box, and cap box upon his belt. His brasses are supposed to be very bright, and his gun like silver without, and clean and smooth within. If his rammer comes up from the bottom, and his white glove can not be stained by it, his gun is supposed to be clean. The last call is sounded at 9 o'clock, when the Orderly marches his squad upon the parade. Here the squad form in line, opening order as they take position, the 1st sergeants standing behind the rear rank. The Sergeant Major now takes command and dresses the two ranks. This done he announces it to the Adjutant, who gives the order, "Officers and non-commissioned officers to the front, march." Those designated thus, step to the front, and the Adjutant assigns them to their respective reliefs. This done, they are ordered back to their posts, and the Adjutant orders "Inspection arms." The guards are then inspected by the lieutenant of the guard, and the man who has the cleanest gun is detailed as orderly. The remainder is like any dress parade. The Adjutant then turns to the Officer of the day, and saluting with his sword reports, "Sir, the Guard is formed." Which being done, that officer directs the guard to pass in review and march to the guard house. The guard is divided into three reliefs, which stand two hours upon post alternately. Thus each relief stands eight hours of the 24, and rest the remainder. There are but two commissioned officers detailed, and these are a Captain as Officer of the day, and a Lieutenant as Officer of the Guard. The guards load at night, and fire off their pieces at a target in the morning. The name of the soldier who makes the best shot is recorded, as is also that of the one selected as orderly. The penalty of neglect of duty in a sentinel is, death. There is no excuse for sleeping upon post. When a man can not walk his post he can call the corporal of his relief, and have another man put in his place. When several men approach a post at night, the sentry halts them and allows but one man to approach and give the countersign, or pass word. If more than one attempt to pass, he fires upon them, and falls back upon the main guard. The rebels tried to surprise our pickets not long since, but it so happened that the guard was changing, hence there were enough upon hand to give them "Jesse," which they accordingly did.

Sprague and Foss, who have had a hard siege of fever, are back in the company. Each got a good thick comforter of Dunkirk manufacture, to keep him warm until strong enough to defy cold weather. Sprague is lying upon a bunk by the fire, looking at me as I write. He would not answer to split for laths, there not being enough of him for two, but he is free from disease, well provided for in every respect, and will soon fat up. Foss is not so much reduced, and will soon be all right. Chapin Lyon, of Co. B, has returned from general hospital, and brings me what intelligence I have respecting it.

Yours as ever,

Arthur

"Jesse": to give one Jesse is to give one hell or beat the hell out of them.

Split for laths, there not being enough of him for two . . . : Wood slats (lath) used to build walls were hewn by the builder on the frontier. This probably referring to how skinny Sprague had become.

Camp Wool Jan. 20th, 1862

Dear Jennie,

I received your letter some time since and you can not doubt that it was warmly welcomed. It is terribly nasty out of doors now but what with Censor correspondence, Lyceum lectures and chess I do not find the time to hang heavy upon my hands. We have a young Lyceum in our company and I can assure you I have heard much poorer addresses from men of celebrity. It is however designed as a school of argument and oratory and is governed by the strictest parliamentary rules. Thus while ingenuity in debate is fostered the usages of the speakers platform become familiar also. All frivolous subjects are avoided as are all of those exciting topics which provoke improper warmth. Forestville can furnish no such debate—Fredonia hardly. I am a member as you may suppose. We meet this evening and determine the title by which it will be known. I have proposed that we call it the Pioneer Lyceum. The question this evening is Resolved that the Pulpit exercises more influence than the Press. I am on the affirmative, and; though against my own conviction; I mean to prove the Pulpit in the ascendant. As a pure school of logic you will rarely meet its equal and all questions are decided from the arguments and not from personal opinion. I am about as muscular now as I ever was and am enjoying myself capitally. Every now and then we get up at night and make a batch of slapjacks and eat them. All hands are getting very expert at that business and a man is just as likely to be up at one hour of the twenty four as another. We get sugar and flour at the Commissary and plum pudding—slapjacks and fried cakes are the order of the night. We don't intend to go hungry but the ration wont keep us clear of it. I've got about two ounces of bread for supper and that's all but "bress de lor" I'll have slapjacks and as "Chub" Booth said "that'll do." Flour is 5 cts. and sugar 10 cts. at the commissarys'. We hoped when Burnsides' Expedition set out that they were coming here but they didn't and we have as little business as ever. The rebels have been firing to day and jarring my table as I wrote to mother but we don't pay much attention to them lately. Well Jennie what is the news from home. So Hattie Dennison is married. Well that is quite on regle and to be expected. Cousin Orra I supposed must be living at Northampton by this time. So you had a visit from Uncle Jim. I had a letter from Uncle Theodore a few days since. The poor old fellow is lonely I know, Elvira is married, Parne learning at trade at Tiffin, and Henry with Elvira. He seems discouraged at the state of things. I hardly wonder at it, though I feel more hopeful myself. The greatest enemy we have yet met is that spirit of speculating upon our nescessities [*sic*]. The sutlers reap their millions and jobbers at Congress their tens of millions and we soldiers are kept in the field that they may do it. Well I must get the flour for those pancakes so with lot of love to John and Millie and John Jr. good bye. I wish I could see those nieces of mine. Tell Millie that she and I will sugar off yet in old Chautauqua.

Your aff. Brother,
Arthur McKinstry

"Bress de lor": "Bless the Lord."

"Chub" Booth: Likely a character from a magazine serial read in the McKinstry home.

Regle: French for "rule" or "prescription."

Sugar off: to reduce maple, say by boiling to make maple syrup, maple sugar, or maple toffee.

Fredonia Censor: Published January 29, 1862

FROM THE THIRD REGIMENT.
Camp Wool, 35 miles below Washington, Jan. 21, '62.

Dear Uncles:—

Here I am, perched upon my bunk in security, and calmly contemplating the sea of mud below. The rain falls steadily by the hour, and even when it does intermit, a heavy mist hangs over the drenched hills and miry valleys of the wooden country. Still we soldiers contrive many and ample means of amusement. Drill is of course not to be thought of, so our only duties are to bring wood and water, and to stand guard. It is a noticeable fact, that soldiers from time immemorial, have been fond of pets, and Company D is no exception to the common rule. In Camp Scott, cats were at a premium, but only one or two survived the removal. In Camp Caldwell, cats were scarce, and the dog star began to be in the ascendant to such an extent that "mongrel, whelp and hound, and curs of low degree" barked, whined and howled, from nearly half the tents in the regiment. The removal from Camp Caldwell rid the regiment of most of these pets, and only those who could boast patrician blood were retained. Thus spaniels, hounds and setters, are about all that remain.—Post keeps a model dog of the setter *persuasion*, which goes by the name of "Ephraim," and which is drilled as strictly as if the "Articles of War" were intended to take effect upon dogs as well as men.

As for amusements, dominoes, chess, checkers, and cards help the day to drag their slow length along, and newspapers, books, visiting and Club meetings, beguile away the evening hours. We have an association here in Co. D, which is of recent origin, and which bears temporarily the title of "Pioneer Debating Club." Matters of general, but not immediate and exciting interest, are the topics of discussion. We have, of course, little authority at command beside our own memories yet the interchange of thought, and the constant calling up of data of general interest, cannot prove otherwise than instructive. The strictest rules of parliamentary debate are enforced, and owing to the exclusion of politics, and other subjects which are likely to awaken latent prejudice, the most marked courtesy and absence of personality prevails.

At the close of each meeting, the Chairman appoints his successor, and the only permanent officer is that of Secretary, which position is filled by Gilbert Lewis, of Forestville. The last two questions were: "Is military service necessarily demoralizing?" and, "Resolved, That the Pulpit exercises a greater influence than the Press." Our next is:—"Resolved, that man is the architect of his own fortunes"; and I expect some pretty keen argument upon it. Disputants are chosen without regard to their individual preferences, and I have known the contestants to take up a train of argument, and follow it so keenly as to cause a material change in *their own* opinions, as well as those of others.

Last Friday evening we heard very heavy firing down at the river, but, as usual, the result was, "nobody hurt." One of our steamers came up from the lower flotilla and deliberately proceeded to sound the channel, in the face, and regardless of, the converging fire of three rebel batteries. She performed her mission at her leisure, and departed unscathed, while the ground jarred for miles to the sound of the enemy guns.

Since then one of the lower flotilla boats came up to the mouth of the Chopawamsic Creek, which is, perhaps, a couple of miles—three, possibly—below . . . [missing text] . . . It is very unsafe to be caught with whiskey, so they discharge that portion of the cargo at some safe rendezvous and peddle their other goods during the day.—But after dark, they trot out the "ardent," and find ready customers, at $1 per bottle. Meanwhile, Col. Taylor is after them with an exceeding sharp stick, and one of our scouting parties found and smashed eight dozen bottles at a single depot. I was one of a party of six who went out under Lieutenant Hinman, and captured a peddler, who, however, had only four bottles on hand. Hinman applied his nose to the bottle, but his air of expectation gave way to one of great disgust, as he exclaimed: "Boys, that will kill at forty rods!" Solemnly the bottle passed from nose to nose, and all were unanimous in the opinion that a man whose stomach was not lined with copper sheathing, or boiler plate iron, had no business with whiskey of that quality. For a short time past, the 3d Regiment scouts have been very active in hunting up these rascals and they are cutting up their trade considerably. I do not believe it within the bounds of possibility to entirely prevent the use of liquor in the army, but I think that ninety-nine per cent of the drunkenness which characterized the early part of the campaign may and will be prevented.

As I expected, the mud is now abominable, and a forward movement in the Department of the Potomac must be attended with great difficulty. As the rebels are subject to the same inconveniences, however, and even greater, I do not see but that the chances balance about as evenly as before.

It seems to be a question with many what we can do with the negroes, even during the campaign. As regards what we can do with them *hereafter*, I leave that question to abler judges; but at present we have more than five hundred regiments in the field, and the general rule seems to be, that in cooking, bringing wood and water, and other extra duty—at least ten per cent of the able bodied men are employed—which necessity takes them from their military duties. Suppose that for this percentage of soldiers you substitute an equivalent of "contra bands." By so doing you provide employment for these poor Africans, who are left destitute by the escape of their masters, and add very extensively to our own military power.

The Paymaster still preserves a respectful distance, though I can't possibly conceive why. We have heretofore reckoned confidently on receiving our pay by the 15th, but he is not here yet. Our hospital record stands as follows:

Died—A. P. Hubbard of Co. B, on the 17th. In hospital, *of Co. B*, E. Hosier, convalescent; V. Zahn, fever; James Bronson, fever; E. Crouch, convalescent; Whitmore, fever.

Co. D—Winsor H. Porter, fever; Rinaldo Stafford, nearly well. Porter is very sick, but is a little better to-day, and we have considerable hope that the first death in Co. D will not soon occur.

Co. E—None in hospital.

Co. G—James Bond, convalescent.

Co. H—Wild, convalescent; Schnider [Schneitter], fever.

The fever has had a very hard run in Co. G, and Co. B is now suffering in its turn. Co. D has had many sick from fever, but thus far we have been so fortunate as to lose none of our number. Those who have the fever seem to be thoroughly acclimated by it, and to have their constitutions completely renovated. At the same [time] there are exceptions, and some will never recover the vigor and hardihood they once enjoyed. In almost all cases, the recovery is very slow, and the patient may be perfectly free from disease for weeks before he can run a hundred yards, or keep his place in the ranks on drill. Lieut. Howard has had a long hard siege of it, but is now able to walk out a little; much to the joy of the company. Foss and Sprague are recovering their weight very rapidly.

Toujours le mem,
Arthur

Lower flotilla boats: probably a sarcastic reference to a smuggler's boat or dingy. Not a member of the Navy's Potomac Flotilla.

Camp Wool Jan. 22nd 1862

Dear Uncle,

At the risk of being thought a bore I will send yet another private letter to your address.

I have devoted a leisure hour in copying for you a map which I have constructed but which I have not had either the time or tools to turn into a sketch. Such as it is however it defines our position much better than anything I have yet seen. From Cockpit Pt. down to Aquia Creek the map is very correct and that embodies all the strong points of the vicinity. As regards Freestone head I believe that I also have that pretty exactly, but the view of Mattawoman Creek is not commanded by any eminence in our vicinity. As however I entered it from the Potomac on my voyage down, and recollect its bearings from Freestone Head. I have a pretty fair idea of its position. Camp Baker, whose position I have laid down, was our last stopping place. The camp ground occupied by the 11th Mass. Regt. is the spot where Rouse, Daily and O'Donahue were injured by that fatal shell explosion. Co. B of Jamestown has a very large amount of sickness just now and more than forty of its men are unfit for duty. In fact the able men do guard duty nearly twice as often as our own. I have to go on guard about twice—no once I mean—in seven days. This is not hard at all, but when

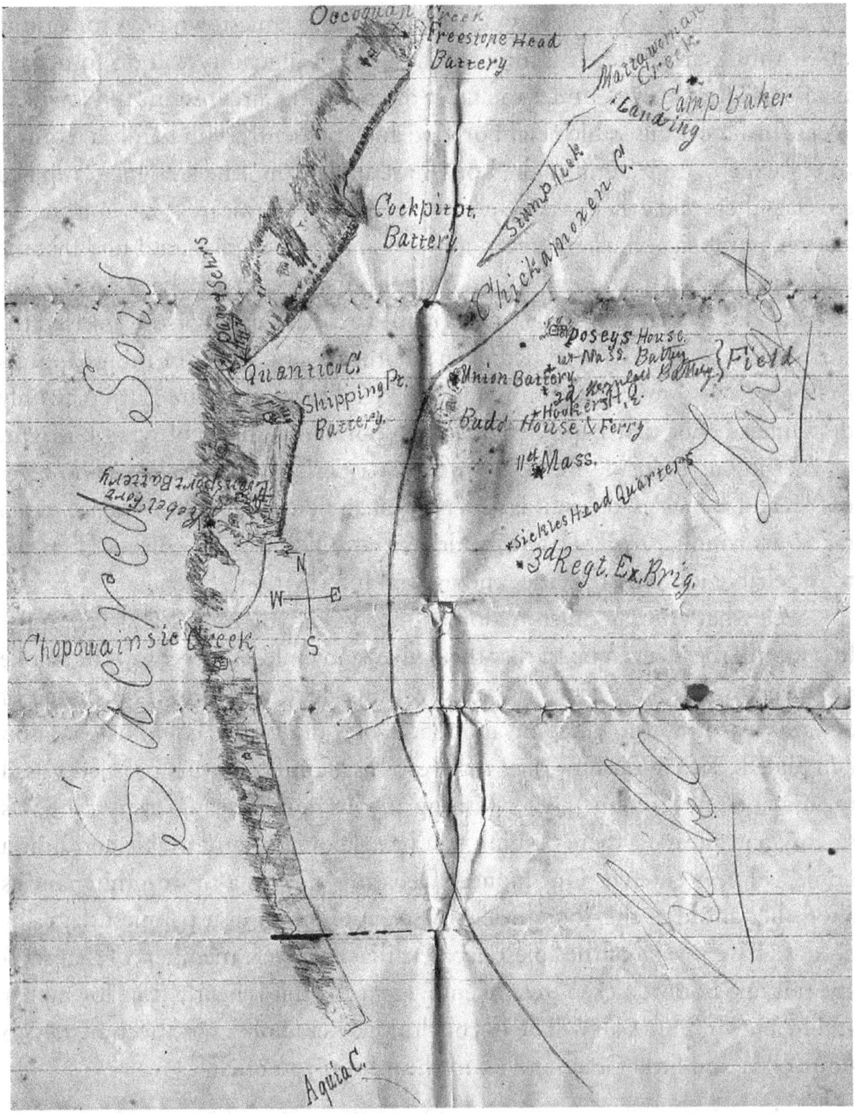

Figure 6.4. Map of Potomac. On January 22, 1862, Arthur wrote his uncle a private letter that included a map of his stretch of the Potomac. On his map Arthur labels Virginia as the "Sacred Soil" and the opposite shore of Maryland as "Rebel Target." The spot marked as the location of the "3rd Regt. Ex. Brig." is Camp Wool where the regiment moved around November 11 after a short stay at Camp Baker near Mattawoman Creek. *Courtesy of Ulysses S. Grant Presidential Library.*

a man has to go on guard every other day as those Jamestown boys sometimes do, it rubs pretty hard. It is a marvel how much ingenuity will do to make a man comfortable even under the most discouraging circumstances. Now here we are in a most miserable neighborhood and apparently with hardly a resource of enjoyment. But comfortable houses are built along the straight turnpiked streets. Chess and other social clubs are instituted. Furniture is hewn from the standing timber, and when I reckon up the sources of enjoyment I find that the greatest drawback just now is that I cannot pursue mathematical studies—not so hard a lot by half as a soldier has a right to expect. Last night we received the stirring news of the Union Victory in Kentucky. The aspect of things appears to brighten very much. According to the Herald the rebels are getting awfully discouraged, but that paper has such an abominable habit of lying outright, or guessing at probable future events, that I perfectly despise it. As however the Herald is Sickles' organ it is generally taken here. The Tribune is not much taken. Its conduct toward our brigade was rascally but still I consider it as the most reliable journal of politics and general information.

Well what is going on at Fredonia. I fancy that you must lead a very quiet life. I think the Spartan boast that their wives and children never saw the smoke of an enemy camp fire may be revived with us. That was shrewd document of Sewards was it not in which he announces that the British could have Mason and Slidell. Well Wint how does that very cosy family of yours prosper. I used to enjoy myself very much when visiting at your house because everything was so cosy and pleasant there. I think you have about as comfortable and neat a home as I ever entered. Our Pioneer Debating Club is a tip top thing and is altogether ahead of the Young Men's Association, even in it palmiest days. Indeed we have several of the ablest debaters that ever were members of that society. It is one of my chief sources of enjoyment. Well it is nearly time for supper and in a few minutes all will be in conclusion. Remember me affectionately to Aunt Ellen and little Grace and let me hear from you often.

Your aff. nephew
Arthur

Editorial Note

With the end of winter anticipated, both Yankee and Rebel commanders grow increasingly anxious about the situation along the Potomac. Confederate commanders at the highest level recognize that McClellan will not keep his gigantic Army of the Potomac idle for much longer and any move south would mean an end to the Potomac batteries, they being either destroyed by direct assault or otherwise cut off from the rest of the army. Confederate forces are stretched thin along that part of Virginia and many companies are suffering from much sickness and want of supplies. Across the river from his position in Maryland, Joseph Hooker is eager to eliminate the opposing enemy artillery once and for all. "The primary object in delivering an attack . . . should be to destroy the batteries, in order to give us the free use of the river," Hooker writes on January 27th outlining his plan.[3]

For Hooker, his divisional level attack will never materialize. As for the Confederates, their position along the river continues to deteriorate in the face of increasing Yankee strength.

Fredonia Censor: Published February 12, 1862

FROM THE THIRD REGIMENT.

Camp Wool, 35 miles below Washington, Jan. 28, '62.

Dear Uncles—

Like the immortal Webster, "I still live," and have as fair a chance of continuance in that state as if I resided in a palace, and fared luxuriously in proportion. Our mode of living still remains tame, but not monotonous. Day before yesterday we were detailed, with three other companies, to work upon the roads, which were becoming impassable. If any doubt existed in my mind as to our boys all being weavers, it was dispelled when I saw the long piece of *corduroy* which was completed by night. All hands laid to with a will, and enjoyed their unwonted occupation extremely well. Beyond the variety of the thing, there was spice of necessity, for it was evident that the teams could not haul our stores over such roads, and the alternative was to dig or starve. I have lately observed—I need not say with what pleasure—that our boys are getting to be thorough philosophers, and seem to be as ready in every emergency as the Imperial Zouaves themselves. When new to the service but very few felt at home, and much sickness was experienced. Trifling annoyances caused despondency, and most of all, there were few who knew how to prepare the food properly. Again, a complete change, both of diet and manner of living, almost invariably results in more or less sickness. But most of this regiment are now at home wherever their tents are pitched. The acclimative fevers have had their course, and their violence is greatly diminished. Every man can cook for himself if need be, and our present arrangements for the company kitchen are about as good as circumstances will admit of. Perhaps you think that I lay too much stress upon culinary and gastronomical matters. I think not. One of the principal reasons of the superiority of the French Army, lies in the fact that they are so skillful in cooking properly, and thereby preserving their health and spirits. Wherever your "Zou-Zou" stops, a fire is soon crackling and blazing, and over it is one of his incomprehensible stews.

In natural spirit, the Zouaves of our brigade do not surpass the American Volunteers. In actual powers of endurance they are decidedly inferior. They are not nearly as well disciplined in field manoeuvers, at least so far as the march is concerned. No orders, however stringent, seem sufficient to keep them in their places in the ranks, and you may depend upon it that every fruit tree within your vision will be loaded with Frenchmen in red breeches and embroidered jackets.

The 2nd Reg. is just now in a ferment on account of one of the soldiers shooting a corporal. There was a free fight, I believe, and the prime cause of the whole was liquor. The result to the murderer can hardly be other than death by sentence of court martial. I am sorry that the sentence may not fall upon the man who soid [*sic*] so fruitful a cause of discord to soldiers with weapons always in their hands or within reach. However useful liquor may be as a medicine, I believe that it has made more sickness than it has cured. When out to day after some milk, I met some thirsty souls, who inquired very anxiously if I could direct them in their search for whiskey. Owing to the active exertions of our scouts I was enabled to give the desired information.

There has been heavy cannonading this evening, but being engaged in a game of chess I did not witness the fireworks. The rebels were very foolish to waste their ammunition, for the night was so dark that I don't believe they could have hit a farm at a hundred yards. As regards the cost of the fun I can give some data. We have here, in Co. D, representatives of almost every occupation which you meet with in ordinary life. Knowing the quality of iron prescribed for shot and shell, I asked an iron moulder, who lives in the next tent, what they were worth. His reply was that, in large quantities, shot were worth $2.00 and shell about $3.00 per cwt. Thus a shot of 32 lbs. is worth about 64 cents, and hollow shot or shell, about 75 cts. The prescribed cartridge for a 32 pr. at medium range—say a thousand yards—is—if my memory does not deceive me—four pounds of powder. This will cost not to exceed one dollar. The primer is worth two cents. Thus the actual cost of shot fired from a 32 pr. is not exceeding $1.66, while the shell which is fired, allowing about 50 cts. for the fuse, costs about $2.75. In this estimate I allow two pounds of powder to fill the shell. We have had lately a long period of very bad weather, and it is not over with yet. Still, as far as actual comfort is concerned, we have no need to complain.

I see that Senator Wilson has introduced a capital bill as a substitute for the late sutler arrangements. His plan is precisely what has long been needed.

Figure 6.5. REBEL BATTERIES, FEBRUARY 1862. A Robert Knox Sneden sketch of the Confederate battery at Budd's Ferry. *Courtesy of Library of Congress.*

The proper manner of supplying men with articles not in their table of allowances, is evidently through the Quarter Master's hands. This course will in a great measure end the abominable course of imposition to which the soldiers have been so subjected. It is not the *necessary* and inevitable privations which the soldier knows to be before him, of which he complains. Send him forth upon a well planned expedition, and whatever he may have to endure, you will not hear from him a murmur. But send him forth upon a useless errand, and subject him to hardships which common foresight might have prevented, and he will complain, and very justly. I do not think there are many soldiers who enlisted for the pecuniary prospects, but still a laborer, of whatever grade, prefers that for pecuniary outlay he receives a proper return. In the life of a volunteer the need of outlay is far greater than many might suppose, and it has been a notorious fact that the soldiers have to pay at least double prices for much which they have received. Senator Wilson's bill provides that the soldier shall receive from the Quarter Master all those articles of which he stands in need, and that not over ten per cent profit shall be demanded. This seems very reasonable and proper.

We have had a smart storm of hail and rain, which was so severe that only eight men stood guard for the entire regiment, and those were hourly relieved. There are still a few small patches of snow about, but the ground is mostly bare, and if it gets tolerably dry I suspect that Maj. Stevens will give us "right smart" of battalion drills. Col. Taylor has gone home on leave of absence.

Jan.: 29th.—We have been out at work upon the road again to day; and have had a pleasant time, as well as made ourselves useful in addition to being ornamental. When Uncle Sam settles up for damaged woodlands I hope that he will be duly credited with that excellent corduroy road we are making. We are straightening out these crooks in the "Maryland miles," so that Charles County ought to be greatly obliged to us. While on my way over I stopped a few moments to see a friend in the Michigan Company of the 1st Regiment. The camp certainly presented a more disorderly appearance than our own, but I must say that those Michigan boys had much more roomy and comfortable habitations than we. Not being restricted, as we are, to uniformity, they built commodious houses, with shingle roofs. While chatting with my friend I observed a brother of Maj. Stevens, and learned to my surprise that he was the 2d Lieut. of that company. The company is certainly one of the finest in the brigade.

The weather is clear again, and we are catching it again in the shape of drill "right smart, I reckon."

Ryther has just obliged me with the hospital list, which is as follows: Died, Jan. 29th, Curtis Wheeler, of Co. B. In hospital of Co. B, Hosier, Zahn, and Bronson, convalescent; and Crouch and Whitmore, who are considered to be doing well. Winson H. Porter, of Co. D, is considered to be also doing well. Bond of Co. G, is convalescing. Wild and Schneider, of Co. H, are considered convalescent. The entire number in hospital is eleven. The general health of the men in Co. B is improving greatly. Being rather restricted as to time, I must bring this letter to a conclusion. Last Saturday we were paid off. Hoping that the next time I write I may have more matter of interest to communicate.

I remain,

Yours as ever, Arthur

"I still live": last words of Daniel Webster, American politician.

Corduroy: a road formed by laying logs or timbers perpendicular to the line of travel. Used in muddy or swampy conditions.

Senator Wilson: from Massachusetts, Henry Wilson was chairman of the Military Affairs Committee, a staunch abolitionist, and served as Grant's vice president.

Camp Wool Jan. 30th 1862

Dear Mother,

We were paid off last Saturday but we have had so much extra duty that I have not been able to write before. Enclosed find $5.00. Of this I wish you to retain a dollar and a half for your own private use and you may promise definitely that at the next pay day the remaining $7.75 will be promptly liquidated. Owing to my funds having run low in consequence of buying my watch and feeling not only the prudence but the necessity of keeping a fair supply on hand; I can not conveniently pay in full now. The next pay is due March 1st but will probably be over to the 15th before the Paymaster can get around to us. I am enjoying myself and weigh about 175 which is very fair for me. My strength is greater than ever before and as for spirits I am as full of the "Old Harry" as Frank when he used to cut up so absurdly. Well how do you all get on. I went to a daguerrean saloon this afternoon that I might get my likeness taken for Jennie, but there was such a crowd that I walked off in disgust. I have received no answer from Lucy and am thinking of trying it again. What do you think?

I was over to the 1st this morning and found Bob as fat as a woodchuck in a clover patch. He had been thinking of hunting me up. Aunt Jane sent me nine numbers of the Springfield Republican with a continued story in them. I received them last night but have had no time to look at them. I feel some symptoms of liver complaint and mean to try a blue pill before I eat again. A timely dose would have saved me Dr. Hortons bill and last falls sickness too. We have now to carry our wood at least a quarter of a mile and a good deal up hill at that. This exercise strengthens the muscles of the legs wonderfully and I feel as active as a colt. As roll call is close at hand I must quit and indeed I am tired for I have worked hard to day and written a letter for the Censor beside. I had a letter from Uncle Theodore a few days ago. He was well as were his children and grandson. How I would like to see the good old soul. What are Frank and Luther doing—are they going to school. How does Newton get on. Does Mary P. teach or study this winter. I am getting behind in some things but I do not think that upon the whole I lose ground, and when this war is over I will show you what hard study can do. When sixteen years old I lacked application but I have the power of concentrating my mind upon studies in a more than ordinary degree now. You can hardly imagine how eagerly I desire to retrieve lost opportunities. I am now at that point where a years study will double the profits of the next. Well I am tired and must leave off so good bye.

You aff. son,
Arthur McKinstry

"Old Harry": Devil, Satan.

to retain a dollar and a half for your own private use and you may promise definitely that at the next pay day the remaining $7.75 will be promptly liquidated. Owing to my funds having run low in consequence of buying my watch and feeling not only the prudence but the necessity of keeping a fair supply on hand, I can not conveniently pay in full now. The next pay is due March 1st but will probably be over to the 15th before the Paymaster can get around to us. I am enjoying myself and weigh about 175 which is very fat for me. My strength is greater than ever before and as for spirits I am as full of the "Old Harry" as Frank when he used to cut up so absurdly. Well how do you all get on? I went to the daguerrean saloon this afternoon that I might get my likeness taken for Jennie, but there was such a crowd that I walked off in disgust. I have received no answer from Lucy and am thinking of trying it again. What do you think?

I was over to the 31st this morning and found Bob as fat as a woodchuck in a clover patch. He had been thinking of hunting me up. Aunt Jane sent me nine numbers of the Springfield Republican with a continued story in them. I received them last night but have had no time to look at them. I feel some symptoms of liver complaint and mean to try a blue pill before I eat again. A timely dose would have saved me Dr. Horton's bill and last fall's sickness too. We have now to carry our wood at least a quarter of a mile and a good deal up hill at that. This exercise strengthens the muscles of the legs wonderfully and I feel as active as a cat. As roll call is close at hand I must quit and indeed I am tired for I have worked hard to-day and written a letter for the Censor beside. I had a letter from Uncle Theodore a few days ago. He was well as were his children and grandson. How I would like to see the good old soul. What are Frank and Luther doing—are they going to school. How does Newton get on. Does Mary E teach or study this winter. I am getting behind in some things but I do not think it is upon the whole a loss to me, and when this war is over I will show you what hard study can do. When sixteen years old I lacked application but I have the power of concentrating my mind upon studies in a more than ordinary degree now. You can hardly imagine how eagerly I desire to retrieve lost opportunities. I am now at that point where a years study will double the profits of the next. Well I am tired and must leave off so good bye.

Your aff. Son,

—Arthur McKinstry.

"Old Harry" = devil, Satan.

Chapter 7

Every Preparation for Immediate and Active Duty

February to April 1862—Lower Maryland and Forays into Virginia

Pace of war accelerates as the Army of the Potomac stirs into action • Raids onto the sacred soil of Virginia • Confederates abandon batteries along the river • Packing up for the great offensive against Richmond

Camp Wool   Feb. 9th, 1862

Dear Mother,

What is the matter with you that you do not write. It must be a month if not more since I heard from you. You cannot plead that you have no tidings from me and I hope you do not think the anxiety all upon your side. We are still here in the old place and doing little beside making ourselves comfortable. There is no excitement here of late and news are pretty scarce. Lowes balloon has been sent for and Major Stevens has promised to use his efforts to procure me a passage. I have no doubt that he will be successful and I look forward to it with considerable anticipation. A journey in mid-air would furnish material for quite a lively Censor article. Well, how do you all get on at Forestville—what news have you to relate—what births deaths and marriages have occurred. Leute Jones is perfectly well and is now doing full duty. He looked pretty slim for some time but is now fat as a woodchuck. Bob McKinstry is hale and hearty and I expect him over to dine with me to day. The health of the regiment is good and I hear but few complaints of any kind. I have never felt better in my life and have at last recovered all the strength and all the activity which I lost in Mexico. I feel ready for a campaign but it will probably be six or eight weeks before business gets very lively. The fact is we are all blockaded "by the powers of mind" we are. I must say that I am really enjoying myself and why shouldn't I when I have good society, good reading, club meetings and chess, to while away the time. As for extras we have now and then a plum pudding or a plate of slapjacks and these are not very expensive. I have a strong suspicion that Col. Taylor is trying to get us transferred from Sickles Brigade—on account of the hard name the other regiments bear. I hope that it will be done for Sickles hangs upon our neck like a millstone. Taylor is a fine officer and has a high reputation. I have got a pretty large stock of clothes and I mean to send some home just before we march. I can spare a good jacket which will last Frank a year and a pair of pants which want a new seat and will then wear a long time. I can also spare a very fine riflemans blouse and a couple of pairs of linen pants and still have two full suits left—all that I want to march with. I calculate to keep two suits by me of good whole clothing so that I may never be left destitute by being ordered to march when I have only oldish clothing on hand. Thus I shall always keep neat and instead of throwing away clothing when it is still good for considerable, I will send it home where it can do long service in the every day work of farming.

I can not get a stamp and shall have to let you pay the postage. Money is not lacking but stamps are scarce.

Give my love to all

Your aff. son
Arthur

Editorial Note

The effectiveness of the Confederates' blockade of the Potomac may have been a matter of opinion, depending on who is asked. Small boats are running the river constantly, keeping Washington supplied with oysters and such, while most large ships stay away, causing shortages of fuel and other bulk items. Railroad traffic into the city is increased dramatically to take up the shortfall, but trains can never match the tonnage ships deliver. Many military men and private ship captains hold disdain for Rebel artillery marksmanship but ships stay away just the same. Increasingly, Washington residents, including the president, are demanding that the Army, by way of McClellan, take action to fully open the river.[1] But even as McClellan seems to be dragging his feet regarding any direct move against the batteries, Confederate planners increasingly recognized their positions as ultimately untenable and make preparations for the day they will need to abandon the shoreline.

Figure 7.1. Federal picket. Federal picket on the Potomac, in front of Confederate batteries. Picket duty along the river was described by Arthur as a dull routine that could be broken up by a Confederate decision to shoot at something. Source: *Illustrated London News.*

Fredonia Censor: Published February 26, 1862

FROM THE THIRD REGIMENT.

Camp Wool, Feb. 10.

Dear Uncles.—

Still the old alternation of weather goes on almost as regularly as clockwork. The programme is generally as follows:—Two days rain—one day cloudy—and one day fair. Well, by six weeks it will be settled weather, and we may reasonably hope for something more exciting. Prof. Lowe's balloon is down by Posey's; just out of the rebel's sight; and there will probably be some more reconnaissances. Prof. Lowe holds the rank of a Colonel, and I dare say there are few officers of that rank who are more useful.

Last night I was on guard between nine and eleven, and the dull routine of duty was agreeably broken in upon by a heavy cannonade. We could see the flash of the rebel guns at Cockpit Pt., and spots of bright crimson when their shells exploded above the river, or on the Maryland shore. It took twenty-five seconds by the watch for the sound to reach my post. I know not what they were firing at, but I feel morally certain that no particular harm was done. I suppose that the feelings of the rebel gunners were anything but agreeable, when the Pensacola escaped so cleverly, and it seems that all sorts of ridicule was heaped upon them. "Why in h—ll didn't you hit her"; bawls the gunner of one battery to another gunner, the ensuing morning. "Damn you! Why didn't you hit her," replied No. 2. All hands felt pretty sore upon the subject, and the Richmond papers did little enough to console them. It is a noticeable fact how much cleaner the boys keep their rifles than they did their old muskets. As an extra incentive, Col. Taylor some time since ordered that the man whose arms and uniform were in the best order should be detailed as orderly, and be exempt from the next tour of guard duty. Barton, Hamilton, O'Donaghey, Palmer, Simpson, Weiler and Zentz, are all celebrated for their luck as orderlies. The man who makes the best shot when the guards discharge their guns in the morning, is also excused from the next tour on guard. In the strife for orderly there is a close contest between Co.'s B and D. At the same time the rivalry is always of that frank and generous nature which may exist between brothers in blood, as well as brothers in arms.

Stores and provisions come in very regularly, and for some time I have heard no complaint about rations. In fact we hold "the powers of mud" in the most supreme contempt; thanks to the firm and durable road we have built. We get our mail matter pretty early I think—in about three days from Chaut[auqua] generally. Lieuts. Hinman and Howard, who have been home are back again and looking quite hearty. Capt. Barrett is also again at the head of his company.

Col. Taylor has been as unhappy as a fish out of water, on account of the deep mud, which effectually checks battalion drills. Thinking that we ought to drill at something, he set us at work to erect an immense building, where we can drill in the manual of arms and the bayonet exercise, though it rain ever so hard. The idea is a good one, and the building is nearly completed. The general health in camp is wonderfully good, when we consider how very unfavorable the weather has been. There is not to-day, a man in hospital whose symptoms are unfavorable. I regret, however, to record the death of John C. Schneider [Schneitter], though a young man, was a veteran soldier, and fought in the trenches in the Crimea. His neatness and good conduct had raised him greatly in the estimation of his Captain.

The hospital list of to-day is as follows: Of Co. B, Zahn and Bronson are about to retire to quarters, and Crouch and Whitmore are convalescing. Of Co. G, Taylor has a severe cold. Of Co. D Porter is convalescing, and Page has a cold. Bond, of Co. G, and Wild, of Co. H, are convalescing.

We enjoy our present free and easy style of living very much, and I verily believe that when we get home we shall now and then run wild, and take the axe and rifle and shoulder our knapsacks for a hunt upon the Pennsylvania mountain ridges. At all events the growing taste for architecture will be manifested in *cottages ornees* for poultry, put up in orthodox soldier style, and log edifices where the annual "sugaring time" can be profitably and merrily spent. At the same time I confess to a growing curiosity as to what would be the sensation produced by a sleep between linen sheets, and upon a feather bed. Roll call is close at hand, and I must close.

Yours as ever,

Arthur

Prof. Lowe: Thaddeus S. Lowe was the driving force behind the Union's fledgling balloon corps. Lowe's balloon provided excellent intelligence when deployed, especially during the Peninsula Campaign. After a series of bureaucratic problems, Lowe resigned in mid-1863 and with it the balloon corps.

Ornees: decorated.

Fredonia Censor: Published February 26, 1862

FROM THE THIRD REGIMENT.

Camp Wool, Feb. 18.

Dear Uncles:—

I sit down to address to you a few hasty lines, and to acquaint you with our present situation and future prospects. All is silent along the river, and the fire of our battery can stir up "nary secesh." The balloon has reconnoitered for a couple of days, but with what results I am as yet unacquainted. I have just seen upon our bulletin the official dispatch announcing the fall of Fort Donelson, and the capture of an army. We are not idle, meanwhile. Arms are being repaired, clothing given out, superfluous stores sent to Washington, and every preparation made for immediate and active duty. Every man has had a chance to get rubber and other blankets, and to prepare in every way for a long journey. I see that the hunters in this grand battue of traitors, are fast closing their circle; and every mail brings the glad tidings of some new and glorious triumph of the Union Army. It is, of course, contrary to regulation to report progress at a point like this; but if some fine morning you should learn that Hooker's Division was upon the "sacred soil," it should not necessarily be a matter of surprise to you. No man knows when the marching orders will come, but there is a deep and settled conviction that our stay here will be a short one.

The books you sent come safely, and are to be found all through the company, as well as at the hospital. As regards the merits of the Army and Navy Express, there are several who claim that title, and I do not know but that one is about as good as another. The American Express generally forwards from New York by Adams & Co., and the box you sent has been also through the hands of Kingsley & Co. The Express is very like the mail—while most articles come through in a reasonable time, some come late or never. I was very glad to find among those books the Tribune Almanac; which is perhaps the most condensed form of national statistics which a soldier can carry. It furnishes in a convenient form, much information which had hitherto been unattainable.

There is a fair sample of snow upon the ground, for this latitude at least.—The other day the regiment was called out, avowedly for the purpose of clearing away a space of ground for the parade to form upon. As soon, however, as the boys got out upon the field, they began to "deploy as skirmishers," and to snowball each other at a furious rate. Charley Loeb was the only commissioned officer who ventured out, and he got well peppered for his presumption. Charley is, however, quite a favorite with his old comrades of Co. D, and got off pretty lightly, when we consider the circumstances.

Meanwhile, though the preparations for an advance are going on, we still continue to amuse our leisure hours in the old way. Our books are not neglected, our Club meetings go on regularly and profitably, and chess receives the same attention as heretofore. Several sets of men have been carved by ingenious whittlers, and I have one here which is made of minie bullets. WE have long feared that we should have no chance to testify our faith by our works, but the prospects just now are very much in favor of our having the motion we have so long and eagerly looked forward to. The sanitary condition of the regiment is excellent, and all are impatient for business. While writing the last sentence, the rebels at Shipping Point opened fire. I presume they have been keeping quiet to avoid balloon observations, and to tempt us into a trap. They will not succeed in doing either. If we do advance, there will be scouts and skirmishers so far in advance as to render it impossible to surprise the main body.

Col. Taylor's huge drill house fell in a few days since, and I cannot say there was any profound regret expressed by the privates who had all along been of the opinion that it was cutting it a little too fat to expect them to work very industriously upon an edifice which would deprive them of the leisure they enjoy in foul weather. It is now so near spring, that by the time the thing could be set to rights, it would be superfluous. At the same time it would make a capital warehouse.

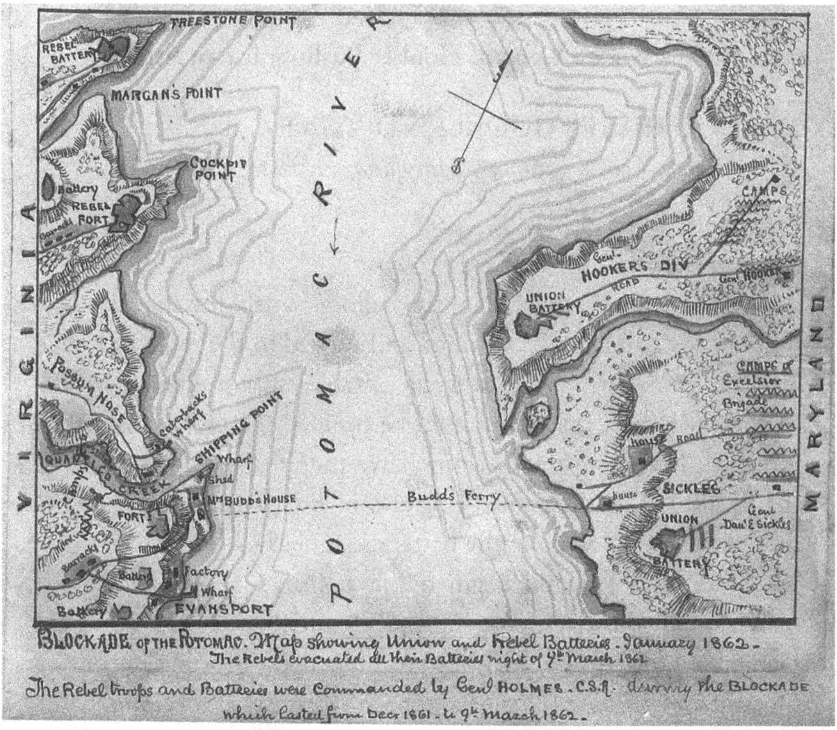

Figure 7.2. ROBERT KNOX SNEDEN'S MAP OF THE POTOMAC. Map showing the proximity of the Excelsior Brigade to Budd's Ferry during the spring of 1862. *Courtesy of Library of Congress.*

The rebels still continue to fire viciously, and I presume that they see more vessels, canal boats, or something of that sort, than they deem compatible with their . . . [text illegible] . . . conjecture, for I have not been out to see. Our Hospital list is as follows:

Band—Frank Stevens, of Fredonia, fever. Frank is pretty sick, but the prospects are rather favorable than otherwise. Of Co. B, G. Taylor and F. Whitmore are convalescing. Porter and Page, of Co. D, are also convalescent, while Newburgher is very sick with fever. Bond, of Co. G, is convalescent, as is also Wild, of Co. H. Leguire, of Co. H., has fever. As the mail is about to close, I hasten to subscribe myself,

Yours as ever,

Arthur

Battue: the driving of game toward hunters by beaters. A hunting party arranged by driving game toward hunters by beaters.

Other Voices: General Hooker Pushing for an Attack

HEADQUARTERS HOOKER'S DIVISION,
Camp Baker, Lower Potomac, Maryland, February 20, 1862.

Brig. Gen. S. WILLIAMS,
Adjutant-General, Army of the Potomac:

. . . My observations from the balloon satisfy me that the batteries in my front can be stormed and carried in the manner I have already communicated whenever a suitable night presents itself for that service; or, if that should not be deemed the most satisfactory mode of destroying them, I now have the means, with the aid of the flotilla, of landing three brigades of my division on the rebel shore and of demolishing the batteries regularly.

To do this I would begin the attack on Cockpit Point, and march down the river, crossing the Quantico by boats. With six Dahlgren howitzers from high ground on the north side of the Quantico I can drive the rebels from the batteries at Shipping Point in two hours. These guns, with ammunition, I can procure from the flotilla.

The Whitworth guns have arrived. If these guns possess the virtues assigned them, I believe that the camps of all the supports of the batteries can be broken up. I will know as soon as I can have them put in position.

The steamer Page will also be in danger, if I am not mistaken.

The free navigation of the river will give us immense advantage over the rebels, particularly so long as the roads remain in their present condition, and the destruction of the batteries will in no way expose future intentions of the Major-General in the conduct of the war.

Very respectfully, &c.,

JOSEPH HOOKER, *Brigadier-General, Commanding Division.*[2]

Fredonia Censor: Published March 5, 1862

FROM THE THIRD REGIMENT.

Feb. 22.

Dear Uncles:—

Company D is out upon picket, and your most obedient servant is out upper post, and is practicing "the position of a soldier," which, in his opinion consists in seating himself upon a log, and drying his shoes at a good cheerful fire. My business for the day is to see that no boat lands upon my beat and to keep all persons from the shore who are not called there by their duties, or who have not the proper pass. Five men are sufficient for the day, but at night the posts are trebled, and the duties are considerably extended. All night long you can see the signal lights of the flotilla, as the gunboats pass silently to and fro upon their reconnoissances.—The lights are presented toward our side, to warn us not to fire upon our friends, and if you could see how completely the river is traversed, you would be perfectly satisfied of the efficiency of this blockade at least.

Not long since, I had an interview with Lieut. Edward P. McCrea, who was in command of the lower flotilla. His flag ship is the *Belle*, and there were two other steamers, the *Resolute* and the *Satellite*. In addition to these were the transport *Columbia*, (side wheel,) and several schooners, formerly attached to the coast survey. Just aft of the cabin of the *Belle* was an eight-inch shell gun, (68 pounder) with which McCrea professed himself perfectly competent to lodge any required number of shells in any battery whose distance does not exceed 1 ¾ miles. He did not feel any hesitation in declaring that he could silence and destroy any of the upper batteries, whenever it so pleased him, and the reason why it was not done was that it was not considered at present a desirable object. It seems to be a studied aim to keep the enemy's right wing upon the river. The wisdom of this is apparent, when we consider that while the enemy has no means of crossing, it is perfectly optional with us. A single night would suffice to throw our whole division across, and that, too, in a place naturally favorable. The Lieutenant seemed to feel a great deal of affection for that 68 pounder, and his voice softened considerably as he alluded to it. It was not, however, his only pet, as he had another on the bow.

It seems that the Aquia Creek batteries are better managed than those above, for one morning the *Belle*, which had been cruising during the night pretty close to the rebels, was fired upon, and a shot struck in direct line about ten feet short of the port (left,) bow, and ricocheted over, just touching the awning. Pray excuse me here, for a moment, while I convert myself into a walking arsenal, and take a turn up and down my territory. All right! I have visited the creek which forms my northern boundary, and elicited a whistle from Charley Miller, who is on the next post below. The only moving object is our sail-boat, tenanted by some ambitious Argonauts of Co. D, who are taking a quiet voyage upon the broad and placid bosom of the Potomac. I can hear the whistle of a railway train down at Aquia, and I have been regaled by the melodious strains of some rebel trumpeter who is deluded by self-conceit into the insane idea that he is a musician. I should judge by the samples I have just heard, that his tunes had been frozen up in his bugle on some frosty night, and were being thawed slowly out in disjointed fragments.

I supposed by this time you are beginning to feel some interest as to our geographical situation. Well, we are located at Sandy Point, which is between Budd's Ferry and Liverpool Point. From Capt. Abell's headquarters and the rendezvous of the company, we can see the flotilla about a mile and a half below, and off Liverpool Point. This latter is not over four or five miles from Budd's Ferry.—Hooker's Division extends from the vicinity of Mattawoman to Liverpool Point, and the picket much farther. From Budd's Ferry down the Potomac begins to assume the appearance of a broad estuary of the sea, or a long lake. Its shores no longer preserve the ordinary course but are indented with large bays, and the semblance to the regular bends of a river disappears. At Budd's Ferry, the river will probably not exceed a mile and a half in width. At Liverpool it is more than four. Aquia Creek lies a little below upon the opposite side, and a shell was thrown thence across to the Maryland shore—over four miles. At this distance, however, no man can aim with any degree of accuracy; and even were that possible, the shell scream of the coming missile would give ample warning to seek shelter or avoid its path. Our present routine of duties is as follows: During the day, five men patrol the beach, or station themselves where they can overlook the boats. At night, these are relieved by about three times as many, who divide the five beats among them, and are relieved every four hours till morning. Thus the company is divided into four reliefs, one of which stands during the entire day, and the other three stand each four hours in the night. There are several signals to be observed by approaching boats, any failure in which exposes them to the pleasing and agreeable operation called the *fusillade*. We are about three miles, I should judge, from the regiment, and get most of the advantages which our comrades enjoy. We consider the variety as ample recompense for the more important duties we now perform, and the increased exposure we must undergo.

I cannot, as heretofore, give all the hospital details, but I can give all that is really important. Frank Stevens is the only patient whose condition was at all critical and he was improving at last account. Porter, of Co. D, is restored to quarters. The books you sent us are at Camp Wool, but we will have them here shortly. The reading will not interfere with our duties during the day, and they will do much to while away hours which would otherwise be tedious.

Ira Lewis had just made me a visit and informs me that C. L. Ryther, Ward Master of the Hospital, and Newburgher, our drummer, are pretty sick, but that they will probably come out all right.

Yours, as ever,

Arthur

Belle: actually, the USS *Jacob Bell*, 141-foot-long sidewheel steamer.

Other Voices: Letter Appearing in the *Fredonia Censor*

Published March 5, 1862

From a private letter
From the Third Regiment
Camp Wool, Feb. 22, '62

On this anniversary of the birth of the immortal Washington, the ears of loyal Americans are greeted by the boom of artillery, celebrating an event which has not, in the history of earth, a parallel for black-hearted ingratitude, and political depravity. The minions of Slavery, with a hypocrisy and effrontery which would shame the devil, have chosen this anniversary, so dear to the lovers of Freedom in America, to attempt to foist into permanent existence their bogus confederacy. As I stand looking across the Potomac, and the ground hallowed by the step of Washington, the places with which he was so familiar, and which he loved so dearly because he had wrenched their jurisdiction from a despot I cannot keep back a "thank God," that he is not alive to-day to witness the utter degeneracy of Virginia. With all the pomp and circumstance which belong to noble and worthy deeds, the rebels inaugurate their head-devil as President to-day, and the announcement comes borne on the breeze, commingled with the booms of our own loyal artillery, commemorating the natal day of a man who loved Freedom with a fervor only equaled by his detestation of tyranny and oppression in every form. Oh! how I wish the Union army of the Potomac could be in Richmond in time to take part in the closing scenes of this day. How it would thrill the hearts of the millions whose blood is wont to flow quicker when Freedom's Star is in the ascendant, to hear that this infamous reptile was strangled before it could count one day its own, that the evening of the day which saw its birth, witnessed its ignominious exit from the face of earth. But from present appearances the result so devoutly wished, will not take place, until Davis's government has numbered its days by the dozen. The orders for which the citizens of the North have been waiting with so much painful anxiety, and which the grand army of the Potomac have been led to believe was part of the plans which are being so successfully developed, have been promulgated. The full extent of the orders have not transpired, but enough is revealed to justify me in saying that a forward movement is meditated. We are ready. The Quartermaster, (who is a model of his kind,) has everything in the shape of baggage, reduced to its smallest capacity, and we are, I think, quite sure to have a chance in the struggle which is to deal the death blow to this infamous rebellion. Our arms and accoutrements have undergone a rigid inspection and the question is asked every man, "did your rifle ever miss?" If "yes," it is thrown aside; for over there we must have every shot effective. At Liverpool Point are 10 of the flotilla, and 20 barges, canal boats, &c. The Stepping Stones is to come to night, with enough to make it forty. What for? We think those rebel batteries must be taken at the point of the bayonet, and we, driving the rebels back, (for we have nothing but the river to fall back on,) to their lines at Centerville, are to unite our forces with Heintzleman's, rush into them with the bayonet, which is now the weapon most depended on, turn their right flank, the center and right wing of our army advancing and thus drive them panic struck to Manassas, for a breathing spell, and finally following them up with the strong arms and courageous hearts of our soldiers, we drive them to Richmond, and as h— is near that place, you can easily see what will become of them.

G. W. S.

Camp Wool Feb. 23rd, 1862

Dear Mother,

Franks and your letter came to hand and were very gladly received. I had begun to grow anxious about you, you had been so long silent. I can and will send you the V. out of my next pay and shall suffer no inconvenience by so doing. We may get our pay anywhere from the 10th to the 20th of March. I think it will be within three weeks. Our company is out on picket along the shore of the Potomac but Camp Wool is still our Post Office. I am on the day relief and the business is not carried on so strictly as at night. Tomorrow I stand four hours night relief. As I can see all that is going on at a glance I sit and toast my shins at a good fire and take a turn up and down the beach now and then. I drew a new rubber blanket so that I might be on hand to march at any time and made a good havelock of a part of the old one. This has already proved a capital thing for it protects my head and shoulders effectually from the rain. I sent a box to Uncle Willard yesterday morning which contained two very fine and heavy riflemen's blouses, 2 prs. good linen pants and my comforter which I do not need longer and am by far too stingy to throw away. The freight is paid and when Frank goes and gets them he and Lute can wear them. They are whole and almost new and cost Government about eight dollars or more. They have stood me a good turn but the weather is growing milder and as I am still well loaded the alternative was to send them away or throw them at the niggers. The reason I sent them by way of Uncle Willard was that some others put in with me which reduced the freight one half per man. The birds have begun to sing today and I don't believe we shall have much more frost. Our present station is a Sandy Point which is perhaps 2 ½ or 3 miles below Budds ferry and about 1 ½ above Liverpool Pt. By this reckoning you can place it upon the map I drew and sent you.

Hookers Division has not moved to Liverpool Point but extends from Mattawoman Creek to Liverpool Pt. Thus the line of regiments extends twelve or fourteen miles and contains about that number of regiments averaging at about 1,000 strong each.

Well I think our chances of getting back to celebrate the 4th of July decidedly better than they were ten days ago. That the rebels are discouraged is evident from their silent batteries. They have been very quiet for a number of days. Well I must get some firewood for it will soon be dark so with love and plenty of it for the old home circle I remain

Your very affectionate son

Arthur

P.S. I weigh 180 and don't look as fat as I did when I left home. The weight is in muscle this time.

Fredonia Censor: Published March 12, 1862

From The Third Regiment.

Headquarters, Co. D, on picket, Sandy Point, Feb. 28th, 1862.

Dear Uncles:—

We are still on picket, as you will see, by the date of this epistle, and have just been mustered for the next two months pay. We have had rather rough weather, but have made out to enjoy ourselves in spite of it. Last Monday we had a tremendous gale, which made us subside into the smallest possible compass in our blankets, and blew our flotilla from its anchorage. One gunboat only stood its ground, and the rest either scudded down the river, or tried to get under the lee of the Virginian shore. One of these last had to do its best, if I am to judge by the volumes of smoke which poured up from its furnaces.

The rebels are very busy across the river to-day, with a new gun which they have placed upon a lofty hill. They have been firing slowly and deliberately, and have made much better practice than heretofore. They have thrown shells over to Liverpool Point, which is distant at least four miles. As we are nearer than that point, we may take our turn at any time. Our gunboats had to get out of the way yesterday and are anchored a half mile below.

We still remain upon the eastern bank of the Potomac, and it may be detailed by good generalship, but God knows that it did not need the glorious news from Burnside and Grant, to stir our blood and cheer us on to action. I suppose that we must patiently await the hour of battle, but we may be pardoned if we regret that we may not share the victories as well as the toils of our fellow soldiers of the west. We have to encounter all the hardships of a soldier's life, and though they are much alleviated, it has been the result of the labor of our own hands, and the Government has done for us absolutely nothing. We are within range of three or four rebel batteries, and cannot act upon the aggressive or even the defensive. Our only alternative is to get out of the way if fired upon, so much for a civilian general. I hope I shall not be accused of cherishing too much *esprit du corps* when I opine that the Excelsior Brigade has never been so well managed as when during the absence of Gen. Sickles, Col. Taylor has been acting brigadier. Sickles displayed great energy and patriotism in the raising and equipment of the brigade. He has governed it however in a civilian manner, and whatever talent and administrative ability he may have, he is evidently incompetent to personally maneuver the brigade. That he has done so well so far is owing to the fact that his counselors were experienced military men, or at least good tactitians. I don't suppose that any general's reputation would transfer this brigade to more active service now, but I think that we might have played some other *role* than that of special policemen, and laborer upon a Maryland highway, if we had been headed by an experienced soldier before we left Washington. Still we may make an early movement, and everything has been put on a good war footing.

Since I commenced writing, the rebels have removed the gun upon the hill. It is a field-piece. Night before last, Corporal Walden seized the bayonet of one of the sentries to try his vigilance, and surprised him into firing upon him and shooting him through the wrist. Dr. Irwin hopes to save the hand, but it will probably disable him even then. This trying to frighten sentries is very well for new recruits in camps of instruction, but it is very much out of place here before the enemy, and when I reflect how often it has been practiced by officers, I am surprised that more accidents have not resulted. The case of Walden is much to be regretted, for he is a good non-commissioned officer, and had only a short time before been promoted on account of his general good conduct.

There have been several shell explosions in our fireplace, but as the (not very) deadly missiles had their origin in one of the Chesapeake oyster beds, the alarm has not been proportionate to the excitement. The blockade of the Potomac is ineffective; witness the luscious bivalves which my gallant comrades of company D are devouring. While a regular express has been commenced between Washington and Camp Wool, we have got an oyster boat manned by a smart likely contraband, bringing those delicious shell fish to our very door. Capt. Abell celebrated the first freight by treating all hands to oyster soup, and I feel bound to admit that his talent as an executive officer elicited much admiration in this instance, and the affair was considered one of the best planned and executed of the campaign.

We are quartered in some old buildings upon the shore, and like most ancient edifices, they have an unlimited ventilation. There are no glass windows, but as there is a large hole in the roof, we do not lack light in the house I live in. Some of the others have neither windows nor holes in the roof, but rejoice in the possession of some very wide cracks, which admit even more air than the occupants find necessary for respiration. After all, we contrive to enjoy ourselves quite as well as our friends in camp. We are so used to each other's ways, that we feel very much like a family, and quarrels are extremely rare. I can imagine no better Elysium for a soldier than to stand picket here, when the leafy woods and opening flowers shall proclaim the fresh and joyous springtime.—The blue hills of the Old Dominion loom grandly up upon the western shore, and the whole scenery along this inland sea, so beautiful new, must soon wear the aspect of a fairy land. Even now, holly, which our British ancestors so highly prized, does much with its bright green leaves and shining berries to relieve the stern aspect of winter, and three or four weeks will bring fresh verdure, and banish these fierce March winds.

This is a beautiful county, but it wants the stirring, active Yankee to develop its resources. Are the Yankees so much more mercenary than their brethren of the South? I suppose the upholder of this idea will, in drawing the parallel, call our attention toward the beautiful homes of the Northern middle class, and laborers even, and then turn to the shift less, tumble-down establishments of our F.F.V. neighbors. Here prolific nature is the only beautifier. With us, the shapeless tree is pruned to symmetry, and our own shoulders vigorously applied to the wheel, scorn the aid of the Hercules these children of idleness implore. A planter lamented to-day that his corn and wheat lay idle in his granary. Why was this, when six or seven tons of flour, and a vast amount of corn were being daily used here within ordinary market distance of his door? Because no vitality existed in this worn, slavery ridden country. Because the *Yankee* is wanted to erect flouring mills, and saw-mills, and school houses—in short, to wake these Rip VanWinkles from their century's sleep, and turn their mismanaged, profit-less district to the garden and pride of Maryland.

There, now! I feel much better. I have had a good oyster supper, and feel charity, peace and good-will toward my fellow men—yes, even charity to the Maryland planter. This is the last night of winter, and the wind howls through every crack and cranny of our ruinous old barracks. The sentries will have a rough time of it, but no boat can live upon the water to-night; so they can wrap their coats closely around them, and seek the shelter of some angle of the rugged bluffs which line the shore. We take our turns so that we come on guard every second day, or night, as the case may be. The guards are summoned and are off for their stations. Jemmy Bowen is among them, and looks but little bigger than a pint of cider. Jemmy, or "Bones," as we call him, is one of the peculiar institutions of Co. D. On a fine, sunny day, you will see Bones out in all his mischief, stalking gravely and solemnly about, with a queer twinkle in the corner of his eye, which warns the by-standers to keep out of harm's way. Pretty soon, Bones becomes tired of his usual style of locomotion, and throwing a half somerset, starts off upon his hands. If you buy a half dozen of apples who is that who comes up in an opposite direction, quietly munching a fine spitzenburg? Bones, of course, and you are astonished to find that six spitzenbergs makes only five apples. Bones is not a strong man to labor, and he cares as little for the articles of war as he does for the old Mosaic law; [but to induce] a laugh from a lot of tired, dispirited men, who can equal Bones? He is equal to a circus, a concert and a theater, combined, and we could as well dispense with our cup of coffee as with the queer adventures and impudent capers of this same "Bones."

Yours, as ever,
Arthur.

Somerset: somersault.

Other Voices: Confederates Prepare to Evacuate Potomac Batteries

Centerville, February 27, 1862.
Brig. Gen. S. G. FRENCH,
Commanding at Evansport:

GENERAL:

It may soon become necessary for you to evacuate your present position and rejoin General Holmes; therefore please prepare, as well as you can, for such a contingency. If you can remove any property of value do so. Endeavor in whatever you attempt in that way to excite as little observation as possible, as it is important that no movement should be suspected beforehand. Any intimation as to time of movement will be made through Brigadier-General Whiting.

Very respectfully, your obedient servant,

J. E. JOHNSTON[3]

Pickets at Sandy Point March 1st 1862

Dear Mother,

As I have a good chance to write I will make the most of it and tell you what little good news I have in store. I got a letter from Lucy the other day via Fortress Monroe. She is at West Pt. Miss. And the family were well with the exception of herself. She considered her personal security ample but her health was poor. I sent her letter at once to Aunt Eliza and it was a very apropos answer to an anxious inquiry from her as to whether any means existed of communicating with the absentees. Lucy said that she had been trying some charlybeate springs but thought my letter (I had condensed in it all the news even to the birth of Emily's boy) a greater panacea than the medicinal waters. I am very hearty and enjoy glorious health. I am on picket with the company and have usually a fine cannonade as a dessert no less than once per diem.

I enclose to you Uncle Willards last letter and in so doing I must say that in my reply (of to-day) I declined any assistance as inexpedient. I am getting along famously and any pressure from the outside is more likely to result in harm than help to me for though it might succeed, if it was ever discovered it would work a good deal of mischief. There is much jealously as to promotions and it is no kindness to the recipient of an unwise choice. I consider my chances of the very best and shall do nothing which if discovered would bring up the complaint of unfairness. The wind is worthy of the day but the birds are here already and though the river's edge is marked by a line of frozen foam, spring is not far behind. I must go on guard to night and though it is pretty cold I am glad that it is at least dry. I shall stand one relief of four hours and sleep the next eight and I am sure that that is no very hard 24 hours task. I have heard once from Uncle Theodore lately and have sent a sheet of foolscap as well as fools idea in reply. He was as democratic as ever and looked through Petermans own spectacles. No matter, the destiny of the nation is in the hands of younger and stronger men and the days of the driveling dotards of Buchanans stamp are over. I will not underrate the wisdom which age is apt to bring but I feel fully satisfied that our army, our navy and our state have suffered incalculable injury from the well meant but feeble management of superannuated warriors and statesmen whose enfeebled brains and unstrung sinews were unfit to calculate and unable to accomplish the parts which they sought to play. Scott has retired and brave warrior and almost revered though he be he would have done us a greater service had he retired earlier. He is competent to command the army in peace but his vital forces are too far spent for the active toils of war.

Well I have done considerable writing to day and feel tired so I will not continue much longer. You must punch that great cub Frank in the ribs and make him write oftener. He is a good writer and the greatest kindness you can do him is to make him exercise his talents in that line. I think Lute too must be able to write now and I want to hear from him too. I heard from Jennie a few days since by way of Alf White and must answer.

As stamps are scarce I will enclose the silver to recompense your outlay. Give my love to all the family and write by self or proxy as soon as you can.

Your aff. son
Arthur

Charlybeate springs: waters, also known as ferruginous waters, are mineral spring waters containing salts of iron.

Foolscap: foolscap folio is paper cut to the size of 8½ × *13½* inches (for "normal" writing paper, 13 × 8 in.). This was a traditional paper size used in Europe and the British Commonwealth.

Direct as before

Camp Wool March 1st 1862

Dear Jennie,

I got a letter from Alf a few days ago and I believe I will answer it in your name. We are about ready to dig out in any required direction and can do so at short order. There has been hard fighting at Leesburgh and the sound of distant but very heavy cannonading still comes booming down the river. The rebels have been firing at our battery at Budd's Ferry this morning but we pay very little attention to such trifles. We are a couple of miles below but could see the operation without paying any quarter. They have guns however which command the picket station where I now am on duty and I confess I am a little surprised that they have not treated our company to a few doses of cold iron. We could scatter and get out of the way but they might smash our building and turn us out into the cold which would not be so very agreeable. I am hale and hearty and feel quite ready to tramp. I hear that we must move next Tuesday but can hardly imagine where. It may be a mere camp yarn or it may [missing text.]

I can make no very good guess as to whether we cross the river or not. I rather hope of the two that we shall and if we do we shall have sharp work as soon as we can land. Well Jennie how do John and those little nieces of mine get on. I would give a quarter "immediately if not sooner" for a good sight at any of them. I supposed that John is making his pile by the fist full on the great demand for beef just now. I eat very little of the articles for I never was partial to salt-horse and so long as pork holds out I leave it alone. I have been very busy this forenoon and I must take a good rest before I go on guard to night. Write yourself and tell Alf that I was glad to hear from him and hope to do so often. Love to all of you

Your aff. brother
Arthur McKinstry

Direct as before to Washington

Other Voices: *New York Tribune*

March 1st, 1862
There has been no safe communication by water between this city and the capital of the nation during all this time—a period of six months. This is one of the most humiliating of all the national disgraces to which we have been compelled to submit. It has been most damaging to us in the eyes of the world . . . And it has helped the confederates just in proportion as it has injured us. It has been their haughty boast that they had maintained steady and effectual sway over the great channel of commerce between this city and Washington, through which the immense supplies of our grand army of the Potomac would naturally have passed . . . The inhabitants of Washington have at times suffered from a scarcity of both food and fuel from the same cause . . .[4]

Figure 7.3 (facing page). March 6, Dear Uncles. Thousands of readers of the *Fredonia Censor* were able to follow the adventures of their Chautauqua County boys thanks to Arthur McKinstry and his uncles. *Courtesy of Darwin R. Barker Historical Library.*

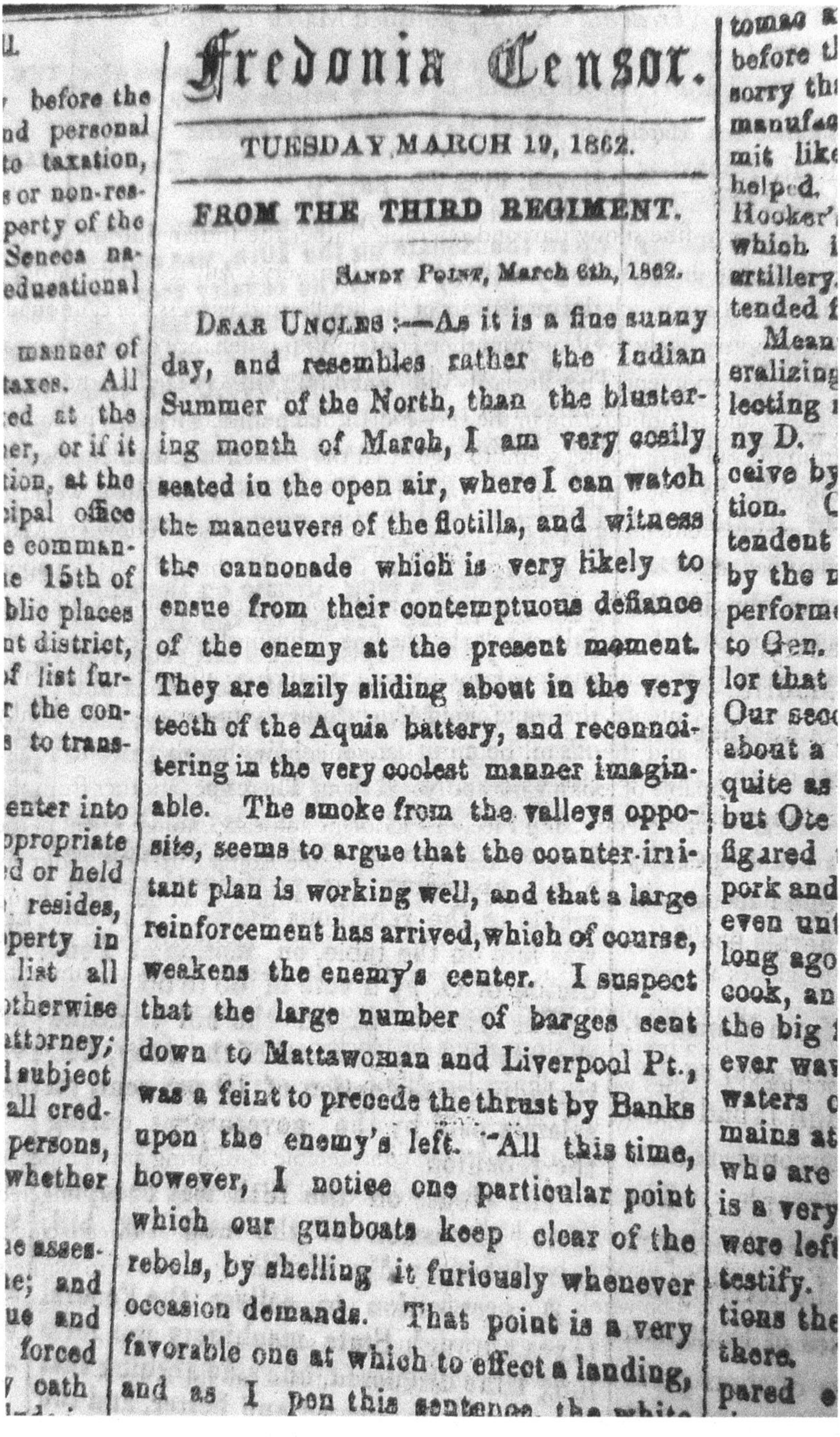

Fredonia Censor.

TUESDAY, MARCH 19, 1862.

FROM THE THIRD REGIMENT.

SANDY POINT, March 6th, 1862.

DEAR UNCLES:—As it is a fine sunny day, and resembles rather the Indian Summer of the North, than the blustering month of March, I am very cosily seated in the open air, where I can watch the maneuvers of the flotilla, and witness the cannonade which is very likely to ensue from their contemptuous defiance of the enemy at the present moment. They are lazily sliding about in the very teeth of the Aquia battery, and reconnoitering in the very coolest manner imaginable. The smoke from the valleys opposite, seems to argue that the counter-irritant plan is working well, and that a large reinforcement has arrived, which of course, weakens the enemy's center. I suspect that the large number of barges sent down to Mattawoman and Liverpool Pt., was a feint to precede the thrust by Banks upon the enemy's left. All this time, however, I notice one particular point which our gunboats keep clear of the rebels, by shelling it furiously whenever occasion demands. That point is a very favorable one at which to effect a landing, and as I pen this sentence, the white

Fredonia Censor: Published March 19, 1862

FROM THE THIRD REGIMENT.

Sandy Point, March 6th, 1862.

Dear Uncles,—

As it is a fine sunny day, and resembles rather the Indian Summer of the North, than the blustering month of March, I am very cozily seated in the open air, where I can watch the maneuvers of the flotilla, and witness the cannonade which is very likely to ensue from their contemptuous defiance of the enemy at the present moment. They are lazily sliding about in the very teeth of the Aquia battery, and reconnoitering in the very coolest manner imaginable. The smoke from the valleys opposite, seems to argue that the counter-irritant plan is working well, and that a large reinforcement has arrived, which of course, weakens the enemy's center. I suspect that the large number of barges sent down to Mattawoman and Liverpool Pt., was a feint to precede the thrust by Banks upon the enemy's left. All this time, however, I notice one particular point which our gunboats keep clear of the rebels, by shelling it furiously whenever occasion demands. That point is a very favorable one at which to effect a landing, and as I pen this sentence, the white cloud which eddies from one of those spunky looking tugs, and the far off boom of cannon, show that she is wide awake and quite capable of looking out for No. 1. Bang! There goes another from the rebels at Shipping Point, and I feel just indolent and easy enough to enjoy the spectacle. Reckoning by the velocity of sound, the Aquia battery is about six miles distant—a fraction short, and my measure is the 25 seconds intervening between the flash and report of the guns. The day is gloriously clear, and the spy glasses are in constant request. We pickets have a splendid opportunity to see the operations upon the river, and a cannonade, unless unusually spicey, is getting to be a pretty old story. As to the blockade, that is all fudge, and upon our night watches we usually see large fleets of vessels passing and re-passing, whenever it is cloudy and dark.

Day before yesterday, the boats did considerable hard firing at the especial point I have just adverted to, and the result seemed satisfactory, as they lingered about some time after firing had ceased. Yesterday morning, at three o'clock, we were roused by very heavy firing, and some of us turned out to witness the spectacle. The whole gun-boat fleet were lying about the place where the firing of the day before had occurred, and were sending shells inland at a rate the sesech gunners have never been known to make an approach to. The illumination was very fine, and I enjoyed it much. You can hardly form an idea of how efficiently this river is guarded. In addition to the pickets which are of themselves impassable, the whole river is alive with boats as soon as darkness falls. Rowboats search every nook of the Virginian shore, and keen ears catch the sound of every movement that takes place. If the Rebels undertake to start fortifications on forbidden ground, one or two gun-boats slide gracefully into the bay, and down comes a perfect hail of eight-inch shell and fixed ammunition, which operation is the precursor of a very active stampede inland.

Song-birds are plenty to-day, and I feel the welcome conviction that they are the forerunners of Spring. I have noticed in many of the letters you have published, some very odd and sometimes un-fortunate mistakes. Now while I am in doubt whether to charge most of them to the printer or to my own very careless chirography, I have noticed some which I am certainly not to blame for. Would it not be advisable that both of us bear one half the blame, and trust to the good sense and indulgence of your readers to supply the meaning which is sometimes undefined or obscure. I have seen in the last Herald a paragraph stating that while Sickles was reviewing the brigade, a shell exploded within a few feet from him. Taking my own legs for the meter, I should say that the point at which the shell that day exploded was distant about three miles from the ground upon which the review took place.

March 7—It is very cold and windy to-day, and I have again sought the sunny sheltered cave where my first letter was indited. It is too rough to-day for the gunboats to play at ball, unless some movement in rebeldom should absolutely require it, and the fleet lies quietly at anchor off Liverpool Point. We read, or rather Simpson read aloud to us (newspapers being rather scarce,) Seward's noble letter disclaiming all future political ambition. The sentiment it expresses could not be more lofty than Benton's in a not wholly dissimilar case, but criticism must vainly seek for an amendment. Many masterly productions have emanated from his pen and brain during his long struggles with the gladiators of the political arena, but the last, in which self is so wholly forgotten in the face of a political necessity, is the noblest of them all; and commands the admiration of his bitterest foes. It is pleasing to see the administration wrung involuntarily from our political enemies by Lincoln's administration. We are fortunate in possessing, for the Republican party, an exponent who so fully carries out the sentiments and wishes of a very large majority of his constituents, and who vindicates his platform so well that our opponents would deny it to be ours, and claim it as their own. Well, if that affords them any satisfaction, so let it be; to me, at least, the principle is of more importance than an empty name. The Philadelphia Inquirer states that we soldiers on the Potomac are not likely to receive any pay before the first of next month. We are sorry that the paper mills are not able to manufacture the needful, but must submit like philosophers to what can't be helped. I hear that reinforcements for Hooker's Division have arrived, among which is a couple of batteries of flying artillery. They cannot, of course, be intended for any use on this side of the river.

Meanwhile, I perceive that I am generalizing so much that I am sadly neglecting my proper subject, to wit Company D. We still hang out, as you will perceive by the date of this, at our old location. Col. Graham, who is Superintendent of the pickets, was so far pleased by the manner in which our duty was performed, that he mentioned it expressly to Gen. Sickles, who requested Col. Taylor that we might remain another tour. Our second tour of ten days will last about a week longer. We do not live quite as well as at the regimental camp, but Ote Luce does his best, and has figured thus far so as not to remit his pork and beans, the fame of which abounds even unto the first regiment. Wright long ago abdicated his position as chief cook, and John Nuepling now flourishes the big fork as bravely as Old Neptune ever waved his trident over the obedient waters of the sea. Wm. Schindler remains at camp and cooks for the sick, who are not at the hospital. Schindler is a very obliging cook, as those who were left so long ago at Camp Caldwell can testify. He gained by his kind attentions the good will of all the invalids there. We lived better while he prepared our food than at any other time since our enlistment.

Yours, as ever,
Arthur.

Seward's noble letter . . . : Secretary of State William Seward, who had lost the 1860 Republican presidential nomination to Abraham Lincoln, wrote a letter in December of 1861 in which he states he would NOT be a candidate for the 1864 presidential nomination. This letter did not appear in papers until March of 1862 however. Senator Thomas Hart Benton of Missouri had written a similar letter many years before regarding his not seeking the presidential nomination.

Editorial Note

While Arthur observes that Confederate attempts to blockade the Potomac from Union ship traffic are futile and that nighttime trans-river traffic by the Rebels is nearly impossible thanks to the efforts of the Navy and Hooker's Division, President Lincoln remains dissatisfied with the lack of progress. Increasingly frustrated with General McClellan's lack of offensive initiative, Lincoln resorts to a policy of issuing firm timetables and direct orders. But those few stirrings the Army of the Potomac does make convince Confederate commanders that defending their batteries is hopeless.

Other Voices: President's Order Regarding Potomac Batteries

PRESIDENT'S GENERAL WAR ORDER,
EXECUTIVE MANSION,
Number 3.
Washington, March 8, 1862.

Ordered, That no change of the base of operations of the Army of the Potomac shall be made without leaving in and about Washington such a force as, in the opinion of the General-in-Chief and the commanders of army corps, shall leave said city entirely secure. That no more than two army corps (about fifty thousand troops) of said Army of the Potomac shall be moved en route for a new base of operations until the navigation of the Potomac from Washington to the Chesapeake Bay shall be freed from enemy's batteries and other obstructions, or until the President shall hereafter give express permission. That any movement as aforesaid, en route for a new base of operations, which may be ordered by the General-in-Chief, and which may be intended to move upon the Chesapeake Bay, shall begin to move upon the bay as early as the 18th March instant, and the General-in-Chief shall be responsible that it moves as early as that day. Ordered, That the Army and Navy co-operate in an immediate effort to capture the enemy's batteries upon the Potomac between Washington and the Chesapeake Bay.

ABRAHAM LINCOLN.[5]

Other Voices:
Confederates Begin to Evacuate Potomac Batteries

HEADQUARTERS,
Brooke's Station, March 9, 1862
General S. COOPER,
Adjutant-General:

GENERAL:

I was notified yesterday by General Johnston that he had ordered General French to abandon Evansport, and that he and General Whiting with their commands would immediately march on Fredericksburg. He advised me to place these troops beyond the Rappahannock and only to hold the Potomac with strong outposts, breaking up the wharf at Aquia and being ready to destroy the railroad from thence to Fredericksburg. As the outpost for the Potomac, I propose to keep General Walker's brigade at Aquia as it is. I am at a loss whether to remove the guns from the batteries there, and will be obliged if you will inform me by telegraph. I have ordered Colonel Brockenbrough's regiment from the Northern Neck to this place. I have not been informed of the object of these sudden and, to me, very unexpected movements, and therefore can only strive to be ready for anything.

I am, general, very respectfully,

TH. H. HOLMES,

Major-general.

P. S.—Since writing the above General French has arrived here and reports his brigade *en route* to Fredericksburg, that all the guns at Evansport have been or will be destroyed before the rear guard leaves, and that the George Page (steamer) will be burned.

T. H. H.[6]

Figure 7.4. General J. E. Johnston. Joseph E. Johnston's command of the Department of Northern Virginia included the Confederate batteries along the Potomac River. With the Federal Army of the Potomac under McClellan beginning to move, Johnston recognized the Potomac batteries could not be defended and ordered them abandoned and destroyed. *Courtesy of Library of Congress.*

Camp Wool, March 9th 1862

Dear Mother,

There has been hard fighting to-day within sight of our pickets but across the river, we have seen the destruction of all the rebel camps which are near us and the demolition total of the so-called blockade of the Potomac. I have no authentic intelligence but I can ascribe these events and the continuous firing which we have heard and whose smoke we have witnessed to no other cause than an advance and a victory by Heintzelman. We can now cross unmolested and I think that we shall do so at very short notice so I dash off these lines to relieve you of any troublesome anxiety concerning your scapegrace son. The batteries opposite us are deserted and in flames and the Potomac is now as safe to navigate as the Connecticut which never saw the smoke of a hostile camp. I am all ready for business having sent home my spare clothing and procured those little trifles—a watch with compass, a revolver, and pocket spy glass which for a small one is very good. Thus my equipment is complete as a soldier and a correspondent. You spoke in your last of the danger of attaching too much importance to my letters. While I attach no importance whatever to them to my comrades I may be excused for reposing a confidence in my mother which I do not extend to any great degree even to McK. and Bro. That they afford pleasure to many I know—by friendly messages from the friends of my companions and by the privileges extended to me here by those who do not want to be "damned by faint praise." I have never in any instance allowed private animosity to leak out in public correspondence and I do not mean to but I have known officers to apprehend something of that sort.

In the meanwhile I exert every care to be quite innocent of any appearance of consciousness and as I never was in a set so generally friendly to me I suppose that I must be successful.

I hear that we are not likely to be paid off before the first of April and I am more sorry on your account than my own . . . I fancy these recent victories must give Uncle Sams "I promise to pay" a good deal livelier circulation. One thing I will bet high upon and that is that they wont be issued four months longer. It is getting to be spring here and the birds sing right merrily though to day they have been sadly eclipsed by the musical whistle of shells. How the folds begin to tighten upon poor "secesh," shells rain down upon them in front, flank and rear and the bloody drama is well nigh over. One or two more death hugs and the grapple will be past and we who love the union so well will return to bright firesides and loving hearts while our rash and beaten assailants will find their homes in ashes and their property wasted . . . by a long and fruitless struggle. Those who raise a devil should beware lest the servant should become the master. In very spite and desperation the rebels opposite have burned the habitations of friend and foe alike and only blackened ruins will mark the sites of some of the fairest homes in the magnificent valley of the Potomac. And all this time our homes are untouched and tenanted by the old familiar faces and they are not so far off as they seemed a month ago. In the victories of science as well as the victories of arms space is annihilated and time is the only true reckoner of distance. Thus New York City more than—[not] just 450 miles away—but linked by rail is nearer to you than Clymer which is but one ninth of the space. Well it is late and I must pace the shore for four long hours to night so good by. I shall give through the Censor later and better information.

I expect to write next from the "Old Dominion." Love to all

Your aff. son,
Arthur

Scapegrace: a mischievous or wayward person, especially a young person or child; a rascal.

Reposing: relying on (archaic).

Other Voices: A Slaveholder Complains of Treatment in Camp

[Portion of letter from John H. Bayne of Charles County to E. M. Stanton, March 10, 1862—RB]

I learned by some of the soldiers my servants were in Camp and soon as my mission became general known a large crowd collected and followed me crying shoot him, bayonet him, kill him, pitch him out, the nigger Stealer the nigger driver, at first their threats were accompanied with a few stones thrown at me which very soon became an almost continued shower of stones a number of which struck me, but did me no serious damage. Seeing the officer who accompanied me took no notice of what was going on and fearing that some of the soldiers would put their threats of shooting me into execution I informed him that I would not proceed any farther, about this time Lieutenant Edmund Harrison came to my assistance and swore he would shoot the first many who threw a stone at me, the soldiers hooted at him and continued throwing. I returned to Col. Grahams quarters but was not permitted to see him again. I left the camp without getting my servants and have not been favored to get them yet.[7]

Editorial Note

On March 9th General Joseph Johnston withdraws from Manassas Junction and repositions his army sixty miles further south to near Gordonsville on the upper Rappahannock River. This move means the batteries along the Potomac can no longer be adequately supported and thus are abandoned. Johnston's redeployment foils General George McClellan's planned repositioning of his army at the small village of Urbana, also on the Rappahannock. But McClellan has a backup plan and by mid-March a vast fleet of six hundred vessels of all kinds assembles near Alexandria to move his massive army to Fort Monroe, which lays between the James and York Rivers, beginning what will come to be known as the Peninsula Campaign.

At the same time McClellan's massive army is assembling in Alexandria, the US Senate is holding its hearings on Sickles's nomination to brigadier general. Because of the toxic relationship with Hooker, a petition by the 72nd New York requesting transfer out of the brigade, or the enormous amount of political baggage Sickles carries, the suspicious Senate rejects his nomination on March 17 by one vote. Hooker immediately places Nelson Taylor of the 72nd in command of Excelsiors, though Sickles argues he is still senior colonel within the brigade and by rights should retain command. Hooker acquiesces to Sickles, leaving the question of brigade command unsettled.[8]

Fredonia Censor: Published March 26, 1862

FROM THE THIRD REGIMENT.

Camp Wool, March 15, 62.

Dear Uncles:—

Here we are again in D street, Camp wool, and I assure you that the place looks very familiar. We find our comrades hard at work drilling in the bayonet exercise, as well as being put through a series of brigade drills by Daniel, who has suddenly come to the conclusion that something of the kind was needed.

We have had no lack of interesting events since the evacuation of Shipping Point by the rebels. In order to bring the history of events in the order in which they occurred, I will refer to my diary, since writing, unlike our uncertain memories does not forget. My last was written upon Monday last. On Tuesday there seemed to be great activity among the gun-boats and I counted nine barges capable of transporting a company each, brought down to Liverpool Point. The clear, sunny weather and singing of birds showed that spring had fairly set in. All at once the transportation of troops seemed to be checked, and we found that Gen. McClellan had ordered that none of this division should cross. During this day we had a view of nearly all the vessels of the Potomac Flotilla. The largest of these is the "Yankee," which mounts a gun which I should judge to be a 68 pr. forward, and a 32 pr. and a couple of brass howitzers aft.

On Wednesday I was on post No. 2, which commands a view of Shipping Pt.; and until noon nothing of moment occurred. A little before 12, however, I thought the little armed tug lying just below my post rather more noisy than the occasion demanded. Fancy my amazement when I beheld the magnificent L.I. Sound boat, Elm City, dashing rapidly up the river. Wonders did not cease here, however, for close after followed sixteen steamers most of them first class and the guard saw there more pass up in the night. On Thursday morning, business began again bright and early, and seventeen steamers and propellers passed up together with two large barges, the Vanderbilt taking the lead.

At noon Capt. Abell took the sail boat for a trip to the "sacred soil." As the Captain knew my penchant for taking notes for your readers, I was offered a seat, and as you may suppose, it was promptly accepted. The wind was against us, but we made Shipping Pt. in a little over an hour. We landed near a large lighter, where Lieut. Thomas Eastman Comd'g str. Yankee, was working his tars in getting off a superb English gun, which had very recently graced Evansport battery. Lieut. Hinman took out his rule and found its caliber to be 7½ inches. Close by lay about three tons of shell; they were conical, and were declared by the sailors to weigh 120 pounds. A part of them were intended for 32 and 42 pr. guns, and were very much elongated. Just beyond and about these, was the balloon Constitution, which was filling for an ascension. Here I turned up the bluff, and in less than two minutes had crossed the fosse, and stood upon one of the magazines of the famous battery of Shipping Point. This fort consisted of a semicircle of magazines, in the shape of a very large potato hole. They measured, perhaps, fifteen feet across, and between them were intervals of three or four feet. From each of these intervals had frowned the muzzle of a cannon, but they had all been removed by this time. The magazines, or at least such as I entered, had been emptied, and their contents destroyed, or transferred to some place where they would be more useful to Uncle Sam. I now walked down to the Evansport battery, which was at a short distance below. Here, in the first embrasure between the magazines, I saw a heavy gun torn from its burned and shattered carriage, and leaning upon the low parapet with its muzzle inclining at an angle of about forty five degrees. In the next embrasure was another English rifled gun, like the one at the landing. Like the others

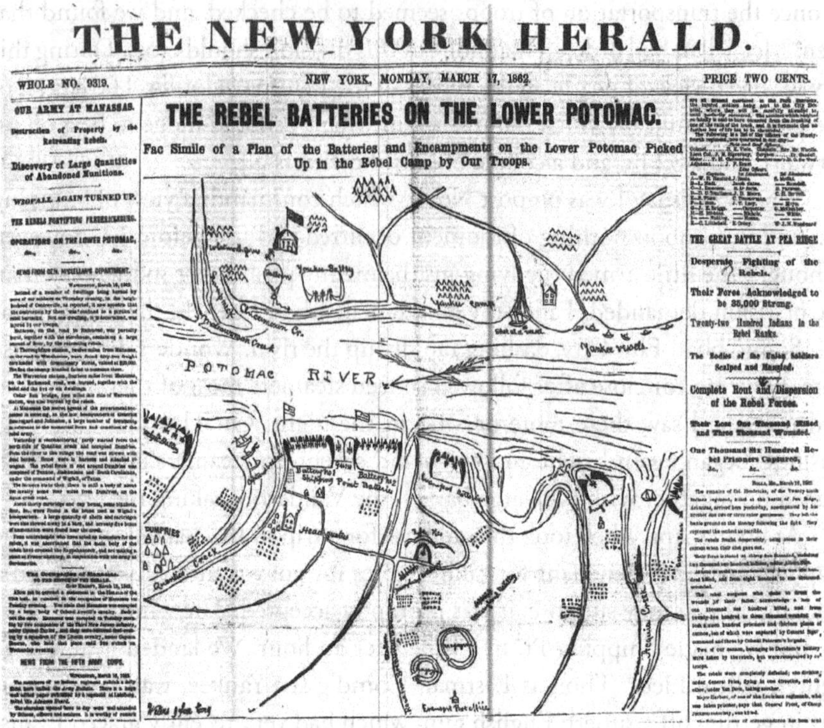

THE NEW YORK HERALD.

WHOLE NO. 9319. NEW YORK, MONDAY, MARCH 17, 1862. PRICE TWO CENTS.

OUR ARMY AT MANASSAS.

Destruction of Property by the Retreating Rebels.

Discovery of Large Quantities of Abandoned Munitions.

WIGFALL AGAIN TURNED UP.

THE REBELS FORTIFYING FREDERICKSBURG.

OPERATIONS ON THE LOWER POTOMAC, &c., &c., &c.

THE REBEL BATTERIES ON THE LOWER POTOMAC.

Fac Simile of a Plan of the Batteries and Encampments on the Lower Potomac Picked Up in the Rebel Camp by Our Troops.

THE GREAT BATTLE AT PEA RIDGE

Desperate Fighting of the Rebels.

Their Force Acknowledged to be 35,000 Strong.

Twenty-two Hundred Indians in the Rebel Ranks.

The Bodies of the Union Soldiers Scalped and Mangled.

Complete Rout and Dispersion of the Rebel Forces.

Their Loss One Thousand Killed and Three Thousand Wounded.

One Thousand Six Hundred Rebel Prisoners Captured, &c., &c., &c.

Figure 7.5. *Herald* FRONT PAGE. The *New York Herald* ran this plan of the Confederate batteries on their front page following their abandonment. The artist's lack of concern for the proper representation of distances, especially regarding Aquia Creek, is evident. Source: *New York Herald*.

it was spiked and the charred fragments of its carriage lay scattered around. The next was, I believe, of the same description. In the next embrasure was a 42 pr. and a pretty looking spectacle it presented. The chase and muzzle still hung by the trunnions to the torn and wrenched carriage while the heavy base lay near, in fragments which might weigh a quarter of a ton. Sticking fast in the bore, and indeed, projecting somewhat beyond it, was a shot which had been rammed only half home and choked well, so that when the gun was fired it must infallibly explode. In the embrasures I saw fragments of the shells our gun boats had thrown, and which I had seen to explode over this very point. The next gun was a 32 pr. and it was half full of grape and canister shot. I should suppose, from its appearance, that the rebels had attempted to burst it, and failing in this had spiked and left it. Its carriage, like all the rest, was charred and broken to such a degree as to totally disable it. In the rear of the 42 pr. was an ammunition case, containing six strapped shells, with loads and fuzes all ready for instant use. The last embrasure had contained the English gun on the shore. In the Evansport battery was a large bomb proof, where the gunners had evidently lived. I entered some of the magazines, and found their construction to be very good, and nearly uniform. Enter a low and narrow door, and follow a passage of like dimensions for about six feet; then turn a right angle, and soon after another, and you are in the magazine. The inside was cased with plank and logs, and the outside was frequently palisaded as an additional security. It was impossible that the powder should be fired by hostile shells, through the zigzag entrance, or the huge mound of earth by which it was overlaid. The guns were protected by low parapets of sandbags, and bundles of faggots, (such as the Catholics used to grill and roast our respected ancestors with,) and the whole works were admirably calculated to resist an attack from the water. In the rear, the works were absolutely defenseless. The batteries were situated near the bank, which is here a bluff of twenty feet or more in height, and generally very difficult to escalade. All the ravines and like salient points were defended by strong palisades, and if the rebels had stood their ground, it would have cost much blood to carry those works. I now took my way to the rear of the works for a look at the rebel quarters. They had built some very good log houses and many were shingled. Most of these, I presume, had belonged to officers. Half burned tents and clothing lay around, and smashed tea pots and frying pans showed that our secesh friends didn't mean that we should profit unnecessarily by their hasty flight. Some tolerably good blankets lay around, but I left them there, on account of an apprehension that they might be peopled by a tribe whose *union* proclivities are never for a moment called in question. The clothing was mostly the homemade, butternut-colored stuff which the rebels wear so extensively and the only article of uniform which I found was a dilapidated blouse, whose buttons had been cut off.

Thinking by this time that I ought to rejoin the rest of the party, I turned my course shoreward. One of the 1st Mass. pickets, who had just returned from a scouting expedition, informed me that they had seen secesh cavalry, and that one of his companions had been captured but had effected his escape. I arrived at the boat just in time to meet the Captain's party, and we soon shoved off for the Maryland shore. Most of us had some trophy or other in the shape of grape shot, or something of that sort. Clark Brooks secured a cartridge-bag which he sports for a night cap.

On Friday morning we began to pickup for our return to Camp Wool. The stream of vessels still continued to shoot past us, four steamers, a propeller, a schooner and a barge having passed us, and several more were in sight. Thus you see that transportation for at least 40,000 men has passed up toward the capital. Some of the vessels were fired at, but without effect, and the last I saw of our gunboats, they were shelling in retaliation the rebels at Aquia.

A little before noon, Co. E of the 4th Reg. came down and relieved us, and after bolting a hasty dinner, we resumed our accoutrements, and again turned our faces toward old Camp Wool. The Spring has so far progressed as to make the roads quite passable, and the journey occupied but a short time. Here we find things very much as we left them.

In answer to a private inquiry, I will make a public reply. It is not our business to return slaves. Citizens, whether black or white, are generally allowed to pass our lines in the day time, and the slave owner has precisely the same privilege as the darkey. We suffer, but we never aid in the capture of fugitives. We are mere passive spectators, though sometimes, when a "Chiv" is scampering hot foot after a contraband, it has occurred that the sentry didn't see the latter until he had got past the lines, while the owner was discovered just in time to bring him up at the point of the bayonet, and send him around to No. 1 post, where he could get out and dash after his property, which had got about a half mile into the woods.

It seems, from all accounts, that the rebels did not have a battle with Heintzleman's forces, and that the sound and smoke which we supposed to be of battle, were in reality the blowing up of magazines, whose roar was multiplied by the numberless echoes of the Quantico and adjacent valleys.

Our Hospital list to-day is as follows: Co. B—Whitmore, convalescent. Co. D—Newburgher, conv. Co. E—Corp. Loftus, general debility. Co. H—Leguire, conv. Frank Stevens of the band has long wavered between life and death, but has lately exhibited such favorable symptoms as to justify considerably hope of his recovery. Every attention has been given him by Drs. Irwin and Leighton. Corporal Walden's wrist is doing finely, and it is probable that he will recover its entire use.

Yours as ever,
Arthur

"Yankee": USS *Yankee*, a side-wheel steam tug of 328 tons and 146 feet long, mounting two 32-pound guns. A landing party from USS *Anacostia* and *Yankee* destroyed abandoned Confederate entrenchments and batteries at Cockpit Point and Evansport, Virginia, on March 9, 1862, the same day as the engagement between ironclads USS *Monitor* and CSS *Virginia*.

Escalade: the scaling of fortified walls using ladders, as a form of military attack.

Other Voices: General Hooker's Frustration with Runaway Slaves

[Portion of letter from Brig. Gen. J. Hooker to Brig. Gen. S. Williams, March 18, 1862—RB]

Contraband are arriving in such numbers at my camp from Virginia as to render it necessary for me to be advised of the disposition I shall make of them. Am I to understand Paragraph 8 General Orders 120.60 dated Head Quarters Army of the Potomac Febr. 21, 1862, as embracing this class of persons? To permit them to go at large in this secession district, would, I have no doubt result in many of them being returned to their rebel masters, and I hope that it will not be permitted. Please advise me.[9]

Camp Wool, March 19th, 1862

Dear Aunt,

I have three letters to write and I think I ought to look to yours first. We are now back from the river and in camp again but we are not idle for we have plenty of drill. I will give you a little diagram of our situation. It is rumored that we are to cross over in a day or two and to march on Fredericksburgh. I hope that is true for I would like to pitch in and get through this war and go about my business.

If Lucy comes home she will not have to travel far to get within the U.S. lines. In a very short time I am inclined to think we shall occupy Miss. And I have no fear of our friends suffering any injury or ill treatment from our forces. Houses of citizens are generally guarded, especially if requested, to prevent pillage. We belong to Heintzelmans division. Gen. McDowell I hear has just come down with 35,000 men and landed below Aquia Creek. I think this portends an advance on Richmond. I have not a doubt that an attack would be perfectly successful.

I am pretty well prepared as regards outfit for an advance—having a compass in my watch, a good revolver, and a very good pocket spy glass. I have also provided myself with all the clothing I need and it is new and good. Some time since I sent Condin Cyrus a map of this vicinity which is much better than I have now time to make. Did you see it when at Uncles. Papers are very uncertain in coming but if you should send me any send the Republican which is the only one worth the postage beside the metropolitan dailies. In fact I like it the best of any I know. I guess though it is better to send none for I don't believe we shall remain here twenty-four hours. Letters are a great comfort to us and are the greatest indeed we have. I have a letter from Mother a few days since. All at home are well and Mother and Frank had been to Fredonia with a few days. All were well there. The weather is a little raw but not severe enough to trouble us much. We have good Sibley tents for the march. We don't keep fire more than half the time and it is really Spring here. A fortnight on, at most three weeks will bring settled weather here. As it is nearly time to drill I must close. Write soon and often and direct as heretofore.

Your aff. nephew
Arthur McKinstry

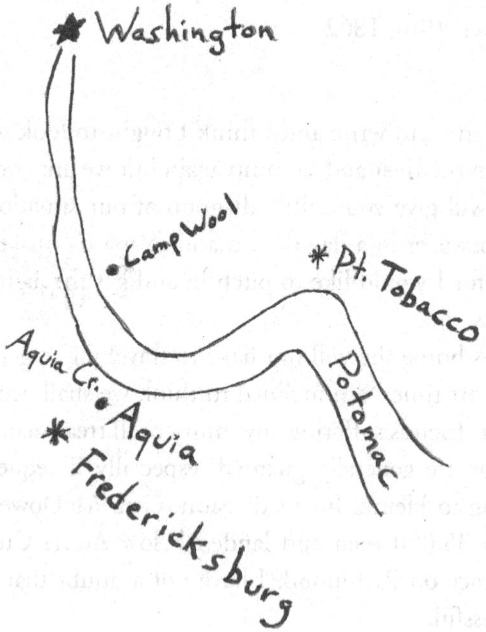

Figure 7.6. McKinstry map, March 19, 1862. Rendering of the map included in the body of the March 19, 1862, letter to his aunt showing the relative positions of Washington, Camp Wool, Aquia, Fredericksburg, and Port Tobacco. *Rendering by the author.*

I will give you a little diagram . . . : Arthur included, embedded in the text of the letter, a small drawing of the lower Potomac showing the locations of Washington, Camp Wool, Aquia, Fredericksburg, and Port Tobacco.

Lucy: Lucy Chapin, a cousin of Arthur moved south prior to the war to teach school, eventually settling in Mississippi.

Heintzelmans division: General Samuel Peter Heintzelman was a career soldier who at this time commanded the 3rd Corps of the Army of the Potomac. Joseph Hooker commanded the 2nd Division of the 3rd Corps to which the 72nd New York belonged.

Gen. McDowell . . . with 35,000 men: McDowell's Union Corps briefly occupied Fredericksburg in anticipation of the offensive against Richmond but was pulled away to the west when Stonewall Jackson's Confederate force moved into the Shenandoah Valley.

Sibley tents: conical shaped tents of about twelve feet high that could house twelve men comfortably and able to accommodate a small central stove for cooking and heating.

Fredonia Censor: Published April 2, 1862

FROM THE THIRD REGIMENT.

Camp Wool, March 28, 1862.

Dear Uncles:—

Still we linger upon the threshold of important changes, and still the respite is employed in war like preparations. The rebels still infest the country below Acquia, and several companies have been out scouting. Company I, of Delaware County, went to Liverpool Point, and went down the river in armed tug Satelite. They landed on the Virginia shore at a distance of 18 miles below, and started inland after a reputed spy, whom they captured just in the nick of time. Among the spoils and trophies of the expedition were a revolver and the finest pattern of a Bowie knife I ever saw. It had the genuine Bowie curved point, and the blade measured 12 ½ inches.

On their re-embarking, three secesh horsemen came down to the shore to watch their movements. In anticipation of such an event the satellite's guns were shotted and several shells were thrown at the horsemen. One of the rebels was seen to fall, and his horse galloped rider less inland. The ensuing day they returned to camp, Willard, of Co. B, led his mudsills upon a similar expedition.—The night was entirely dark, and under its cover they were landed by the Satelite at Boyd's Hole, which is situated at some distance below Aquia. They traveled back from the river perhaps a mile and a half, and drove in one of the enemy's outpost after a brief exchange of shots. One of the rebel pickets, in his hurry, left a very fine double barreled shot gun. One barrel was loaded with ball and the trifle of 22 buck shot. About this time however they discovered a regiment drawn up in line to receive them with all that hospitality for which the old dominion is celebrated; when Capt. Willard concluded that the 3d Excelsior would look very badly upon parade with so fine a company as B absent, and returned with all the expedition which military etiquette would allow of.

We drill constantly when the ground is dry. Lieut. Hinman has been instructing Co. D in the bayonet exercise. This drill is very fatiguing to a novice, but under our present instructor, who affords us the needed rest and change of position; the boys progress rapidly. It is this quiet but constant regard for the comfort of his men which has made Lieut. Hinman's one of the exceptional cases in which a man may exercise strict military authority over social companions, and retains *all* the respect and *all* the friendship which were enjoyed as a civilian.

I have read the foregoing paragraph to a group of my companions, and it was approved without a dissenting voice. If the company were canvassed the result would be the same. We are under marching orders and expect to leave soon. When and where we are to go, is and will be, a secret. That we are, however, to depart soon is evinced by the fact that all who are not able to endure the hardships of a march has been sent to a division hospital. From our hospital were sent the following volunteers from Chautauqua: Whitmore, Co. B, Newburgher, Co. D, Leguire, Co. H, Wilder, of Co. D, was not in the hospital, but being unfit for duty, went with the others. His wrist is doing very well, and we hope that disability may be only temporary. Frank Stevens did not go, but remains here until sufficiently recovered to visit home.—His furlough is ready and will probably be used by next week. His recovery is no longer doubtful. In addition to those removed from hospital, there were a number sent from the companies who were in no need of medical treatment, but were not strong enough to warrant their being taken upon a march. It again becomes my unpleasant duty to record the death of a Chautauqua volunteer. On the 17th, Wild, of Co. H, expired very suddenly. He had recovered from an attack of typhoid, and was back in his company, but was carried off by heart disease.

It is difficult, indeed, to even conjecture what movements are in contemplation. We hear of wars and rumors of wars, and all sorts of improbable tales are in circulation. One of the latest is that, the Merrimac had made fast to fortress Monroe and towed it into Norfolk harbor, and though we do not place absolute confidence in the report, it is quite as plausible as the majority.

I imagine that we shall move in the direction of Fredericksburg, upon the Rappahannock, as it is the nearest place where the rebels are found in force.—Gen. Holmes is said to command the enemy in front of us.

We had only one mail during the past week. This was owing to the seizure of the mail steamer by Government as a transport. I see published a general order, prohibiting the soldiers from sending letters home. As this applies to the advanced post only, I am still free to transmit to you the news current, but it is very probable that we shall, by another week, come under the title of advanced posts, when my correspondences will be interrupted partially if not totally. If, therefore, our friends should find that this end of the correspondence fails, they must remember that it is from necessity and not from choice, and we hope that we shall continue to receive the letters from home, which are so cheering to the soldier's heart. Do our friends at home rightly estimate the comparative facilities for letter writing? My knees are my table, and my portfolio is my desk. I may at any time be summoned to drill or to labor, and whatever of sport or cheerful gaiety there may be in the soldier's life must be self-sustaining. But *you* can write; *you* can draw your chair to your writing table, and suffer no interruption by extra duty, by roll call or by parade. Our time by day is demanded by drill and cleaning of arms and accoutrements. Our Sunday is by no means a day of rest, for it generally brings us harder drill than any other in the week. Our evenings are generally our own, and you can readily conceive the writing facilities which twelve men enjoy in a room whose dimension are about 12 by 14 feet, by the light of one candle. At least one-half of the inmates of a tent pull off their boots and climb upon their beds to eat or write. I do not say this in a complaining spirit, for it is not unexpected nor is it avoidable.

We did not suppose when we enlisted that we were departing upon a pleasant summer jaunt, that Delmonico was to supply our table. I simply mention these facts that you may not expect of us that which is beyond our power.

Yours, as ever,
Arthur.

Figure 7.7. CAMP OF THE 8TH NEW JERSEY. Camp of the 8th New Jersey near Mattawoman Creek, part of the 3rd Brigade of Hooker's Division. *Courtesy of Library of Congress.*

Other Voices: From the *Fredonia Censor*

Published April 2, 1862

A member of the Excelsior Brigade writes from the Camp to a friend in this village, from which we make the following extract:

Camp Wood, March 28, 1862

Dear Sir:—

Since my last letter to you, another move has been made on the military Chess Board, and affairs on the Potomac have been very much changed. Our martial Paul Morphy is playing his game with consummate skill, and as a strong evidence of the fact, I may here remark that one of the first fruits of his masterly combinations has been to compel the rebels to raise the blockade of the Potomac. Two weeks ago to-day the weather was beautifully fine, I took the occasion to stroll up to Run Point and get a breath of fresh air. As I neared the camp of the New Jersey 5th, which is located about one mile below the Point, I came across a party of men intently watching some object on the River. As a matter of course I made one more of the party of site seeking. The object of our curiosity proved to be one of the gun-boats which was boldly standing in towards the batteries of the enemy on Cock Pitt Point. As she came silently gliding down the river, a puff of white smoke curled in graceful folds from her forward deck and a moment after a shell from her bow gun burst directly over the Battery Parapet. She halted a moment to see what response this would awaken from the secessionists on the bank.

None came, so once more under way she neared the shore rapidly, eagerly, feeling her way by sending shell after shell to awaken the secessionists. She was now so close to the shore that the high hills seemed to over top her deck, when a boat shot out from under the stern, and before we could scarcely credit our eyesight they had landed, and from the flag staff where so long had hung in diabolical defiance the boasted flag of secession, soon was floating the glorious stars and stripes. Such a cheer as then rent the air rose from our crowd now grown large and enthusiastic that made the hills of old Virginia ring again with its gladsome music. Now dense volumes of smoke are seen rising from the batteries at Shipping Point some four miles further down the River and then again from the one on Quantico Creek, and a smaller work below, and the steamer George Page together with the schooner which long ago had taken refuge in the creek were discovered to be on the fire. What this meant was past our comprehension, but soon the truth burst on our minds. The Rebels were leaving their batteries and destroying everything inflammable and the blockade of the Potomac was raised. And so it was, and as I strolled back to camp musing upon the exciting scenes I had witnessed, I admiringly blessed the strategic skill which had forced our foes to abandon such a stronghold of defence and offence, which to have broken would have cost our division many valuable lives.

Yours &c.

Paul Morphy: born in 1837, Morphy is considered one of the greatest chess players of all time. He retired from the game in 1859 after getting a law degree.

Editorial Note

While Arthur has great admiration for Sickles early on, the general's habitual absenteeism and subsequent poor management of the brigade causes McKinstry's opinion of Sickles to decline. Though Arthur does recognize Sickles is taking the role of general more seriously, for McKinstry it may be a case of too little, too late.

Fredonia Censor: Published April 9, 1862

FROM THE THIRD REGIMENT.

Camp Wool, March, 30, 1862.

Dear Uncles:—

"All quiet along the Potomac," and the rain falling in a perfect deluge upon the God-forsaken country. This, however, is a source of self gratulation among the soldiers, for it puts a temporary veto upon the tedious and abominable course of drill to which we have lately been subjected. We were lately reviewed by Gen. Hooker, and went through a long bayonet drill and some battalion evolutions. The General was so far pleased by our proficiency that he exclaimed: "This regiment is not only the best drilled in the Division, but it is the best I ever saw." It is very pleasing to us that we are so unequivocally complimented by a veteran soldier like Gen. Hooker, but, after all, I think that one half the drill we go through, would have answered much better. I can readily see the propriety of maintaining the athletic training but do not so kindly take to the drudgery of a pack mule. A reasonable drill engages the attention of the soldiers, and they endeavor earnestly to improve, but when it is pushed beyond all reason, the only care or wish of the men is to get through the day in any shape or manner. All ambition is lost, and when they ought to be dressing on the right or left, they are measuring with the eye the sun's distance from the horizon. When the soldiers of the 3d *choose*, they execute their field evolutions with the precision of clock-work, but when they are tired by unreasonable tasks, neither man nor devil can compel it of them. If a half of the drill of the U.S. volunteers had been applied to the legitimate task of quelling the rebellion, I fully believe that Jeff Davis' horde of traitors would not only be subdued but utterly exterminated from the face of the earth. We have had some more brigade drills lately, and Gen. Sickles has done much better than his former management would have justified our expecting. I cannot but admire his indomitable resolution, and have no mean opinion of his talent. If the time spent at Washington in intriguing for the confirmation of the Generalship had been employed as at present, I believe that his nomination would have been more favorably received. Meanwhile, one of the best disciplined brigades in the service is drawing (not very regularly) Government pay, and eating Government rations, (what they are not cheated out of,) until it can be ascertained whether we have a General or not. If Sickles is to be our General why not confirm him and let him apply himself to his business? If he is not to be, why not at once appoint his successor and let him assume his harness as promptly as possible. It should be to us a source of humiliation, that military experience and signal ability have weighted so lightly when opposed to political trickery and partizan prejudices. The fortunes of our Generals have been made or marred by powerful political friends or foes, rather than by faults or merits of their own. There is strong hope that Stanton's appointment as Secretary of War will work important and beneficial changes, but Enceladus bore upon his breast no such burden as the mass of red tape beneath which Stanton must struggle for some time to come. If he is successful, we must accord to him the praise of regenerating a system which is unsound in every part, and not the less difficult task of organizing a new. If he cleanses the Augean stable, he has accomplished the labor of a Hercules. If he fails, we can say of him as of Phaeton, that he fell but perished in a great attempt.

I have not been down to the river for some time, but those of our boys who have, tell me that armies are being transported down the Potomac. Navigation is certainly very brisk, and the masts and sails of vessels are almost constantly to be seen from the vicinity of the guard house, which commands a view of a bend of the river.

It is now a certain fact that we are recognized as the 72d N. Y. Volunteers. This is substantially a triumph to Gov. Morgan, and an embarrassment to Gen. Sickles. In their personal quarrel I can sympathise but little, and that little would not be in Gov. Morgan's favor, but the result of it is evidently beneficial to us. If we were classed as U.S. Volunteers, we should in all probability be retained to garrison disaffected localities, and not be discharged at the close of hostilities until all the State Volunteers had been sent home, and the very last drudgery of warfare accomplished.

We have been on no reconnoissances since I wrote to you last, and nothing of moment has occurred. Everything of value, however, which we cannot carry, has been sent away for storage until we start homeward. Those who are unable to march with their equipments upon their backs have been sent to the Division Hospital and remain there. Of the sick in our regimental hospital there were only Whitmore, of Co. B, and Leguire of Co. H; Walden, of Co. D, is with them, and so also are a number who were sent there on account of weakness, and not for medical treatment. In comforts and attendance, the Division Hospital is far inferior to that of our regiment, and it is a good thing that none of our boys there are seriously ill. Frank Stevens is still here, but is improving fast.

A battery of light artillery was on our parade ground a few days ago and drilled there. They changed front and maneuvered considerably, loading and firing blank cartridges.

The Paymaster avoids us as if we had the pestilence.

Last night we had a snow-storm, and for a Maryland spring it was a *right peert* one. For several days before it had been so pleasant that we kept hardly any fire.

McClellan does not seem to ride so buoyantly upon the wave of popular favor as some months since. If the recent Union successes are legitimately the fruits of his strategy, the facts must eventually be proven, and his fame will be great and enduring. If they are owing only to the skill and bravery of his subordinates, they and not he should wear the victor's laurels. The whole will doubtless be cleared up in time, and it is our common duty to wait patiently until the proper period arrives. Meanwhile, though one of the Army of the Potomac, of whom Gen. McClellan expects such extraordinary deeds, I should thank the kind fortune which would cast my lot with Burnside or Shields. I do not think the slow policy of starving out an enemy either prudent, humane or glorious. The final result will prove that not a life is saved, while the expense and injury of property are multiplied in an alarming ratio. I am a soldier, and I look my chances in the face, and I am not alone in the desire that if my days are to be ended in this campaign, that it may be by the short and comparatively easy death of the bullet, rather than by the slower and not less deadly hand of disease. The carnage of the battle-field may be terrible, but more by far are lost or disabled by sickness in a long campaign that are killed in the course of a shorter and more bravely contested war. More than this, I believe that the traitors with whom we are contending will need the force of a terrible warning to restrain them from similar demonstrations in the future. They are like their own bloodhounds which only attack in the rear, and they need a lesson which shall last them not now only but forever. Fort Donelson, Newbern, Pea Ridge, and Strasburgh are not idle warnings, and it is only my ardent desire for a speedy and enduring peace which prompts in me the desire that a yet severe scourging is in store for the enemies of our country and their own interests.

I should like to acquaint you with our prospects, but for the present I have done with speculating upon such a dissolving view as the destiny of the Excelsior Brigade.—Should we leave our present situation there are three points to which we might be sent. First in the direction of Fredericksburgh, Va. Second, to Fortress Monroe. Third, to reinforce Burnside. I have seen nothing of the "wooden guns" on the rebel fortifications at Shipping Point. On the contrary the guns were of the most approved sort, and sufficient in number for the embrasures. There were several kegs and half barrels of loose canister shot in the batteries. It would be strange indeed if the rebels had not all the necessary implements and materials of war when the Portsmouth Navy Yard, with its ample resources was so convenient. I am surprised that the Nashville has again run the blockade.—Since our European friends have so suddenly discovered the virtues of privateering we should at least have profited by former and present experience, and allowed the idle vessels of our merchant service to plug the ratholes of the southern coast. It would have been done gratuitously by mercantile associations, and effectually, too. Or was it to pay some surplus millions to such brokers as Morgan, that so great an element of national strength has been so studiously neglected.

Yours, as ever,

Arthur

Enceladus: one of the Gigantes, the Giants, in Greek mythology, son of Gaea and Uranus.

Augean stable: the stables, which belonged to King Augeas, housed a large herd of cattle and had not been cleaned for years. Hercules was ordered to clean out these filthy stalls.

Phaeton: son of Helios, the Sun god. Attempted to drive his father's chariot across the heavens but failed mightily in the effort.

Peert: variation of peart, lively.

Morgan: businessman John Pierpont Morgan financed the purchase of five thousand surplus rifles at $3.50 each, which were then sold back to the government for $22 each. The 1861 incident became renowned as a scandalous example of wartime profiteering (not to be confused with New York governor Edwin D. Morgan).

Camp Wool April 1st 1862

Dear Mother,

It is a splendid spring morning and the boys are as merry as crickets. The sun shines bright and warm and the wags of the camp are celebrating "All Fools Day" in the most approved fashion. Well, all this don't affect me very much and I can occupy my time better in writing to you. So Frank goes to Edwards to work. It is a good place and I do not know of so model a farmers establishment in any other place. Uncle Truman has the science of doing a big days work and doing it in season and that is just what a youngster like Frank wants to know. Our mail does not run very regularly now on account of the regular boats being seized by Government as transports. We expect however a mail this evening and I shall look for the Censor and hope to get a letter from you. I must write to Frank and will do so to-day if I can get a stamp to pay its postage. We expect to be paid off this week and have some hope of drawing three months pay instead of two. In justice we ought to get it but it is by no means certain yet. If we should get it I could spare you an X and not miss it at all. I will send you the five whether or no.

I get along here very pleasantly—as much so as any who don't carry a commission. Frank spoke in his letter of wooden guns. I saw nothing but the most approved kind of ordnance in the rebels fortifications and plenty of it. I think I can get Douglas Stevens of Fredonia to carry home some little souvenirs of my trip to secessia. He can take them to Uncle Willard. It now occurs to me that you wanted to lend Uncle Henry my hammock. Lend it to him for the season if you like. I do not wish however to lose any of the companions of my journeyings, so do not give it away.

We were reviewed a week ago by Gen. Hooker, and though we had no warning at all, but turned out at five minutes notice: we came out in such neat order and drilled so accurately that he exclaimed—This is not only the best drilled regiment in the Division but by God it's the best I ever saw. Hooker is an old soldier and knows his business well, hence we value such a compliment. We are all ready to move at any time and may go to-morrow, or stay here a month. Meanwhile we are getting rather impatient of McClellans style of doing business. There is nothing made in a long campaign, for more lives are lost by disease than are saved by avoiding actual battle. I am acclimated pretty thoroughly and don't fear disease but I am looking at the general rule. Isn't Burnside doing slashing work. I have not heard from any-body for a long time. Last week I got a proper letter from Phebe Morgan. I had sent to the girls—Ellen, Phebe, and Abbie several numbers of the Censor containing my letters, and Phebe sent me a Republican in return. It was like seeing an old friend and I must say that it is the best conducted paper I know of far or near.

I have now and then a game of chess and stand my hand with any I have played with as yet. I can get plenty of good reading and don't fail to improve my chances. It is a fine day and I expect a wretchedly hard drill to day. We have no fire in the tent and don't need it to day. We shall doubtless keep one however to night. What is John up to this season. I supposed that you will try to raise considerable wheat this summer. I hope that it will be a more favorable season than the last. How much stock do you keep this season. Don't ever get caught in the fall with more stock than you can winter for it is dear business. Whenever I get a farm it will be where hay is out of fashion. How does Father stand it. I hope his health is good. I hope to see you all before many months but none can say when our labors will end. Write as often as you can and direct as formerly.

Your aff. son
Arthur

Burnside doing slashing work: Brigadier General Ambrose E. Burnside, assisted by the US Navy, executed a series of engagements along the North Carolina coast aimed at closing blockader-running ports inside the Outer Banks. Also known as the Burnside Expedition.

Figure 8.1. *Elm City*. A civilian ship prior to the war, the *Elm City* was used extensively to move Federal troops and supplies. The 72nd New York regiment was transported from Lower Maryland to Hampton Roads and the safety of Fortress Monroe at the tip of Virginia Peninsula aboard the *Elm City*. Source: *Historical Digressions* blog site.

Chapter 8

We Expect a Big Fight Very Soon

Mid-April to Early May 1862—
Move to the Peninsula and Battle at Williamsburg

Excelsior Brigade moves to the Virginia Peninsula minus Dan Sickles • Siege in front of Yorktown • Arthur and many others killed at Williamsburg

Editorial Note

After months of delay, the Army of the Potomac is finally on the offensive. Since mid-March, General McClellan has gathered the army at the tip of a peninsula in Virginia formed by the York River to the north, and the James River to the south. From here the army expects to push all the way to Richmond and final victory. But with the Confederates dug in around the town of Yorktown, the cautious McClellan begins time-consuming siege operations designed to eventually reduce the town and open the way toward Richmond.

With his division now on its way to join the gathering army on the peninsula, Hooker uses the move as an opportunity to rid himself of Sickles once and for all, issuing orders on April 5 relieving Dan from command of the Excelsior Brigade. A day later, Sickles pens a farewell to the brigade he had raised and then heads to Washington to attempt another resurrection of his career.[1] With Nelson Taylor now appointed to lead the Excelsiors, Arthur takes time to ruminate on Sickles's fate and what lies ahead.

Fredonia Censor: Published April 23, 1862

FROM THE THIRD REGIMENT.

U.S. Transport, Elm City, April 11, '62.

Dear Uncles:—

I believe I left off at Sickles being superseded by Col. Taylor in command of the brigade. It was the greatest thing I ever saw, for the order came when most of the troops were embarked, so that Daniel couldn't even close them in mass to hear his last dying speech, before his official head rolled off his shoulders. I have no doubt but what the state of the brigade at that time presented a disgraceful scene, for Sickles was half insane with fury. During Sunday afternoon the ocean steamer *Hero* came down from Washington, bringing Maj. Gen. McDowell, and Brigadiers Wadsworth and Negley. Col. Taylor went on board and shook hands with the party, and conversed with them for some time. On Monday we had two more days rations served out, but lay unmoved at anchor. While Capt. Doyle was going his rounds as officer of the day, he found a little stranger in Mrs. Collins state room, which was not named upon any enlistment roll. The *Elm City* is a New Haven boat, and we ought to class the new recruit as a true blue Yankee, by virtue of the vessel, rather than to claim him as a citizen of Maryland, from the waters in which she lay. By all means give the accused the benefit of the doubt. Tuesday found us in *status quo*, but Col. Taylor's patience now began to ooze out of his fingers' ends. The difficulty was that the brigade must go together, and there was not yet sufficient transportation. By Col. Taylor's orders, the next two steamers passing up were brought to by a gunboat, and taken *nolens volens* to transport our brigade. In so doing, it would seem that Col. Taylor exceeded his authority, but this fact only renders the proceeding the more creditable to his humanity, for the lower part of the vessel was like the forty-seven separate stinks of Cologne turned loose in a stable. The boat will accommodate three or four hundred very well, but it is piling it on pretty steeply to quadruple that number.

At 4 P.M. on Wednesday, we at last got off and steamed down as far as the mouth of Port Tobacco creek, where we dropped anchor for the night. We had two barges and two schooners in tow, and the *Elm City* kept their hawsers as taut as fiddle strings. On Thursday morning we steamed down as far as Point Lookout, at the mouth of the Potomac. As the seas were running high in the bay, we lay at anchor until they should subside, fearing that the tow lines would part.

Figure 8.2. *Monitor* AND *Merrimac* FIGHT, BY CURRIER AND IVES. The ironclads USS *Monitor* and CSS *Virginia* (formally, *Merrimac*) had just fought their epic duel at Hampton Roads as the first clash of iron ships only days before the arrival of Arthur and his mates. *Courtesy of Library of Congress.*

At dark, signal rockets were sent up, and away we dashed for Fortress Monroe, into the harbor, and dropped anchor a few rods off the *Monitor*, and under the guns of Fortress Monroe. The harbor was full of vessels of war of every description, and we were close to the celebrated Fortress, but the lion of the place was the very quiet, unpretending little craft with a big cheese box on the top, which passes by the name of *Monitor.*—None would suppose at first sight what a terrible adversary she really is, [just when you witnessed her plan of unattraction, you will admit the hidden strength and manifest] impregnability which was her attribute. No one would suppose, to look at her, that she had been so recently exposed to the *Merrimac*'s heavy Columbiads.

Our stay here, however, was short indeed, for a signal gun announced strange vessels toward Norfolk, and three or four huge steamers were seen looming up through the blue haze of the morning.—At some distance in their rear came a thick cloud of smoke and steam, which was supposed to proceed from the *Merrimac*. A scene of great activity ensued in the harbor, and the vessels in front of the Fortress got out of the way to leave her guns a clear field, as well as to look out for No. 1. The *Monitor* began to spit steam like an enraged cat, but laid quietly at anchor, apparently to coax her enemy under the

Fortress' heavy guns. The *Elm City* was taken outside, and the sequel of the affair we do not know, for we soon steamed off to our present location. We are now up a creek some distance, which I suppose must be near the York River. A large army are around us, and among them are the 49th Buffalo boys. We disembark in the morning, and expect a pretty good day's march.—A battle is expected very soon, and if successful—which every thing would augur—a very large tract is lost to the rebels. Our forces are ample, and made of better stuff than to wish to *play* at soldier longer. The change of latitude makes a sensible difference in the climate, and we can see from our vessel peach orchards are in full bloom. Think of that, you poor shivering samples of humanity, and wrap your beaver and pilot coats around you, while *our* overcoats are rolled upon our knapsacks until we need them some damp evening on guard. The mouth of the river is commanded by forts, which the rebels built and we occupy. Well, that is better than making good Union soldiers do it, I think you will allow. All is bustle on board, and many jogs of the elbow, as well as trampled toes fall to my share, so as I have told you about all which has occurred since I wrote you last, I will close. I am suspicious that this will not travel as readily as its predecessors have done, but I will give it a chance—All well on board.

Yours, as ever,

ARTHUR

Nolen volens: willing or unwilling, like it or not.

47 separate stinks of Cologne: probably a reference to a traditional German perfume called 4711 produced in Cologne since at least 1799.

Monitor: USS *Monitor* was an ironclad ship that had an innovative revolving turret placed midship on its low freeboard deck.

Merrimac: Confederate ironclad ship built upon the burned hull of the USS *Merrimac*, renamed the CSS *Virginia.*

Elm City: A large passenger ship that was put into United States service transporting troops.

49th Buffalo Boys: 49th New York Infantry, formed out of Buffalo, New York, September 18, 1861.

Other Voices: Sickles's Farewell to Excelsior Brigade

Headquarters, Excelsior Brigade
Second Hooker's Brigade On Board Transport "Elm City,"
April 6, 1862
General Orders, No. 6

Soldiers:

Special Orders No. 132 will announce to you that I am relieved from further duty in the Brigade, by order of the Brigadier General commanding this division.

My last act of duty is to bid you farewell. After a year of service with you, it is hard to yield to the necessity which separates me from so many brave and devoted companions-in-arms, endeared to me by more than ordinary ties.

While protesting that it is unlawful and unjust, I obey this command, because obedience to superior authority is the first duty of a soldier.

It is my earnest hope that a prompt appeal for redress, to the General commanding the army, will permit me to share with you the honors of the campaign now so auspiciously begun.

Whether we are separated for a day or forever, the fervent wishes of my heart will follow your fortunes on every field. You have waited patiently for the hour now at hand, when the Army of the Potomac will move upon the stronghold of the enemy.

Your discipline, courage and bearing will place you among the foremost of our legions. The glory which surely awaits you will help to reconcile me to the pain it costs me to say again—Farewell![2]

Steamer Elm City, off Fortress Monroe,

Dear Mother,

April 11th, 1862

We arrived in port this morning and as there will probably be a mail sent ashore I will improve a leisure hour. We dropped anchor within a few rods of the Monitor and under the guns of Fortress Monroe. We didn't stay there long though for a signal gun announced suspicious sails toward Norfolk. Three large steamers were seen and the tail of a very large rat was seen in the shape of a cloud of steam and smoke whose origin could not be well made out. Taking all things into consideration we dug outside to be ready for a run and left an open field for the Monitor and the guns of the Fortress. The Monitor's steam is up but she lies quiet and seems to be trying to get the Merrimac within range of the Fortress. All on board the Elm City are on the qui-vive to witness the anticipated combat. The Monitor is a very unpretending little craft and no one would suppose to look at her that she was the best vessel of our navy.

I have but little idea where we are going but should not wonder if we should go up the York River. I enclose you a rude drawing of the Monitor which will give you as good an idea of its exterior as if you were here. I could finish it better if I had the proper drawing pencil but this is a faithful sketch of its outline. There is not a shot mark to be seen. The Monitor is certainly the greatest triumph of Naval architecture and I should not fear to sail in her under fire of the heaviest guns.

We have been on board the Elm City ever since Saturday last—six days used up when it might just as well have been done in one. That is a fair sample of the way U.S. transportation is done.

Sickles was decapitated in the neatest style I ever saw. The brigade was mostly embarked so that he couldn't even assemble them to hear his "last dying speech and confession." Col. Taylor is in command and it is my firm belief that it will be wisely exercised. We have had no mail or papers for some time so that I don't know at all what is going on in the outside world. Write often and direct to Washington and it will be sent on. I will write to you and Frank as soon as we get to our destination.

Your aff. Son
Arthur

Fredonia Censor: Published April 30, 1862

FROM THE THIRD REGIMENT

Camp of 72nd N.Y.V., April 15th 1862.

Dear Uncles—

As I presume that you are now upon the anxious seat, concerning the fortunes of our migrating organization; I will hasten and do what little lies in my power to appease your anxiety and curiosity. Since my last epistle was written, we have disembarked and moved four or five miles from the landing toward Yorktown. Wc expect to move forward to-morrow, and take our position in the advance; where the 49th already are. We have been visited by many of the Stoneman Cavalry, but have as yet, had no opportunity to communicate with the 49th.

I presume that the final rejection of Sickles has created some surprise among your readers. The other regiments of the brigade accuse us of being the cause of his rejection. I have no doubt that they are correct in their opinion, though the movement which caused his downfall was not initiated with any intention of creating that result. It was a petition, signed almost unanimously by our line officers, requesting that the regiment might be transferred to the command of an experienced officer; which, instead of affecting the desired transfer, defeated Sickles' confirmation. A daily (The *Herald*, I believe,) states that he was deposed by Gen. Hooker. General Hooker was as powerless to do that as the undersigned "high private in the rear rank." The fact that Sickles so unaccountably retained his command, caused a little inquiry, and the result was that the order that he should be superseded was sent directly from the War Office, and *promulgated*, not *originated*, by Hooker.

And now, for a few further words of explanation. When this brigade was organized, our feelings were strongly enlisted in favor of Gen. Sickles, and Governor Morgan's double dealing with him, created against the latter a feeling of distrust and prejudice which still holds good as originally. We gave Sickles the credit of a great energy and patriotism, and we do not yet see cause to deny him those attributes. But Bull Run and Big Bethel forced upon us the reflection that something more than mere civilian talented shrewdness were necessary in a military commander. Gen. Sickles was not a soldier, and you might as well suppose the babe an hour old to perform the labors and duties of experienced manhood, as for a peaceful citizen to assume the responsibilities of a grade which in a lifetime of service most frequently fails to attain. His labors and responsibilities deserved a high reward, but are the lives and fortunes of five thousand men to be risked on that account? Did Sickles risk his fortune and life to a greater extent than a host of men who cheerfully shoulder their muskets in the ranks? Such was the position of affairs at Camp Scott, and Marsh. We then removed to Camp Caldwell. McClellan now ordered a course of Brigade drills. Gen. Sickles was busy at Washington with politics, and the regimental commanders conducted the drilling. This was Sickles' first grand error, and his political efforts could balance the . . . [illegible.]

Relying upon the political aid which so long sustained him, he continued to absent himself from his post and his duties, and while the soldiers of his command attained military excellence, their leader could not boast of the warlike knowledge which is indispensable to a company officer, and his palpable errors called forth the sneers of the privates in the ranks. Then came the stunning blow of his rejection, but as he was not immediately relieved of his command, he commenced a series of Brigade drills, and during their course manifested more of an aptitude than previously. Doubtless he supposed that this sudden zeal, coupled with the same latent aid which had thus far preserved him in his situation, would sustain him still, and would eventually bear him out. But political power and a certain personage who shall be nameless, infallibly desert their friends at last. The official axe descended—Sickles was no longer a general. And the most capable officer of the Brigade is now its leader. Some few officers of other regiments resigned when those events transpired, but as they were mere adventurers, it did not create any profound sensation.

Enough, however, of Sickles, and let us dismiss him, and return to the 72d. We are in a low, and unhealthy region, but thus far the consciousness of being in a fair way of doing something has sustained our spirit, and our health, to such a degree, that the sick list is much smaller than ever before. If we advance to morrow we shall reach a more elevated region, and consequently, a more healthy one. I expect within twenty-four hours to be within range of the enemy's guns. Our officers have at last received their commissions. They were sent long ago, but were retained by Gen. Sickles. Gov. Morgan, however, sent a line to Col. Taylor, apprising him of the fact of their having been sent. As no commissions came to hand, Col. Taylor wrote a line of inquiry to Gen. Sickles. The answer apprised Col. Taylor that the proper mode of communication with his general was through the assist. Adj. Gen. Col. Taylor complied with these insulting, though strictly legal terms, and received in answer that the commissions had been received and used as waste paper. Col. Taylor enclosed this obscenely worded communication to Gov. Morgan, and duplicate commissions were sent directly to himself.

It now occurs to me that I have hitherto forgotten to mention that our little burial place at Camp Wool was enclosed by a neat and substantial railing, by the Colonel's orders. The little cemetery presents a much more creditable appearance than those in many parts of Maryland and the names of the sleepers were carved deeply upon cedar or other durable posts.

Yours as ever—

Arthur.

P.S.—We have just received a mail, and we shall be glad to have our friends write often, as their letters will not reach us less surely, though somewhat delayed. We are now encamped within four or five miles of the enemy, and can hear the cannon both of Yorktown and Fortress Monroe.

—Arthur.

Other Voices: From the *Fredonia Censor*

Published April 30, 1862

GEN. SICKLES—

We see it announced that the President has re-nominated Gen. Sickles as a Brigadier General. By what maneuvering he was induced to do this in the face of unanimous rejection of Sickles' previous nomination by the Senate is a mystery which the people would like to have unraveled. Sickles, friends pretend that his rejection was brought about by a misapprehension of facts. Which has been explained away. But no explanation can do away with the damaging fact that Sickles has not the confidence of his men, and that his best officers signed a petition to be transferred from his command. In time of war no one ought to be appointed to a military position unless fully competent for the discharge of his duties. The lives of 5,000 men are too much value to be hazzarded recklessly, for the purpose of rewarding politicians ambitious of military glory. We believe that President Lincoln has been bamboozled in making this re-appointment, and trust that the Senate will again save the country from the disgrace, and the army from the hazard which must result from investing Sickles with such a responsible position.

Camp Winfield Scott, near Yorktown, Va. April 16, 1862

Dear Brother,

Your and Mother's letter reached me last night and very glad I was to hear from home again. As you are probably already aware we have emigrated from Camp Wool and are now upon the sacred soil of Virginia, and within four or five miles of one of the principal strongholds. Our forces are . . . Yorktown in overwhelming . . . and our siege guns are now mostly in position. We have also several gun boats upon the York River ready to cooperate with us. McIntosh (the rebel General) in answer to McClellans order to surrender declared that he would first make every house in Yorktown a hospital. As things look just now he . . . some his bacon a bit by doing that for we have the men and the implements to whip him in short metre. There has been heavy firing to day and I presume that our gunners have been getting the range of the artillery preparatory to a general assault. Our Brigade is south east of Yorktown and is encamped upon Cheasemans [Cheesemans] Creek, which flows into the Poquosin [Poquoson] River. We are not yet in sight of the enemy but we expect to move up to the advance in a day or two. We expect a big fight very soon but our artillery will probably do most of the work. There are a very great numbers of field and siege guns [and they are] mostly rifled. Steel guns or brass howitzers, whose large [bore] will scatter the grape and canister beautifully. We had a very slow passage down on the Elm City and were just a week in performing the journey of a day. That is a fair sample of the way Government transportation is carried on with vessels hired at from $500.00 to $1,000.00 per day. The tide flows here to the height of three or four feet and all those who like clams and oysters can have them if not too lazy to pick them up and cook them. I don't fancy them myself and have not eaten any except one day that we were short of provisions when I baked a few on the coals.

While you are probably hugging the fire around the sap kettles I have sneaked off into the shore to escape this hot Virginian sun. . . . are in full blossom here and the air is soft and mild. Gen. McClellan is on the other side of. . . . has the command. . . .

And so you are trying your luck at my old. . . . I don't think you could well have got a better. . . . After living so long with Father it is high time that you should begin over again and learn the farmers trade at a place where work is not only done well but done in season. A man can do his best days work between sunrise and sunset and I am glad that you are at a place where you will see it, and learn to be wiser than . . . enough after sunrise to make it good. You must remember me to Mr. and Mrs. Edwards and to [Mick] and Jerry and last but by no means least to Mrs. Jerry. I can think of nothing more of importance so hoping to hear from you early—letters will come safely enough and you and Mr. Edwards folks must write directing to Washington, —I remain

Your affectionate brother

Arthur McKinstry
3d Reg't., Excels. Brig.
Washington D.C.

P.S. It is reported that the firing to day was at one of the rebel batteries which our men carried, with the loss of Gen. Porter. I do not know if it is true or not. There is smart cannonading this evening.

Fredonia Censor: Published May 7, 1862

FROM THE THIRD REGIMENT

Outposts Near Yorktown, April 22.

Dear Uncles:—

Our Regiment is out on picket to-day, and as I anticipated some leisure, I brought on my portfolio. We started from our beds at 4 o'clock this morning, and swallowed a cup of coffee and some "Shingles" and then buckled on our belts and seized our rifles for a day on picket. Several shells have exploded—one now, within a few rods to our left. We are concealed by woods, and I suppose the enemy are trying a few "feelers" to ascertain our position. Berdan's Sharp Shooters are ahead us, and we hear the frequent crack of their deadly rifles. Last Thursday Co. D was upon guard, and as nearly all our regimental marches have taken place on such occasions, we argued that we should get orders to advance. Sure enough we did march that afternoon.—

We took the road to Yorktown, and Hooker's Division is encamped in a lump together, in the advance at the center.

We are in easy range of the enemy's rifled guns, as a shell thrown half a mile beyond our camp testified on Saturday last. The 9th Cavalry are encamped half a mile in our rear, the Ellsworth Avengers on our right, and a little in advance; and the 49th are five or six miles to our left. A few visits have been exchanged, but the distance, the mud, and the Provost Guard, are serious obstacles to frequent intercourse. The 49th have lost up to date, one man killed.

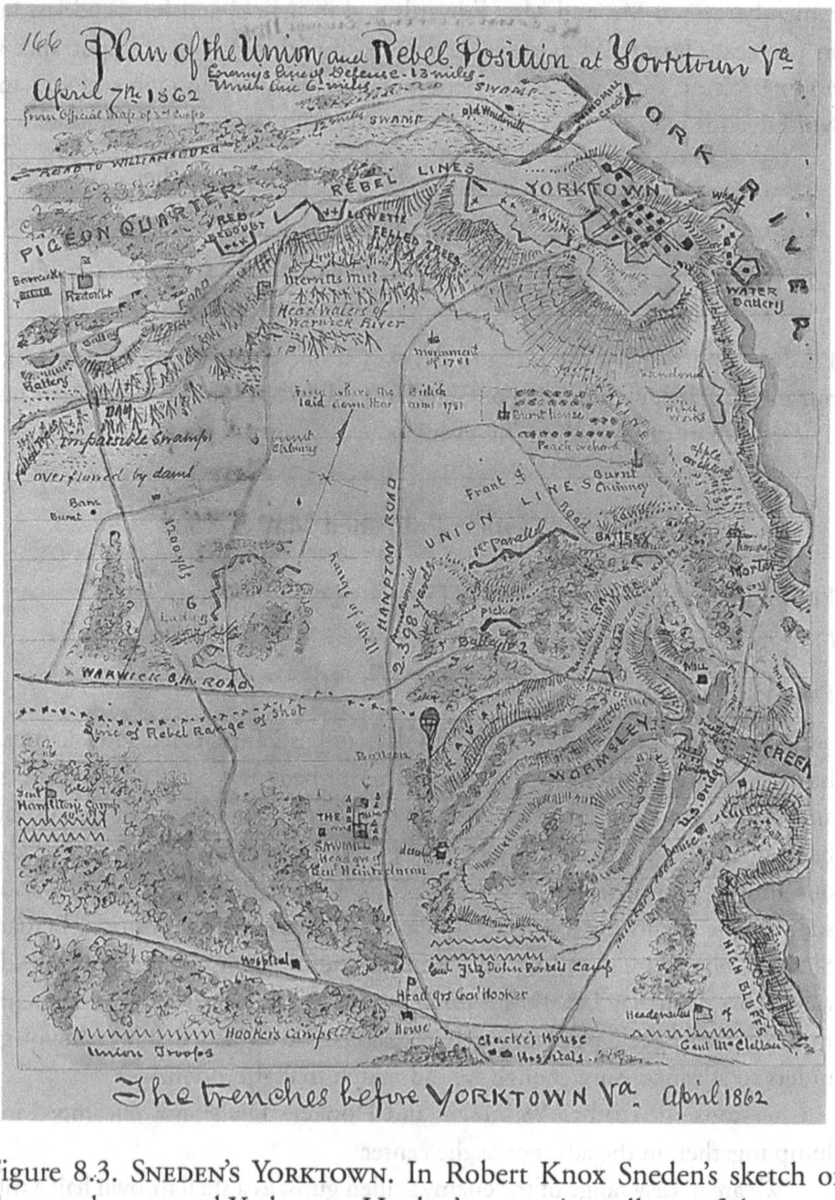

Figure 8.3. SNEDEN'S YORKTOWN. In Robert Knox Sneden's sketch of the trenches around Yorktown, Hooker's camp sits well out of the range of Confederate cannon fire. The dangerous work of advancing the line of trenches and establishing siege batteries happens above Wormsley Creek. It is most likely any encounters with Confederate sharpshooters or artillery is happening near the Warwick Road and east of Hampton Road. The ravine marked out by Sneden provided a safe staging area for Federal troops. *Courtesy of Library of Congress.*

The last Censor was duly received, and your private epistle was gladly read last night. Sunday was too wet for an inspection so we went (Cos. B, D & H,) down to Col. McLeod Murphy's regiment of Engineers, and took thence a large number of gabions to an earth-work where siege guns are being mounted. A "gabion" is a circular wicker frame, without a bottom, which is set upon end and filled with earth. It is used for building earthworks, and is stronger, though less portable than sand bags. Bang, rattle and crash go the volleys of small arms to our left, and in rifle shot of our present position. I shouldn't wonder if we had to fall in and try the efficacy of our Belgian rifles, with live secesh for targets, but having got my hand in, I will keep on writing, unless interrupted.

After all the abuse they have borne as being fastidious in their choice of weapons, Berdan's Sharp Shooters prove to be one of the most useful organizations of our service. I have heard of many of their exploits as marksmen, and am not at all surprised to hear of the annoyance they cause the enemy, when I recollect the extraordinary test they had first to undergo. Not long since, a secesh gun was fired at the U.S. forces, and while the gunners were sponging the piece, each dropped with a hole through his carcass. The sponge staff was still sticking from the muzzle, and as fast as men came to take it out, they got their tickets to the next world from the watchful sharp shooters. Supposing that we Yankees had a fraternal affection for "the innocent cause of the war," a darkie was sent for the sponge. Down tumbled the unhappy African, and like poor Tray, for being found in bad company. This was a very bad state of things, for all efforts to work the gun proved unavailing, so in true secesh faith, a flag of truce was hoisted and negotiations opened for the burial of the dead. While this was going on, the rebels attempted to remove the gun to another position. This open breach of faith met a fitting response—a couple of shells from one of our batteries right among the rebels.

I have heard an amusing anecdote of a secesh, who took a "contraband" and placed him in front as a shield. Berdan's men did not shoot the poor devil, till at last the master got incautious, and exposed a part of his body, which was at once perforated by a bullet. The best shooting is of course done with the telescope sighted target rifles, and no national arm has been or ever will be invented which equals even the hunting rifles with globe sights. Many sharp shooters are armed with Colt's revolving rifles, but they are not accurate enough for the hunters who wield them. The sharp shooters are out in advance of our pickets, and keep behind logs and mounds, annoying the enemy until night, when they return within our lines.

2 ½ P.M.—sure enough, we had to fall in and proceed to reinforce Capt. Chadwick; in front of whom considerable firing had been going on. No attack,

however, taking place, we had to return after firing nary shot. When we went it was with the fullest expectation of a fight, and the boys leaned forward and stretched their necks out to the greatest possible extent, as if that would bring them a little nearer. Every man looked as placid as a cat with a pitcher of cream; but the net proceeds of the affair were summed up by one of Chadwick's men getting his eyes full of sand thrown by a rebel shell, while nary secesh came within sight of us. We then returned to our old positions, and got behind all the big trees for shelter from a lively April shower. The shower soon blew over, and we began to cast about for some new excitement. As if purposely for our gratification, Gen. McClellan and staff rode up to a battery near, and after inspecting the progress of its erection and defenses, he walked over to our party and held a confab of some length with our officers, and Maj. Stevens, who was with us.

The sun shines hotly between the showers, and the wild trees about us are in full blossom. Grass, mandrakes and cowslips are sprouting greenly around us, and the violets and other spring flowers are in bloom. We must be about six weeks ahead of you, for peach trees were blossomed out by the 1st of April. While at our two former camps we were in little danger of suffering from hunger, for we had only to walk to the shore and dig clams, oysters, and mussels, in quantities to suit the consumer. We of course enjoyed the privilege of salt water bathing, and the water was so far warmed as to render the operation an agreeable one.

The rebels have just sent a shell plump into our battery, within a dozen rods of us. It did not explode, but it finished the whistling of "Dixie" with a thump of considerable emphasis. They are at it again, but their shells burst too soon.

The sky is as clear now as we can reasonably expect in so fickle a month as April, and I believe I will stretch myself upon the ample couch which kind Mother Earth furnishes even to such a scapegrace as a Union Volunteer.

Camp Winfield Scott, April 23d.

Being back again in camp, without any loss either of killed or wounded, I will add a little more to this epistle and send it upon its travels. We are near enough to the rebels for them to shell us if only they could know our position. We have the very best of spring water, and as healthy a position as we can desire. The sickness which used to be so prevalent in time of brigade and regimental drills has suddenly disappeared, and now that the whistle of shot and shell are "familiar to our ears as household words," and there is not room to drill, our boys have not so many sick in the whole regiment as used frequently to be found in the morning report of a single company. The following list embraces the sick of our regiment who are away in hospitals:

Of Co. E, Frank Mathews and Patrick O'Brien were left at Division hospital on the Potomac: Edward Cook is at the Division hospital here, and Corporal Milton Hadley was sent sick to Washington at the time of our embarkation at Liverpool point. Of Co. H, Leguire was left at the above Division Hospital. Of Co. B, R. Griffin and J. Patchin are in Brigade hospital, here, with measles. Of Co. G, Robert Duncan remains in Georgetown Hospital as a nurse since his recovery. By private sources I learn that Frank Matthews, whom I just referred to, is dangerously and it is feared, hopelessly ill, at last accounts.

I would like to give you more definite information about the situation of things here, but present military law compels me to confine myself to personalities and matters of purely local interest. Thus in giving some little history of our adventures, I have carefully avoided giving any information which an enemy could possibly profit by. Cook who formerly worked in your office is visiting us this morning. A deserter from sesech came over to Co. E this morning, while out on picket. Co. D still flourishes finely, and the only absentees are Sergt. Chapman, who is on sick furlough, Riley, who assists in the Alexandria Hospital, and Walden, whose wounded wrist detained him at Camp Wool.

Yorktown, April 27th

We are now quietly waiting until the siege guns can be got into position, which is being done with all possible dispatch. The guns are mostly long rifled Parrots, and the earthworks in which they are placed, are concealed by the timber.—

When the proper time arrives, an hour's work with axes will reveal guns by hundreds, in a huge semi-circle, within easy range of the doomed city. I think that the taking of Yorktown will be a bloody achievement, but that the loss will be almost entirely on Jeff's side. Many sesech have deserted, and they tell us that it takes one half of Jeff's forces to keep the other half straight, and that swarms of them would yield at once if they could. We have had a rough time of it lately, and have had to work pretty hard, but it did not awaken one tithe of the dissatisfaction that the fatiguing and useless battalion drills did. We will work like slaves, and fight like tigers, when common sense shows us that some desirable end will be attained thereby.

Yesterday the 1st and 20th Massachusetts were annoyed by sharp-shooters, from a rebel earthwork, and took it at the point of the bayonet, with a loss of three killed and twelve wounded. They were giving the sesech "fits," when seventeen of them, displayed white handkerchiefs, crying, "don't shoot us; we are not fighting you." They left the rebel service voluntarily, and are now in our custody.

Yours as ever,
Arthur.

Berdan's Sharp Shooters: Hiram Berdan was the force behind the creation of two regiments of specially trained and equipped sharpshooters.

9th Cavalry: Stoneman's Cavalry; Westfield Cavalry. Formed primarily from Chautauqua County. Left the state: November 26, 1861.

Like poor Tray, for being found in bad company: Tray is the innocent spaniel in Aesop's "The Spaniel and the Mastiff," who is set upon by angry villagers for the bad deeds of his traveling companion, Tiger.

Capt. Chadwick: Isaac L. Chadwick of Company C raised out of New York City.

Fredonia Censor: Published May 14, 1862

FROM THE THIRD REGIMENT
Camp Winfield Scott, April 29.

Dear Uncles:—

We have had such a round of balls and parties lately that I have had but little time to devote to the Censor and its readers. We have not, however, enjoyed a season of so unmixed pleasure as you might infer by the foregoing; for the parties were of that kind so justly termed in military parlance, "fatigue," while the balls were mostly ten pound rifled, and obligingly got up by our hospitable Virginia neighbors. We are kept on the qui vive, as a brief summary of the last few days will show. On Thursday last we were roused somewhere in the small hours, and told to prepare for action. Our belts were accordingly buckled on, our boots and shoes were resumed, and our rifles placed in easy reach. Thus, being ready to fall in at a quarter of a minute's notice, we turned in all standing, and slept soundly till daybreak. At night we were ordered to work on battery No.—, from which we returned at 3 A.M. Friday.

Friday, which was cold and rainy, was devoted to sleep. Saturday was cold and rainy, but we had to turn out and choke with corduroy the miry ruts of one of these Virginia roads. All day we worked through a drenching storm, and at

Figure 8.4. Hooker's Division in the ravine in front of Yorktown. The ravine occupied by the picket reserves of Hooker's Division. Arthur described the ravine as "created expressly for the reserve of our line of pickets." *Courtesy of Library of Congress.*

night, chilled and wearied, sought our camp couches. Sunday passed very quietly, with only *two* inspections. On Monday morning, at three o'clock, we were roused for another day on picket. Out we turned, our breakfast was bolted, dinner and supper were laid by in our haversacks, and by six we were posted in a ravine which seemed created expressly for the "reserve" of our line of pickets. Several companies were now posted in a rifle pit, which extends along the front of our lines, as the advance, while the reserve lay concealed until some demonstration by the rebels should require their support for the advance. Many shells were thrown by the rebels, but without effect.

At 4 P.M., Co. D fell in and relieved Capt. Bliss' men, who had been in the advance all day. We were now in plain view of the enemy, and could see them by looking over the wall beyond the trench. Great care was necessary, however, that the observer did not get hit by the enemy's sharp shooters. On the right, Burdan's sharp-shooters had tormented the enemy very much, and when darkness fell, their artillery began to play at our woods, to disturb the men who were working upon our batteries. Another object was probably to draw our fire, and thus discover the situation of our principal works, which are still masked by trees but can be unmasked at very short notice, when all is ready. Growing tired of this fruitless business, they began to depress their guns until they bore directly upon the rifle pit where our pickets lay. Their aim was perfect, but so too was our shelter. A few men were thrown out in advance of the pit as look-outs. Averill and Babcock were sent out from the squad I was in, and as they lay close to the ground, a shell with blazing fuze rolled within a few feet and stopped.—The boys lay low as possible, and the shell, exploding, scattered its fragments near them, but left them unharmed. At midnight, Babcock, who felt quite unwell, came in and I went out in his place.—Averill and I lay just in the rear of a slight swell of ground, so that shot or shell which was coming toward us might strike the earth in front and *ricochet*, or bound over us. Many did so, and passed closely enough over us to have made mince meat of us if we had stood up. Once we had a close shave of it, for a shell burst directly in front of us, but luckily the fragments did not diverge soon enough to reach us, but went humming over our prostrate bodies and crashing among the timber in our rear. While many shells passed close to us, this was the only time in which I considered myself in danger, for the rising ground was a sufficient protection from the flying shell, and the trench in the rear could only be entered by bombs flying from a mortar. Like a seaman who is tranquil so long as a plank is between him and the water, the soldier is content that shot shall pass within a yard of him, so long as the known laws of mathematics and gunnery *insure* that yard of interval.—Two bombs were fired from a mortar, but they fell wide of the mark. While the enemy were amusing themselves with a round of three guns every half-hour or so, one of our gunboats sent a shell over into one [of] the grand encampments of the rebels, where it burst with a loud explosion. At intervals though the night, the vessel continued to hurl its huge iron globes through the air and into the rebel camp. One of the ten pound solid shot, fired by the enemy, tore a tree fourteen inches in diameter so that it fell. The shot was brought up to camp by Capt. Doyle's men, three of whom it would have killed had it not been for the tree.

This morning we were relieved and returned to camp. While we cannot of course fathom the plans of Gen. McClellan, what we have seen of the outworks and their plan of construction ought to satisfy us with our present quiet state. It is very evident that Yorktown will soon be at our General's mercy, and that while our tremendous system of batteries are showering their iron rain from shot-proof defences, our army, secure in well and ingeniously planned covers, will be able to repulse with the utmost ease any sorties of the beleaguered forces. Our new line of works enclose the entrenchments which were constructed by Washington's forces in the war of the Revolution.

Quite a gunboat fleet lies in the river, and it takes about twenty seconds for a shell to travel from their guns to Yorktown.

3 ½ *A.M., Wednesday.*—Ordered to guard a working party, and must march immediately. Time presses, so Adieu.

Yours, as ever,
Arthur

Camp Winfield Scott, May 2nd

Dear Uncle Wint,

I received your letter a few days since and have not had time to reply until now.

We have been very busy of late but I will leave the details for my next public letter. I set everything down in my diary and my public correspondence is very like posting a ledger. Thus dates are accurate and the whole thing much more complete. I send by this mornings Express thirty dollars ($30.00) which belongs in sums of ten dollars each to Tate, Hamilton, and myself. I owe you something by way of Express charges. Give Hamiltons money to his father. Tates to D. J. Pratt, and send five dollars to my mother. There will be remaining five dollars and I wish you to apply that to the payment of the freight bills which you have incurred on my account. If any balance remain, send it to me in postage stamps as early as possible. We have seen some pretty lively times on picket and Doyles company have skirmished a little. Our county volunteers acquit themselves more than creditably under fire and the only trouble yet has been with a company of N.Y. City men under Capt. Chadwick who broke and ran like a flock of sheep. Co. D was in the reserve that night and Chadwick's men came helter skelter to our position and many rallied upon our company. They were scared to death and did not even answer our challenges much less give the countersign and if our boys had not possessed a more than ordinary degree of cool common sense they would have riddled them with bullets. They reserved their fire however and made sure that they were friends, (If cowards can be termed such) but they would have been strictly justified by military law, and perhaps by moral, if they had shot them down. We have just got two months pay, and a similar amount is still due to us. I hope it will soon be paid us and it looks rather small that we should only get the pay of two months on the very day that two more months pay became due. Your remarks about Sec. Stanton explains to my mind much which had appeared hitherto unaccountable in the conduct of the campaign. Does the man indeed entertain so absurd a fancy as to suppose that he can fill the presidency—the jackal may indeed partake of the lions fare but only at the second table, and cold fragments at that, Honest Old Abe has that berth at pleasure if I rightly interpret the signs of the times. Are you surprised at the duration of the siege of Yorktown? Being somewhat behind the scenes I am not. I believe that McDowell will, in cooperation with Banks, menace, if not conquer, Richmond. I imagine that the crisis of the war will take place within about three weeks, and that a simultaneous attack upon Norfolk, Richmond, and Yorktown, will give the coup de grace to Jeff's mushroom Confederacy. Our works here are simple but impregnable so long as they are even tolerably defended and an enemy can only attack at a great disadvantage. First there is a huge crescent of extensive batteries which throw shells of all sizes from ten pounders to ten inch, next a system of mortar batteries and in advance of all a trench which can be manned by a large army: which is safe from our own shot which will pass over; and which is a complete defense against everything excepting the enemy's mortars. These last may enter a trench occasionally but they must be sent with a degree of skill which the Confederates have given no earnest of yet, to lodge in a trench at right angles with the line of fire and not over ten feet wide. No gunner in the world could do much execution at such disadvantage. Thus you see when the signal is given, our batteries can open fire and the rain of shell upon the doomed city will be absolutely terrific, while a formidable army lies in the trench to repel a rebel sortie, and another army in the ravines in reserve. I feel a perfect confidence in the result for I have the proofs before my eyes. The Mass. 11th who behaved gallantly at Bull Run, and since here acquitted themselves shamefully the other night for they were seized by some unaccountable panic and ran past us while we were on reserve and some rallied on our company. Capt. Abell was cool, calm, and sensible. While as a man he has many enemies, and justly, as an officer I prefer him as my commander in danger to any I know. I am extremely . . . [unreadable] . . . was greatly in error and that was in supposing that our embarkation would interfere with a visit from you. We lay four or five days off . . . Pt. but I will message more about it for it makes me feel fairly sick when I think what a game of cross purposes it was. I send you the general idea of a section of our line of works. Lots of love to all our friends. Tell Thomas Chandler that it is . . . [unreadable] The enemy are . . . very spitefully today and may bring on a fight.

Your aff. Nephew,
Arthur

We have just got two months pay . . . : at the beginning of the war, pay for Union privates was $13 per month and to be paid every two months. Pay increased with rank. A colonel earned $212 per month.

Mushroom Confederacy: upstart confederacy.

Editorial Note

Since arriving on the peninsula, Arthur and his mates are engaged in siege operations in front of Yorktown. Unexpectedly, Confederate commander Joseph E. Johnston orders a withdrawal from the Yorktown line. On the morning of May 4th, the 3rd Corps, with Hooker's Division in the lead, begins a pell-mell pursuit of the Rebel army. Twelve miles beyond Yorktown, near the town of Williamsburg, lay a series of prepared trenches and earthworks awaiting the retreating Confederates. It will be here that the enemy rear guard will make its stand. The battle will be joined the next day.[3]

72nd N.Y.V. Before Yorktown, May 4th, 1862

Dear Uncles,

My time is extremely short but what I have shall be at your disposal. My knapsack is packed and I sit upon it awaiting the order to pursue the enemy who have evacuated Yorktown.

Where on earth do these men of straw intend to go now? Since I wrote you last we have done another tour of picket duty and labored for a day in the trenches. On Wednesday at 5½ A.M. we went out on picket, or rather as a reserve to support those more advanced. We lay concealed in a deep ravine during the day and read whatever we could scrap together of books and papers, or ventured a quiet rubber at whist, while the rebel shells were crashing through the timber in our immediate vicinity. At night we were sent out in companies for the pickets to rally upon in case the enemy should press them hard. Company was posted upon a hill which was completely swept by the enemy's guns and as they held the position without flinching until morning it is very remarkable that none were injured. During the night the enemy drove in our pickets and some of them, a large body . . . came back upon our position. To Capt. Abell's challenge they were too much excited to reply and only a rare degree of coolness and caution on the part of our boys saved them from a destructive fire from their own friends. By every law of warfare we should have been justified in firing upon them when they advanced upon us without halting and responding to the challenge. The pickets skirmished not a little and amid the screams of shell we could frequently hear the low but not so very soothing hum of the minie bullets. They approached within shot of Doyle whose company was posted in a mortar battery and exchanged a few balls. One bullet grazed the neck of Ralph Doty, reddening but not breaking the skin. Co. D had a good many close shaves and one of these may be instanced in a 32 pr. round shell which struck the ground just before us, ploughed a small trench six or eight feet long, and stopped within a few feet of the main group of our company . . . that it traveled a little farther some of us would have been smashed. Thursday morning we returned to camp, signed the pay roll and got our shinplasters, and were mustered for two more months pay. The 4th Reg't. of our brigade who were on picket, gave three regiments of the rebels who approached them a severe drubbing. Nothing of moment occurred on Friday, excepting that the rebels shelled our camp a little. Yesterday a detail of a hundred went out to work in the trenches and we did a days task by noon. So we worked [and] were shelled by a rebel fort and the frequent sound of exploding shells and the low hum of flying fragments kept us pretty close to the breastwork we were throwing up. Upon the bank behind us lay specimen bricks of Jeff's "Chateau en Espagne" in the shape of shot and shell of various sizes up to 120 prs. It is seldom that a fragment of their . . . back upon its . . . One, which was too far spent to inflict any harm struck two of Capt. Bliss' men, and was straightway pocketed. The other piece struck the embankment. The greater portion of the shells thrown were the old fashioned round 32 pr. Of a thousand men who were at labor near me and in plain sight, not one was killed. Our labor completed we returned to the camp. The balloon ascended during the afternoon directly in front of us, and drew the shells of the rebels into our camp. One passed over the head of Lucius Jones and stuck between McGinness and Holland, of Co. H. It did not miss either by more than a foot.

A quiet rubber at whist: popular trick-taking card game in the 1700s and 1800s using two sets of partners.

Shinplasters: privately issued paper money, usually of little value. Likely used sarcastically here by McKinstry.

"Chateau en Espagne": castles in Spain. The phrase "to build castles in the air, or in Spain," means to attempt unattainable projects. From poetry of the Middle Ages.

Other Voices: From the *Fredonia Censor*

Published on May 7, 1862

EVACUATION OF YORKTOWN.

The rebels have again "Skedaddled" without a fight. Abandoning their strong position at Yorktown on Saturday night, they departed for parts unknown, leaving a large number of guns, and quantities of camp equipage and supplies in our hands. This movement will take the country by surprise. The siege of Yorktown was looked forward to as likely to prove a protracted, desperate and bloody undertaking. Why did the rebels run? We think the statement in the letter of our army correspondent, in another column, throws some light upon the subject. Deserters from their army say "it takes one half of their forces to keep the other half straight." Plainly they have no confidence in their ability to hold their position, and though their flight can only serve to increase their demoralization, it enables them to put off a little longer their inevitable doom. Where they will endeavor to make a second stand is un-known, but it would not be surprising if this movement was made with reference to an entire abandonment of Virginia, and an attempt to escape into the Cotton States before the avenues are all closed. McClellan promises to "drive them to the wall," but his army will have to make good time, or the rebels will distance them "in the long run."

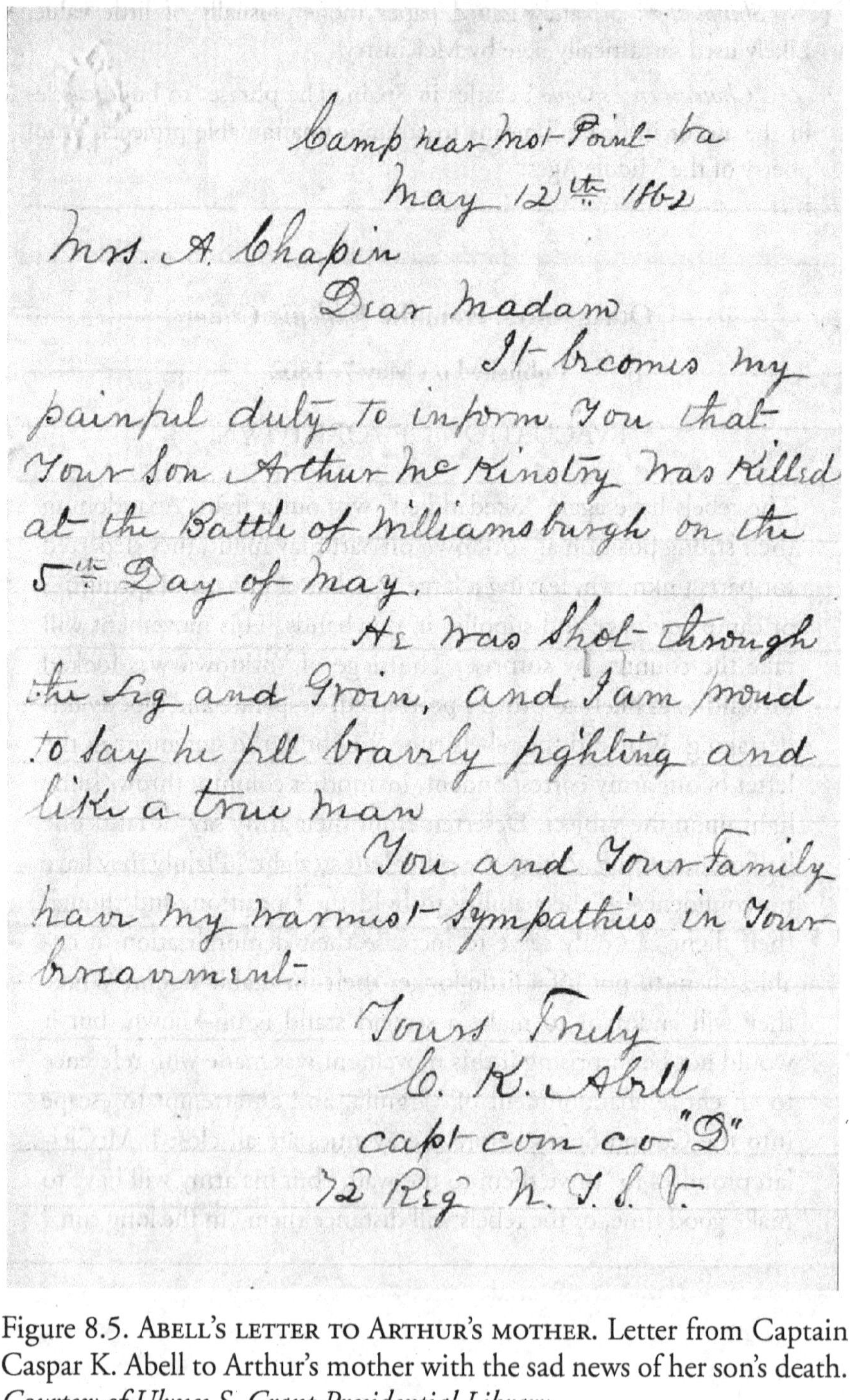

Camp near West Point Va
May 12th 1862

Mrs. A. Chapin

Dear Madam

It becomes my painful duty to inform You that Your Son Arthur McKinstry Was Killed at the Battle of Williamsburgh on the 5th Day of May.

He was Shot through the Leg and Groin, and I am proud to say he fell bravely fighting and like a true man

You and Your Family have my warmest Sympathies in Your bereavement.

Yours Truly
C. K. Abell
capt com co "D"
72 Reg N. Y. S. V.

Figure 8.5. Abell's letter to Arthur's mother. Letter from Captain Caspar K. Abell to Arthur's mother with the sad news of her son's death. *Courtesy of Ulysses S. Grant Presidential Library.*

Other Voices: Captain Abell of Co. D Writes to Arthur's Mother

Camp near Wst Point Va
May 12th 1862

Mrs. A. Chapin,
Dear Madam

It becomes my painful duty to inform you that your son Arthur McKinstry was killed at the Battle of Williamsburgh on the 5th Day of May.

He was shot through the leg and groin, and I am proud to say he fell bravely fighting and like a true man.

You and Your Family have my warmest sympathies in Your bereavement.

Yours Truly

C. K. Abell
Capt. Com. Co. "D"
72 Reg N.Y.S.V.[4]

Other Voices: From the *Fredonia Censor*

Published May 14, 1862

THE BATTLE OF WILLIAMSBURGH.

The enemy, on his retreat from Yorktown, made a desperate stand at Williamsburgh, some 12 mile from Yorktown and came near defeating our advance army corps, commanded by Heintzelman, before assistance could arrive. The 3d Regiment of the Sickles' Brigade, which is represented to have fought so desperately, contains five companies of Chautauqua County boys. Hence the report of the fight will be perused with great interest by our readers. The Baltimore American's account of the battle of Monday says it was a most warmly contested engagement. Owing to the roughness of the country, and the bad condition of the roads, but a small portion of our troops could be brought into action. Sickles' brigade, in Gen. Hooker's division, bore the great brunt of the battle, and fought most gallantly, though greatly overpowered by the numbers, superior position, and earthworks of the enemy. The approaches to their works were a series of ravines and swamps, whilst rain fell in torrent all day. The men had also been lying on their arms all the night previous, and were soaked with rain and chilled with cold. The battle raged from early in the morning till 3 o'clock P.M., when McClellan arrived with fresh troops, relieving Hooker's division, who were nearly prostrated with fatigue and exposure, while the third regiment of Sickles' brigade had its ranks badly thinned by the balls of the enemy. They are represented as having fought with such imprudent bravery that not less than 200 were killed and wounded. After the arrival of McClellan the enemy was fiercely charged by Hancock's brigade, and were driven within their works before nightfall, with heavy loss. Nearly 700 of their dead were left on the field, with many wounded, though most of the latter were carried into Williamsburg. Our loss is less than 300 killed, about 700 wounded. Night having come on we occupied the battle field, the rebels having been driven within their works, and our forces laid on their arms prepared to storm their works in the morning at daylight. On Tuesday McClellan sent out scouts, whilst preparing to move on the enemy's works, who soon reported that the rebels had again taken to flight. The works of the enemy and Williamsburg were then taken. Fort Magruder was a most extensive work, capable of prolonged defense; but the enemy abandoned it in the night, retreating in great alarm and confusion.

THE KILLED AND WOUNDED

The friends of Chautauqua Companies in the Sickles Brigade, have waited with the most anxious solicitude for the list of killed and wounded in that engagement. Up to this date but a partial report has been received, which we copy below. It is likely that many names of the wounded, and perhaps some of the killed, remain as yet unreported. The mortality in Co. D leaves reason to infer that such is the case.

COMPANY D—KILLED

Martin Boyden, Ellery.
Frank Halsey, Laona.
Chas. H. Miller, Silver Creek.
Arthur McKinstry, Forestville.
C. L. Rowe, Cherry Creek.
Wm. Simpson, Dunkirk.
Jerome C. Sprague, Pomfret.
Chas. F. Sisson, Gowanda.
Percival R. Moon, Villenova.

WOUNDED

Barnard Goetz, Dunkirk.
Jacob Kramer, Dunkirk.
Allen Richard, Ellery.
Geo. F. Parker, Versailles.
Aug Schluter, Buffalo.
Chas. H. Wribourg, Dunkirk.
A. M. Wright, Elmira.

COMPANY E.

Capt. P. Barrett, Dunkirk, killed.
Michael O'Brien, Dunkirk, wounded

COMPANY H.

Lieut. L. Marcus, Dunkirk, wounded.
Wm. Lavigne, Dunkirk, killed.
Francis Carr, Dunkirk, killed.
Charles Wolf, Dunkirk, killed.
Charles Gauther, Dunkirk, killed

COMPANY B.

Capt. Darwin Willard, Jamestown, kill'd.
Lieut. S. Bailey, Dunkirk, severely w'n'd.

The body of Capt. Willard was rifled of his watch and money by the enemy, as were many of our dead. It has been forwarded to Jamestown for interment.

If the report that the regiment lost over 200 in killed and wounded, is correct—and the partial returns of the killed seem to warrant the supposition—the carnage must have been truly frightful. As the effective strength of the regiment could not have been much over 800, full one-fourth would seem to have been stricken down.

Capt. Barrett's body has been received in Dunkirk, and will be buried with military honors on Thursday forenoon next.

OBITUARY

In the long, sad list of victims of the sanguinary battle at Williamsburg, given in the Daily Tribune of Monday, appears the name of ARTHUR MCKINSTRY. The readers of the Censor will know to whom the announcement refers. The pen which has so often enlivened the columns of this paper with clear and faithful limning of life in camp, has dropped from the clay-cold fingers, our genial, talented and warm-hearted correspondent, "ARTHUR," is no more.—We are unnerved, and have no heart to write, after this terrible announcement. The blow will fall with crushing effect upon a devoted mother and sister, and a large circle of relatives. Of the thousands of victims who have offered up their lives upon the altar of their country, Death has claimed no spirit more noble, more truly and unselfishly devoted to the great cause in which he had enlisted. When the call was made for volunteers to fill the ranks of Co. D, although he had but just risen from a long and protracted illness, in which the scale had nearly balanced between life and death, and vigorous strength had not returned to his frame, he hastened to enroll his name among those who were prompt to go forth and peril life in the sacred cause. From that time, through his frequent correspondence, the readers of the CENSOR have formed a partial acquaintance, and learned to appreciate his manly and sterling qualities. The last letter received from him, written for the public, appears in another column of our paper. The only alleviation which his surviving friends can feel in their terrible bereavement is the knowledge that he died as he would prefer to die, if he must pass the dread ordeal in his manly prime, upon the field of conflict, and in the cause of that country which so many of the bravest and best have yielded up their lives to preserve.

"How sleep the brave who sink to rest
By all their country's wishes blest;
When Spring, with dewy fingers cold,
Returns to deck their hallowed mould;
She then shall dress a sweeter sod
Than Fancy's feet have ever trod.
By fairy hands their knell is rung;
By forms unseen their dirge is sung,
There Honor comes—a Pilgrim gray,
To deck the turf that wraps their clay;
And Freedom shall awhile repair
To dwell a weeping hermit there."

Other Voices: *Fredonia Censor*
Published May 21, 1862

Arthur McKinstry—The Dunkirk Union of the 14th, in noticing the victims of the battle of Williamsburg, pay the following tribute of respect to our deceased relative:

ARTHUR M'KINSTRY

Aged 22 years, enlisted as a private in Co. D, and was one of the first to respond to the call for volunteers. He was a nephew of the Messrs. McKinstry, proprietors of the Fredonia *Censor*, and is well known to the readers of that paper as the writer of the excellent letters from Camp, which have appeared regularly in that paper. We remember well his coming into our office the day Co. D left, and taking us by the hand, bid us good-bye in a cheerful manner, expressing his determination to stand by the old flag and never turn his back to the foe. But we little thought we should never see him again. He was a young man of more than common ability, and his sad end will be sincerely mourned by all who had the pleasure of his acquaintance.

Other Voices: George Tate, Incident at Williamsburg

On the night of the disastrous battle of Williamsburg, in the rain and mud, the scattered members of Co. D and of the 3d reg. tried to gather themselves together around a smouldering fire, wet and chilled and wounded. Without food or shelter. As one by one they came around the camp fire, to report themselves among the living, and tell of the comrades who were among the fallen, the question was asked: "How many are present?" The Captain asked Sergeant Billy Post to call the roll, so that those present could answer to their names. Post began the roll, intending to omit the names of those known to be among the slain, but long practice had made roll call mechanical and when he reached McKinstry he called it, then Miller, then Moon. He could go no farther, but broke down amidst a tempest of sobs from the comrades who surrounded him.[5]

Editorial Note

Most of the day of the fourth and all of the fifth, rain falls. On the night of the fourth, Arthur and the rest of the Excelsiors camp in the wet and mud. Struggling to make progress on the roads, Hooker's Division is spread out, but the aggressive general orders his first brigade to the attack. Eventually the Excelsiors and New Jersey men follow as the battle escalates as brigades of Confederate troops, already beyond Williamsburg, counter march and join the swirling and stubborn fight. Throughout much of the day and now severely outnumbered, Hooker's calls for reinforcements go unanswered while his division teeters on the verge of collapse. Only the timely arrival of Philip Kearney's division saves Hooker. [6] Eventually, darkness and exhaustion end the fighting. In the night, the Confederates withdraw again, leaving Williamsburg in Yankee hands.

Figure 8.6. Battle of Williamsburg, *Harper's Weekly*, May 1862, Hooker Division. A. R. Waud image from *Harper's Weekly* showing Hooker's Division in action at Williamsburg. This image correctly depicts the rainy and wet conditions under which the battle was fought. Source: *Harper's Weekly*.

Four of the five regiments of the Excelsior Brigade are engaged in the battle and collectively suffer the loss of 772 men, the size of an entire regiment. The 70th New York loses 330 men, nearly half the regiment, along with the capture of its commander, Colonel William Dwight, though he is subsequently released. The 72nd New York, for its part in the battle, loses 195 men. Sixty-one men are killed outright with another twenty-three dying later from their wounds. There are sixty-seven men wounded, some of whom recover and return to the ranks. Yet there are another forty-four men listed as missing, mostly captured, with some whose fate is never fully known.[7]

Williamsburg is the biggest battle of the war so far. The losses come as a shock to all involved. But there is still a war to fight and there will certainly be more men lost. Official federal losses at Williamsburg amount to 2,239; 1,575 coming out of Hooker's three brigades. "History will not be believed when it is told that the noble officers and men of my division were permitted to carry on this unequal struggle from morning until night unaided in the presence of more than 30,000 of their comrades with arms in their hands," writes Joe Hooker, adding, "nevertheless, it is true. If we failed to capture the rebel army on the plains of Williamsburg, it surely will not be ascribed to the want of conduct and courage in my command."[8]

Chapter 9

The Low but Not So Very Soothing Hum of Minie Bullets

The 72nd New York and Excelsior Brigade after Arthur McKinstry

History of the Excelsior Brigade • Personal accounts by other Chautauqua men • The fate of Arthur's mates

On July 2, 1893, survivors of the Excelsior Brigade, their friends and families, gathered in Gettysburg to dedicate a monument raised in honor of that brigade. Located on what is now known as Excelsior Field, the assembled listened to speeches and prayers recounting not only the actions of the brigade members while on the Gettysburg Battlefield, but a summation of their three full years of service to the Union. John N. Coyne of the 70th New York, who had risen from the enlisted ranks to lieutenant colonel, provided the centerpiece of the day's commemorations, a history of the Excelsior Brigade. Coyne's oration was published in the three-volume work *New York at Gettysburg.*

ORATION OF LIEUT. COL. JOHN N. COYNE, OF THE FIRST EXCELSIOR.

COMRADES OF THE EXCELSIOR BRIGADE:

As we stand on this historic ground with a summer's sun bathing in a golden light the peaceful landscape, and the soft air filled with the fragrance of the meadowland and the song of the birds,

"You would not dream that once this tranquil spot
Had felt the burning hail of the rifle shot;
Or heard the screaming of the deadly shell,
Or the wild echo of the Rebel yell.

"It should be haunted. Phantom hosts should rise
And cloud with battle-smoke the smiling skies.
The clash of meeting bayonets we should hear;
And booming cannon shock the listening ear.

"Hark! Is not that the marshalling of men?
Does not a war-like bugle wake the glen?
Is not the trampling of ten thousand feet
Heard, keeping rhythm to the drummer's beat?

"No, not an infant in its mother's arms
Breathes freer than this scene from war's alarms.
The record of that awful day is writ
In human hearts. Here is no trace of it."

How peaceful and lovely the scene as we stood here on the morning of the 2d of July, thirty years ago. The same golden sunlight and fragrance of wood and meadow greeted us as we arose from our slumber that morn; but, ere darkness again covered the earth it was all changed. These fair fields were turned into a crimson tide of blood; these hills that had stood unshaken for ages, trembled with the shock of war, and the sun was darkened with the smoke of battle.

On that fair morning the Excelsior Brigade, numbering 1,701 sturdy forms, the survivors of Yorktown, Williamsburg, Fair Oaks, The Seven Day's Battle, Bristoe Station, Bull Run, Fredericksburg and Chancellorsville, stood in martial array ready to face the foe who had marched into this fair land in their treasonable design of invasion. On all these fields, hundreds of your comrades had given their lives in defence of the Union that these invaders had been battling to destroy; and now the Rebel host had entered this peaceful Northern State in a final effort to accomplish their purpose. But it was to be otherwise, and the waves of the Rebellion were to be dashed into fragments against the rocks of Round Top, and the soldiers of Longstreet, Hood, McLaws and Barksdale were to suffer annihilation in their efforts to break through the storm of fire at the Peach Orchard.

The banners of the Excelsior Brigade were in the heart of this volcano, and you won imperishable renown by your unflinching courage and heroism in the desperate struggle.

As the sun sank over the distant hills on that eventful day, and the shades of night began to fall, your depleted ranks were withdrawn from the ground you had so stubbornly contested. For hours you had been battling over this very ground where now you stand, and your dead lay in scores on the extreme front of the day's conflict. Your standards were still unsullied, and history had to add another to tell of your valor.

I will now take up in chronological order our battles and losses, but in a paper of this kind, written to illustrate the deeds of our brigade, and to briefly give an account of its heavy sacrifices, it will be impossible for me to dwell upon the details of our campaigns.

Formation of the Brigade

On May 18, 1861, Hon. Daniel E. Sickles was authorized by President Lincoln to organize a brigade for service in the field. To this task he devoted all his energies, and, after surmounting many difficulties, he completed the organization of five regiments.

The first Regiment was organized with General Sickles as a temporary colonel, he being succeeded by Col. Wm. Dwight, Jr.; the Second Regiment, under Col. Geo. B. Hall and Lieut. Col. H. L. Potter; the Third Regiment under Col. Nelson Taylor; the Fourth Regiment under Col. James Fairman, who was succeeded by Col. Wm. R. Brewster; and the Fifth Regiment under Col. Charles K. Graham. The regiments were organized independently of all State authority and were known as United States volunteers until December 5, 1861—long after they had been mustered into service—when orders were issued by the War Department for their incorporation in the volunteer forces of the State of New York. It was for this reason that their numerical designation became so high.

The first Regiment was mustered into the United States service at Camp Scott, on Staten Island, June 20 and 22, 1861. The Second Regiment, originally the Jackson Light Infantry, was mustered by companies at Camp Scott between June 20th and July 18th. The Third Regiment was mustered by companies at Camp Scott between June and October. The Fourth Regiment, which was recruited as the Second Fire Zouaves, was mustered between July 8th and October 8th at Camp Scott; and the Fifth Regiment was mustered at Camp Scott between June 30th and October 6th.

Washington and Lower Maryland

When the Excelsior regiments reached Washington, they were placed in camp in the vicinity of the Capitol.

Late in the fall, the brigade was sent to the Lower Potomac, near Liverpool Point, where it did excellent service guarding the river. The regiments were regularly drilled in marching, bayonet exercise, and musketry practice, and passed the winter in perfecting themselves for the sterner duties that were to follow when the spring should open.

You were now the Second Brigade of the Second Division, Third Corps of the Army of the Potomac, or Sickles' Brigade, Hooker's Division, Heintzelman's Corps.

Other Voices: Memories of Lucius "Leute" Jones Jr., Co. H

We had a rigid examination; they were very careful whom they took. I was pronounced sound O.K., so was given a suit of soldier's clothes. Was then told I would have to get my father's consent to go, being under the required age. The next day I went home and got the consent of my father. Went Monroe's photography rooms and had my picture taken . . . There were a lot of men enlisted in our Company who worked in the Brooks car shops—big, stout fellows. I was small, and they made all manner of fun of me and a few others of my size. They would tell us to go home and let our mothers take care of us, and all such things.

Our Company being filled, we were off for the front or seat of war. All those big fellows were pretty well soaked with whiskey before we left Dunkirk, and when we arrived at Baltimore they drank so much water it made them sick. The next morning we arrived Washington and were taken across the river to the Maryland side, where we went into camp two or three days . . . [Eventually] we made camp forty miles down the Potomac River from Washington, where we were in training all winter . . .

We left Maryland in the spring and were put aboard large boats. The whole army was on transports; they struck out for Fort Monroe . . .[1]

The Peninsula Campaign

On the 9th of April you were on transports on your way to the Peninsula, and on that dark and bloody ground you were to prove that the motto on your banners was well deserved.

You were soon before the formidable works of Yorktown, where the brigade was thrown well to the front, and was almost constantly engaged in building redoubts and intrenchments, or on duty on the skirmish line. You were ever vigilant in the performance of this duty, and always ready to take advantage of any carelessness of the enemy. Your vigilance was rewarded, for at early dawn on the morning of the 4th of May, after a night of terrific artillery fire from the enemy, our enterprising comrades of the Fourth Regiment, becoming suspicious of the unusual quiet-ness in their front, made up their minds to find out the cause of it, and, pushing forward, were soon climbing over the Rebel works, thus being among the first to announce their evacuation.

The loss in the brigade during the siege of Yorktown was slight, being 1 killed and 2 wounded.

Hooker's Division is selected to lead in pursuit of the retreating foe. Many of you remember that March,—the heavy roads, the driving rain as night descended, and the comfortless bivouac in the woods, as weary and exhausted, we sank to rest.

Early the next morning, May 5th, you resume your march, and you do not fail to notice that your commanding officers keep the columns well closed up, and that they have an air of expectancy which does not usually mark their faces.

The rain is still falling, and the roads and woods are dismal; the air is heavy with moisture and seems like a pall. At last we are halted, and as the noise of jingling accoutrements ceases, we hear peculiar sounds and reverberations. Our cheeks flush, and we begin to tighten our belts and inspect our arms. We know what it means. Hooker, with the leading brigade, has overtaken the enemy and he is contesting our advance, and the increasing noise indicates that the resistance is becoming serious. We are on the eve of our first battle, my comrades, and our minds wander to our far-off homes where our loved ones are, and as the vision comes before us, a feeling heretofore unknown pervades our hearts, and the eye becomes moist with the tender reflection.

The gentle breeze that brings to our ears the noise of conflict unfolds our banners, and the motto upon them dispels the vision. Our lips become compressed and our brows knit, and the light deepens in our eyes. The sound of battle increases, and the atmosphere becomes heavy with its smoke as we stand by the roadside awaiting orders.

Hooker's advance has been severely contested all the morning. Longstreet, who has the command of the enemy's forces on the field, has thrown into the contest regiment after regiment, and is fighting desperately to hold the ground where he has made his stand. The iron bolts from Fort Magruder and the heavy musketry fire from masses of the enemy's infantry have decimated the ranks of the gallant New Jersey regiments, who have been bearing the brunt of the battle up to his hour, and they feel that unless succor comes they will have to abandon the ground covered with the bodies of their comrades.

At this critical moment, about 2 p.m., Hooker calls upon the Excelsior Brigade, and soon the command, which now becomes a welcome one, is given and we move forward.

Our arrival on the field is opportune. Longstreet has been heavily reinforced, and he has thrown forward several regiments into a dense wood on our front and left, apparently with a view of cutting off the remnants of the Jersey Brigade. At this moment we confront him, and we have advanced so far that when his line emerges from the edge of the woods we are within short range. There is a moment's hesitation, as if the Angel of Death shrank from the harvest before him. But more than human life is at stake—the fate of the battle is wavering in the balance, and the duel is to be a bloody one.

The enemy now opens upon us along his whole line, and we return his fire with calm deliberation. The months of drill and musketry practice on the Lower Potomac give you confidence and firmness. There is no shrinking, no wavering. You stand to your work, and with your deadly buck-and-ball soon throw his lines into confusion, and they are driven into the woods.

Again Longstreet throws forward fresh regiments, and the contest is renewed. The musketry fire is terrific, and Fort Magruder lends its thunder and hurls an iron hail into our ranks. For hours you have held at bay thrice your number; you begin to find your cartridge-boxes empty, and use those of the comrades who have fallen around you. These soon become exhausted, and you slowly fall back, loathe to surrender the field; but your heroism and heavy sacrifices have not been in vain—succor is at hand. Kearny comes to the rescue, and the enemy soon give way before his enthusiastic and gallant troops, and the victory is ours.

The story of the battle of Williamsburg is an interesting one to the soldiers of Hooker's Division, for upon them fell the brunt of the fighting. The reports of that battle did not do justice to our gallant leader. They were brilliantly colored when referring to other parts of the field, but here in front of Fort Magruder the vision of the author of the report was obscured by the smoke of battle and the volcano of fire that whirled around the vicinity.

Col. William F. Fox in his work on Regiment Losses says: "The battle of Williamsburg was fought almost entirely by the Third Corps. Of the 2,239 casualties on that field, 2,002 occurred within its ranks, and three-fourths of them in Hooker's Division; the brunt of the battle having fallen on the Excelsior Brigade and Jersey Brigade, both in Hooker's Division."

Your proportion of the loss was enormous; the First Regiment losing 330 in killed, wounded and missing; the Third Regiment, 195; Fourth Regiment, 104; and the Fifth Regiment, 143; a total loss in the four regiments, in killed, wounded and missing, of 772.

Editorial Note

The fighting at Williamsburg had not been kind to the men of Chautauqua County. A number of Arthur McKinstry's comrades would die along with him in the battle. Of the men who joined Arthur on one of "these glorious moonlight evenings" in late August of '61 to raise "Ned," Percival Moon, Charles Miller, and William Simpson would all not survive Williamsburg. Martin Boyden, who had been wounded in the hand when that live coal was put into a cannon ball, would not survive either. Neither would John Nuepling, who had been complimented for having one of the cleanest guns in the regiment. The man whom McKinstry favored to win the regimental shooting contest, James Van Hautten, would die in the battle along with others from the Chautauqua. Bob McKinstry in the 70th New York, who was no relation to Arthur but with whom he had built a friendship, was wounded in the battle and was eventually discharged for disability in September of 1862.[2]

The brigade was commanded by Col. Nelson Taylor in this battle, General Sickles' nomination as brigadier general having failed of confirmation in the United States Senate. This is no time to criticize the gross injustice of that act, but we can remember the bitter resentment we felt when our general was relieved of his command as we were about to be embarking for the Peninsula; and it spoke well for your loyalty to your country that you still remained true and faithful soldiers.

After the battle of Williamsburg this act of injustice was repaired, and General Sickles was confirmed as brigadier general, and he resumed command of the brigade while we were encamped at Bailey's Crossroads.

On the 31st of May, we were at Bottom's Bridge engaged in the usual routine of camp duty, and looking forward to a quiet Sabbath on the morrow, when suddenly an aid from headquarters dashes up, and soon the command to fall in is passed along. The "assembly" is sounded, and the men hasten to form company. With your usual promptness you are soon in line, and receive the first intimation of the battle which has been raging across the Chickahominy, at Fair Oaks, and of the disaster that has befallen Casey's troops. Leaving tents and knapsacks you are off on the double-quick, and do not cease your rapid march until you reach the field. The shades of night have now descended, and the battle has ceased, leaving the enemy in possession of Casey's intrenchments, and confident of success on the morrow.

At early dawn the battle is resumed, and the rattle of musketry is heard all along the line. It increases in violence on the Williamsburg Road, and the order comes for you to move forward. General Sickles is now in command and you bear yourselves proudly as his eye wanders along your ranks. The Second Regiment, owing to a detail which kept them near Yorktown, was not with us at Williamsburg, and are now anxious to show of what mettle they are made. The opportunity soon comes, and in a gallant bayonet charge cover themselves with glory and win the commendation of the commanding general of the army for their gallantry. The other regiments of the brigade press forward, and soon come in contact with the foe, and the enemy is driven from the field. Night finds you occupying Casey's old intrenchments, and the commanding general thinks you have done so well that he leaves you there for three or four days, evidently believing that the men of the Excelsior Brigade are insensible to fatigue and hunger, and that coffee, hardtack and bacon are luxuries that they abhor. General Sickles, however, loses his patience, so the story goes, and sends word to the rear that if they want him to take Richmond alone, he will have to go to New York and raise another brigade. The hint was sufficient, for that afternoon the brigade was relieved from duty at the front.

Though closely engaged with the enemy two or three times during this battle, our loss was not severe, the brigades only losing 74 in killed, wounded and missing.

Other Voices: Memories of Lucius "Leute" Jones Jr., Co. H

We were after the Rebels as fast as we could move until we came to Fair Oaks, in front of Richmond. There the Rebels made a stand. We moved up Saturday night to the front line of battle, where Casey's division was driven back that morning. Sunday morning we made a charge and drove the Rebels back from the grounds they had captured the day before. The battle raged all day; we were losing men fast. Night put a stop to the fighting. Soon as it was dark pickets were called for, and I was one of them. We were taken out in front in a strip of woods; it was in a swamp. We were posted along a line about ten feet apart, with orders not to talk, but to keep a sharp lookout. James P. Knox was next to me; we had to stand in the water up over our shoes. We took turns standing on a big root of a tree to keep out of the water—only room enough for one at a time. We were glad when morning came.[3]

During the month that we remained on this field the brigade was called upon to do almost constant picket duty, and the duty was arduous for us, as the regiments we would relieve were frequently forced back by the enemy and we had the line to retake. Thus it was, that whenever we were seen going to the front, the comrades in other regiments would commence to look to their arms, and grumble about Sickles' men always raising a fuss. Thus it became almost a daily battleground for the Excelsior Brigade, and our losses were serious. The twin Houses would often be filled with our wounded, and the rattle of musketry as you pressed back the foe would echo through the woods like a general engagement.

You lost in these brief but severe contests, which included the engagement at Oak Grove and Peach Orchard, 322 killed, wounded, and missing.

I will not dwell on the Seven Day's Battles which followed; they are too full of blood and misery. All your heroism and your glorious deeds which had shed so much lustre on our arms had been in vain. You looked upon your banners with Yorktown, Williamsburg and Fair Oaks emblazoned upon them with a proud glance, but your hearts grew heavy as you gazed upon your depleted ranks and remembered the hundreds of your comrades who were buried on those fields.

You were in action at Glendale, June 30th, and rendered gallant service in the severe Battle of Malvern Hill on July 1st, in which engagements your loss was 26.

Editorial Note

The Seven Days Battle, of which Malvern Hill was the last major engagement, would claim eighty-seven killed, wounded, and missing from the 72nd New York.[4] Among those killed at Malvern Hill was Captain Stephen M. Doyle. Doyle had joined the regiment as a lieutenant and served as adjutant until taking command of Company H. Doyle had paid Arthur McKinstry a high compliment early on by recognizing Arthur as a "writing man." McKinstry in turn always thought Doyle to be of the highest quality of officer.

Other Voices: Memories from David B. Parker, Co. D

At Malvern Hill there seemed to be but little reason for our losing as many men as we did. The position was a wonderfully strong one. Our artillery was massed on a hill. The Confederates came through the white oak swamp and charged across a valley. The morning of the battle Captain Doyle of Dunkirk, Captain of Company H of our regiment, a highly educated and accomplished gentleman, came to me and gave me a tin box, saying, "I want you to take this and if anything happens to me send it to Steven Caldwell. It contains (he opened the box) money, my watch and a diamond cross which was my mother's, which I have worn next my body suspended by a chain around my neck."

"Captain," I said, "why do you give it to me?"

"I expect to be killed this day."

"Oh," I said, "you can't believe in presentiments."

"I never have, but I expect to be killed this day, and I want you to take this and send it home if anything happens to me."

He was killed that day, I think the only officer of our regiment that was.[5]

On the 2nd of July, you were at Harrison's Landing, and on August 14th, on your way to Yorktown to embark for Alexandria. On your arrival there you were sent on to Warrenton Junction to reinforce Pope, and on August 27th, were severely engaged at Bristoe Station with a superior force of the enemy under Ewell, who was strongly posted along the railroad and in the woods. After a severe contest which lasted from between 3 and 4 o'clock in the afternoon until dusk, you drove the enemy from his position and across Broad Run, and were victors of the field, the enemy leaving his dead and many of his wounded in your hands. This was a brilliant action and proved that you were still capable of great deeds. Your loss in this engagement was severe, numbering 307.

You were engaged at Groveton on the 19th; at Bull Run on the 30th; and at Chantilly on September 1st. Your losses in these engagements, however, were slight, only numbering 20.

After this campaign you were stationed near Alexandria with the rest of the Third Corps, and, owing to your depleted ranks, you were not called upon to participate with the rest of the Army of the Potomac in its march into Maryland, nor in the sanguinary battle of Antietam which followed. You were not idle, however, as you were constantly employed in building intrenchments and in picket duty.

During the latter part of October, the enemy having made a demonstration in the vicinity of Fairfax Court House, you were selected for the hazardous duty of a reconnaissance, and on November 1st, broke camp and marched for Manassas Junction. On our arrival there the Third Regiment was thrown forward to Warrenton Junction; the First and Fifth to Bristoe Station, and the Second and Fourth Regiments remained at the Junction. You remained in this vicinity some three weeks, when you took up your line of march with the rest of the army for the Rappahannock. This march was a severe test of your endurance. It began in a heavy rain, which continued until we reached Wolf Run Shoals. Here the sun came out, the roads dried up, and a sharp frost coming on, marching became comparatively easy. A few days after leaving this camp you were in front of Fredericksburg.

On the 13th of December you were across the Rappahannock engaged in the campaign which resulted so disastrously to our arms, but were not called upon to sustain a severe loss, only losing 16.

Chancellorsville

Burnside was soon relieved of the command of the Army of the Potomac, Hooker superseding him. Under this leader the army soon recovered from the effects of its recent defeat. With wonderful courage and elasticity it responded to his efforts, and was soon in a condition equal to its palmiest days.

On May 1, 1863, you cross the United States Ford, on the Rappahannock, to participate in the Chancellorsville campaign. With the rest of Hooker's old division, you were held in reserve near the Chancellor House, and rest quietly on your arms in the woods to the left of the road that leads from the United States Ford. Fighting and skirmishing were going on around you, and you wondered how it was that you were not called upon to lead the advance and to bear the brunt of the storm of shot and shell that your comrades were facing. But your commander knew your value, and was reserving you for a much more serious duty if the occasion should arise.

The 2nd of May dawned, and the splutter on the skirmish-line was all that disturbed the tranquility of the scene. As the early hours passed this gave place to a heavy musketry fire on Hancock's front, which soon involved Couch and Slocum. It was now discovered that this attack was only intended to conceal the movement of a large body of the enemy that was rapidly passing to our right, and Sickles, to develop the intention of the enemy, threw forward Birney's Division, supported by Whipple's.

This movement resulted in the capture of the Twenty-third Georgia, and the discovery that Jackson, with a large force, was rapidly moving in the direction of Howard's position. Howard was immediately advised of this and cautioned to be prepared for an attack.

About 6 o'clock a crash of musketry was heard, and before we had time to realize what was the cause of the uproar, word came to us to fall in. We now knew that the emergency had come, and that we were to be thrown into the breach. You will remember with what alacrity we seized our arms and formed in the road in light marching order, and impatiently awaited the signal to advance. The word came, and as we started off on the double-quick evidences of disaster to our right flank increased, and soon we were among the fleeing troops of the Eleventh Corps.

General Doubleday, in his work on the Chancellorsville campaign, says: "The constantly increasing uproar and the wild rush of fugitives past the Chancellor House told Hooker what had occurred. It was not easy to find an adequate force for this emergency, for the whole line was now actively engaged. Fortunately, Berry's Division was held in reserve and was available.

"They were true and tried men, and went forward at once to the rescue. Few people appreciate the steadiness and courage required, when all around is flight and confusion, for a force to make its way through crowds of fugitives, advance steadily to the post of danger in front, and meet the exulting enemy, while others are seeking safety in the rear. Such men are heroes, and far more worthy of honor than those who fight in the full blaze of successful warfare."

Through the superhuman exertions of Sickles and the gallant Pleasanton the tide was turned, and, a sharp contest, Jackson's forces sullenly fell back.

As darkness fell upon the battlefield, the gentle moon shone forth, lighting up with weird shadows the depths of the forest in which our line is formed. Availing ourselves of her soft light, we gathered logs and earth and strengthened our position as best we could, knowing that the contest on the morrow would be a desperate one.

While thus engaged, a heavy musketry and artillery fire opened on our left near the Plank Road and involved the Fourth Regiment of our brigade. In this storm of missiles Stonewall Jackson was mortally wounded, and the South lost one of her greatest generals.

On the morning of the 3d the contest was renewed, and the storm of fire ran along the whole line. The enemy worked around on our left flank, and, the Third Maryland giving away, our position became untenable. We were forced, after desperate resistance, to give ground. We fell back to the artillery reserve and formed in support, but were not allowed to remain, as our commander, General Revere, notwithstanding our earnest protest, marched us to the rear. It was the only instance in our history of our having been marched from the field while under fire. As soon as this was discovered General Revere was relieved, and Colonel Farnum of the First Regiment was placed in command. Under this gallant soldier we were marched back to the battleground, and remained at the front until the army re-crossed the Rappahannock. Our losses in this battle amounted to 250.

The enemy, flushed with his recent victory and confident of his superiority, soon determined on a bold, aggressive movement. Collecting his forces and abandoning our front, he made a detour and marched rapidly towards the Potomac. Hooker followed with energy, and we were soon passing over our old battlefields of Bristoe, Groveton and Manassas, and the enemy was allowed to cross the Potomac without molestation.

Other Voices: Lucius Jones Remembers Chancellorsville

Sunday morning we were attacked in front and flank, and by some means a gap occurred in our line, and some of the enemy taking advantage had flanked us; we took it front flank and rear. It seemed all over with us, and our prospects for Rebel prison was very flattering. We made a desperate attempt to escape the bagging. How we got out of it I can hardly tell, as the Rebels came over our breastworks on our flank like so many sheep getting over a stone wall. At one time we were all mixed up; they ordered us to surrender. Our Captain, John W. Holmes, asked us what we were going to do. We told him we were going to stick to him. He said he would run the chances of getting out, so we took leg bail and started—the Rebels after us. None of us had our guns loaded. The Rebels caught two of my company and held them. As we came to the open field we could see our artillery on the other side. When we got almost across, we were signalled to lie down. In a moment we were flat on our faces. Hell seemed to let loose over our heads, and the ranks of the pursuers seemed fairly to vanish.[6]

Other Voices: Tribute to Colonel William Stevens, Killed at Chancellorsville

HEAD QUARTERS 3D REGT. EX. BRIG.,
May 18, 1863.
At a meeting of the officers of the Excelsior Brigade, held at the Head Quarters 3rd Regiment Excelsior Brigade, Colonel William R. Brewster, Commanding Brigade, presiding, preambles and resolutions were adopted as expressing the feelings of the entire brigade.

Whereas—it has pleased God, in his all wise providence, to remove from us our late Commander, Colonel William O. Stevens, who fell on the morning of May 3d, at the battle of Chancellorsville, Va. while nobly performing his duty, we, the surviving officers of the regiment and brigade with which he has so long been connected wish to pay this slight tribute to departed worth, while expressing our heartfelt sympathy for the afflicted family in bereavement.

In the loss of Colonel William O. Stevens, the regiment and the army has been deprived of the services of a most gallant and efficient officer, an accomplished gentleman and a true patriot, who has sealed with his life his devotion to his country, and our highest aspirations for the future shall be to emulate the noble example of fidelity to trust that he has bequeathed to us.

Through all the vicissitudes of the service in which he has been engaged, he has manifested a steady and hopeful bearing, stimulating by an exalted zeal and patriotism the hopes of the wavering, and encouraging all by the noble example to stand firmly in the great struggle, trusting to the righteousness of their cause for the attainment of permanently beneficial results.

To the afflicted family, in their bereavement, words of condolence and sympathy are all we can bestow; our loss has been great, theirs has been greater. A parent now mourns the offering of a second son to the altar of his country, while a devoted wife with her fatherless children deplores the loss of a kind and generous protector. We trust that a Higher Power may sustain them in their bereavement, and enable them to support with becoming fortitude their deep distress, realizing that though he sleeps, his memory will not be forgotten, but will descend to posterity with names of the illustrious dead, which a grateful country will render immortal.

Resolved, that copies of the above be sent to the family of Colonel Stevens, Washington Chronicle, Lawrence Boston Journal, New York Herald, Chicago Times, New York Tribune, Dunkirk Journal, Jamestown Journal and Westfield Republican for publication.

Resolved, That the proceedings of the meeting be placed in the records of the brigade.

WM. R. BREWSTER, Col. 4th
Excelsior,
President.[7]

Gettysburg

As we passed into Maryland and across the Pennsylvania line, your eyes brightened and you marched as you never marched before. The Pennsylvania boys in our ranks had an air of confidence, and the seal of grim determination was upon their faces. They were on their own soil, and they held their lives of little value, if by their sacrifice they could deal a deathblow to the invader.

It would be idle for me to dwell upon the battle of Gettysburg. You, the survivors of this field know its history. The heroism of the Army of the Potomac, and the fruitless efforts of Lee, Longstreet, and Pickett, are well known to you. These hills and woods and valleys are eloquent with the story of your victory and the saving of a Nation. This was the high tide of the Rebellion, and the hope of the Confederacy was blotted out in the blood of the brave but mistaken soldiers who battled against you on this field. Thirty years have passed since the battle, and we have assembled here to dedicate to the memory of our dead who fell in this field this beautiful monument, which stands like a temple of fame on the front line of the second day's contest.

They are sleeping in their soldiers' graves, my comrades, but they are not for-gotten, for we have in our hearts a tender love, a fond undying remembrance of them.

The First Regiment carried into action on the 2d of July, 22 officers and 349 men, and lost 1 officer and 32 men, killed or died of wounds; 7 officers and 73 men, wounded, and 4 men missing; total, 117.

The Second Regiment carried into action 13 officers and 320 men, and lost 1 officer and 13 men, killed or died of wounds; 6 officers and 58 men, wounded, and 13 men, missing; total, 91.

The Third Regiment carried into action 22 officers and 283 men, and lost 1 officer and 10 men, killed or died of wounds; 6 officers and 69 men, wounded, and 28 men, missing; total, 114.

The Fourth Regiment carried into action 27 officers and 480 men, and lost 5 officers and 47 men, killed or died of wounds; 10 officers and 92 men, wounded, and 8 men, missing; total, 162.

The Fifth Regiment carried into action 17 officers and 258 men, and lost 1 officer and 16 men, killed or died of wounds; 5 officers and 64 men, wounded, and 3 men, missing; total, 89.

These figures make a total loss on the brigade of 573 killed, wounded and missing.

The night of the 3d found Lee vanquished at all points, and his decimated battalions soon retreated and re-crossed the Potomac, with the Union army in close pursuit.

Editorial Note: Aftermath of Battle

Though Gettysburg was the largest battle of the war, fewer men within the regiment were killed here and at Chancellorsville than at Williamsburg. Billy Post, who had won the shooting contest back in Maryland and had risen through the ranks to captain of Company F, was wounded at Chancellorsville and discharged four months later. William Pugh, another one of the boys who "raised Ned" back in summer of '61, was captured at Chancellorsville and then paroled in time to be wounded at The Wilderness.

Of the men mentioned by McKinstry, only Charley Foss, the man said to have one of the cleanest guns in the regiment, was killed at Gettysburg, having first risen to the rank of second lieutenant of Company C.[8]

On the afternoon of July 23d we overtook the enemy at Manassas Gap, where we found him strongly posted on Wapping Heights, supported by artillery. General Meade determined to dislodge this force if possible, push through the gap, and compel him to give battle.

The Excelsior Brigade was selected for this duty, and you moved forward, climbed the heights and charged the foe. General Spinola, commanding the brigade fell seriously wounded, and the gallant Farnum took command. You pressed on with determination, and drove the enemy from his position, the cheers of the onlookers echoing from hill to hill as you planted your colors on his defences.

This following morning the Fifth Regiment was thrown forward to feel the enemy, but he had abandoned the Gap, leaving his dead unburied and many of his wounded in your hands. The brigade lost in this action 74 in killed and wounded.

You were soon resting in camp near Brandy station, and were not brought in contact with the enemy again until November 27th, at Locust Grove, during the Mine Run campaign, where the brigade lost 45 in killed and wounded.

The Overland Campaign

During the winter of 1863 and 1864 reorganization and consolidation is the order of the day, and when the campaign opens in the spring we were marching with the standards of the Second Corps,—all that was left of the old Third Corps having been consolidated.

The fierce and sanguinary struggle in the wilderness began on the 5th of May. As Lee would not leave his defences, we had to attack him in his works, and the contest promised to be fierce and bloody.

For two days the struggle continued. The musketry fire exceeded in violence any experienced before. In this vast jungle the enemy was like a tiger in his lair and not easily driven forth; therefore, the left flank movement, which was to be-come such a feature of this campaign, was adopted. The brigade lost in this battle 140 in killed, wounded and missing.

At Spotsylvania we found the enemy strongly fortified in an almost impregnable position from which he could not be tempted, and after a series of desperate en-counters, the Second Corps was called upon to assault his works. On the morning of May 12th, at the first light of dawn, you charged his intrenchments, and a hand-to-hand struggle took place which had no parallel in the history of the two armies. The enemy fought gallantly, but was driven from his position, which has become known in history as the Bloody Angle, leaving 3,000 prisoners, several pieces of artillery, and 30 battleflags in our hands. Our loss in this battle in killed, wounded and missing was 148.

On May 23d, you were engaged at North Anna; on the 30th you were under fire at Totopotomoy, and on the morning of June 3d, participated in the assault at Cold Harbor. The loss in the brigade in these engagements was 76.

In the movements upon Petersburg your marches were long and exhaustive, and the James River as you approached it spread out invitingly like an oasis in the desert to the weary Arab. You were not allowed to halt, however, and refresh yourself in its cooling waters. You crossed the river and pushed on for Petersburg, where you arrived on the night of the 15th, and participated in the assault on the works around that city on the 16th, in which action you lost 86.

Other Voices: Lucius Jones Remembers the Wilderness

Our regiment was detailed to guard the division ammunition train. On the 5th we crossed the Rapidan river. This was the first day's Battles of the Wilderness. About four in the afternoon, I with a few others of my company, went over the battlefield of May 3rd, 1863. We went where our regiment fought on that Sunday morning near Chancellorsville. There we found the skeleton of Henry Heyl of my company, lying by a big log. His cap was found by his side with his initials upon it. He was a fine young man, and a good soldier.[9]

The time had now come, my comrades, when the Excelsior Brigade shall cease to exist, your three years' term of service having expired.

The First Regiment was withdrawn from the field on June 22d, and honorably mustered out under Lieut. Col. Thomas Holt, July 1, 1864. The men not entitled to discharge were transferred to the Eighty-sixth New York.

The Second Regiment was honorably mustered out under Lieut. Col. Thomas Rafferty, July 30th, 1864, and the men not entitled to discharge were transferred to the One hundred and twentieth New York.

The Third Regiment was honorably mustered out under Lieut. Col. John Leonard, June 19 and 20, 1864, and the men not entitled to discharge were transferred to the One hundred and twentieth New York.

The Fourth Regiment retained its organization, a sufficient number of the men having re-enlisted, and it remained to fight on other fields and to participate in the Grand Review on Washington on the cessation of hostilities.

The Fifth Regiment was honorably mustered out under Lieut. Col. Wm. H. Lounsberry, from June 10th to August 3d, and the men not entitled to discharge were assigned to the Fortieth New York.

During your term of service the total enrollment in the brigade was 6,442, divided as follows: The First Regiment had 1,462; the Second Regiment, 1,170; the Third Regiment, 1,250; the Fourth Regiment, 1,350; and the Fifth Regiment, 1,210.

The brigade lost during its term of service, in which I include the losses in the Fourth Regiment and among the veterans of the brigade who were transferred to the Fortieth, Eighty-sixth and One hundred and twentieth New York, after the brigade ceased to exist and in several minor affairs not mentioned in this history, 3,028, which severe loss places you among the 300 fighting regiments in Colonel Fox's valuable work, "Regimental Losses in the Civil War."

My task is done. I have, as briefly as the remembrance of your glorious career would allow, carried you along from the time of your first muster until you stacked arms after your last battle.

As you followed me in your history, many scenes not mentioned and of almost equal interest have come before you; some personal deed of gallantry, some incident of the march and camp, which would all go to make up a marvelous story, and which should not perish.

And now for the years that remain to us let "the tie that binds" be drawn closer. Let our motto be Fraternity, Charity and Loyalty to one another, and let us so live that the honors gained while following glorious banners shall never be dimmed by an unworthy act, so that when the time comes to lay down our arms and answer to the last roll-call can explain, "Excelsior!"

Other Voices: Lucius Jones and Mustering Out

The term of service of our Regiment—the 72nd N.Y.—expired on the 21st of June, 1864. We were relieved from the picket line on the 22nd of June, and went back to the rear to be mustered out—that is, all of those who didn't re-enlist as veterans. There was not enough re-enlisted to hold the organization, so the dear old 72nd Regiment was mustered out. Then the parting came, with goodbye to all; and off the boys went, wishing us good luck, and we the same to them. Then all of us veterans were transferred to the 120th Regt. N.Y. Vol., and put into different companies. I was assigned to Company A., 120th, Captain James A. Hyde. He was a fine man. Then we wished we hadn't re-enlisted, but it was now too late, and the boys were off for home. And we veterans turned our faces to the enemy.[10]

At the close of Colonel Coyne's oration, General Daniel E. Sickles, president of the Excelsior Brigade Association, made a few remarks. He said:

"Colonel Coyne in his admirable address has carried you through all of your campaigns. He has accomplished in thirty-five minutes what it took the Army of the Potomac four years to do. This eloquent story of your heroism and never-faltering courage shall not perish with the hour; it shall be preserved in the annals of the State whose motto you bore upon your banners, for future generations to read."

Here followed a notable event. Gen. Jos. B. Carr upon being called upon for an address, in few felicitous words referred to the gallantry of the Excelsior Brigade, its discipline and reliability in action, and turning to General Sickles, said:—

"I congratulate you, General Sickles, in having been the creator of a brigade that carried its banners unsullied through all the campaigns of the Army of the Potomac; and now, General Sickles, as a souvenir of this day, and as a testimonial of the affection and loyalty of your comrades of the Third Corps, I have been selected to present you with this gold medal, which is made from the same die from which are struck the beautiful bronze medals the State of New York has bestowed upon the veterans who represented the State upon this field thirty years ago."

General Sickles was so much overcome by this unexpected mark of affection on the part of his comrades in arms, he could only briefly respond. Among other things, he said that he would preserve the medal as a priceless treasure and wear it near his heart as long as he lived.[11]

Other Voices: *Fredonia Censor*

Published July 13, 1864

RETURN OF THE 72D REGIMENT.

The remnant of old companies D and E, belonging to the 72d, N.Y. (3d Excelsior Regiment.) having received an honorable discharge at the expiration of three years term of service, arrived in Dunkirk on Thursday last. The news of their coming having preceded them, a large throng of friends and citizens from Dunkirk and the towns adjoining assembled at the Depot to greet the war-worn heroes on their arrival. The occasion was painfully suggestive of the scene witnessed at the Depot three years before, on the memorable 30th day of May, 1861, when these gallant companies, with full ranks, over 200 strong, left their homes with all their pleasant associations and endearments, to peril their lives in defence of the honor of the National flag. Then, as now, a large throng assembled to witness the event. They were sorrowful, yet hopeful. Could their eyes have then pierced the veil of the future, and followed the career of the devoted band to the finale of its glorious three years of service, keenly as they felt the trial of parting, their anguish would have been yet keener. STEVENS, BARRETT, DOYLE, and a host of gallant spirits then waved their adieus as the long train swept from the Depot to the gay music of "Girl I left behind me." Of that brave array, the first precious contribution of our County to the cause of the Union, a handful only—some 25 or 30—returned on Thursday last to receive the greetings of their friends, amid old familiar scenes. A few others remain in hospitals, unable to endure the fatigues of the homeward trip, and still another remnant have re-enlisted, animated with a determination to see the struggle through, and are now adding new laurels to the reputations won in the old "Fighting Brigade," in the trenches fronting Petersburg. The following description of the reception ceremonies we condense from the Dunkirk Journal: At a little past 3 o'clock, the booming of cannon announced that the train had been signalled, and immediately upon its arrival, the ceremonies of the occasion were put in charge of George M. Abell, Esq., who had been appointed Marshal of the day, assisted by Messrs. Horatio G. Brooks, and T. C. Thompson, and were conducted in the following order:

Procession led by Pioneers on horseback.
Dunkirk Brass Band.
President and Council of Dunkirk.
Chaplain and Orators of the day.
Committee of citizens.
Fire Companies in double column,
enclosing the surviving Heroes of Co.'s D and E.
Citizens and visitors.

The procession marched down Lion street to Front, up Front to Center, up Center to Fourth, down Fourth to Buffalo, up Buffalo to Park, where a stand had been erected for the village officers, speakers and Chaplain.

The Chaplain, Rev. L. J. Fisher, addressed the Throne of Grace in a most fervent and effective prayer.

Hon. James Sheward was then introduced to the assemblage and made a fitting and eloquent speech.

At the conclusion of the speech, the procession marched through several streets to the Depot Dining Saloon, where a sumptuous dinner had been provided for the occasion. Rev. Mr. Fisher, at the request of the Volunteers, expressed their thanks, and high appreciation of the welcome they were receiving. Hon. F. S. Edwards, in behalf of the Common Council of Dunkirk, then made a speech of welcome, after which they all fell to heartily upon the comforts for the inner man, provided by Jas. Gerrans, Esp., of the Depot Saloon.

Company D 3d Excelsior, Sickle's Brigade.

"How sleep the brave who sink to rest
By all their country's wishes blessed!
When Spring, with dewy fingers cold
Returns to deck their hallowed mould,
She then shall dress a sweeter sod
Than Fancy's feet have ever trod.

"By fairy hands their knell is rung;
By forms unseen their dirge is sung;
There Honor comes, a pilgrim gray,
To bless the turf that wraps their clay,
And freedom shall awhile repair
To dwell a weeping hermit there."

BY ARTHUR McKINSTRY.

Killed at Williamsburg, Va., May 5th, 1862.

Roam the world over,
You'll never discover
'Mid infantry, rifles, or cavalry bold;
On land or on sea,
There did never agree,
Such a gay merry party as here are enrolled.

Oh where, I would ask you,
Though sorry to task you,
With what it is clear must impossible be,
Could your eye, if you ran it,
Over all our great planet,
Find such a gay party as Company D.

There is Captain Cass Abell,
Quite as staunch as a cable,
Will stand like a rock by the colors, we know;
How wide his eyelashes,
How fierce his mustaches
Whenever there's prospect of meeting the foe.

Hugh Hinman beside him,
Good fortune betide him,
And young Johnny Howard stands stifly as starch;
Quite certain the fact is
The three will not practice
In face of the rebels, the right about march.

There is Billy Post, standing,
To look from the landing,
At the boats on the water so misty and dark;
Their cannon are crashing,
He sees their red flashing
And grins with delight, like a shovel-nosed shark.

In Brooks, too, our hope is,
And Harvey T. Lopez,
Who bears the Excelsior colors you know,
And Foss and Van Houten,
There rests not a doubt in
In the line of file closers, they will dash at the foe.

There is Corporal Luce,
Who may go to the deuce
Or to China; it is immaterial to me;
And Corporal Ellis
A prince of good fellows,
With pirates by legions to windward and lee.

There is Ludlow so jolly,
Who brings with him "Cully,"
And Barley, or queer little Corporal Pugh;
And Walden and Tate,
Who are mentioned so late
Must go with the others collectively through.

There is bluff Red Lewis,
And nothing more true is,
Than that, if you tease him, he is certain to swear.
No teamster so brave is,
As jolly "Jeff Davis,"
Who will run you a heat upon time, if you dare.

There is Henry Brevier,
Like a bold grenadier
With Newberger, scarcely more tall than his knees.
If the foe should come nigh
They must certainly fly,
Or be stifled at once with his Limburger cheese.

There is little Jim Bowen,
So wicked and knowing,
Like Barton, he sports a miraculous gun.
And though Floyd were himself
To keep watch of the elf,
He'd be stolen quite blind, for the sake of the fun.

And Moon, with his capers,
Should have place in these papers,
An excellent judge of these Maryland crops;
He is certain the way to
Live well on potato,
Is to draw them while tender and green, by the tops.

Though Stevens has left us
He has not bereft us,
Of a captain that is equally as good as our old;
And Marcus and Loeb are,
Since last year's October,
By Doyle in a different muster enrolled.

And Doyle, the brave fellow,
So genial and mellow,
We graduate him with a captain's degree.
But if evil befall him,
We will quickly recall him;
Warm welcome awaits him in Company D.

Each sticks to the other
Quite as close as a brother,
And our style has been always so easy and free;
Our hearts never sinking,
We ever are thinking—
Oh who would not soldier in Company D.

FARIBAULT (MINN.) REPUBLICAN PRINT.

Figure E.1. McKINSTRY POEM. This poem/song written by Arthur was recovered among his belongings upon his death and was later printed by his uncle Winthrop. *Courtesy of Ulysses S. Grant Presidential Library.*

Epilogue

The battle at Williamsburg had been a rude baptism of fire for the Excelsior Brigade. Official losses approximated one-fourth of those engaged. Casualties in the 72nd had been nearly two hundred of the estimated eight hundred or so men who went into action that day. Hooker's division had not been completely wrecked, but it had been shaken to its core, requiring several days to reorganize before it could effectively rejoin the rest of the army moving against Richmond.[1] Losses among the Chautauqua companies had been as heavy as in any other, but it is easy to speculate that the sense of grief felt by the entire county could not have been more profound, thanks to the frequent epistles of Arthur McKinstry and other county men that appeared in the *Censor* and other nearby papers. Outpourings of condolences to Arthur's uncles, Willard and Winthrop McKinstry, came from throughout the county, as readers of the *Censor* sensed a connection to Arthur beyond merely a name on the casualty list. But there would be more casualty lists to follow.

George Tate, another Company D man, known to the McKinstry brothers as a "reliable young man & a member of the Presbyterian church in this village," took responsibility for getting Arthur's belongings sent home.[2] It would not be till mid-June before Tate could assemble all of Arthur's things and find adequate time from active campaigning to have all of the possessions sent home. In a June 16th letter marked "Camp six miles from Richmond," George Tate inventories for the brothers McKinstry what has been sent:

> As I have today sent off the effects of Arthur by Express to you, I take this opportunity to write you. The box contains his bible, revolver, housewife & two scrap books, in one of which you will find the song you allude to. There are also in the box two pictures & two volumes of Hardee's Tactics which belong to Almond Hamilton [Hamilton was later wounded at Gettysburg] whom you will oblige by handing them to his father or brother John.

Figure E.2. George Tate. Company D man George Tate took it upon himself to see that Arthur's possessions made it home. *Courtesy of the U.S. Army Heritage and Education Center.*

Arthur's daily memorandum which he always carried with him must have been taken by the thieving rebels who robbed his pockets as I have been unable to find it.

His haversack which contained his portfolio was picked up the day after the battle by a member of our company of which fact I had no knowledge until three days ago when the person who had it called me into his tent & handed me this, last, unfinished letter of Arthur's for the Censor which I have here inclosed [*sic*] to you [see chap. 8, May 4th letter]. He had left the haversack but had the portfolio & said it contained nothing else which he got it but a few envelopes which were in it yet. The portfolio is somewhat dilapidated & too large to go in the box which is the only one I could procure.[3]

Few other details about the battle or Arthur's death would come to light in the weeks following the battle. J. Horton of the 49th New York who was not engaged in the battle had visited the camp of the 72nd and relayed what he had learned to the McKinstry brothers, who in turn passed the information to Arthur's mother. During the peak of the fighting, Arthur's platoon was fired upon by the enemy, causing Arthur and two others to fall. "The bodies were brought in the next day & buried side by side, wrapped in their blankets, & a board placed at the head of each with the name, company & Regiment so that all can be designated. It would appear that the field on which he fell was in possession of the rebels or between armies," according to Horton's reporting.[4] On May 14, the McKinstry brothers made an appeal to Congressman Reuben E. Fenton, who represented Chautauqua County and who would be elected New York's governor in 1864. The brothers penning, "We write you to see if the remains can be obtained & forwarded to us," continuing, "if his remains may be returned & deposited in our own Forest Hill Cemetery, we will be content. You are in a situation to ascertain whether it can be done & any effort on your part to effect this will be gratefully remembered by us & his afflicted mother."[5] However, unable to obtain Arthur's body, a cenotaph was erected in the family plot at Forest Hills memorializing Arthur's life and death while acknowledging his body remained in Virginia. At some point, Arthur's remains were moved to what is now the Yorktown National Cemetery. This cemetery was officially established in 1866 but soldiers, particularly those killed during the Peninsula Campaign, had been buried there prior to this time. Arthur McKinstry lies in grave number 143.[6]

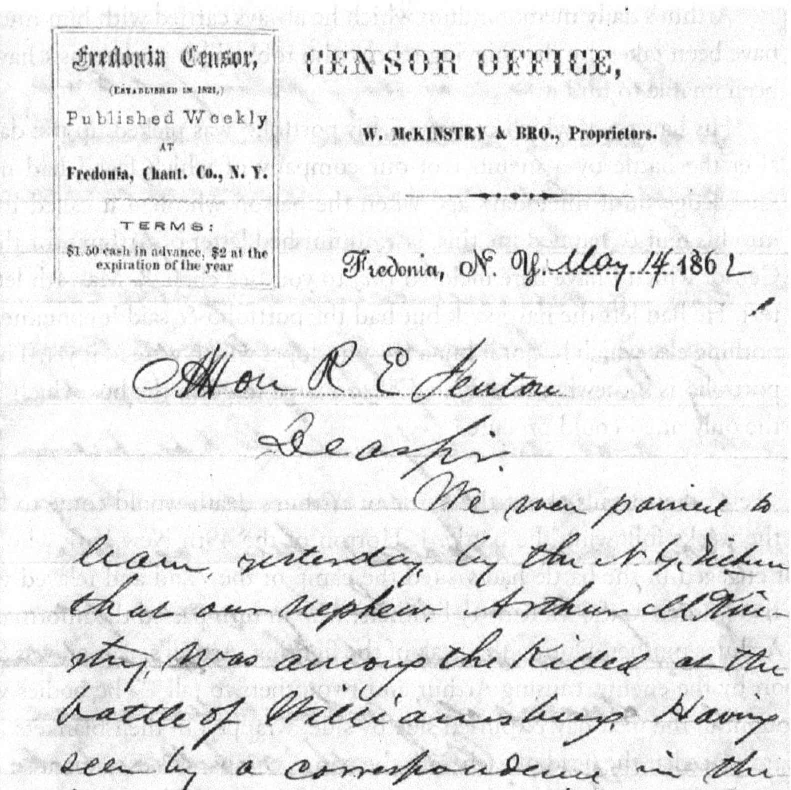

Fredonia Censor,
(Established in 1821,)
Published Weekly
at
Fredonia, Chaut. Co., N. Y.
TERMS:
$1.50 cash in advance, $2 at the expiration of the year

CENSOR OFFICE,
W. McKINSTRY & BRO., Proprietors.

Fredonia, N. Y. May 14 1862

Hon R E Fenton
Dear Sir:
We were pained to learn yesterday by the N. Y. Tribune that our nephew Arthur McKinstry was among the killed at the battle of Williamsburg. Having seen by a correspondence in the Dunkirk Journal that you had sent Mr. D G Morgan to the place to look after the sufferers in that dreadful conflict, we write you to see if the remains can be obtained & forwarded to us. He was a private in Co. D. Capt. Abells, 2d Regiment Excelsior Brigade.

Figure E.3. McKinstry brothers to Fenton. The McKinstry brothers wrote Congressman Reuben E. Fenton requesting his help to have Arthur's body returned home. Fenton would be elected governor of New York in 1864. *Courtesy of Ulysses S. Grant Presidential Library.*

With the death of Arthur McKinstry, coverage of the 72nd New York Regiment in the *Fredonia Censor* seemed to fade. There were no letters from Arthur to be sure, but there seemed to be fewer letters published from other Chautauqua men as well. Whether the pace of the war precluded such letters be written and sent, or the McKinstry brothers lost interest in such war coverage, or were perhaps distracted by other pursuits, one can never be fully sure.

In April of 1863, senior editor Willard McKinstry left the paper to his younger brother to fully pursue his position as Fredonia Post Master, a position that he had actually held since July of 1862. Winthrop carried on and in April of 1865, Willard returned to lead the paper again. In November, with his brother back in charge, Winthrop moved to Faribault, Minnesota, where he bought the *Faribault Republican*, which he edited for many years. Willard remained in his senior position until July of 1867, when his older son, then twenty-two years old and also trained in the newspaper business, bought a half interest from his father. They ran the paper together until Willard's death in 1899.[7] By the time of Willard's death, many of the early editions of the *Censor* had already begun to be housed at the Darwin R. Barker Historical Library, located in Fredonia, which was established in 1884. After years of financial difficulties, the *Censor* closed in April of 1964 and by 2010 the Barker Library had acquired nearly all *Censor* editions. And it is there at the Barker that the *Censor* editions of old, now fully digitized, wait ready to enlighten the next researcher or ambitious curiosity seeker.

Arthur's mother, Mary Theodosia Frink McKinstry Chapin, moved soon after the war from New York to Kansas. In 1870, Arthur's sister, Laura Jane McKinstry White, moved her family to Kansas too, but soon found the farming difficult. Eventually, Laura Jane moved to Mississippi with the urgings of a cousin who had moved there from Massachusetts a few years before the war, while Arthur's mother remained in Kansas, passing away there in 1892. In 1888, Laura Jane and her son, John McKinstry White, purchased 840 acres of farmland and an antebellum home in Oktibbeha County, Mississippi, where a family member had farmed and lived continually until 2008. The White family continues to farm and live in and around Starkville, Mississippi. From here, the letters sent home by Arthur McKinstry made their way to the Mississippi State University, when John White's youngest daughter, Frances Morgan White Rhodes Nowell Oakley, donated the collection to the Ulysses S. Grant Presidential Library, housed at MSU, in 2015.[8]

There are millions of Americans who are descended from someone who soldiered in the Civil War. Many are no doubt unaware of any Civil War

Figure E.4. McKinstry memorial at Fredonia. With Arthur's body remaining in Virginia, the family erected this monument at the family plot in Fredonia. *Photo by David Brown.*

Figure E.5. McKinstry marker at Yorktown. Arthur McKinstry is buried at the Yorktown National Cemetery in Virginia. *Photo by Jeff Joyce.*

connection they may have. Many others may know a name and a unit or perhaps a battle in which their relative participated, and nothing else. Fewer still may have a letter or two from their soldier that may offer a peek into their term of service or their personality. But indeed, the very fortunate few can look to an archive such as that created by Arthur McKinstry. While he was prolific indeed, one cannot discount the contribution of Arthur's mother for saving his letters home and then the respect of subsequent generations for holding these letters in reverenced safety. So detailed are Arthur's letters that it is easy for many of us, without actual letters from our soldier-ancestor, to imagine the nature of the service undertaken by our relative all those many years ago. So let us offer a collective round of thanks to both Arthur and the extended McKinstry family for allowing us all to share in his experience so that we all may learn and, more importantly, remember.

Appendix

Report of Brig. Gen. Joseph Hooker, U.S. Army, commanding Second Division.

MAY 5, 1862.—Battle of Williamsburg, Va.

HEADQUARTERS HOOKER'S DIVISION,

Third Army Corps, Williamsburg, Va., May 10, 1862.

CAPTAIN:

I have the honor to report that under the instructions received through the headquarters Third Army Corps, dated May 4, to support Stoneman and aid him in cutting off the retreat of the enemy, my division marched from its camp before Yorktown about noon that day. We marched toward Williamsburg. After advancing 5 or 6 miles on this road I learned that Brigadier-General Stoneman had fallen upon the rear of the enemy's retreating column, and was then awaiting the arrival of an infantry force to attack him. This was 5 or 6 miles in advance of me, and immediately I left my command and galloped to the front in order to see what disposition it would be necessary to make of my force on its arrival. While here I was informed that Brigadier-General Smith's division had filed into the road in advance of my command, and that in consequence my division would be compelled to halt until after Smith's had passed. I immediately returned to the head of my column, where I found my division halted, and as Smith's was extended, it was between three and four hours in passing. As soon as this was ascertained, and feeling that Stoneman would require no additional support, I applied to Brigadier-General Heintzelman, the senior officer charged with the advance on the Yorktown road, for authority to throw my command on to the Hampton road, which intersected that on which Brigadier-General Stoneman had halted at the identical point his enemy occupied.

The angle formed by the two roads is a little less than a right angle. Obtaining this permission the head of my division left the Brick Church about dark, and it pressed forward, in order, if practicable, to come up with the enemy before morning. This, however, I soon found would be impossible, for the roads were frightful, the night intensely dark and rainy, and many of my men exhausted from loss of sleep and from labor the night before in the trenches. The troops were halted in the middle of the road between 10 and 11 o'clock p.m., resolved to stop until daylight, when we started again, and came in sight of the enemy's works before Williamsburg about 5.30 o'clock in the morning.

Before emerging from the forest the column was halted, while I rode to the front to find what could be learned of the position of the enemy. The first work that presented itself was Fort Magruder, and this was standing at the junction of the Yorktown and Hampton roads, and on each side of it was a cordon of redoubts, extending as far as could be seen. Subsequently I found their number to be thirteen, and extending entirely across the Peninsula, the right and left of them resting on the waters of the York and James Rivers. Approaching them from the south they are concealed by heavy forest until the observer is within less than a mile of their locality. Where the forest trees had been standing nearer than this distance the trees had been felled, in order that the occupants of the redoubts might have timely notice of the approach of an enemy and early strike him with artillery. The trees had been felled in this manner on both sides of the road on which we had advanced for a breadth of almost half a mile, and the same was the case on the Yorktown road. Between the edge of the felled timber and the fort was a belt of clear arable land 600 or 700 yards in width. This was dotted all over with rifle pits. In connection with the redoubts themselves I may be permitted to state that I found them standing near the eastern and southern verge of a slightly-elevated plain, the slopes of which were furrowed with winding ravines, with an almost boundless, gently-undulating plain reaching across the Peninsula,—and extending to the north and west as far as the eye could reach. The landscape is picturesque, and not a little heightened by the large trees and venerable spires of Williamsburg, 2 miles distant. Fort Magruder appears to be the largest of the redoubts, its crest measuring nearly half a mile, with substantial parapets, ditches, magazines, &c. This was located to command the Yorktown and Hampton roads, and the redoubts in its vicinity to command the ravines which the guns of Fort Magruder could not sweep.

Being in pursuit of a retreating army, I deemed it my duty to lose no time in making the disposition of my forces to attack, regardless of their number and position, except to accomplish the result with the least possible sacrifice of life. By so doing my division, if it did not capture the army before me, would at least hold them, in order that some others might. Besides, I knew of the presence of more than 30,000 troops not 2 miles distant from me, and that within 12 miles—four hours' march—was the bulk of the Army of the Potomac. My own position was tenable for double that length of time against three times my number.

At 7.30 o'clock Brigadier-General Grover was directed to commence the attack by sending the First Massachusetts Regiment as skirmishers into the felled timber to the left of the road on which they were standing, the Second New Hampshire to the right, both with directions to skirmish up to the edge of the felled timber, and there, under cover, to turn their attention to the occupants of the rifle pits and the enemy's sharpshooters and gunners in Fort Magruder. The Eleventh Massachusetts and the Twenty-sixth Pennsylvania Regiments were then directed to form on the right of the Second New Hampshire, and to advance as skirmishers until they had reached the Yorktown road, and when that was gained to have word sent me.

Under my chief of artillery, Web's battery was thrown forward in advance of the felled timber and brought into action in a cleared field on the right of the road and distant from Fort Magruder about 700 yards. No sooner had it emerged from the forest on its way to its position than four guns from Fort Magruder opened on it, and after it was still farther up the road they received the fire from two additional guns from a redoubt on the left. However, it was pushed on, and before it was brought into action two officers and two privates had been shot down, and before a single piece of the battery had been discharged its cannoneers had been driven from it despite the skill and activity of my sharpshooters in picking off the rebel gunners. Volunteers were now called for by my gallant chief of artillery, Major Wainwright, to man the battery now in position, when the officers and men of Osborn's battery sprang forward, and in the time I am writing had those pieces well at work. Captain Bramhall's battery was now brought into action under that excellent officer on the right of Webber's, and before 9 o'clock every gun in Fort Magruder was silenced and all the troops in sight on the plain dispersed.

Between my sharpshooters and the two batteries the enemy's guns in this fort were not heard from again until late in the afternoon. One of the regiments of Brigadier-General Patterson's brigade, the Fifth New Jersey, was charged with the especial care of these batteries, and was posted a little to the rear of them. The remaining regiments of Patterson's brigade, under their intrepid commander, were sent to the left of the road from where they were standing, in anticipation of an attack from that quarter. Heavy forest trees cover this ground and conceal from view the enemy's earthworks about a mile distant. The forest itself has a depth of about three-fourths of that distance. It was through this that Patterson led the Sixth, Seventh, and Eighth New Jersey Regiments. Bodies of the enemy's infantry were seen drifting in that direction, and the increased musketry fire proved that many others were flocking thither whom we could not see. Prior to this moment Brigadier-General Emory had reached my position with a light battery and a body of cavalry, which were promptly placed at my disposal by that experienced and gifted soldier; but as I had no duty on which I could employ those arms of service, and as I was confined for room in the exercise of my own command, I requested that he would dispatch a party to reconnoiter and observe the movements of the rebels to the rear of my left. This was executed to my satisfaction.

It was now reported to me that the skirmishers to the right had reached the Yorktown road, when word was sent to Colonel Blaisdell to proceed with the Eleventh Massachusetts and Twenty-sixth Pennsylvania Regiments cautiously down that road to destroy any rebel force he might find, and break down any barrier the enemy might have thrown up to check the advance of our forces in that direction, and when this was executed to report the fact to the senior officer with the troops there, and on his return to send me word of the result of his mission. This was done, and word sent me through Adjutant Currier, of the Eleventh Regiment.

Up to this moment there had been a brisk musketry fire kept up on every part of the field, but its swelling volumes in the direction of Patterson satisfied me from the beginning of the engagement that the enemy had accumulated a heavy force in his front. Grover had already anticipated it, and had moved the main portion of the First Massachusetts Regiment to receive it, while, first, the Seventy-second New York Regiment of Taylor's brigade, and soon after the Seventieth New York Regiment of the same brigade, were ordered to strengthen Paterson.

Colonel Averred, of the Third Pennsylvania Cavalry, had with great kindness and gallantry tendered me his services and executed for me with great promptness several important services; while Lieutenant McAlester, of the Engineers, volunteered to make a reconnaissance of such of the enemy's works as were hidden from view, preparatory to carrying them by assault should a suitable opportunity present itself for that object. For this service I am under many obligations to that accomplished officer.

From the earliest moment of the attack it was an object of deep solicitude to establish a connection with the troops in my immediate neighborhood on the Yorktown road, and as that had been accomplished, and as I saw no signs of their advance, at 11.20 a.m. I addressed the subjoined note to the assistant adjutant-general Third Corps, under the impression that his chief was still there. It is as follows:

I have had a hard contest all the morning, but do not despair of success. My men are hard at work, but a good deal exhausted. It is reported to me that my communication with you by the Yorktown road is clear of the enemy. Batteries, cavalry, and infantry can take post by the side of mine to whip the enemy.

This found General Heintzelman absent; but it was returned opened, and on the envelope indorsed, "Opened and read," by the senior officer on that field. A cavalryman took over the note, and returned with it by the Yorktown road after an absence of twenty minutes.

To return. It was now after 1 o'clock, and the battle had swollen into one of gigantic proportions. The left had been re-enforced with the Seventy-third and Seventy-fourth New York Regiments—the only remaining ones of my reserve—under Colonel Taylor, and all were engaged; yet its fortunes would ebb and flow, despite the most determined courage and valor of my devoted officers and men. Three times the enemy approached within 80 yards of the road, which was the center of my operations, and as often were they thrown back with violence and slaughter. Every time his advance was made with fresh troops, and each succeeding one seemed to be in greater force and determination.

The Eleventh Massachusetts Regiment and the Twenty-sixth Pennsylvania were ordered to the left. The support of the batteries and the Second New Hampshire Regiment were withdrawn from their advanced position in front to take post where they could look after the front and left at the same time. The orders to the Twenty-sixth Pennsylvania Regiment did not reach it, and it remained on the right.

At this juncture word was received from Colonel Taylor that the regiments of his command longest engaged were falling short of ammunition, and when he was informed that the supply train was not yet up a portion of his command presented an obstinate front to the advance of the enemy with no other cartridges than were gathered from the boxes of the fallen.

Again the enemy were re-enforced by the arrival of Longstreet's division. His troops had passed through Williamsburg on their retreat from Yorktown and were recalled to strengthen the rebel forces before Williamsburg. No sooner had they joined than it was known that they were again moving to drive in our left. After a violent and protracted struggle they were again repulsed with great loss. Simultaneous with this movement an attempt was made to drive in our front and seize the batteries by the troops from Fort Magruder, aided by re-enforcements from the redoubts on the left. The withdrawal of the supports invited this attack, and it was at this time that four of our guns were captured. They could have been saved, but only at the risk of losing the day. Whatever of dishonor, if any, is attached to their loss belongs to the brigadier-general commanding the division, and not to his chief of artillery or to the officers or men serving with the batteries, for truer men never stepped upon the field of battle.

While this was going on in front Captain Smith, by a skillful disposition of his battery, held complete command of the road, which subsequently, by a few well-directed shots, was turned to good account.

The foregoing furnishes a faithful narrative of the disposition of my command throughout this eventful day. Between 4 and 5 o'clock Brigadier-general Kearny, with all his characteristic gallantry, arrived on the ground at the head of his division, and after having secured their positions my division was withdrawn from the contest and held as a reserve until dark, when the battle ended, after a prolonged and severe conflict against three times my number, directed by the most accomplished general of the rebel army, Maj. Gen. J. E. Johnston, assisted by Generals Longstreet, Pryor, Gholson, and Pickett, with commands selected from the best troops in their army.

The lists of the killed and wounded attest the character of the contest. The killed of the enemy must have been double my own. Of the wounded we cannot estimate. Eight hundred were left in hospitals at Williamsburg, and others were distributed among the private houses of this city, while all the available tenements in the vicinity of the field of battle are filled with them. Three hundred prisoners were taken.

I have omitted to mention the arrival early in the afternoon of Brigadier-General Heintzelman, commanding the Third Army Corps, with his staff, and to express my very grateful acknowledgments for the encouragement inspired by his presence and for the aid and support he gave me by his counsel and conduct.

As soon as darkness concealed their movements the rebels retreated in a state of utter demoralization, leaving behind artillery, wagons, &c.

History will not be believed when it is told that the noble officers and men of my division were permitted to carry on this unequal struggle from morning until night unaided in the presence of more than 30,000 of their comrades with arms in their hands; nevertheless it is true. If we failed to capture the rebel army on the plains of Williamsburg it surely will not be ascribed to the want of conduct and courage in my command.

The field was marked by an unusual number of instances of conspicuous courage and daring, which I shall seek an early opportunity to bring to the notice of the commander of the Third Corps.

At this time I can speak but in general terms of the regiments and batteries engaged in the battle of Williamsburg. Their list of the killed and wounded from among their number will forever determine the extent of their participation in this hard-fought and dearly-contested field. Their constancy and courage are deserving all praise. My profound and grateful acknowledgments are rendered to them.

I am under great obligations to the officers of my staff for eminent serves, and especially to Capt. Joseph Dickinson, my assistant adjutant-general, and my aides-de-camp, Lieuts. William H. Lawrence and Joseph Abbott, who were with me throughout the day.

JOSEPH HOOKER,
Brigadier-General, Commanding Division.

Capt. CHAUNCEY McKEEVER,
Assistant Adjutant-General, Third Army Corps.

[Addenda.]

Letter to Captain McKeever, inclosing dispatch dated "Front of Williamsburg, May 5, 1862, 11.20 a.m.," in regard to the contest during the morning.

May 7, 1862.

I send you herewith a dispatch which was addressed and sent you by me, as dated, under the impression that you were in the vicinity of General Sumner. The orderly went and returned by the Williamsburg and Yorktown road, and was not absent more than twenty minutes. You had left. General Sumner opened the note, read it, and returned on the envelope that he had done so. The envelope was destroyed by the rain. I request that you will, after reading it, return the within to me. It speaks for itself, and will have much to do in history hereafter.

Respectfully,

JOSEPH HOOKER,

Brigadier-general.

Captain McKEEVER,

Assistant Adjutant-General, Third Corps.

[Inclosure.]

IN FRONT OF WILLIAMSBURG,

May 5, 1862—11.20 a.m.

I have had a hard contest all the morning, but do not despair of success. My men are hard at work, but a good deal exhausted. It is reported to me that my communication with you by the Yorktown road is clear of the enemy. Batteries, cavalry, and infantry can take post by the side of mine to whip the enemy.

Very respectfully, your obedient servant,

JOSEPH HOOKER,

Brigadier-general, Commanding.

Capt. CHAUNCEY McKEEVER,

Assistant Adjutant-General.

——

HDQRS. HOOKER'S DIVISION, THIRD ARMY CORPS,

Camp near White Oak Swamp, Va., May 27, 1862.

CAPTAIN:

My attention has been called to that part of Brigadier-General Kearny's official report of the battle of Williamsburg which states "and enabled Major Wainwright, of Hooker's division, to collect his artillerists and reopen fire from several pieces," and I give it my positive and emphatic denial. This statement admits of no application to any battery of mine except Smith's, and I deny that any men of his were driven from their pieces, or that the fire from his battery was suspended from the proximity or fire of the enemy's skirmishers at any time during that day. I request that this statement may be forwarded, in order that it may be placed on record with my official report of the battle on the 5th instant.

Very respectfully, your obedient servant.

JOSEPH HOOKER,
Brigadier-general, Commanding Division.

Capt. CHAUNCEY McKEEVER,
Assistant Adjutant-General, Third Army Corps.[1]

Fredonia Censor: Published May 21, 1862

THE BATTLE OF WILLIAMSBURG

The Errors and Responsibility—Formidable Nature of the Rebel Defenses—The Fiercest and Hardest Fight of the War.

Brady should instantly send a corps of photographers here, to take the actual likeness of the vast lunette of forest-tree *chevaux-de-frise*, in which over 25,000 of the rebels, in ambush, and under the protection of a rear line of forts of vast strength, with heavy cannon in position awaited the advance of the Union troops, for no description with the pen, no painting of words, nor use by artist of pen or brush, can possibly convey even an approximately accurate idea of the nature of the ground, which the rebels first picked out, then ingeniously prepared with axes, wielded by slaves, and directed by West Point engineers. No Imagination of the densely thicketed and wooded pens in which Braddock was defeated and St. Clair lost his army and his reputation, can prepare the mind for the realization of the difficulties of the rebel defenses before Williamsburg. Standing upon the parapets of Fort Magruder—a bastioned work as large as Fort Monroe, with a wide moat, filled with water, and having a sweep of the plains at every point of the compass—and, looking toward Yorktown, you see a horseshoe shaped sweep of a forest, a mile and more around—you see it is fringed on the inside with a gigantic abattis of fallen timber, against which the eyes fairly ache, in their sweep of a mile or more of look[ing]—you see for a part of the way, beginning at the end nearest Williamsburg, a deep, wide ravine, constructed but little by stumps, and having a hard bottom, you say instantly "their reserves could be held secure from the fire of a million rifles"—you look to the left and you see upon the plain one fort, two forts, three forts— forts away to a dammed up body of water, bounded next an impassable ravine swamp by a high and narrow mill dam, commanded by a battery overlooking it, and the passage of which would be a labor that the warriors who crossed the bridge at Lodi would have been swept from like oat-chaff. Go down from the high parapets of Fort Magruder and go away over to the right (western) part of the horse-shoe of the rebel position, pass through that ravine (so convenient and secure for the reception of the reinforcements to be marched up from Williamsburg,) and enter, if you can, the *chevaux-de-frise* of forest trees, tumbled with cowardly and savage ingenuity five hundred feet wide, and stretching further than you can see to the west upon an arc of difficulty that would appall the bravest troops that England, France, or Russia ever sent into the field. The fallen timber was mostly hemlock and pine. Grown on a swamp, it was thick and Rank. The trees were put so as to interlock their branches. They lapped each other. The ingenuity of the chopping is astonishing. But you soon study out a craftier arrangement; in little alleys leading into this terrible cover—going straight—seemingly ending—turning right angles—advancing again—terminating anew in a mass of limbs and trunks and branches, through which a tiger could not force himself—alleys leading in from the open space before Fort Magruder, and made for the rebels to conveniently go and come in their labor of sheltered massacre of unprotected Northerners. Get through this monstrous cover if you have a change of clothes, and the hopes of a second growth of skin—get into the thick standing forest of which it was last week a part. Here is a dead Alabamian. Five rods beyond him, a sharp visaged Virginian, barefooted and naked now to the waist, turns up to the sunlight a breast with the blue-rimmed bullet hole, and proves that in this dense forest, beyond the timber *chevaux-de-frise*, the rebels first fought us under cover, and practiced their barbarous civilization of robbing and stripping their own dead. Far, far into this tangled, swampy forest, you keep coming upon the ragged and dirty barbarians, lying upon their backs, in every form of bloody death—their faces without a single exception, denoting a race of people from those of the

North—a race below the negroes, in reducing whom to slavery that have brutalized themselves.

Now go back to Yorktown, southeast, and to Lee's Mills, southwest, and let the time be Sunday noon, and the occasion our pursuit of the retreating rebels, and the principal *dramatis personae* Sumner and Heintzelman. Sumner who ranks Heintzelman in the date of his commission, had in his pocket an order from McClellan, which in its substance and effect was to halt on the left. Heintzelman carried a written order to go straight up the Yorktown road to Williamsburg—which would have brought him on the right. Nightfall carried our troops up to the rear of the enemy, and brought Sumner past his proper position, the left, and on the right, and in a dense, wet wood, that not a man in the army had entered or knew anything about.—Where were the enemy? How many were they? Beyond these, in the dark, were their entrenchments? What was there that a corps of 80,000 troops might run disastrously against? Military questions all. A close coming storm wholly obscured the sky. On my night ride to the front, so dark was it that the better sight of my horse only saved me from tramping the fallen soldiers that lined the road for miles. Diverted into the woods by artillery trains and ammunition wagons, I was repeatedly, almost swept from the saddle by unseen branches of trees. Yet in such darkness, in the such ignorance of his ground, and such ignorance of his foe, Sumner was stumbling around in the forest, where his 30,000 men were waiting for daylight to enable them to find the rebel rear, which they had been ordered to attack the evening before—stumbling around to find his way back to Adams House, his headquarter—stumbling until nearly day dawn—while one of his divisions, 10,000 strong, lay down, among the trees, cursing the mismanagement which had ordered them to march without a mouthful of food in their haversacks, and another division, also 10,000 strong, wrathfully thought of their knapsacks, which they had been ordered to leave behind in their camp, and exhausted ingenuity in avoiding the moisture of the swampy ground. Before daylight a heavy down-pour of cold rain set in from the southeast.

When Sumner, at 5 o'clock, the evening before, communicated to Heintzelman his purpose to commence the attack immediately, the latter, who had no control over him, but did have control of Hooker, ordered the latter to post his division immediately on the left—the ground that Sumner should have occupied with his large command. He did more—he instantly sent back for reinforcements, anticipating that Sumner would be repulsed. He did more yet—did his duty to the army and cause, by sending one of his aids [*sic*] to the front, to say to Sumner that Gen. Hooker would attack the enemy at daybreak on the left, and to suggest to him to defer his own attack in the center till that time. The aide hunted faithfully for Sumner through the tangled forest for over an hour, and then returned and reported him *non est inventus*. It was not to be wondered at—for so dense was the woods, and so dense was the dark, that Sumner, with his staff, had even run against the enemy's pickets and were fired on. Fortunately, none of them were killed. More fortunately yet, his regiments marching into the wood, and coming upon each other in the night gloom, did not commence a destructive battle of Union troops upon Union troops. The intelligence and discipline of American private soldiers saved the army from a horrible disaster. More yet—at the conference between Sumner, Heintzelman, Keys, Stoneman, Smith and Hancock, Gen. Heintzelman, I am assured, refused to offer a suggestion until a reconnaissance had been made, and insisted upon one being made. It was not ordered. Night fell, as I have said before, ere the preparations by Sumner for his attack had been made, and before his regiments had disappeared into the woods. At the time it was evident to the commonest teamster in the army, that upon the narrow and wretched road from Yorktown, choked with cavalry, infantry, artillery and wagons, supplies of food and re-enforcement of men, aye, and supplies of ammunition even, could not be got up in time for use before the next noon.

Monday—A chill northeast rainstorm was in full sweep over the country—Sumner did not commence the attach which he had spent the night before in wandering the forest to make, but he commenced a conference. Heintzelman earnestly advised a reconnoissance. It was ordered. While in progress from east to west, the officers conducting it sent back word that on the enemy's extreme left were two unoccupied forts, part of a chain stretching away across, below Williamsburg. Negroes accidentally at headquarters, offered to guide us to them by a road which was in part a mill dam. Sumner intimated that he should wait until the reconnoissance was finished before he acted. On Heintzelman's suggestion that in the mean time the enemy might occupy these forts, Hancock was ordered to pour his troops into them. This laid the foundation for the victory of Williamsburg. Freed now from headquarters, and alarmed by the heaviness of the battery firing from Hooker's division, Heintzelman instantly went to the nearest practicable road to his position, and about 1 o'clock found the gallant General sorely pressed and in great danger. Hooker inquired for the reinforcements he had sent for, by a path through the woods only a mile long—sent to Heintzelman for. His written message was received and read by Sumner soon after Heintzelman left headquarters. Heintzelman instantly sent two orderlies with another message to Sumner for a portion of his 30,000—sent two, so that if one was killed the other could go through. He also began sending to the rear, to hurry up the march of the brigades floundering through the mud. Officer after officer he sent to the rear, on this painfully anxious mission—till he was frequently wholly alone on the field. I told yesterday how he encouraged the troops—how he rallied and led back broken companies—how he gathered the fragments of two bands of music, and while awaiting the coming of the reinforcements from Sumner on the right, or from out of the mud in the rear, animated the drooping courage of Hooker's outnumbered and almost overmastered men, with "Yankee Doodle" and the "Star Spangled Banner." To the repeated messages he sent to Sumner for aid, *he got no reply whatsoever*. At 5 o'clock, and not before, Sumner ordered Hancock to the front. Before five, Berry had come up with his brigade, and saved us from the most imminent ruin that has lowered on our cause since Bull Run.

The thousands who unnecessarily wear mourning in the North and West, for our victory at Williamsburg, will now understand the causes of the terrible mortality which accompanied the demonstration of our superiority to these barbarians. To further elucidate them—regard the plan of the field, and see where the Yorktown road comes upon the corn-field, directly in front of the bastioned fort Magruder. That was our direct line to Williamsburg. The swampy woods on both sides are a mile deep, the abattis of fallen trees about 500 feet deep; beyond that there were rifle pits away round the horse shoe–shaped plain; beyond them were batteries of flying artillery; the Magruder beyond all, vomiting shell, canister and grape. In that mile depth of thick woods, Heintzelman and Hooker, and their brave comrades, fought the principal part of the battle. It was principally there, that in the long struggle from 8 o'clock in the morning until 2 o'clock in the afternoon, 8,000 men held their own against 25,000. But the battle rages with desperate courage on the edge of the woods in front of the abattis, in the infernal abattis itself, and through it, up to the rifle pits, and beyond them, and finally in triumph, into one of the forts. The only ground on which we could use artillery was a small angle of the corn field, where the road debouches upon the plains, and which our infantry had cleared of the rebels to admit of our gunners wading with their pieces into position. No sooner were those unlimbered; than men and horses began to fall—the recoil of the guns soon buried them almost to the hubs in the soft earth—down went more men and more horses—the enemy made a dash at the batteries and they were lost. The assistance Heintzelman received from Kearney's Division, enabled him to do what he had vainly tried and hoped to do, all day—to attack in flank. The 88th and 40th New York charged through the abattis upon the rifle pits, and threw the rebels out with their bayonets in double quick. Berry's charge at the same time all along the front, settled a part of the dispute between the North and the South. The rebels were whipped.

Now this was purely an infantry fight. And how well Hooker's Division did fight! Those much abused—those wronged, derided, and suspected Fire Zouaves—the Sickles Brigade—they were heroes all. Every man of them had reason to be proud of the organization. I have just returned from the spot where Lieut. Col. Lewis Benedict Jr. was last seen.—It is in the densest heart of the abattis, and close to the front of the rifle pits. The bark of the trunk and branches of the trees is checkered white with musket bullets and grape. Standing up to his full height, and waving his men forward with his pistol, he was heard to shout, "Fight men! Fight to the last." The idea prevailing in his regiment is, that he got to the front—that a charge drove his men back, that he was too brave and too proud to run—that he was captured for his exchangeable value, instead of being killed. A negro woman saw him on his way to Richmond the next morning, leaning on the shoulders of two soldiers, and walking lamely. Out of his regiment, a small one, 1 captain and 2 lieutenants, and 19 privates were killed; 54 privates were wounded, 37 are missing, and their manly Lieutenant Colonel was captured. The same proportional mortality marked the courage and the fighting of all the Sickles Brigade. The Williamsburg battle was, indeed, as I have said, an infantry fight. Very much of it was hand to hand. Bayonet to bayonet, musket-butt to musket-butt. After Berry's brigade came up, and after Ward and Riley led the 38th and 40th New York into rifle pits, swarming at the time with the savage tatterdemalions, the battle was purely a hand-to-hand conflict. As soon as we got them where we could reach them, the question of the comparative manhood of Northern and Southern men received a speedy solution. Sixty-three rebels lay in a heap in one section of the rifle pits—fury and outlay of the last and the best powers of their savage natures set with iron hardness by death upon their course in brutal faces. Not a corpse of a Union man was near them.

On both sides was ten times as desperate as at Bull Run.

Now on to the Gulf of Mexico!

INCIDENTS OF THE BATTLE OF WILLIAMSBURG

There can be no question that the rebel savages bayoneted our wounded. Lieut. Brush of the New York Seventy-third was seen to fall dead. He was shot through the heart. When his body was received, the next day, it was wholly naked, *and bayoneted.*

All the wounded Zouaves, all having red shirts who fall on ground which the rebels pushed us from, were found to have been bayoneted. They turned the pockets of their own dead inside out, and took off their shoes and stockings.[2]

Figure A.1 (following pages). 3rd Corps Organizational Chart. Organizational and command chart for Hooker's Second Division of the 3rd Corps starting on March 13, 1862, with the establishment of the corps. *Courtesy of the author.*

Organization and Leadership Command Chart for Hooker's Second Division of the 3rd Corps

III Corps

S.P. Heintzelman, Brig. Gen.	Mar. 13, 1862–Oct. 30, 1862
Geo. Stoneman, Brig. Gen.	Oct. 30, 1862–Feb. 5. 1863
D.E. Sickles, Maj. Gen.	Feb. 5, 1863–July 2, 1863
W.H. French, Maj. Gen.	July 7, 1863–Mar. 24, 1864

First Division

Fitz John Porter, Brig. Gen.	Mar. 13, 1862–May 18, 1862

Division transferred to 5th Provisional Corps May 18, 1862

Reorganized from Third Division, III Corps, Aug. 5, 1862

Philip Kearny, Brig. Gen.	Aug. 5, 1862–Sept. 1, 1862
D. B. Birney, Brig. Gen.	Sept. 1, 1862–Sept. 13, 1862
Geo. Stoneman, Brig. Gen.	Sept. 13, 1862–Oct. 30, 1862
D.B. Birney, Maj. Gen.	Oct. 30, 1862–Mar. 24, 1864

Second Division

Joseph Hooker, Brig. Gen.	Mar. 13, 1862–Sept. 5, 1862
D. E. Sickles, Brig. Gen.	Sept. 5, 1862–Jan. 12, 1863
J.B. Carr, Brig. Gen.	Jan. 12, 1863–Feb. 8, 1863
H.G. Berry, Brig. Gen.	Feb. 8, 1863–May 3, 1863
J.B. Carr, Brig. Gen.	May 3, 1863–May 23, 1863
A.A. Humphrey, Maj. Gen.	May 28, 1863–July 9, 1863
Henry Prince, Brig. Gen.	July 10, 1863–Mar. 24, 1864

Third Division

C.S. Hamilton, Brig. Gen.	Mar. 13, 1862–Apr. 30, 1862
Philip Kearny, Brig. Gen.	Apr. 30, 1862–Aug. 5, 1862

Designation changed to First Division.

Reorganized Nov. 8, 1862

A.W. Whipple, Brig. Gen.	Nov. 8, 1862–May 3, 1863
C.K. Graham, Brig. Gen.	May 3, 1863–June 20, 1863
W.L. Elliott, Brig. Gen.	July, 10, 1863–Oct. 5, 1863
J.B. Carr, Brig. Gen.	Oct. 5, 1863–Mar. 24, 1864

First Brigade, Second Division
Old Hooker Brigade

H.M. Naglee, Brig. Gen.	Mar. 13, 1862 – Apr. 27, 1862
C. Grover, Brig. Gen.	Apr. 27, 1862 – Sept. 16, 1862
J.B. Carr, Brig. Gen.	Sept. 16, 1862 – Jan. 12, 1863
Wm. Blaisdell, Col. 11th Mass. Inf.	Jan. 12, 1863 – Feb. 8, 1863
J.B. Carr, Brig. Gen.	Feb. 8, 1863 – May 3, 1863
Wm. Blaisdell, Col. 11th Mass. Inf.	May 3, 1863 – May 23, 1863
J.B. Carr, Brig. Gen.	May 23, 1863 – Oct. 5, 1863
R. McAllister, Col. 11th N.J. Inf.	Oct. 5, 1863 – Dec. 1863
Wm. Blaisdell, Col. 11th Mass. Inf.	Dec., 1864 – Mar. 24, 1864

1st Michigan Inf.	Mar., 1862–Mar., 1862
1st Mass. Inf.	Mar., 1862–Mar., 1864
11th Mass. Inf.	Mar., 1862–Mar., 1864
2nd New Hampshire Inf.	Mar., 1862–Feb., 1863
26th Penn. Inf.	Mar., 1862–Mar., 1864
16th Mass. Inf.	June, 1862–Mar., 1864
120th New York Inf.	Oct., 1862–Dec., 1862
11th New Jersey Inf.	Nov., 1862–Mar., 1864
84th Penna. Inf.	June, 1863–Mar., 1864
12th New Hampshire Inf.	June, 1863–July, 1863

Second Brigade, Second Division
Excelsior Brigade

N. Taylor, Col. 72nd N.Y. Inf.	Mar. 13, 1862–May 11, 1862
J. J. Abercrombie, Brig. Gen.	May 11, 1862–May 24, 1862
D. E. Sickles, Brig. Gen.	May 24, 1862–July 16, 1862
N. Taylor, Col. 72nd N. Y. Inf.	July 16, 1862–Sept. 5, 1862
Geo. B. Hall, Col. 71st N. Y. Inf.	Sept. 5, 1862–Dec. 24, 1862
J. W. Revere, Brig. Gen.	Dec. 24, 1862–Feb., 1863
J. E. Farnum, Lt.-Col. 70th N.Y. Inf.	Feb., 1863–Feb., 1863
C. K. Graham, Brig. Gen.	Feb., 1863–Mar., 1863
J. W. Revere, Brig. Gen.	Mar., 1863–May 3, 1863
J. E. Farnum, Col. 70th N. Y. Inf.	May 3, 1863–May, 1863
W. R. Brewster, Col. 73rd N. Y. Inf.	May, 1863–July 11, 1863
F. B. Spinola, Brig. Gen.	uly 11, 1863–July 23, 1863
Thos. Rafferty, Maj. 71st N. Y. Inf.	July 23, 1863–July 24, 1863
J. E. Farnum, Col. 70th N. Y. Inf.	July 24, 1863–Aug. 10, 1863
W. R. Brewster, Col. 73rd N. Y. Inf.	Aug. 10, 1863–Jan., 1864
John Leonard, Lt.-Col. 72nd N.Y. Inf.	Jan., 1864–Feb., 1864
W. R. Brewster, Col. 73rd N. Y. Inf.	Feb., 1864–Mar. 24, 1864

70th New York Inf.	Mar., 1862–Mar., 1864
71st New York Inf.	Mar., 1862–Mar., 1864
72nd New York Inf.	Mar., 1862–Mar., 1864
73rd New York Inf.	Mar., 1862–Mar., 1864
74th New York Inf.	Mar., 1862–Mar., 1864
120th New York Inf.	Dec., 1862–Mar., 1864

Third Brigade, Second Division
New Jersey Blues

S. H. Starr, Col. 5th N. J. Inf.	Mar. 13, 1862–May 3, 1862
F. E. Patterson, Brig. Gen.	May 3, 1862–May 31, 1862
S. H. Starr, Col. 5th N. J. Inf.	May 31, 1862–June 1, 1862
J. B. Carr, Col. 2nd N. Y. Inf.	June 1, 1862–June 6, 1862
F. E. Patterson, Brig. Gen.	June 6, 1862–Nov. 22, 1862
J. W. Revere, Col. 7th N. J. Inf.	Nov. 22, 1862–Dec. 25, 1862
Gershom Mott, Brig. Gen.	Dec. 25, 1862–May 3, 1863
W. J. Sewell, Col. 5th N.J. Inf.	May 3, 1863–June, 1863
G. C. Burling, Col. 6th N.J. Inf.	June, 1863–Aug. 29, 1863
Gershom Mott, Brig. Gen.	Aug. 29, 1863–Feb. 16, 1864
G. C. Burling, Col. 6th N.J. Inf.	Feb. 16, 1864–........, 1864*
Gershom Mott, Brig. Gen.	........, 1864–Mar. 24, 1864*

*as indicated in Dyer's Compendium

5th New Jersey Inf.	Mar. 1862–Mar., 1864
6th New Jersey Inf.	Mar., 1862–Mar., 1864
7th New Jersey Inf.	Mar., 1862–Mar., 1864
8th New Jersey Inf.	Mar., 1862–Mar., 1864
2nd New York Inf.	June, 1862–May, 1863
115th Penna. Inf.	July, 1862–Mar., 1864
2nd New Hampshire Inf.	June, 1863–July, 1863

III Corps disbanded in March, 1864
Second Division transferred to II Corps

Notes

Introduction

1. Mississippi State University, University Libraries Digital Collections, *The Letters of Pvt. Arthur McKinstry*, McKinstry letter September 1, 1862.

2. Chautauqua County Offices website, History of Chautauqua County, https://chqgov.com/live-work-play/History, accessed April 16, 2020.

3. Douglas H. Shepard, *Fredonia Censor* (1821–1964), submitted April 2011, Darwin R. Barker Historical Museum.

4. Alice McKinstry Hawes, *The McKinstrys of Chicopee [Massachusetts]* (Stonington, ME: Penobscot Press, 2002), 50.

5. Mary Frances Smith, *Arthur McKinstry Letters to Mother, Letter from Mother to Arthur from September 1854 to May 1855*, unpublished, and United States Naval Academy, *Minute Book of the Academic Board, June 1855*, Nimitz Library, US Naval Academy, Annapolis, MD.

6. Rick Barram, *The 72nd New York Infantry in the Civil War: A History and Roster* (Jefferson, NC: McFarland, 2014), 11–13.

7. William A. Swanberg, *Sickles the Incredible* (Gettysburg: Stan Clark Military Books, 1956), 50–55.

8. Barram, *72nd New York Infantry in the Civil War*, 14.

9. "From the Camp," *Fredonia Censor*, June 19, 1861.

10. Chautauqua History Company, ed., *The Centennial History of Chautauqua County: A Detailed and Entertaining Story of One Hundred Years of Development*, vol. 1 (Jamestown, NY: Chautauqua History Company, 1904), 540–563.

11. Mississippi State University, *Letters of Pvt. Arthur McKinstry*, Letter from Arthur McKinstry to Mother, November 17, 1861.

Chapter 1. Installed among Fine and Gentlemanly Fellows

1. William A. Swanberg, *Sickles the Incredible* (Gettysburg, PA: Stan Clark Military Books, 1956), 118–120.

2. Biographical Directory of the United States Congress website, Nelson Taylor.

3. New York State Military Museum and Veterans Research Center website, 70th NY newspaper clipping.

4. Swanberg, *Sickles the Incredible*, 117–118, 123.

5. New York State Military Museum and Veterans Research Center website, 70th NY.

6. Henry LeFevre Brown, *History of the Third Regiment, Excelsior Brigade, 72d New York Volunteer Infantry, 1861–1865* (Jamestown, NY: Journal Print, 1902), 15.

Chapter 2. As Far as the Eye Can Reach

1. Rick Barram, *The 72nd New York Infantry in the Civil War: A History and Roster* (Jefferson, NC: McFarland, 2014), 15–20.

2. Peter Messent and Steve Courtney, eds., *The Civil War Letters of Joseph Hopkins Twichell* (Athens: University of Georgia Press, 2006), 47.

3. Henry LeFevre Brown, *History of the Third Regiment, Excelsior Brigade, 72nd New York Volunteer Infantry, 1861–1865* (Jamestown, NY: Journal Print, 2006), 17–18.

4. Francis T. Lynch and Samuel C. Sandoli, comp., *Come Cry with Me: The Letters of Emerson F. Merrell, Native of the Town of Coventry in Chenango County, New York, Who Served in Company I. 72nd. Regiment, New York Infantry, New York Excelsior Brigade, Army of the Potomac, 1861–1863* (Self-published, 2001), 3–4.

5. Barram, *72nd New York Infantry in the Civil War*, 19.

6. Brown, *History of the Third Regiment*, 19–20.

7. Barram, *72nd New York Infantry in the Civil War*, 139, 270.

8. *72nd Regiment N.Y. Vol. Inf., Civil War Newspaper Clippings*, Unit History Project, New York State Military Museum.

9. Barram, *72nd New York Infantry in the Civil War*, 22–23.

10. Messent and Courtney, *Civil War Letters of Joseph Hopkins Twichell*, 60.

11. David B. Parker, *A Chautauqua Boy in '61 and Afterward: Reminiscences by David B. Parker, Second Lieutenant, Seventy-Second New York*, introduction by Albert Bushnell Hart (Boston: Small, Maynard, 1912), x.

Chapter 3. Into the Doubtful Part of Maryland

1. Rob Orrison and Bill Backus, "War on the Potomac, May 1861–March 1862," Blue and Gray 32, no. 5 (2016): 6–24, 38–42.

2. The War of the Rebellion: A Compilation of the Official Records of the Union and Confederate Armies, series 1, vol. 5 (Washington, DC: Government Printing Office, 1880–1901), 590.

3. War of the Rebellion, series 1, vol. 5, 17.

4. Official Records of the Union and Confederate Navies in the War of the Rebellion, series 1, vol. 4 (Washington, DC: Government Printing Office, 1897), 726–727.

Chapter 4. Down the River and Opposite the Rebels

1. Rick Barram, The 72nd New York Infantry in the Civil War: A History and Roster (Jefferson, NC: McFarland, 2014), 30.

2. Peter Messent and Steve Courtney, eds., The Civil War Letters of Joseph Hopkins Twichell (Athens: University of Georgia Press, 2006), 75–76.

3. *The War of the Rebellion: A Compilation of the Official Records of the Union and Confederate Armies*, series 1, vol. 5 (Washington, DC: Government Printing Office, 1880–1901), 637.

4. Mary Alice Wills, *The Confederate Blockade of Washington, D.C., 1861–1862* (Shippensburg, PA: Burd Street Press, 1998), 86–87.

5. Messent and Courtney, *Civil War Letters of Joseph Hopkins Twichell*, 85.

6. James F. Rusling, *Men and Things I Saw in Civil War Days* (New York: Eaton & Mains, 1899), 206–207.

Chapter 5. Where the Bon Vivants Assemble

1. *The War of the Rebellion: A Compilation of the Official Records of the Union and Confederate Armies*, series 1, vol. 5 (Washington, DC: Government Printing Office, 1880–1901), 951.

2. James F. Rusling, *Men and Things I Saw in Civil War Days* (New York: Eaton & Mains, 1899), 208–209.

3. Charles W. Mitchell, ed., *Maryland Voices of the Civil War* (Baltimore, MD: Johns Hopkins University Press, 2007), 250–251.

Chapter 6. All Frivolous Subjects Are Avoided

1. *The War of the Rebellion: A Compilation of the Official Records of the Union and Confederate Armies*, series 1, vol. 5 (Washington, DC: Government Printing Office, 1880–1901), 1033.

2. *Official Records of the Union and Confederate Navies in the War of the Rebellion*, series 1, vol. 5 (Washington, DC: Government Printing Office, 1897), 17.

3. *War of the Rebellion*, series 1, vol. 5, 710.

Chapter 7. Every Preparation for Immediate and Active Duty

1. Mary Alice Wills, *The Confederate Blockade of Washington, D.C., 1861–1862* (Shippensburg, PA: Burd Street Press, 1998), 97–104, 118–146.

2. *Official Records of the Union and Confederate Navies in the War of the Rebellion*, series 1, vol. 5 (Washington, DC: Government Printing Office, 1897), 725.

3. *The War of the Rebellion: A Compilation of the Official Records of the Union and Confederate Armies*, series 5, vol. 50½, 4 (Washington, DC: Government Printing Office, 1880–1901), 82.

4. J. Thomas Scharf, *History of the Confederate States Navy from Its Organization to the Surrender of Its Last Vessel* (New York: Rogers & Sherwood, 1887), 103.

5. *War of the Rebellion*, series 1, vol. 5, 50.

6. *War of the Rebellion*, series 1, vol. 50½, 497.

7. Charles W. Mitchell, ed., *Maryland Voices of the Civil War* (Baltimore, MD: Johns Hopkins University Press, 2007), 374.

8. Walter H. Hebert, *Fighting Joe Hooker* (Lincoln: University of Nebraska Press, 1999; originally published, Indianapolis: Bobbs-Merrill, 1944), 67–68.

9. Mitchell, *Maryland Voices of the Civil War*, 274.

Chapter 8. We Expect a Big Fight Very Soon

1. Rick Barram, *The 72nd New York Infantry in the Civil War: A History and Roster* (Jefferson, NC: McFarland, 2014), 47–48.

2. Daniel Sickles, "General Sickles Farewell to His Soldiers, 1862," *New York Times*, April 10, 1862.

3. Walter H. Hebert, *Fighting Joe Hooker* (Lincoln: University of Nebraska Press, 1999; originally published Indianapolis: Bobbs-Merrill, 1944), 80–83.

4. Mississippi State University, University Libraries Digital Collections, *The Letters of Pvt. Arthur McKinstry*, Capt. Abell to Mrs. Chapin.

5. Mississippi State University, *Letters of Pvt. Arthur McKinstry*, Incident at Williamsburg.

6. Herbert, *Fighting Joe Hooker*, 83–87.

7. Barram, *72nd New York Infantry*, 62.

8. *Official Records of the Union and Confederate Navies in the War of the Rebellion*, series 1, vol. 11/1 [S# 12] (Washington, DC: Government Printing Office, 1897), 464.

Chapter 9. The Low but Not So Very Soothing Hum of Minie Bullets

1. Lucius Jones Jr., *In the War of the Rebellion from 1861 to 1865* (Fredonia, NY: [No pub.], 1913), 1–4.

2. *Annual Report of the Adjutant-General of the State of New York for the Year 1901* (Albany: J. B. Lyon, State Printers, 1902), 485.

3. Jones, *In the War of the Rebellion*, 8.

4. Henry LeFevre Brown, *History of the Third Regiment, Excelsior Brigade, 72nd New York Volunteer Infantry, 1861–1865* (Jamestown, NY: Journal Print, 1902), 145.

5. David B. Parker, *A Chautauqua Boy in '61 and Afterward: Reminiscences by David B. Parker, Second Lieutenant, Seventy-Second New York*, introduction by Albert Bushnell Hart (Boston: Small, Maynard, 1912), 20–21.

6. Jones, *In the War of the Rebellion*, 14–15.

7. Brown, *History of the Third Regiment*, 96–97.

8. *Annual Report of the Adjutant-General,* 782, 866, 867.

9. Jones, *In the War of the Rebellion*, 22.

10. Jones, *In the War of the Rebellion*, 25, 28.

11. William F. Fox, *New York at Gettysburg*, vol. 2 (Albany: J. B. Lyon, 1900), 586–597.

Epilogue

1. Walter H. Hebert, *Fighting Joe Hooker* (Lincoln: University of Nebraska Press, 1999; originally published Indianapolis: Bobbs-Merrill, 1944), 92.

2. Mississippi State University, University Libraries Digital Collections, *The Letters of Pvt. Arthur McKinstry*, Letter from McKinstry Bros. to Mother of A. McKinstry, May 16, 1862.

3. Mississippi State University, *Letters of Pvt. Arthur McKinstry*, Letter from Geo. Tate to Mr. McKinstry, June 16, 1862.

4. Mississippi State University, *Letters of Pvt. Arthur McKinstry*, Letter from McKinstry Bros. to Mother of A. McKinstry, May 16, 1862.

5. Mississippi State University, *Letters of Pvt. Arthur McKinstry*, Letter from McKinstry Bros. to Jenton [Fenton], May 14, 1862.

6. Yorktown National Cemetery website and Mississippi State University, *Letters of Pvt. Arthur McKinstry*, Mabel L. White to War Department.

7. Douglas H. Shepard, *The Fredonia Censor (1821–1964)*, Darwin R. Barker Historical Museum, 9–12.

8. Mary Frances Smith, various correspondence with Rick Barram regarding McKinstry family history.

Appendix

1. *Official Records of the Union and Confederate Navies in the War of the Rebellion*, series 1, vol. 11/1 [S# 12] (Washington, DC: Government Printing Office, 1897), 464–470.

2. *Fredonia Censor*, May 21, 1862, Morning Edition.

Bibliography

Books

Annual Report of the Adjutant-General of the State of New York for the Year 1901. Albany: J. B. Lyon, 1902.

Barram, Rick. *The 72nd New York Infantry in the Civil War: A History and Roster*. Jefferson, NC: McFarland, 2014.

Battles and Leaders of the Civil War: The Opening Battles, Volume 1. New York: Castle, 1887.

Bauer, K. Jack, ed. *Soldiering: The Civil War Diary of Rice C. Bull*. Novato: Presidio Press, 1977.

Boynton, Charles B. *The History of the Navy during the Rebellion*. New York: D. Appleton, 1867.

Brown, Henri Le Fevre. *History of the Third Regiment, Excelsior Brigade, 72nd New York Volunteer Infantry, 1861–1865*. Jamestown, NY: Journal Printing, 1902.

Bryan, Charles F., and Nelson D. Lankford, eds. *Eye of the Storm: A Civil War Odyssey, Written and Illustrated by Private Robert Knox Sneden*. New York: Free Press, 2000.

Chautauqua History Company, ed. *The Centennial History of Chautauqua County: A Detailed and Entertaining Story of One Hundred Years of Development*, vol. 1. Jamestown, NY: Chautauqua History Company, 1904.

Cowles, Calvin D., ed. *The Official Military Atlas of the Civil War*. New York: Barnes & Noble, 2003.

Cudworth, Warren, H. *History of the First Regiment (Massachusetts Infantry), from the 25th of May, 1861, to the 25th of May, 1864*. Boston: Walker, Fuller, 1866.

Donald, David H., ed. *Gone for a Soldier: The Civil War Memoirs of Private Alfred Bellard*. Boston: Little, Brown, 1975.

Dougherty, Kevin J. *Encyclopedia of the Confederacy*. San Diego, CA: Thunder Bay Press, 2010.

Floyd, Claudia. *Union Occupied Maryland*. Charleston, SC: History Press, 2014.

Fox, William F. *New York at Gettysburg*. Albany: J. B. Lyon, 1900.

Fox, William F. *Regimental Losses in the American Civil War, 1861–1865: A Treatise on the Extent and Nature of the Mortuary Losses in the Union Regiments, with Full and Extensive Statistics Compiled from the Official Records on File in the State Military Bureaus and at Washington.* Albany: Albany, 1889.

Freeman, Douglas Southall. *Lee's Lieutenants: A Study in Command Volume 1.* New York: Charles Scribner's Sons, 1942.

Guernsey, Henry M., and Alfred H. Alden. *Harper's Pictorial History of the Civil War.* New York: Fairfax Press, 1886.

Hasting, Earl C., Jr., and David S. Hastings. *A Pitiless Rain: The Battle of Williamsburg, 1862.* Shippensburg, PA: White Mane, 1997.

Haynes, Martin, A. *A History of the Second Regiment, New Hampshire Volunteer Infantry in the War of the Rebellion.* Lakeport, NH: [No pub.], 1896.

Hayward, John. *Give It to Them, Jersey Blues! A History of the 7th Regiment, New Jersey Veteran Volunteers in the Civil War.* Hightstown: Longstreet House, 1998.

Hawes, Alice McKinstry. *The McKinstrys of Chicopee [Massachusetts].* Stonington, ME: Penobscot Press, 2002.

Hebert, Walter H. *Fighting Joe Hooker.* Lincoln: University of Nebraska Press, 1999; originally published Indianapolis: Bobbs-Merrill, 1944.

Jones, Lucius, Jr. *In the War of the Rebellion from 1861 to 1865.* Fredonia, NY: [No pub.], 1913.

Katcher, Philip R. N. *The Civil War Source Book.* New York: Facts on File, 1982.

Keneally, Thomas. *American Scoundrel: The Life of the Notorious Civil War General Dan Sickles.* New York: Nan A. Talese, 2002.

Kostyal, K. M. *Field of Battle: The Civil War Letters of Major Thomas J. Halsey.* Washington, DC: National Geographic Society, 1996.

Leech, Margaret. *Reveille in Washington, 1860–1865.* New York: Carroll & Graf, 1941; reprint 1991.

Lynch, Francis T., and Samuel Sandoli, comp. *Come Cry with Me: The Letters of Emerson F. Merrell, Native of the Town of Coventry in Chenango County, New York, Who Served in Company I, 72nd. Regiment, New York Infantry, New York Excelsior Brigade, Army of the Potomac, 1861–1863.* Self-published, 2001.

Mathless, Paul, ed. *Voices of the Civil War: The Peninsula.* Alexandria, VA: Time-Life Books, 1998.

McClellan, George B. *McClellan's Own Story.* New York: [No pub.], 1887; reprint Big Byte Books, 2014.

McPherson, James M. *War on the Waters: The Union and Confederate Navies, 1861–1865.* Chapel Hill: University of North Carolina Press, 2012.

Merriam-Webster's Deluxe Dictionary, Tenth Collegiate Edition. New York: Reader's Digest Association, 1998.

Messent, Peter, and Steve Courtney, eds. *The Civil War Letters of Joseph Hopkins Twichell: A Chaplain's Story.* Athens: University of Georgia Press, 2006.

Mitchell, Charles W., ed. *Maryland Voices of the Civil War*. Baltimore, MD: Johns Hopkins University Press, 2007.

Murray, R. L. *Excelsior Brigade at Williamsburg in the Army of the Potomac Journal*. Wolcott: Benedum Books, 2005.

Naval History Division. *Civil War Naval Chronology, 1861–1865*. Washington, DC: Office of the Chief of Naval Operations, Navy Department, 1961.

New York Monuments Commission. *Final Report of the Battlefield of Gettysburg, Vol. II*. Albany, NY: J. B. Lyon, 1902.

Oates, Christopher Ryan. *Fighting for Home: The Story of Alfred K. Oates and the Fifth Regiment, Excelsior Brigade*. Cornelius, NC: Warren, 2006.

Official Records of the Union and Confederate Navies in the War of the Rebellion. Washington, DC: Government Printing Office, 1897.

Parker, David B. *A Chautauqua Boy in '61 and Afterward: Reminiscences by David B. Parker, Second Lieutenant, Seventy-Second New York*. Introduction by Albert Bushnell Hart. Boston: Small, Maynard, 1912.

Pickerill, William N. *History of the Third Indiana Cavalry*. Indianapolis, IN: Aetna Printing, 1906.

Porter, David D. *The Naval History of the Civil War*. New York: Sherman, 1886.

Rafuse, Ethan S. *McClellan's War: The Failure of Moderation in the Struggle for the Union*. Bloomington: Indiana University Press, 2005.

Reed, Rowena. *Combined Operation in the Civil War*. Annapolis, MD: Naval Institute Press, 1978.

Rhodes, James Ford. *History of the Civil War, 1861–1865*. New York: Macmillan, 1917.

Rusling, James F. *Men and Things I Saw in Civil War Days*. New York: Eaton & Mains, 1899.

Sandburg, Carl. *Abraham Lincoln: The War Years*. New York: Harcourt, Brace, 1939.

Scharf, J. Thomas. *History of the Confederate States Navy from Its Organization to the Surrender of Its Last Vessel*. New York: Rogers & Sherwood, 1887.

Sifakis, Stewart. *Who Was Who in the Civil War*. New York: Facts on File, 1988.

Street, Owen. *The Young Patriot: A Memorial of James Hall*. Boston: Massachusetts Sabbath School Society, 1862.

Swanberg, William A. *Sickles the Incredible*. Gettysburg, PA: Stan Clark Military Books, 1856.

Tagg, Larry. *The Generals of Gettysburg: The Leaders of America's Greatest Battle*. Cambridge: Da Capo Press, 2003; originally published Sacramento, CA: Savas, 1998.

Toomey, Daniel Carroll. *The Civil War in Maryland*. Baltimore, MD: Toomey Press, 1983.

Twichell, Joseph H., Chaplain of the Second Excelsior. *Oration at Dedication of Excelsior Brigade Monument at Gettysburg, July 2, 1888, in New York at Gettysburg*. Albany, NY: J. B. Lyon, 1900.

Warner, Ezra J. *Generals in Blue: Lives of the Union Commanders*. Baton Rouge: Louisiana State University Press. 1964.

The War of the Rebellion: A Compilation of the Official Records of the Union and Confederate Armies. Washington, DC: Government Printing Office, 1880–1901.

Wert, Jeffry D. *The Sword of Lincoln*. New York: Simon & Schuster, 2005.

Wiley, Bell Irvin. *The Life of Billy Yank*. Baton Rouge: Louisiana State University Press, 1952.

Wills, Mary Alice. *The Confederate Blockade of Washington, D.C., 1861–1862*. Shippensburg, PA: Burd Street Press, 1998.

Wright, John D. *The Timeline of the Civil War*. San Diego, CA: Thunder Bay Press, 2007.

Websites

Biographical Directory of the United States Congress. https://bioguideretro.congress.gov.

Browne, Patrick. "Steamship 'Elm City,' A Civil War Work Horse." *Historical Digression* (blog). https://historicaldigression.com/2021/07/28/steamship-elm-city-a-peninsular-campaign-work-horse/.

Chautauqua County Offices. *History of Chautauqua County*. https://chqgov.com/live-work-play/History. Accessed April 16, 2020.

Chautauqua County, New York. https://en.wikipedia.org/wiki/Chautauqua_County,_New_York. Accessed April 16, 2020.

The Civil War in America from The Illustrated London News. Emory University: iln.digitalscholarship.emory.edu.

Collection of Civil War letters comes to Grant Library. http://lib.msstate.edu/news/2015/oakley.php. Accessed April 16, 2020.

Delaware County, New York, Genealogy and History Site. https://dcnyhistory.org.

Mississippi State University. University Libraries Digital Collections. *The Letters of Pvt. Arthur McKinstry*. https://www.library.msstate.edu/collections/digital/letters-pvt-arthur-mckinstry.

NavSource Naval History. Photographic History of the U.S. Navy. https://www.navsource.org.

New York State Military Museum and Veterans Research Center. https://museum.dmna.ny.gov.

Sample, Jason. "Recalling William Seward in Chautauqua County." *McClurg Museum* (blog). https://mcclurgmuseum.org/blog/2013/01/03/recalling-william-seward-in-chautauqua-county/. Accessed September 5, 2020.

72nd Regiment N.Y. Vol. Inf., Civil War Newspaper Clippings. Unit History Project, New York State Military Museum. https://museum.dmna.ny.gov/unit-history/infantry-1/72nd-infantry-regiment.

Newspapers

Bloomville Mirror

Fredonia Censor

Jamestown Journal

New York Times

Other Material

Bailey, George. *War Time Letters of George Bailey, Company H, 72nd NYSV*. Unpublished. Courtesy of the Gowanda Area Historical Society.

Compiled Military Service File: Nelson Taylor, 72nd New York. National Archives.

Compiled Military Service File: William O. Steven, Company D, 72nd New York. National Archives.

Darwin R. Barker Historical Library. *Fredonia Censor Newspaper Collection*. Fredonia, NY 14063-1891.

Dyer, F. H. *A Compendium of the War of the Rebellion*. New York: T. Yoseloff, 1959.

Historical Data Systems. Various analyses of regimental enrollment and casualties. Kingston, MA.

New York State Library. *Grand Army of the Republic Records, 70th NYV*. Preservation Unit.

New York State Library. *Grand Army of the Republic Records, 72nd NYV*. Preservation Unit.

Shepard, Douglas H. *Fredonia Censor* (1821–1964). Submitted April 2011, Darwin R. Barker Historical Museum.

Smith, Mary Frances. Arthur McKinstry Letters to Mother, Letter from Mother to Arthur from September 1854 to May 1855. Unpublished.

United States Naval Academy. *Minute Book of the Academic Board, June 1855*. Nimitz Library, U.S. Naval Academy, Annapolis, MD.

Walters, Maxwell, curator at Darwin R. Barker Historical Museum. Various Communications with Rick Barram Regarding *Fredonia Censor* and Collections.

Periodicals

Gould, C. W. "The Battleground of Virtue." *Civil War Times Illustrated* 40, no. 5 (October 2001): 26, 68, 71, 74, 76, 79.

Orrison, Rob, and Bill Backus. "War on the Potomac, May 1861–March 1862." *Blue and Gray* 32, no. 5 (2016): 6–24, 38–50.

Sassaman, R. "The Washington Tragedy." *American History*, October 1998.

Tocin, Kerry R. "To Hell and Back: Companies D, E, and H; 72nd New York Volunteers Dunkirk, New York (1861–1864)." *Niagara Frontier* (Winter 1974): 80–95.

Index